**THE HARBRACE CASEBOOKS IN POLITICAL SCIENCE**

Under the General Editorship of
ALAN F. WESTIN, *Columbia University*

*The Uses of Power* (1962)

*The Third Branch of Government* (1963)

# The Third Branch of Government

8 Cases in Constitutional Politics

# CONTRIBUTORS

*Lucius J. Barker*
UNIVERSITY OF WISCONSIN

*Sister Candida Lund*
ROSARY COLLEGE

*David R. Manwaring*
HOBART & WILLIAM SMITH COLLEGES

*Leonard G. Miller*
UNIVERSITY OF CHICAGO

*Richard E. Morgan*
COLUMBIA UNIVERSITY

*George R. Osborne*
MEMBER, NEW YORK BAR

*Barrett Prettyman, Jr.*
MEMBER, DISTRICT OF COLUMBIA BAR

*Frank J. Sorauf*
UNIVERSITY OF MINNESOTA

A HARBRACE CASEBOOK IN POLITICAL SCIENCE

# The Third Branch of Government

## 8 Cases in Constitutional Politics

EDITED BY

*C. Herman Pritchett* UNIVERSITY OF CHICAGO

*& Alan F. Westin* COLUMBIA UNIVERSITY

NEW YORK · BURLINGAME

Harcourt, Brace & World, Inc.

# ARTICLE III

SECTION 1. The judicial Power of the United States, shall be vested in one supreme Court, and in such inferior Courts as the Congress may from time to time ordain and establish. . . .

THE CONSTITUTION OF THE
UNITED STATES

# CONTENTS

# The Supreme Court Since 1937

## Alan F. Westin and C. Herman Pritchett

THIS book explores the politics of judicial review in America since 1937. In choosing to portray this aspect of our constitutional process, and to do so through a set of eight depth-studies of leading cases, the editors have made two basic assumptions that ought to be set out in advance to guide the reader. Summarized briefly, these assumptions are:

(1) The year 1937 marks a major divide in the constitutional jurisprudence of the American nation and in the decisional philosophy of the Supreme Court. This is so much the fact that future histories of the Supreme Court may very well divide the Court's development since 1790 into two fundamental periods, pre- and post-1937.

(2) Students who are limited solely to the edited opinions of Supreme Court Justices and expert commentary on those opinions will not be able to obtain a clear image of this modern Court and its role in the American political process. To opinions and commentary must be added materials that trace constitutional disputes from their beginnings in a corporate executive suite, sheriff's office, city council, or Congressional investigation, to their point of decision by the Supreme Court, and then out again into the political process.

Each of these assumptions could easily be written about at length, but for the purposes of our introduction, a brief development of them ought to suffice.

### From the Jurisprudence of Property to a Jurisprudence of Status

From the first period of major doctrinal development of the Constitution under Chief Justice John Marshall down to the Supreme Court crisis of 1937, the overwhelming majority of constitutionally sensitive cases decided by the Court involved issues of property rights. Land claims, contract enforcement, the property rights of slave-owners, chartering of corporations, regulation of enterprise, antitrust laws, labor-management conflicts, work conditions, taxation: these were the economic-core context of the leading constitutional cases. Even when the issues involved distribution of power between state and nation, or among the three branches of the Federal government, an underlying question of whether property would be regulated, and in what way, often lurked in the jurisdictional question and was perceived as such by the more self-conscious Justices guiding the Court.

During this 130 years of property-focused constitutional jurisprudence, the Supreme Court's basic decisions supported the owners and users of property against the successive tides of reformers and liberals who sought to regulate economic enterprise for the general welfare. This was not because the Supreme Court was corrupted or bribed by the business community. It was because the ideas inherited from John Locke, recast by the Founding Fathers, and applied by judges steeped in the "higher law" concepts of rights of property produced a widely supported notion in the old-stock, middle-class America of these years that this was the right role for the national judiciary.

One way to test the validity of this description, as well as to add another dimension to it, is to note who supported and who attacked the Supreme Court's basic philosophy of decision in constitutionally sensitive cases from 1800 to 1937. The major critics of the Court's role in property and economic regulation cases were the reformer and liberal groups in American history. The Jeffersonians, the Jacksonians, the antislavery forces and the Lincoln Administration, the farmer alliances and Granger groups of the 1870's, the Populists and Bryan Democrats in the 1890's, the progressives and Theodore Roosevelt's Bull Moose movement in 1912, the LaFollette and labor-union forces in the 1920's, and the New Deal critics in the 1930's —these liberal-reformer elements were constant critics of the Court's property jurisprudence. They complained that the Court was an unelected, irresponsible body that defied the will of the majority through its elected representatives, and, decade after decade, struck down key property controls that the public felt to be both necessary and wise. When the Court did not completely block, as unconstitutional, such regulatory legislation, the liberal-reformers alleged that the Court delayed reform measures in a way that harmed society greatly, and that it gave hostile interpretations to measures that often defeated the basic purposes of the legislation.

At the same time that these critics of the Court were attacking the Justices and seeking to limit or curtail the Court's power by constitutional amendment or Congressional controls over the Court's appellate jurisdiction, the property-conservative elements in America were staunch and constant in the Court's defense. They were the beneficiaries of the Court's rulings—the New England merchants and bankers, western land speculators, southern planters, the new industrial captains who emerged from the Civil War, and the leaders of the corporate community and its Main Street merchant allies in the 1920's and 1930's. The property-conservatives were not always the winners in Supreme Court litigation, of course, and sometimes the Court majority disappointed its trusted supporters and upheld reform measures. But the recurring center of gravity of Supreme Court rulings from 1800 to 1937 provided judicial intervention to secure property-owners greater protection and more rights than these men could win in the political arenas of the states and nation. Naturally, the property-conservatives praised the Court as the voice of independence and the guarantee of those precious rights deliberately installed in the Constitution to protect them from majority whim and passion. The Justices were described as the wise, sober-second-look agency of our government, a nonelected agency necessary to hold American legislators to their constitutional limits.

Thus, every time the Court faced serious attacks upon its powers, both in election campaigns and in Congressional sessions, the property-conservatives were usually its champions and the liberal-reformers its critics. No twenty-five-year period has passed in American history since Marshall's day without such a liberal-conservative debate over the proper place of the Court in our governmental system.

Since 1937, a revolution has taken place in the relations of the Supreme Court to property questions and interest groups in America. Space does not permit a discussion of the antecedents to this revolution, the development of the crisis between Court and nation in the mid-1930's, or the specific unfolding of the unsuccessful Roosevelt Court-reform proposal in 1937. The fruits of these developments are what concern us here.

First, the post-1937 Court has virtually erased from its *constitutional* agenda the regulation-of-property cases. No Congressional act since 1937 regulating property has been declared unconstitutional, and very few state laws regulating industry or providing welfare programs have been invalidated as interferences with contract rights or private property. The expansion of the commerce clause, spending power, and other sections of the Constitution has given the Federal government broad authority to govern economic relations in the nation. The Court no longer substitutes its judgment as to the wisdom of economic measures for that of Congress or the state legislatures. Of course, if we moved into an era of novel economic measures or major nationalization programs, the Court might reassert its authority; but the decades since 1937 have been years of consolidation rather than innovation in economic regulation, and the Court's withdrawal from constitutional intervention is therefore not likely to change in the immediate future. At present, the Court's primary impact on economic disputes within the business community and between labor and management comes largely through interpretation of Federal statutes or Federal regulatory agency rulings. Here, the Court's authority is intermediate rather than final in character, since Congress—if it does not agree with a judicial interpretation of a statute— can simply amend or alter the law to have its policy wishes respected. Congress has done this continually since 1937, and economic groups have often transferred to Congress their basic efforts to win favorable positions for themselves in the new setting of economic public law.

Second, the post-1937 Court has replaced its property agenda with a central constitutional preoccupation with issues of status. These issues present three major matters: There are (1) problems of equality involving the minority rights of racial and nonwhite groups such as Negroes, Oriental-Americans, and Puerto Ricans; discrimination against urban and suburban voters through gerrymandered election districts; unequal treatment in public affairs of religious minorities such as Jews, Jehovah's Witnesses, Seventh Day Adventists, or Catholics. There are (2) problems of liberty involving the freedom of expression and association rights of persons or groups that reject the American political and economic consensus, such as Communists, atheists, the American Nazi party, or pacifists, as well as those who reject the moral and literary consensus and choose to go beyond the general canons of good taste in movies, books, plays, or magazines. Finally, there are (3) problems of justice or due process involving the procedural fairness afforded to persons investigated by the police, tried for crime, or judged in their suitability by government; especially involved here is due process for the disfavored groups caught up in the equality and liberty conflicts described above.

In all of these cases, it is the quality of American life and the status afforded to those within the society that is at stake, and the Court's role has been as a register of profound intergroup changes in American society since the 1930's. Thus, if any recent Term of the United States Supreme Court is examined, the overwhelming majority of constitutional cases decided by the Justices with full opinions will be seen to be in the status sector of equality, liberty, and justice cases, where once they were in the property sector. And in these status cases, despite disagreements over degree and means, the Justices have adopted since 1937 a broadly liberal philosophy that has aided considerably the interests of Negroes, political dissenters, minority religious groups, etc. As with the business community in the pre-1937 period, the groups seeking equality and liberty rights do not always prevail in the Supreme Court. But they achieve victories there that they could not have won or defended in the political arenas of state or nation, and thus have the balance of power tipped toward their causes by the judiciary.

Third, the result of this switch in the Court's docket and in those who are the prime beneficiaries of the Court's intervention has been a reversal in those who defend and those who attack the Court. Today, it is the liberals in the universities, in the magazines, and in the political arena who praise and defend the Court. The Americans for Democratic Action, National Association for the Advancement of Colored People, American Civil Liberties Union, Liberal Party of New York, American Jewish Congress, AFL-CIO —this is the organizational chorus that can be found extolling the Court. It now tells the American public that the Court is a wise, sober-second-look agency that protects our precious constitutional rights from being man-handled by majority whim and passion, and holds legislators to their constitutional limits.

By the same token, it is the conservatives who now lash out at the Court —the National Association of Manufacturers, the Chamber of Commerce, the American Legion, the Daughters of the American Revolution, the American Bar Association, the National Association of Chiefs of Police, and the *National Review* magazine. Their deep lament is that the Court—an unelected and irresponsible body of nine lawyers—is substituting its notion of wisdom for that of the elected branches of state and national government, and striking down those anti-Communist and anti-crime measures that the majority of a state or of the nation consider to be both necessary and wise for the preservation of our society. While this is going on, the conservatives add, the court is failing to protect American business from "socialist measures" that are destroying our free-enterprise system and failing to respect the rights of the states to govern their own police and courts, or their special internal security and race-relation problems. The editorial cartoons collected here, spanning the years from 1896 to 1962, illustrate nicely this shift in liberal-conservative relationship to the Supreme Court. Readers will note that the theme of majority will versus restraint on majority coercion remains fairly constant. Only the authors of the theme have changed.

This shift is all the more striking in that leading political and civic spokesmen and interest groups have made the reversal from friend to foe of the court, or vice versa, within one generation. In 1937, when President Franklin Delano Roosevelt tried to enlarge the Court's membership to 15 in order to end the Court's vetoes of key New Deal economic measures, the conservatives defended the Court, and many liberals supported the Roosevelt Court-reform legislation in Congress. In 1957, when the new Court's decisions in the areas of internal security, censorship, criminal procedure, antitrust, labor relations, and segregation prompted Senators William Jenner, John Marshall Butler, James Eastland, and others to sponsor bills to "curb the Court" by curtailing its jurisdiction, many newspapers, political leaders, and group spokesmen were to be found on the exact opposite side of the 1937 "legislative-reform, hands-off" debate. The David Lawrence who authored *Nine Honest Men* in 1937 and championed the "old Justices" was in 1957 the man who placed his magazine, *U.S. News and World Report,* in the forefront of the attack on the Warren "runaway" Court.

Fourth, the shift from property to status issues on the Court's constitutionally sensitive docket reflects major changes in American political, economic, racial, religious, and intergroup life that promise to sustain the Court in its present role. Since 1937, the Court's majority has been reconstituted fully (five or more appointments out of the Court's nine) by both a Democratic President who represented the liberal-reform movement

Gale in the Los Angeles *Times*

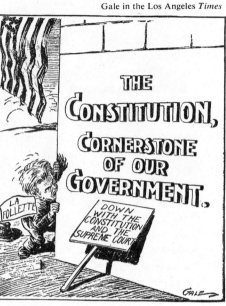

ON A POPULISTIC BASIS.

A FORECAST OF THE CONSEQUENCE OF A POPOCRATIC VICTORY TO THE SUPREME COURT OF THE UNITED STATES.

**Biting on granite**

## 1896–1930: Conservative Defenses of the Supreme Court Against Its Liberal Critics

TOP LEFT: Populist party and Democratic party attacks on the Court's corporate decisions were a major issue in the 1896 Presidential campaign. Here, *Harper's Weekly* depicts the Court staffed by radicals.

TOP RIGHT: Senator Robert La Follette and the American Federation of Labor made the Court's antilabor and antiwelfare rulings part of the Progressive party's platform in the 1924 Presidential contest.

BOTTOM: In 1912, Theodore Roosevelt, running for President on the Bull Moose ticket, urged recall of judicial decisions and raised the hackles of conservatives.

*"UMPH! YOU STILL HANGING AROUND?"*

Duffy in the Baltimore *Sun*

Seibel in the Richmond *Times-Dispatch*

### 1933—1937: The Old Court Blocks the New Deal and the New Deal Proposes Court-Reform

TOP LEFT AND RIGHT: Conservatives saw the Court as a check to an "unconstitutional" New Deal while liberals saw the Court as a threat to national economic recovery.

Elderman in the Washington *Post*

SUPREME COURT—1937

*"Furnishing the Supreme Court some practical assistance"*

LOWER LEFT AND RIGHT: In 1937, FDR proposed "reform" and conservatives beat down the "packing plan."

AID FOR THE HUNGRY ELEPHANT — OR FOR THE NEW DEAL?

Spencer in the Omaha *World-Herald*

### Strange Ditch Diggers

Sandeson in the Fort Wayne *News-Sentinel*

### 1957–Present: The Conservative Disenchantment with the New Court

A TREE GROWS AND GROWS IN WASHINGTON

Warren in the Cincinnati *Enquirer*

TOP LEFT AND RIGHT: Conservatives now insist that popular and majority will is imperiled by the Court's rulings in the status-sector cases.

LOWER LEFT AND RIGHT: Support for Congressional proposals to curb the Court's powers comes from conservative spokesmen while liberals and "Commies" are shown as the Court's allies.

Fitzpatrick in the St. Louis *Post-Dispatch*

"YOU MAY COME BACK NOW"

## 'STILL THE CORNERSTONE'

Crawford in the Newark *News*

### 1957–Present: Liberal Defenses of Judicial Review and the New Court

TOP LEFT AND RIGHT: Liberals applauded the Court's rulings in the mid-1950's supporting civil liberties and equality rights .

LOWER LEFT AND RIGHT: Liberals defended Court and Constitution against the Court-curb proposals in Congress.

"'Tis I, Justice! Here With A Point Of Law"

Haynie in the Greensboro *Daily News*

"..IT'S OUR GOOD DEED FOR THE DAY..!"

Conrad in the Denver *Post*

(Franklin Roosevelt, 9 appointees) and a Republican President who represented business-conservative forces (Dwight Eisenhower, 5 appointees). Both Presidents named the Chief Justice of the United States among their appointees. Yet the basic trend described above as "the post-1937 shift" continued steadily in the late 1930's, 1940's, and 1950's, and is operative today in the 1960's. While there are debates about how far to go in the status cases the basic elimination of the property docket and the interventionist concept in the status area have remained constant. Let us hasten to say that no one is suggesting here that the post-1937 Court is radically new in the type of Justice who sits on the Court, in the way in which the Court goes about deciding cases (which will be described later in this introduction), in the importance of prior decisions and history for the decisions in specific cases, or even in the types of conflicts among the Justices and between the Court and its critics. Such elements are continuing aspects of the Court's development as an institution and in the growth of American constitutional law. What we are saying is that the Court's focus of constitutional decisions and its relation to the economic, social, and political groups of the nation have both undergone profound changes since 1937. It is this change that ought to be the primary area of attention by students of American Government. To provide such a focus, we have turned to the "depth-study" of leading cases.

### The Use of Depth-Studies To Probe the New Setting of Constitutional Politics in America

In the post-1937 setting of judicial review, the best insights into what the judges do, what effect their decisions have on the political process and the conduct of government, and how the judicial process relates to political life in America may be had by looking at a representative group of leading cases in depth. Depth, in this context, means that the case must be reconstructed in all its complexity, background, color, conflict, strategic dilemmas, and ramifications. The real parties to disputes and how their disputes arose; the struggles in private and public arenas that preceded the transfer of the dispute to the courts; the background of any statutes or regulatory action involved; the strategic and doctrinal battles during the litigation process; the way in which political and private forces affect the litigation as it progresses through the courts; the rules of the game by which judges shape political, economic, and social issues into form for judicial decision; the impact of public opinion upon the judiciary in its consideration of cases and its scope of decision; the response of the parties, government, and the public to the judicial rulings once they are issued; the compliance, noncompliance, or modification of judicial rulings by elected and appointed officials; the response of the courts when new facts and new situations raise problems about the meaning of a leading case and its application—these and a host of other questions must be explored in order to achieve a sophisticated understanding of what the role of the courts is in contemporary America.

Ideally, one would like to have students trace these elements in each case from the original documents. There is no substitute for looking at the Congressional statute, the letter from a loyalty-security board to a Federal employee, the transcript of a trial in a court or a hearing before an administrative agency, the briefs and motions of the parties, the oral argument before the Supreme Court, or the memoirs of participants in great constitutional cases. One major case is available for such an inspection of edited documentary sources, the Steel Seizure decision of 1952.[1] However, treating enough cases in this way to provide a full portrait of the contemporary Supreme Court and the judicial process would require a book of from 1,600 to 2,000 pages, and a commitment of time from college students that is simply not available.

Our response, therefore, has been to attempt a compromise between edited opinions and analyses on the one hand and documentary reconstruction on the other. We have assembled here eight detailed narratives, each a story in itself and each incorporating considerable documentary material throughout the account. At its chronological place in the narrative, we have inserted the edited opinions themselves, as much to give the reader the experience with the style and debating format of the Justice as to let readers decide for themselves what the response of the Justices was to the issue thrust up to them for judgment.

The topics represented in this collection span the major areas of Supreme Court work, both constitutional and nonconstitutional. Two case studies deal with economic affairs—the Portal-to-Portal Pay Case and the Offshore Oil Cases—and a third, the Sunday Closing Cases, provides a fascinating mixture of commerce and religion. Due process is probed in a case from the state courts involving a claim of cruel and unusual punishment, the Electric-Chair Case, and in the Government Loyalty-Security Program Case, involving fair procedure in the administrative process. The Released Time Case and the Sunday Closing Cases show the Court engaged in drawing the line between church and state, while the Flag-Salute Cases and the Government Loyalty-Security Program Case raise problems of freedom of expression and the compulsion of loyalty exacted by government under the pressures of war and cold war. The deep stakes of the conflicts between state and nation are mirrored in the Offshore Oil Cases, as well as in the NAACP Case, which takes readers into the heart of the segregation dispute and explores the south's response to the Supreme Court's desegregation rulings since 1954. All of the cases show the special role of organized groups in

---

[1] Alan F. Westin, *The Anatomy of a Constitutional Law Case* (New York, Macmillan, 1958).

sponsoring litigation and carrying it through the state and Federal courts as part of the group's general political operations in American society. All of the cases show the interaction of law and politics, precedent and change, personality and institutions, and defiance of or obedience to law that make the study of the constitutional process such a challenging exercise in self-examination of a democratic society and its basic dilemmas.

With this explanation of the post-1937 setting of judicial review and the special values of using depth-studies, there remains only one more item for treatment in this introduction. Many of those who read this book will already have had some material dealing with the American judicial system. Yet some may be using the book who have not had a basic description of how the courts are organized and how the Supreme Court goes about its decisional process. Since all eight cases unfold against this structural and procedural background, a brief sketch of fundamentals will be useful.

The Supreme Court stands at the head of the Federal judicial branch, created directly by Article III of the Constitution, which also provides for the office of Chief Justice of the United States. The other members of the Court, the Associate Justices, do not have their number fixed by the Constitution: this is left for determination by Congress. The First Congress provided for a membership of six on the Court, but since 1869 there have been nine members—despite efforts by President Franklin D. Roosevelt to secure legislation increasing the total to fifteen.

While a system of Federal courts "inferior" to the Supreme Court was authorized by Article III, the Constitution left the creation of these lower tribunals to Congress. By various judiciary acts from 1789 to recent decades, Congress has provided two levels of lower Federal courts. The trial court level is made up of 91 district courts, at least one in each state, with more than 300 district judges. A single judge hears cases in these courts, except when the constitutionality of a Federal statute is questioned. Then, and in a few other situations, three judges sit in trial.

At the intermediate level are the courts of appeals for each of the 10 judicial circuits and the District of Columbia, with a total of some 80 judges. Appeals here are heard by a panel of three or more judges. The courts of appeals review the decisions of the district courts and of Federal administrative agencies such as the National Labor Relations Board and the Federal Communications Commission.

The Supreme Court, of course, is the final court of appeals in the Federal court channel. It also stands as the final reviewing authority for the state courts. This derives from Article VI of the Constitution, which provides that the Constitution, laws, and treaties of the United States "shall be the supreme law of the land" and that "the judges in every state shall be bound thereby, any thing in the constitution or laws of any state to the contrary notwithstanding."

The First Congress, carrying out this principle in the Judiciary Act of

1789, authorized the Supreme Court to review the decisions of state courts which ruled adversely on rights claimed by parties under the Federal Constitution, national laws, or treaties. In the first decades of the Republic, some state supreme courts were embittered at having their decisions reviewed by the Supreme Court, and in a few instances states threatened disobedience to Supreme Court decrees. Again in our own era, implementation for the Supreme Court's decision declaring racial segregation unconstitutional has been resisted in various ways by state courts. The case of *National Association for the Advancement of Colored People* v. *Alabama* in this volume is an eye-opening demonstration of state judicial recalcitrance.

Thus far we have been talking about the Supreme Court as though its job were entirely that of hearing appeals from decisions of state and lower Federal courts. This is not entirely true, for the Constitution does define two categories of cases which can be heard in the Court's original jurisdiction, that is, without prior consideration by any other court. These are cases in which a state is a party, such as the Offshore Oil Case, and those affecting ambassadors, public ministers, and consuls. However, the Court generally does not have to accept a suit invoking its original jurisdiction unless it feels that there is a compelling reason of public policy for taking the case.

All the remaining business of the Supreme Court comes to it in its appellate jurisdiction, which it exercises, as the Constitution says, "with such exceptions, and under such regulations as the Congress shall make." In theory, this language gives Congress authority to completely cut off the Supreme Court's appellate jurisdiction, leaving that august body with nothing to do except decide those few cases that might arise in its original jurisdiction. In fact, however, Congress has actually used this power on only one occasion—during the post-Civil War period. All attempts in Congress since the 1860's to "punish" the court by curtailing its jurisdiction to hear cases in sensitive areas have failed.

Before a case can get to the Supreme Court (except for the original jurisdiction cases) it must have gone through whatever lower courts are proper for it. The role of the Supreme Court is then to correct errors of law—that is, mistakes in defining, interpreting, or applying the law—made by the Federal or state courts below. But not all judicial errors are important enough to require correction by the Supreme Court. Consequently, Congress has, for the most part, given the Court discretion to pick and choose what cases it will hear. Litigants who are dissatisfied with a lower court decision must file a petition for the writ of certiorari with the Supreme Court. This Latin word can be translated as "made more certain" or "better informed." It comes from the formal language of an old English writ, by which a higher court ordered a lower court to send up the record of a case because the higher court wished to be better informed or more certain about the proceedings below.

Certiorari is a discretionary writ. The Supreme Court does not have to grant a petition for certiorari and in most cases does not. The writ is granted only if at least four of the nine Justices agree that issues of special importance are presented by the case. What are the "special and important" reasons the Justices look for in considering a petition for certiorari? Rule 19 of the Rules of the Supreme Court provides:

(1) A review on writ of certiorari is not a matter of right, but of sound judicial discretion, and will be granted only where there are special and important reasons therefor. The following, while neither controlling nor fully measuring the court's discretion, indicate the character of reasons which will be considered:

(a) Where a state court has decided a Federal question of substance not theretofore determined by this court, or has decided it in a way probably not in accordance with applicable decisions of this court.

(b) Where a court of appeals has rendered a decision in conflict with the decision of another court of appeals on the same matter; or has decided an important state or territorial question in a way in conflict with applicable state or territorial law; or has decided an important question of Federal law which has not been, but should be, settled by this court; or has decided a Federal question in a way in conflict with applicable decisions of this court; or has so far departed from the accepted and usual course of judicial proceedings, or so far sanctioned such a departure by a lower court, as to call for an exercise of this court's power of supervision.

The Supreme Court typically grants less than 20 per cent of the petitions for certiorari filed annually; sometimes it grants even as few as 8 to 10 per cent in a given year. Even when reasons such as those mentioned in Rule 19 are shown, the Court may still decline to take up the case, for the exercise of the Court's discretion in deciding whether to grant or deny certiorari often involves as much judicial statesmanship as the decision of a case on its merits. As Justice Frankfurter once wrote, "Wise adjudication has its own time for ripening."

In addition to the cases which come to the court on certiorari, there are some categories of cases in which Congress has granted a right of *appeal* to the Supreme Court. In effect Congress had decided that such cases are so important that the Court should have no choice but to hear them. For example, there is a right of appeal from a Federal court of appeals in cases where a state law has been invalidated because of a conflict with Federal law, or where a Federal statute has been held unconstitutional. There is also a right of appeals from state court decisions which deny a litigant's claim of Federal right, that is, where the state court has upheld a state law against a contention that it violates the Federal Constitution, or where a state court invalidates a Federal statute or treaty on which one of the parties is relying.

While the Supreme Court is supposed to have no choice but to hear appeals in such cases, actually the Court requires appellants to file a preliminary "jurisdictional statement," on the basis of which the Court may determine that no "substantial Federal question" is present and dismiss the appeal.

The Supreme Court meets for business in October of every year, and the "October Term" continues until the following June. The usual pattern of the Court's operation is to hear the arguments of counsel in cases before it for about two weeks at a time and then to recess for two weeks or so to study the cases and write opinions.

On Fridays during the Term, the Justices meet in conference to discuss and decide pending cases. At the conference the Chief Justice presents each case along with his views, and discussion then moves to the Associate Justices in order of seniority. When the vote is taken, the order is reversed, the most recent appointees to the Court voting first, and the Chief Justice last. Following the vote, the Chief Justice assigns the writing of the Court's opinion to himself or to one of his colleagues. If the decision was not unanimous and the Chief Justice voted in the minority, the senior Associate Justice who voted in the majority controls the assignment of the opinion. Drafts of opinions are circulated among the Justices, and the author may revise the final draft on the basis of comments by his colleagues.

In the Court's early days it was the custom for all Justices to give their opinions seriatim in a case, and there was no single opinion "for the Court." However, when John Marshall became Chief Justice in 1801, he decided that the Court's prestige and power would be increased if a single opinion was prepared, and in fact he himself wrote the opinion of the Court in almost all important cases. Justices were still free to write concurring or dissenting opinions, but there was a tendency for them to go along with the Court in silence unless their disagreement was sharp. More recent practice permits dissents to be registered much more freely, and during many Terms the unanimous decisions have been considerably fewer than the nonunanimous ones.

The Justices who sit on the Supreme Court are men of widely varying abilities, backgrounds, and political preferences. With very few exceptions, the President appoints to the Court men of his own party, and usually men who have held political positions and have been active in party affairs. Among recent appointees to the Court, Byron White (1962) had helped organize President Kennedy's 1960 campaign and served as Deputy Attorney General. Arthur Goldberg (1962) was Secretary of Labor in the Kennedy Cabinet, formerly general counsel for the A.F.L.-C.I.O., and a strong Democratic party supporter ever since the New Deal period. Earl Warren (1953) had been a candidate for the vice-presidency on the Republican ticket and Governor of California. Hugo Black (1937), James F. Byrnes (1941), Harold Burton (1945), and Sherman Minton (1949) had been United States Senators. Tom Clark (1949), Robert H. Jackson (1941), and Frank Murphy (1940) had been Attorneys General, and Stanley F. Reed (1938) was Solicitor General.

How members of the Supreme Court will interpret the Constitution and decide cases depends in part upon what kind of men they are and how the world looks to them. This has not always been understood. During many periods of American history there has been a popular impression that when men were appointed to the Supreme Court, they somehow became depersonalized and disembodied of all ordinary prejudices and passions. In the rarefied atmosphere of their chambers they were presumed to be at work discovering the law by the exercise of pure reason. This myth, however, was finally and irretrievably destroyed in the years from 1935 to 1937, when it became all too apparent that the doctrine which the Supreme Court majority was expounding was determined by their personal laissez-faire economic beliefs. As Max Lerner said, the public learned then "that judicial decisions are not babies brought by constitutional storks."

It would be an error as grave as that made by the traditionalists, however, to jump to the conclusion that Supreme Court Justices typically decide cases merely by consulting their personal preferences. There is an institutional ethos about the Court that cannot fail to have a restraining effect upon its most opinionated members. One of these institutional factors, for example, is *stare decisis,* the rule of precedent. The literal translation for this Latin phrase is "stand by the things decided." It is a fundamental principle of American and English jurisprudence that a decision by the highest court in a jurisdiction is a binding precedent on the questions of law involved in the case. The court making the decision and all of the courts subordinate to it are expected to follow the precedent and to give similar answers to similar questions whenever they arise thereafter.

Although *stare decisis* is an ancient and fundamental principle, the Supreme Court does not always follow it. Particularly in constitutional cases, the Court may find it necessary to disregard or overrule its own prior decisions. If the Court will not change its interpretation of the Constitution, a formal amendment is the only alternative, and this is a difficult process. Justice Brandeis once wrote:

> *Stare decisis* is usually the wise policy, because in most matters it is more important that the applicable rule of law be settled than that it be settled right. . . . This is commonly true even where the error is a matter of serious concern, provided correction can be had by legislation. But in cases involving the Federal Constitution, where correction through legislative action is practically impossible, this Court has often overruled its earlier decisions. The Court bows to the lessons of experience and the force of

better reasoning, recognizing that the process of trial and error, so fruitful in the physical sciences, is appropriate also in the judicial function.[2]

The great strength of the Supreme Court's decision-making process is its recognition of the claims of rationality. The individual Justice may think that a particular precedent is wrong or outmoded. If so, he may follow his personal preference and state his reasons for voting to overrule the earlier holding. He is free to do that. But he is not free to ignore the precedents, to act as though they did not exist. He must dispose of them by rational arguments. He has free choice, but only among limited alternatives and only after he has satisfied himself that he has met the obligations of consistency and respect for settled principles which his responsibility to the Court imposes upon him.

Now, the time for introductory matter has come to an end, and each reader can move for himself into the real world of constitutional politics since the New Deal.

---

[2] *Burnet* v. *Coronado Oil & Gas Co.,* 285 U.S. 393 (1932).

# 1

# The Flag-Salute Case

## David R. Manwaring

IN 1943 the United States was at war—a war whose outcome remained doubtful for some time. The United States Supreme Court, however, was going about its business in its time-honored fashion. Harlan Fiske Stone presided over the Court as the twelfth Chief Justice of the United States. A former dean of Columbia University Law School, he had been elevated to the Court from the Attorney General's post by President Coolidge in 1925, and had promptly joined with Justices Holmes and Brandeis as the liberal minority of a conservative Court. President Roosevelt chose this liberal Republican as Chief Justice in 1941 on the resignation of Charles Evans Hughes.

With one exception, all the Associate Justices on the 1943 Court had also been appointed by Roosevelt; Owen J. Roberts was a holdover from the Hoover regime. Roosevelt had appointed Hugo Black, liberal Democratic Senator from Alabama; Stanley F. Reed, a cautious Kentuckian, who as Solicitor General had defended the early New Deal legislation before the Court; Felix Frankfurter, famous professor of the Harvard Law School; William O. Douglas, outdoorsman, former Yale Law professor, and Chairman of the Securities and Exchange Commission; Frank Murphy, a liberal Catholic, friend of labor, former governor of Michigan, and Attorney General; Robert H. Jackson, a brilliant New York State lawyer, a man of considerable political stature and a notable writing style, who had risen through the ranks of the Justice Department to the Attorney Generalship; and Wiley B. Rutledge, a more scholarly type who had been Dean of the University of Iowa Law School and judge on the District of Columbia Court of Appeals.

By 1943 the Stone Court was in considerable trouble. The Chief Justice did not manage the weekly conferences very well, personal animosities arose among the justices, and the number of disagreements and dissents in the Court's decisions had increased sharply. With the exception of Roberts, all the members of this Court were economic liberals who accepted the idea of moderate government intervention in the economy. Consequently, they had no trouble with the issues that had split the Court on New Deal issues from 1933 to 1937. However, they had other basic differences about the role of the Court, particularly the nature of the judicial responsibility to protect civil liberties. The members of the Court were still working their way through these new problems by 1943, but already a polarization was apparent around the judicial restraint position of Justice Frankfurter and the judicial activism of Justices Black and Douglas.

Of all the civil liberties cases decided by the Roosevelt Court, none was more significant for the intellectual development of the Court than the flag-salute issue, which, complicated by the passions of patriotism in wartime, the justices had to look at twice before they knew their own minds.

THE FLAG salute is by far America's most common and popular form of homage to the national emblem. In the period under study here, participants stood and recited: "I pledge allegiance to the Flag of the United States of America and to the Republic for which it stands; one nation, indivisible, with liberty and justice for all." ("Under God" was added in 1954.) At the words "to the Flag," they extended their right hands, palms up and slightly raised, and held them in that position until the end of the pledge.

The ceremony originated in 1892 as part of nation-wide public school observances honoring the four hundredth anniversary of Columbus' discovery of America. It immediately became popular, and soon was in local use by schools in every state. Nor was this always a matter of choice. By 1935, twenty-four states had statutes requiring instruction in flag respect; nine of these explicitly required that the flag-salute ceremony be conducted regularly in all public schools.

The theory implicit in the "flag-salute" and "flag-respect" statutes was very simple and undoubtedly quite effective. School children were to learn patriotism and reverence for the flag by repeated exposure to patriotic situations involving the flag. Another motive underlying the stronger flag-salute laws was to minimize the influence of "red" or "disloyal" teachers by forcing them to include patriotic material in their instruction.

The flag ceremony was supported mainly by civic groups interested in overt displays of patriotism—and generally suspicious of teachers. The American Legion, supporter of the pledge of allegiance since 1923, when it sponsored the first National Flag Conference, has been active in promoting public school use of the ceremony. Also very active have been the Patriotic Order of the Sons of America, Veterans of Foreign Wars, and Daughters of the American Revolution. Other groups endorsing the ritual and defending it against attack included the United Daughters of the Confederacy, Ku Klux Klan, Sons of the American Revolution, Junior Order United American Mechanics, Order of DeMolay, Elks, Grand Army of the Republic Federation, and Improved Order of Red Men.

For several decades after it first appeared no opposition to the flag-salute ceremony was voiced. Teachers were cool toward it, both because of the frequently hostile auspices under which it was introduced to them, and because they considered it another "gimmick," like Leif Erickson Day and temperance instruction, delaying their educational instruction. Because a protest might easily be misconstrued, they contented themselves with performing the unwelcome duty quickly and perfunctorily. When the question later changed to the compulsion of pupils to salute, several teachers' organizations moved into open opposition.

None of the flag-salute laws explicitly demanded that pupils participate in the flag ceremony, for it seemed inconceivable that anyone might refuse. Following World War I school authorities were totally unprepared and lacked statutory guidance to handle the many religious objections raised against the ceremony in many areas. The Mennonites had refused the salute and pledge as early as 1918 and remained the most numerous class of objectors up to 1935; they felt the pledge implied a promise to bear arms. Several members of the Church of God, which did not recognize earthly government, refused to salute; members of the Elijah Voice Society refused on both grounds. The Jehovites in Colorado considered the ceremony idolatrous. These early disputes ended inconclusively. School authorities often chose to exempt the objectors, while others expelled them from school, only to readmit them later; sometimes the objectors gave in. In no instance did the conflict lead to litigation testing the legality or constitutionality of the expulsion since all the sects involved had conscientious scruples against suing in a court of law. As yet, the flag-salute controversy had been sporadic and mild, with little overt ill will. All this was changed in 1935 with the entry of Jehovah's Witnesses.

### Jehovah's Witnesses: A Distaste for Satan

Jehovah's Witnesses are a missionary sect whose doctrines center around the end of this world, expected momentarily. The Witnesses believe that all existing worldly institutions—church, state, the economy—are hopelessly corrupt, under the direct control of Satan. In this generation all except Jehovah's Witnesses will be blotted out at the great Battle of Armageddon (as described in the book of Revelation). This small band of faithful Christians will then live forever in perfect health on an earth restored to Edenic perfection. The Witnesses now are engaged in the great task of warning the world of its danger and showing all who would be saved their only road to salvation. Everyone must have his choice: to join "God's organization" and take part in the "witness work," or to adhere to old ways and suffer destruction at Armageddon. This proselytization is the Witnesses' first and only religious activity and is carried on mainly by door-to-door selling of religious books and magazines published by their corporate head, the Watchtower Bible and Tract Society of Brooklyn. Auxiliary methods include street-corner distribution of literature and the playing of recorded Bible lectures on portable phonographs and through sound trucks. The sect is strictly hierarchical in organization; the leaders merely passive instruments through whom God makes known his commands.

During the 1930's and early 1940's Jehovah's Witnesses were extremely unpopular. Their sense of divine mission and their contempt for existing institutions led them into intrusive and aggressive proselytizing methods that were unsettling at best. Equally offensive to many people were their repeated and drastic condemnations of all other religious denominations—particularly the Roman Catholic Church, which the Witnesses still consider as Satan's chief agent on earth. Witness patriotism was already suspect because of their insistence on exemption from military service as ministers of the gospel. The Witnesses' leader during this period, "Judge" Joseph F. Rutherford, continually encouraged his followers in their alienation from their surroundings.

The hostility of this sect was speedily reciprocated. Many localities, exasperated by their message and methods, struck at the "witness work" with a variety of "anti-peddling" ordinances. The Witnesses fought back, appealing hundreds of convictions and winning most of the appeals. In *Lovell* v. *Griffin* (1938), the Supreme Court struck down a local permit ordinance granting blanket discretion to the licensing authority. In *Schneider* v. *Irvington* (1939), the Court held that pamphleteering on the public streets could not be prohibited altogether, even for the ostensible purpose of preventing littering. Armed with these victories, Jehovah's Witnesses were on the way to solving their local troubles. Then came World War II and a resurgence of the flag-salute issue.

Witness opposition to the flag salute is a more or less accidental by-product of their refusal to "heil" Hitler in Germany. Individual members in Massachusetts saw an obvious parallel and stopped saluting. On October 6, 1935, "Judge" Rutherford backed their stand unreservedly. Soon, all Witnesses stopped saluting. Jehovah's Witnesses look upon saluting as a form of worship; one who salutes ascribes salvation to the object saluted. Since Satan rules this world and all its nations, one who salutes a flag is worshiping the devil. This argument was true to their world-view, but was a hard one to maintain in the face of the rising nationalism attending the start of World War II. Eventually, official doctrine receded to a more defendable position. In worshiping—that is, saluting—a flag, however worthy, one violates God's command in Exodus 20:3–6: "You shall have no other gods before me. You shall not make yourself a graven image, or any likeness . . . you shall not bow down to them. . . ." This scruple became a matter beyond compromise for any Witness; for one who has received the truth and joined God's organization is in a covenant to do God's will. A Witness transgressing divine law in any respect is absolutely doomed. This applies with full rigor to the children, who generally become full members of the sect before the age of ten.

### Religious Minorities and the State

Jehovah's Witnesses' quarrel with the school authorities involved what remains an unsolved problem in the law of religious freedom. The First Amendment to the United States Constitution provides that "Congress shall pass no law respecting an establishment of religion, or prohibiting the free exercise thereof. . . ." Originally applicable only to the Federal government, this restriction has been fully binding on the states at least since 1940. (There were hints even earlier through judicial extension of that clause of the Fourteenth Amendment forbidding any state to "deprive any person of life, liberty, or property, without due process of law.") This general prohibition was quite effective against the general run of religious persecution —such as compulsory church attendance, test oaths, and civil disabilities. But it offered no solution when a religious sect raised objections to a regulation that, on the surface, had nothing to do with religion. Such conflicts are far from rare: many sects object to military service; Jews object to jury duty on their sabbath; Quakers will not swear an oath. Where the sect is otherwise "respectable," the law is fairly quick to make adjustments—examples are the draft exemption of conscientious objectors, and the "affirmation" permitted Quakers. Where a sect is so truculent in manner or drastic in its innovations that it is rejected by society, it lives in a virtual state of siege. It runs afoul of old laws and is the target of new ones, ostensibly nondiscriminatory, but carefully designed to harass. Eventually, accommodation must be made—a softening of public attitude or substantial concessions by the sect—or the sect will die or be driven underground. Since the Civil War, three major sects, aside from Jehovah's Witnesses, have found the road to public acceptance rocky, but passable: the Mormons, the Christian Scientists, and the Salvation Army.

The Church of Jesus Christ of the Latter Day Saints, whose adherents are known as "Mormons," was established in 1829 by Joseph Smith, Jr., in Harmony, Pennsylvania. Smith claimed a divine commission to restore the true worship and re-establish Zion in North America. From the very beginning Smith and his little band of Saints were extremely unpopular for many reasons: their generally humble origins, exalted pretensions, frequent financial irresponsibility, and alleged use of violence and terrorism against both internal and external enemies. The last straw, which finally brought down the wrath of the Federal Government, was Smith's revelation that polygamy (plural marriage) was the right and religious duty of any Saint who could afford to support more than one wife and family. Shortly after Utah became a United States territory, Congress struck with a series of hostile statutes: punishing bigamy with increasing stringency and inclusiveness, disfranchising all practicing Mormons, dissolving the Morman church corporation and confiscating all its properties. Physically outmatched and facing total disaster, the Mormon leaders gave in. Late in 1890 the church officially renounced polygamy as an article of religious duty. A small minority refused to accept this decision and went underground. To the present time small colonies of fundamentalist Mormons still are being smoked out by state and Federal police. With increased maturity and with the polygamy issue out of the way, the Church of Jesus Christ of the Latter Day Saints has become eminently respectable.

The key tenet of Christian Science, founded by Mrs. Mary Baker Eddy in the late 1860's, is spiritual healing. Man can cure himself of most "physical" diseases, she taught, through faith, prayer, and cultivation of proper mental attitudes; he can cure others by inculcating similar faith and attitudes. This healing mission met the determined hostility of the medical profession, which considered Mrs. Eddy a positive menace to the health of the gullible. More serious, the Christian Scientists ran afoul of the various state laws licensing and prescribing qualifications for practitioners of medicine. States without such laws quickly passed them under the urging of worried doctors. Christian Scientists were incapable of qualifying for the legally required licenses—to receive the necessary medical instruction would impair or destroy their own healing power. They could not compromise since this dilemma struck at the very core of their faith; they could only await developments. Eventually, state legislators came to see that Christian Scientists were different from the general run of quacks and patent medicine salesmen. Now every state provides exemption for bona fide faith healers. Christian Scientists still have sporadic trouble over their unwillingness to submit themselves or their children to a physician's care, or even to physical examinations; on the whole, however, they have ceased to be controversial.

The Salvation Army first reached American shores in 1879. The "Army" is strictly nontheological in bent. Its sole mission is to rescue the derelict urban poor—too often ignored by regular churches—from the great moral snares of urban life: vice, narcotics, gambling, and especially liquor. Resented by many churchmen, hated with good reason by saloon-keepers, and a source of amusement to most people with its uniforms and music, the Salvation Army had many difficult early years. Toughs broke up Army meetings under the benevolent eyes of the police. A favorite target was the sect's custom of preceding each worship meeting with a parade through town, playing and singing to attract a congregation. Many cities passed ordinances either prohibiting parades entirely (with numerous exemptions for "respectable" groups) or subjecting them to a discretionary licensing system, which amounted to the same thing as far as the Salvationists were concerned. Eventually, the Salvation Army won out. Many hostile ordinances were declared unconstitutional by the courts because of their discriminatory character. More important, the Salvationists' nonsectarian good works and steadfast good humor, despite extreme provocation, profoundly impressed the more responsible community members. The Army's assistance at disaster areas and its selfless efforts to feed hundreds of thousands during the great depression have made it not only a respectable, but a respected, part of the American religious community.

Religious freedom has not been mentioned in these narratives. The Mormons, Christian Scientists, and Salvation Army all appealed to the state and Federal religious freedom guaranties in case after case; however, these appeals failed in every instance. State and Federal courts adhered consistently to a traditional rule: *that there could be no constitutional right to a religious exemption from a general regulation dealing on its face not with religion, but with the ordinary secular affairs of the state.* The various enactments at issue here dealt with matters—medicine, bigamy, traffic— traditionally within the ambit of governmental authority; it was irrelevant that some people might have religious reasons for violating these regulations. This was the state of the law in 1935. Against this background we must view Jehovah's Witnesses' struggle against the compulsory flag salute.

### The Flag Salute in Court: The Gobitis Case

"Judge" Rutherford's endorsement of nonsaluting in 1935 sparked a wave of Witness refusals across the country. School authorities responded with disciplinary action. Pennsylvania and Massachusetts led the way, and by 1939 over two hundred Witness children had been expelled. This relatively low total indicates that many school districts preferred to seek a compromise. Pressures on the Witnesses to make concessions were great. Aside from the direct hardship of the expulsions, the threat of school law and delinquency proceedings hung over all Witnesses unable to afford private schooling; they were faced with a hopeless choice between incarceration and damnation.

Lacking any perceptible political influence—being both few and unpopular—Jehovah's Witnesses turned naturally to action in the courts;

they had none of the scruples against litigation that had hamstrung their predecessors in the flag-salute controversy. In six states they brought suits for injunction or mandamus to compel readmission of their children to school without the flag salute. The state courts ruled against them each time. On four occasions before 1940 the United States Supreme Court rebuffed appeals from these rulings, without oral argument or written opinion. The Witnesses and their sympathizers kept trying, firmly convinced that total victory would be theirs if they could once secure a full hearing on the merits of the case in the Supreme Court.

Witness persistence was finally rewarded, in a sense, in the case of *Minersville School District* v. *Gobitis* (1940). Walter Gobitis had brought suit before a Federal district judge in Philadelphia, Pennsylvania, for an injunction compelling the readmission of his two expelled children to the Minersville public schools. What made this case different was that Gobitis won; the District Court held that the compulsory flag salute violated religious freedom when enforced against Jehovah's Witnesses. The Circuit Court of Appeals affirmed. The Minersville School Board went to the Supreme Court on a writ of certiorari, and the Witnesses had their test case.

"Judge" Rutherford, doubling as legal counsel (he had just fired the regular incumbent), filed a brief in the Supreme Court on behalf of Jehovah's Witnesses. It appealed at great length to the scriptures and hardly at all to the Constitution and must have had little value for the justices. More substantial arguments were advanced in the so-called *amicus curiae* (friend of the court) briefs filed in the Witnesses' behalf by the American Civil Liberties Union and the Committee on the Bill of Rights of the American Bar Association. It was urged that the compulsory salute violated the sect's religious liberty and was so harsh and self-defeating as to be a denial of "substantive due process of law"—that is, it was arbitrary and unreasonable.

On June 3, 1940, to the great surprise of the Witnesses and many civil libertarians, the Supreme Court reversed the decisions below, with only Justice Stone dissenting. Justice Frankfurter, writing for the majority, rejected the religious freedom argument out-of-hand on the basis of the standard rule:

> Conscientious scruples have not . . . relieved the individual from obedience to a general law not aimed at the promotion or restriction of religious beliefs. The mere possession of religious convictions which contradict the relevant concerns of a political society does not relieve the citizen from the discharge of political responsibilities. . . .

Against the substantive due process argument, he relied heavily on the strong presumption of constitutionality that attaches to all legislation, emphasizing that where the end is legitimate the legislature has a wide discretion in choosing means.

> We are dealing with an interest inferior to none. . . . National unity is the basis of national security. . . .
>     . . . Surely . . . the end is legitimate. And the effective means for its attainment are still so uncertain . . . as to preclude us from putting the widely prevalent belief in flag saluting beyond the pale. . . . The wisdom of training children in patriotic impulses by those compulsions which necessarily pervade so much of the educational process is not for our independent judgment. . . . [T]he courtroom is not the arena for debating issues of educational policy. . . . So to hold would in effect make us the school board for the country. . . .

Frankfurter closed with a general warning against bringing such "policy" disputes into the courts:

> Where all the effective means of inducing political change are left free from interference, education in the abandonment of foolish legislation is itself a training in liberty. . . .
>     . . . [T]o the legislature no less than to courts is committed the guardianship of deeply-cherished liberties. . . .

In view of what came later, it bears emphasis that there was nothing revolutionary in Frankfurter's opinion; the principles he invoked had been good law for over a century. Indeed, by refusing to follow the liberalizing trends that even then were transforming the other freedoms in the First Amendment, Frankfurter played an essentially conservative role. His zeal for completeness, however, partially obscured his own argument. Many people felt that in his *Gobitis* opinion he had laid down a new and dangerous doctrine: that religious freedom might be suppressed with impunity so long as the ballot box remained free.

### 1940–1943: The Road to Barnette

*Public Reception of the* Gobitis *Decision*

The *Gobitis* decision ushered in a bad period for Jehovah's Witnesses. The times were tense; Hitler was marching into France and the Low Countries. American opinion was nervous, confused, sullen—ripe for scapegoats. The Witnesses, with their ubiquitous offensiveness and already "doubtful" patriotism, were obvious candidates; the wide publicity given their flag-salute stand by *Gobitis* set off the explosion. While they probably faced a rough summer whichever way the decision went, Frankfurter's opinion, with its apparent endorsement of the salute and its implied rebuke of the Witnesses, aggravated the already charged situation.

The most spectacular manifestation of anti-Witness hostility was a sharp outbreak of violence. In June, 1940, several hundred incidents occurred in which force was directed against Jehovah's Witnesses; violent incidents continued at a rate of almost a hundred a month through most of 1940, all following a fixed pattern. Hundreds of street fights broke out. A Jehovah's Witness, distributing tracts on a street corner, was approached by several toughs carrying an American flag. When he refused their command to salute the flag, they beat him and destroyed his literature. Where the approach was made to a group of Witnesses, the affair turned into a full-scale brawl.

Often the violence transcended mere street-fighting, especially in the period immediately following the *Gobitis* decision. On June 9, 1940, an angry mob sacked and burned a Witness "Kingdom Hall" at Kennebunk, Maine. On June 22 a Witness was tarred and feathered in Parco, Wyoming. On June 27 a mob of veterans forcibly deported a large number of Witnesses from Jackson, Mississippi, eventually dropping them off at Dallas, Texas. In August a Nebraska Witness was abducted from his home and partially castrated. While the frequency of violent incidents tapered off after 1940, nasty cases continued to occur.

Less obvious but even more serious was the high degree of official persecution directed at Jehovah's Witnesses. This took many forms, the simplest of which was the refusal or failure either to prevent assaults upon the Witnesses or to prosecute the assailants afterward. Often, police and other officials would join the mobs. Deputy sheriffs took an active part in the Jackson, Mississippi, exodus, for example. It became a sort of national sport among small-town police and sheriffs to arrest Jehovah's Witnesses on sight and hold them incommunicado, without charges, for days or weeks. Beatings often were administered during custody. At Richwood, West Virginia, a deputy sheriff detained a group of Witnesses while he gathered a mob. He then forced the Witnesses to drink large doses of castor oil, tied them together with a police department rope, and marched them through and out of town. Ever increasing efforts were made to stamp out the Witnesses' door-to-door distribution of tracts through the application of various local antipeddling ordinances.

Much official hostility was aimed explicitly at the Witnesses' flag-salute stand. Hundreds of school districts made the flag ceremony compulsory for all pupils for the first time. By the end of 1942 expelled Witness children numbered over two thousand. Widespread attempts were made to imprison expellees for delinquency or their parents for school-law violation and contributing to delinquency. A court in Connersville, Indiana, sentenced two elderly ladies to ten years' imprisonment for "riotous conspiracy" because of their avowed opposition to the flag salute. In 1942 the Mississippi legislature made it a felony punishable by imprisonment for the duration of the war to advise "stubborn refusal" to salute the flag; scores of Witnesses were in jail by the end of the year.

The Witnesses fought back through the courts, but with limited success. They did get a large number of permit ordinances invalidated under the *Lovell* and *Schneider* precedents (p. 22), but the courts were not helpful against violence and discriminatory law enforcement. Suits to enjoin state or local prosecutions succeeded only occasionally; general Federal judicial practice was against such actions. Finally, New Hampshire dealt the Witnesses two defeats in the United States Supreme Court. In *Cox* v. *New Hampshire* (1941), the Court unanimously upheld a statute requiring a permit for all parades, which the state court had interpreted so as to give no discretionary power to the licensing authority. In *Chaplinsky* v. *New Hampshire* (1942), another unanimous Court upheld the abusive-language conviction of a Witness for calling the city marshal a "God-damned fascist"; the state's failure to prosecute the marshal, who had called the Witness much worse, was legally irrelevant.

Despite outbursts of zeal in states like Mississippi, persecution of Jehovah's Witnesses was decidedly on the wane by the last half of 1942. A most important reason for this trend was the active intervention of the Civil Rights Section of the Department of Justice. The main statutory weapon at its disposal was a section of the old post-Civil War civil rights legislation, making it a misdemeanor for anyone acting "under color of any law" to deprive any person of his Federal constitutional or statutory right. Under this provision, the Civil Rights Section prosecuted the deputy sheriff involved in the castor oil incident, securing a conviction and maximum sentence (a year in jail and a thousand-dollar fine), and attempted several other prosecutions. More important, however, was the Section's mediative function. Persecution fell off sharply in northern Texas after United States Attorney Clyde Eastus, under Civil Rights Section prodding, pleaded on radio with local authorities and American Legionnaires to respect the Witnesses' constitutional rights.

Meanwhile, unfavorable press reaction to the *Gobitis* decision grew. The hostile writers did not meet Frankfurter's legal arguments directly or precisely; they dismissed them as elaborate rationalizations for throwing the Witnesses to the wolves. Legal niceties aside, the decision was considered intolerable in its direct effect. The St. Louis *Post Dispatch* termed it "A Terrible Decision." The *New Republic* acidly noted Frankfurter's zeal in "heroically saving America from a couple of school children. . . ." "Courts that will not protect even Jehovah's Witnesses will not long protect anybody," snapped the liberal Protestant journal *Christian Century,* which waged a long campaign against the *Gobitis* ruling. Catholic magazines, led by the Jesuit organ *America,* were bitter in denouncing the decision.

Especially impressive was the solid hostility of scholarly comment, particularly in the law reviews. Of thirty-five scholarly writings taking a definite position on the decision (eleven mentioned it without comment), thirty-one were clearly critical, only four favorable. Edward S. Corwin, dean of American constitutional law writers, called the decision "distasteful." Robert E. Cushman, in the *American Political Science Review,* was more emphatic:

> All the eloquency by which the majority extol the ceremony of flag saluting as a free expression of patriotism turns sour when used to describe the brutal compulsion which requires a sensitive and conscientious child to stultify himself in public. . . .

### Judicial Reactions: The Decline of Gobitis

The *Gobitis* decision was also unenthusiastically received by the state courts. In three years after June, 1940, it gave rise to no line of decisions, but was rather effectively quarantined. As pointed out earlier, numerous proceedings had been brought against Witness children and their parents under the laws governing truancy and delinquency. Under existing law these prosecutions should have succeeded; under *Gobitis* the religious scruple giving rise to the violation should have been irrelevant. Actually, however, the courts systematically blocked all attempts at further punishment of either children or parents. Defendant parents were pictured as being helpless to change the stubborn religious views of their offspring. Defendant children were held innocent victims of parental religious instruction. The courts apparently viewed nonsaluting as different from other violations of school regulations. Judges who originally had written opinions upholding the compulsory salute became increasingly impatient with official obtuseness.

Finally, two state courts rebelled outright. Here again, the cases involved attempts at further punishment. In *State* v. *Smith* (1942), the Kansas Supreme Court upset a pair of school law prosecutions by holding that the state's flag-salute law had never authorized the compulsory flag salute, and that it would violate the state constitution if it did. In *Bolling* v. *Superior Court* (1943), the Washington Supreme Court stopped a group of delinquency proceedings against Witness children by declaring that state's flag-salute statute unconstitutional as applied, under both the state and Federal Constitutions. Both decisions were unanimous.

The flag-salute controversy became more complex on June 23, 1942, when Congress, under the urging of the American Legion, passed a joint resolution—commonly referred to as "Public Law 623"—codifying the rules of flag etiquette. Not a law in the strict sense, this resolution was important as an expression of Congressional policy. Significant for present purposes was Section 7:

> That the pledge of allegiance to the flag . . . be rendered by . . . the standard procedure. . . . However, civilians will always show full respect

to the flag when the pledge is given by merely standing at attention, men removing the headdress. . . .

It seems clear, in retrospect, that this section was not intended to alter the controversy then raging. The precise language had been in the American Legion's own code of flag respect since 1924 and was never discussed at all in Congressional debate. Probably the section was meant to apply to spectators at a flag-salute ceremony. However, many enemies of the compulsory salute seized upon these ambiguous sentences as a Congressional declaration that "full respect" could be shown the flag without the salute and pledge. On July 18, 1942, the Civil Rights Section, with departmental approval, threw its weight behind this interpretation, advising all United States attorneys that it was "a very real question whether any local regulation . . . prescribing a different measure of respect to the flag can be enforced." The attorneys were advised to call this conflict to the attention of local school authorities.

By mid-1942, *Gobitis* was under fire from all sides. On June 16 that precedent was undermined still further—by the Supreme Court itself. *Jones* v. *Opelika* (1942) involved a set of local ordinances imposing flat-rate license taxes on door-to-door peddlers. Jehovah's Witnesses challenged the application of such ordinances to their distribution of tracts as a violation of freedom of religion and the press. The Supreme Court held the ordinances constitutional as applied, by a bare five-to-four vote. In an unprecedented step Justices Black, Douglas, and Murphy, dissenting along with Chief Justice Stone, went out of their way to announce a change of heart on the flag-salute issue.

> This is but another step in the direction which *Minersville School District* v. *Gobitis* . . . took against the same religious minority and is a logical extension of the principles upon which that decision rested. Since we joined in the opinion in the *Gobitis* Case, we think this is an appropriate occasion to state that we now believe that it was also wrongly decided. . . .

The anti-*Gobitis* tide was strengthened still further in early 1942, when Appeals Judge Wiley Rutledge replaced Justice James F. Byrnes on the Court. Byrnes, a 1941 appointee, had not taken part in *Gobitis,* but could, from his record, be expected to support Frankfurter's position. Rutledge, while serving on the Court of Appeals for the District of Columbia, had voted in favor of the Witnesses in a case exactly parallel to *Jones* v. *Opelika* and had shown general distaste for *Gobitis*. On May 3, 1943, Rutledge cast the deciding vote in *Murdock* v. *Pennsylvania,* as the Court overruled *Jones* v. *Opelika* in language flatly inconsistent with Frankfurter's *Gobitis* reasoning.

The *Gobitis* decision was as good as dead; all that remained was an official burial. That opportunity was not long in coming; another flag-salute case, *West Virginia State Board of Education* v. *Barnette,* was already pending before the Court.

### The Barnette Case in the District Court

West Virginia law requires that the public schools give instruction in history and civics "for the purpose of teaching, fostering, and perpetuating the ideals, principles, and spirit of Americanism," and grants the State Board of Education wide authority to prescribe courses of study adapted to that end. Exercising this statutory discretion, the State Board resolved on January 9, 1942, that

> [T]he commonly accepted salute to the Flag of the United States . . . now becomes a regular part of the program of activities in the public schools . . . and that all teachers and pupils in such schools shall be required to participate in the salute . . . provided, however, that refusal to salute the Flag be regarded as an act of insubordination, and shall be dealt with accordingly.

The attitude of the West Virginia school authorities toward the flag-salute ceremony was actually more than a little ambiguous. During the month after Pearl Harbor, the State Board of Education allowed itself to be persuaded (by whom is not clear) that with a war on something had to be done about Jehovah's Witnesses. The Board then reached rather mechanically for the weapon offered them by the *Gobitis* decision. That the January 9 resolution was aimed at Jehovah's Witnesses was obvious; the long "whereas" portion quoted at two-page length from Frankfurter's *Gobitis* opinion. As we shall see, however, the Board had no real emotional commitment to its anti-Witness position. Feeling for the salute was intense in the rural areas of the state, but at the scene of our lawsuit, the Charleston area, the picture was quite different. Teachers and principals were reluctant to resort to expulsion and tried by persuasion, and even subterfuge, to procure the minimum "compliance" that would enable the children to stay in school.

Since the *Gobitis* defeat the Witness legal office had abandoned all direct challenges to the compulsory flag salute and concentrated on helping individual Witnesses protect themselves against the by-products of that decision. After hearing the opinions in *Jones* v. *Opelika,* however, Hayden Covington (chief legal counsel since Rutherford's death early in 1942) knew that another test case was in order. He immediately contacted attorney Horace Meldahl to lay plans for an injunction suit to be brought in the District Court at Charleston.

It should be stressed that this was Covington's lawsuit—initiated, controlled, briefed, and argued by him—on behalf of Jehovah's Witnesses as a national organization. Meldahl's main functions were to do the basic paper work and get Covington admitted to the local District Court bar for purposes of this case. The individual plaintiffs—Walter Barnette, Paul Stull, and Mrs. Lucy B. McClure—had no very special status among aggrieved West Virginia Witnesses; somebody's name had to go on the bill of complaint, and these three were conveniently near Charleston.

The three plaintiffs were related: Mrs. McClure was Barnette's sister, and Stull was his brother-in-law. All three were poor: Barnette and Stull were pipefitters' helpers, and Mrs. McClure's husband was a shipping clerk. Seven children were in the three families, and all had been expelled from school for "insubordination," as defined by the January 9 resolution. Nor was this the end of their troubles. West Virginia law required that children between seven and fourteen years of age be enrolled in some school. Parents neglecting this duty were liable to fine or imprisonment; a "habitually truant" child might be proceeded against as a juvenile delinquent. A 1941 amendment to the school laws increased the legal threat by expressly providing that such sanctions were applicable where a child was unable to attend school as a result of noncompliance with any school rule.

Paul Stull obtained private schooling for his children; Walter Barnette and Lucy McClure could not find any such school that they could afford. In the summer of 1942, Barnette and Mrs. McClure were convicted and fined for violating compulsory school laws. The fine was never collected, however, and the state abandoned the case on appeal. At about the same time, Paul Stull retained Meldahl—one of the few friendly lawyers in the whole state— to bring an action in the West Virginia Supreme Court for a writ of prohibition against further enforcement of the flag-salute regulation. This suit was dismissed without a hearing.

The Barnette suit was filed by Meldahl in mid-August before Judge Ben Moore of the Federal District Court for the Southern District of West Virginia. This was a "class" action—that is, an action on behalf of the plaintiffs and all others within the state similarly situated. The bill of complaint asserted that the West Virginia regulation was an arbitrary and unreasonable deprivation of personal liberty and a violation of freedom of speech and religion—all contrary to the due process clause of the Fourteenth Amendment. An injunction was requested forbidding enforcement of the regulation against Jehovah's Witnesses anywhere in West Virginia.

The Federal judicial code provides that an injunction against enforcement of a state statute or state-wide administrative regulation can be issued only by a specially constituted three-judge tribunal. Joining Moore as the tribunal for this case were District Judge Harry Watkins of the Northern and Southern Districts of West Virginia, and Circuit Judge John J. Parker of the Fourth Circuit. Parker was to dominate the conduct of this case in the

District Court. A veteran of seventeen years on the bench, he was well-known because in 1930 the Senate narrowly rejected his appointment to the Supreme Court.

At the first hearing of the *Barnette* case before the three-judge tribunal on September 14, 1942, Assistant Attorney General Ira J. Partlow moved that the action be dismissed on the controlling authority of *Gobitis.* He frankly admitted dissatisfaction with the State Board's stand and said he would have preferred some sort of compromise. Judge Parker was even more displeased. He urged the Board to amend its regulation to exempt conscientious objectors and recessed the hearing to allow consideration of his suggestion. The following morning the State Board voted to stand by its original position.

The decisive hearing took place on the afternoon of September 15. Parker was openly disgusted, commenting on how unfortunate it was "that a case of its kind should be in court at a time when national unity is paramount." He curtly brushed aside Partlow's reliance on *Gobitis,* refused to dismiss the action, and set the case for trial on the facts. However, since the facts were undisputed, there was no trial, the case being submitted by the lawyers for final judgment on the pleadings and briefs that had already been filed.

On October 6, 1942, the three-judge court handed down its unanimous decision, permanently enjoining all the defendants "from requiring the children of the plaintiffs, or any other children having religious scruples against such action, to salute the flag of the United States, or any other flag, or from expelling such children from school for failure to salute it; and that plaintiffs recover from the defendants the costs of suit. . . ." Judge Parker's opinion began by disposing of *Gobitis.* While a Supreme Court decision, not overruled, generally is absolutely binding on lower Federal courts, he held that the *Gobitis* precedent had been deprived of this binding force by its treatment in *Opelika.* Parker's opinion on the merits was based entirely on the lower-court opinions in *Gobitis.* First, he rejected out-of-hand the traditional religious freedom rule holding that since the children invoked religious scruples against saluting, religious freedom was relevant to the case; the state must show some necessity justifying its decision to override such scruples. For Parker, the dividing line between permissible infringements on religious liberty and forbidden invasions was summed up in the "clear and present danger" test generally used in free-speech cases. Did refusal to salute the flag create a clear and present danger to the state? "[T]o ask these questions is to answer them. . . . The salute to the flag is an expression of the homage of the soul. To force it upon one who has conscientious scruples against giving it, is petty tyranny . . . and forbidden, we think, by the fundamental law."

On October 23 the State Board of Education voted to take an appeal to the United States Supreme Court. The case was docketed on December 16, and most of the briefs were filed by January 4. By this time Partlow had become Acting Attorney General. Unwilling either to argue the appeal or to jettison it, he handed the task to a subordinate, W. Holt Wooddell.

Since they planned an appeal, state school authorities could have obtained an order maintaining the status quo—that is, delaying the effect of the injunction—simply for the asking; such an order is standard practice in this sort of case to avoid unnecessary disruption. The authorities requested no delay; instead, they complied with the injunction fully and immediately. On October 7 Superintendent Trent issued a general statement to the press:

> In compliance with the ruling of the . . . Federal Court . . . children belonging to religious sects whose belief prohibits their participating in giving the Flag Salute may attend school and will, pending further court rulings, be considered as fulfilling the regulation . . . by standing at attention with hats off while the Salute is being given.

The Barnette, McClure, and Stull children were readmitted to school almost immediately. Only the Barnette children had difficulty: they had missed a promotion because of time lost and were snubbed by many classmates. School authorities throughout the state complied quickly with Trent's directions. Meldahl had to threaten one Charleston area school district with contempt proceedings, but no other trouble occurred. A few enthusiastic Witnesses forbade their children even to stand during the flag ceremony. Covington and Meldahl sharply rebuked these extremists, foreseeing new and serious trouble if overt disrespect of the flag were to spread among Witnesses.

### The Justices Reconsider: Briefs and Arguments in the Supreme Court

Five briefs were filed in the Supreme Court in the *Barnette* case, those of the principal parties and three *amicus* briefs. The American Civil Liberties Union and the Committee on the Bill of Rights of the American Bar Association filed briefs supporting the Witnesses; the American Legion, entering the judicial arena for the first time, filed a short brief, urging that the decision below be reversed. Virtually no fresh discussion arose on the constitutional merits of the West Virginia regulation; at every stage the parties refought the *Gobitis* battle. The real-life parties in *Barnette* faded into the background; they were mere late-comers, spectators at the last battle of an eight-year war.

The briefs and argument in *Barnette* must be viewed in the light of the peculiar situation prevailing. Four justices—Stone (now Chief Justice), Black, Douglas, and Murphy—were committed to overruling *Gobitis*. Of the justices appointed after *Gobitis,* Rutledge certainly shared their views, and Jackson's position was unclear, but seemed to lean toward overruling. Only

Frankfurter, Reed, and Roberts seemed reasonably sure to stick by their *Gobitis* votes. The Witnesses and their allies, then, could count on at least five votes. The task of their brief-writers was to hold that majority, and overcome any judicial reluctance to overrule such a recent precedent. Writers for the other side had a harder task: to persuade one or two justices to subordinate their personal views on the constitutionality of the compulsory salute to their respect for precedent.

### Briefs for Appellants: "Nothing New Here"

W. Holt Wooddell's brief on behalf of the State Board of Education was very short. His main contention was that the complaint should have been dismissed on the basis of *Gobitis,* "which said decision has in no manner been overruled or modified." He emphasized that this case was simply *Gobitis* over again; nothing new had been added. A second section of the brief advanced the cryptic proposition that "the regulation of appellants is not inimical to public safety and good order," citing *Gobitis* as the only authority. Whatever this section was intended to accomplish, it had the unfortunate effect of supporting the Witnesses' complaint that *Gobitis* had sanctified the various official proceedings against flag-salute expellees and their parents. A closing section denied that Public Law 623 had changed the legal situation, since it was not a "law" in any binding sense, and in other sections not cited by the Witnesses actually endorsed the standard ceremony as the proper mode of showing respect.

Ralph Gregg of Indianapolis filed a very short brief *amicus curiae* for the American Legion, duplicating the first and third sections of Wooddell's brief. Its main purpose was to throw the Legion's authoritative weight against the antisalute interpretation of Public Law 623.

### Briefs for Appellees: "Gobitis *Must Go"*

The American Bar Association's Committee on the Bill of Rights had no regular dealings with Jehovah's Witnesses and had not come to their aid in any of their other legal difficulties. Its sole purpose here was to clarify the law of religious freedom—and to clarify it against the compulsory flag salute. The Committee's argument on this point was a short restatement of its strong brief in *Gobitis*. First, flatly rejecting the traditional rule, the committee insisted that religious freedom was applicable to this dispute because the Witnesses had invoked religious scruples against the salute; it was the nature of the objection, not of the regulation, that was decisive. Second, a conflict between religious scruple and secular regulation must be resolved by weighing the public interest in universal compliance with the regulation against the public interest in religious freedom. Third, and crucial, the usual presumption of constitutionality should be reversed in such cases, placing a heavy burden on the state to justify its interference with freedom of conscience. Religious scruples could be overridden only where such a course was necessary to the achievement of a sufficiently important public interest.

The balance of the Committee's brief dealt with the adverse professional legal reaction to *Gobitis*. The hostile law review articles were carefully tallied and copiously quoted. The Committee described in detail the alacrity with which state judges had ignored, avoided, and even flouted that precedent. There undoubtedly was another purpose to this than merely helping the justices see themselves as others saw them. The Court had been severely criticized for its willingness to overrule precedents. Here, it was suggested, was a precedent that would be mourned by no one if it were discarded.

The American Civil Liberties Union had been involved in the flag-salute controversy since 1925, when it went to the aid of the Jehovites and Elijah Voice Society; it had been working closely with Jehovah's Witnesses since 1935. An ACLU representative had filed a brief and participated in oral argument in *Gobitis*. Neither the brief nor the argument had been well received; therefore, the Union's *Barnette* brief was all new. The ACLU's religious freedom argument was largely patterned on that of the Bill of Rights Committee. Following Judge Parker's lead, however, it went one step further, urging that religious scruples could be overridden only in the event of a "clear and present danger" to the state. If grown men could urge overthrow of the government, the brief insisted, surely the Witnesses' harmless scruples should be immune. The ACLU sharply attacked Frankfurter's reliance on judicial self-restraint in *Gobitis*. "A persecuted minority may suffer long before it can alleviate its burdens by way of the ballot box." As proof, the brief detailed the widespread persecution of Jehovah's Witnesses since *Gobitis* and the many prosecutions brought against expelled children and their parents. Finally, the ACLU appealed to Public Law 623.

Hayden Covington's brief for Jehovah's Witnesses was long, discursive, vigorous, and a veritable anthology of quotations (generally unacknowledged) from previous flag-salute briefs. He borrowed Rutherford's assertion in *Gobitis* that the compulsory salute was void because it was contrary to divine law, and followed this by reproducing in its entirety the religious freedom section of the Bill of Rights Committee's *Gobitis* brief.

Covington further argued that the compulsory salute violated freedom of speech. Since the Court had held in *Stromberg* v. *California* (1931) that one could not be punished for saluting a hostile foreign flag, surely it must be equally allowable merely to refrain from saluting the American flag. The basic assumption was that freedom of speech included the right to refrain from uttering opinions or sentiments not held. Finally, Covington urged that the compulsory salute violated substantive due process of law.

Covington devoted almost a third of his brief to a blistering attack on the decision and opinion in *Gobitis,* particularly Frankfurter's long panegyric on judicial self-restraint. He condemned Frankfurter as an enemy of Jehovah and freedom, who had sought to make local school boards the supreme court of the nation. He described minutely the various forms of persecution to which the Witnesses had been subjected and included a long list of hostile comments on *Gobitis* in law reviews and newspapers. He closed with a bitter attack on the "un-American" position of the American Legion in this case.

*Oral Argument: A Terse Word to the Court*

Wooddell's oral argument for appellants was quite short. He simply re-emphasized his main point—that this case was on all fours with *Gobitis*—and declined to take up any more of the Court's time. Covington's argument for Jehovah's Witnesses was longer and far more vigorous. A big man and an eloquent speaker, Covington was noted for his natty dress, almost calisthenic gestures, a truculent manner, and a sublime disregard of consequences. He came to Washington determined, win or lose, to berate the justices for their *Gobitis* ruling. He did so, calling the decision one of the Court's greatest mistakes, a fit companion for the *Dred Scott* case, and an act of judicial abdication. The justices received his strictures largely in silence.

On June 14, 1943—Flag Day—the Supreme Court affirmed the decision below and overruled *Gobitis* by a vote of six to three.

---

*WEST VIRGINIA STATE BOARD OF EDUCATION* v. *BARNETTE*
319 U.S. 624, 63 S. Ct. 1178, 87 L. Ed. 1628 (1943)

MR. JUSTICE JACKSON delivered the opinion of the Court.

Following the decision by this Court on June 3, 1940, in *Minersville School District* v. *Gobitis,* 310 U.S. 586, the West Virginia legislature amended its statutes to require all schools therein to conduct courses of instruction in history, civics, and in the Constitutions of the United States and of the State "for the purpose of teaching, fostering and perpetuating the ideals, principles and spirit of Americanism, and increasing the knowledge of the organization and machinery of the government." Appellant Board of Education was directed, with advice of the State Superintendent of Schools, to "prescribe the courses of study covering these subjects" for public schools. The Act made it the duty of private, parochial and denominational schools to prescribe courses of study "similar to those required for the public schools."

The Board of Education on January 9, 1942, adopted a resolution containing recitals taken largely from the Court's *Gobitis* opinion and ordering that the salute to the flag become "a regular part of the program of activities in the public schools," that all teachers and pupils "shall be required to participate in the salute honoring the Nation represented by the Flag; provided, however, that refusal to salute the Flag be regarded as an act of insubordination, and shall be dealt with accordingly." . . .

Appellees, citizens of the United States and of West Virginia, brought suit in the United States District Court for themselves and others similarly situated asking its injunction to restrain enforcement of these laws and regulations against Jehovah's Witnesses. The Witnesses are an unincorporated body teaching that the obligation imposed by law of God is superior to that of laws enacted by temporal government. Their religious beliefs include a literal version of Exodus, Chapter 20, verses 4 and 5, which says: "Thou shalt not make unto thee any graven image, or any likeness of anything that is in heaven above, or that is in the earth beneath, or that is in the water under the earth; thou shalt not bow down thyself to them nor serve them." They consider that the flag is an "image" within this command. For this reason they refuse to salute it.

Children of this faith have been expelled from school and are threatened with exclusion for no other cause. Officials threaten to send them to reformatories maintained for criminally inclined juveniles. Parents of such children have been prosecuted and are threatened with prosecutions for causing delinquency. . . .

The freedom asserted by these appellees does not bring them into collision with rights asserted by any other individual. It is such conflicts which most frequently require intervention of the State to determine where the rights of one end and those of another begin. But the refusal of these persons to participate in the ceremony does not interfere with or deny rights of others to do so. Nor is there any question in this case that their behavior is peaceable and orderly. The sole conflict is between authority and rights of the individual. The State asserts power to condition access to public education on making a prescribed sign and profession and at the same time to coerce attendance by punishing both parent and child. The latter stand on a right of self-determination in matters that touch individual opinion and personal attitude. . . .

The compulsory flag salute and pledge requires affirmation of a belief and an attitude of mind. It is not clear whether the regulation contemplates that pupils forego any contrary convictions of their own and become unwilling converts to the prescribed ceremony or whether it will be acceptable if they simulate assent by words without belief and by a gesture barren of meaning. It is now a commonplace that censorship or suppression of expression of opinion is tolerated by our Constitution only when the expression presents a clear and present danger of action of a kind the State is empowered to prevent and punish. It would seem that involuntary affirmation could be commanded only on even more immediate and urgent grounds than silence. But here the power of compulsion is invoked without any allegation that remaining passive during a flag salute ritual creates a clear and present danger that would justify an effort even to muffle expression. To sustain the compulsory flag salute we are required to say that a Bill of Rights which guards the individual's right to speak his own mind, left it open to public authorities to compel him to utter what is not in his mind.

Whether the First Amendment to the Constitution will permit officials to order observance of ritual of this nature does not depend upon whether as a voluntary exercise we would think it to be good, bad or merely innocuous. Any credo of nationalism is likely to include what some disapprove or to omit what others think essential, and to give off different overtones as it takes on different accents or interpretations. If official power exists to coerce acceptance of any patriotic creed, what it shall contain cannot be decided by courts. . . .

Nor does the issue as we see it turn on one's possession of particular religious views or the sincerity with which they are held. While religion supplies appellees' motive for enduring the discomforts of making the issue in this case, many citizens who do not share these religious views hold such a compulsory rite to infringe constitutional liberty of the individual. It is not necessary to inquire whether non-conformist beliefs will exempt from the duty to salute unless we first find power to make the salute a legal duty.

The *Gobitis* decision, however, *assumed,* as did the argument in that case and in this, that power exists in the State to impose the flag salute discipline upon school children in general. The Court only examined and rejected a claim based on religious beliefs of immunity from an unquestioned general rule. The question which underlies the flag salute controversy is whether such a ceremony so touching matters of opinion and political attitude may be imposed upon the individual by official authority under powers committed to any political organization under our Constitution. We examine rather than assume existence of this power and, against this broader definition of issues in this case, reëxamine specific grounds assigned for the *Gobitis* decision.

1. It was said that the flag-salute controversy confronted the Court with "the problem which Lincoln cast in memorable dilemma: 'Must a government of necessity be too *strong* for the liberties of its people, or too *weak* to maintain its own existence?' " and that the answer must be in favor of strength. . . .

Government of limited power need not be anemic government. Assurance that rights are secure tends to diminish fear and jealousy of strong government, and by making us feel safe to live under it makes for its better support. . . .

2. It was also considered in the *Gobitis* case that functions of educational officers in States, counties and school districts were such that to interfere with their authority "would in effect make us the school board for the country." . . .

The Fourteenth Amendment, as now applied to the States, protects the citizen against the State itself and all of its creatures—Boards of Education not excepted. These have, of course, important, delicate, and highly discretionary functions, but none that they may not perform within the limits of the Bill of Rights. . . .

3. The *Gobitis* opinion reasoned that this is a field "where courts possess no marked and certainly no controlling competence," that it is committed to the legislatures as well as the courts to guard cherished liberties and that it is constitutionally appropriate to "fight out the wise use of legislative authority in the forum of public opinion and before legislative assemblies rather than to transfer such a contest to the judicial arena," since all the "effective means of inducing political changes are left free." . . .

The very purpose of a Bill of Rights was to withdraw certain subjects from the vicissitudes of political controversy, to place them beyond the reach of majorities and officials and to establish them as legal principles to be applied by the courts. One's right to life, liberty, and property, to free speech, a free press, freedom of worship and assembly, and other fundamental rights may not be submitted to vote; they depend on the outcome of no elections. . . .

In weighing arguments of the parties it is important to distinguish between the due process clause of the Fourteenth Amendment as an instrument for transmitting the principles of the First Amendment and those cases in which it is applied for its own sake. The test of legislation which collides with the Fourteenth Amendment, because it also collides with the principles of the First, is much more definite than the test when only the Fourteenth is involved. Much of the vagueness of the due process clause disappears when the specific prohibitions of the First become its standard.

The right of a State to regulate, for example, a public utility may well include, so far as the due process test is concerned, power to impose all of the restrictions which a legislature may have a "rational basis" for adopting. But freedoms of speech and of press, of assembly, and of worship may not be infringed on such slender grounds. They are susceptible of restriction only to prevent grave and immediate danger to interests which the State may lawfully protect. It is important to note that while it is the Fourteenth Amendment which bears directly upon the State it is the more specific limiting principles of the First Amendment that finally govern this case.

Nor does our duty to apply the Bill of Rights to assertions of official authority depend upon our possession of marked competence in the field where the invasion of rights occurs. True, the task of translating the majestic generalities of the Bill of Rights, conceived as part of the pattern of liberal government in the eighteenth century, into concrete restraints on officials dealing with the problems of the twentieth century, is one to disturb self-confidence. . . . These changed conditions often deprive precedents of reliability and cast us more than we would choose upon our own judgment. But we act in these matters not by authority of our competence but by force of our commissions. We cannot, because of modest estimates of our competence in such specialties as public education, withhold the judgment that history authenticates as the function of this Court when liberty is infringed.

4. Lastly, and this is the very heart of the *Gobitis* opinion, it reasons that "National unity is the basis of national security," that the authorities have "the right to select appropriate means for its attainment," and hence reaches the conclusion that such compulsory measures toward "national unity" are constitutional. . . . Upon the verity

of this assumption depends our answer in this case.

National unity as an end which officials may foster by persuasion and example is not in question. The problem is whether under our Constitution compulsion as here employed is a permissible means for its achievement.

Struggles to coerce uniformity of sentiment in support of some end thought essential to their time and country have been waged by many good as well as by evil men. Nationalism is a relatively recent phenomenon but at other times and places the ends have been racial or territorial security, support of a dynasty or regime, and particular plans for saving souls. As first and moderate methods to attain unity have failed, those bent on its accomplishment must resort to an ever-increasing severity. . . . Those who begin coercive elimination of dissent soon find themselves exterminating dissenters. Compulsory unification of opinion achieves only the unanimity of the graveyard.

It seems trite but necessary to say that the First Amendment to our Constitution was designed to avoid these ends by avoiding these beginnings. . . .

The case is made difficult not because the principles of its decision are obscure but because the flag involved is our own. Nevertheless, we apply the limitations of the Constitution with no fear that freedom to be intellectually and spiritually diverse or even contrary will disintegrate the social organization. To believe that patriotism will not flourish if patriotic ceremonies are voluntary and spontaneous instead of a compulsory routine is to make an unflattering estimate of the appeal of our institutions to free minds. We can have intellectual individualism and the rich cultural diversities that we owe to exceptional minds only at the price of occasional eccentricity and abnormal attitudes. When they are so harmless to others or to the State as those we deal with here, the price is not too great. But freedom to differ is not limited to things that do not matter much. That would be a mere shadow of freedom. The test of its substance is the right to differ as to things that touch the heart of the existing order.

If there is any fixed star in our constitutional constellation, it is that no official, high or petty, can prescribe what shall be orthodox in politics, nationalism, religion, or other matters of opinion or force citizens to confess by word or act their faith therein. If there are any circumstances which permit an exception, they do not now occur to us. . . .

*Affirmed.*

MR. JUSTICE ROBERTS and MR. JUSTICE REED adhere to the views expressed by the Court in *Minersville School District* v. *Gobitis,* 310 U.S. 586, and are of the opinion that the judgment below should be reversed.

MR. JUSTICE BLACK and MR. JUSTICE DOUGLAS, concurring.

We are substantially in agreement with the opinion just read, but since we originally joined with the Court in the *Gobitis* case, it is appropriate that we make a brief statement of reasons for our change of view.

Reluctance to make the Federal Constitution a rigid bar against state regulation of conduct thought inimical to the public welfare was the controlling influence which moved us to consent to the *Gobitis* decision. Long reflection convinced us that although the principle is sound, its application in the particular case was wrong. . . .

No well-ordered society can leave to the individuals an absolute right to make final decisions, unassailable by the State, as to everything they will or will not do. The First Amendment does not go so far. Religious faiths, honestly held, do not free individuals from responsibility to conduct themselves obediently to laws which are either imperatively necessary to pro-

tect society as a whole from grave and pressingly imminent dangers or which, without any general prohibition, merely regulate time, place or manner of religious activity. Decision as to the constitutionality of particular laws which strike at the substance of religious tenets and practices must be made by this Court. The duty is a solemn one, and in meeting it we cannot say that a failure, because of religious scruples, to assume a particular physical position and to repeat the words of a patriotic formula creates a grave danger to the nation. Such a statutory exaction is a form of test oath, and the test oath has always been abhorrent in the United States. . . .

The ceremonial, when enforced against conscientious objectors, more likely to defeat than to serve its high purpose, is a handy implement for disguised religious persecution. As such, it is inconsistent with our Constitution's plan and purpose.

MR. JUSTICE MURPHY, concurring.

I agree with the opinion of the Court and join in it. . . .

The right of freedom of thought and of religion . . . includes both the right to speak freely and the right to refrain from speaking at all, except in so far as essential operations of government may require it for the preservation of an orderly society,—as in the case of compulsion to give evidence in court. . . .

MR. JUSTICE FRANKFURTER, dissenting.

One who belongs to the most vilified and persecuted minority in history is not likely to be insensible to the freedoms guaranteed by our Constitution. Were my purely personal attitude relevant I should wholeheartedly associate myself with the general libertarian views in the Court's opinion.

. . . It can never be emphasized too much that one's own opinion about the wisdom or evil of a law should be excluded altogether when one is doing one's duty on the bench. The only opinion of our own even looking in that direction that is material is our opinion whether legislators could in reason have enacted such a law. In the light of all the circumstances, including the history of this question in this Court, it would require more daring than I possess to deny that reasonable legislators could have taken the action which is before us for review. . . .

The Constitution does not give us greater veto power when dealing with one phase of "liberty" than with another. . . . Our power does not vary according to the particular provision of the Bill of Rights which is invoked. The right not to have property taken without just compensation has, so far as the scope of judicial power is concerned, the same constitutional dignity as the right to be protected against unreasonable searches and seizures . . . [or] freedom of the press or freedom of speech or religious freedom. In no instance is this Court the primary protector of the particular liberty that is invoked. . . .

Under our constitutional system the legislature is charged solely with civil concerns of society. If the avowed or intrinsic legislative purpose is either to promote or to discourage some religious community or creed, it is clearly within the constitutional restrictions imposed on legislatures and cannot stand. But it by no means follows that legislative power is wanting whenever a general non-discriminatory civil regulation in fact touches conscientious scruples or religious beliefs of an individual or a group. . . .

Conscientious scruples, all would admit, cannot stand against every legislative compulsion to do positive acts in conflict with such scruples. We have been told that such compulsions override religious scruples only as to major concerns of the state. But the determination of what is major and what is minor itself raises questions of policy. . . . Judges should be very diffident in setting their judgment against that of a state in determining what is and is not a major concern, what means are appropriate to proper ends, and what is the total social cost in striking the balance of imponderables. . . .

The constitutional protection of religious freedom terminated disabilities, it did not create new privileges. It gave religious equality, not civil immunity. . . .

The essence of the religious freedom guaranteed by our Constitution is therefore this: no religion shall either receive the state's support or incur its hostility. Religion is outside the sphere of political government. This does not mean that all matters on which religious organizations or beliefs may pronounce are outside the sphere of government. . . .

Law is concerned with external behavior and not with the inner life of man. It rests in large measure upon compulsion. Socrates lives in history partly because he gave his life for the conviction that duty of obedience to secular law does not presuppose consent to its enactment or belief in its virtue. . . . One may have the right to practice one's religion and at the same time owe the duty of formal obedience to laws that run counter to one's beliefs. Compelling belief implies denial of opportunity to combat it and to assert dissident views. Such compulsion is one thing. Quite another matter is submission to conformity of action while denying its wisdom or virtue and with ample opportunity for seeking its change or abrogation. . . .

We are told that a flag salute is a doubtful substitute for adequate understanding of our institutions. The states that require such a school exercise do not have to justify it as the only means for promoting good citizenship in children, but merely as one of diverse means for accomplishing a worthy end. We may deem it a foolish measure, but the point is that this Court is not the organ of government to resolve doubts as to whether it will fulfill its purpose. Only if there be no doubt that any reasonable mind could entertain can we deny to the states the right to resolve doubts their way and not ours.

The right of West Virginia to utilize the flag salute as part of its educational process is denied because, so it is argued, it cannot be justified as a means of meeting a "clear and present danger" to national unity. . . . To talk about "clear and present danger" as the touchstone of allowable educational policy by the states whenever school curricula may impinge upon the boundaries of individual conscience, is to take a felicitous phrase out of the context of the particular situation where it arose. . . .

The flag salute exercise has no kinship whatever to the oath tests so odious in history. For the oath test was one of the instruments for suppressing heretical beliefs. Saluting the flag suppresses no belief nor curbs it. Children and their parents may believe what they please, avow their belief and practice it. It is not even remotely suggested that the requirement for saluting the flag involves the slightest restriction against the fullest opportunity on the part both of the children and of their parents to disavow as publicly as they choose to do so the meaning that others attach to the gesture of salute. . . .

I am fortified in my view of this case by the history of the flag salute controversy in this Court. Five times has the precise question now before us been adjudicated. Four times the Court unanimously found that the requirement of such a school exercise was not beyond the powers of the states. . . .

[E]very Justice—thirteen in all— who has hitherto participated in judging this matter has at one or more times found no constitutional infirmity in what is now condemned. . . .

In view of this history it must be plain that what thirteen Justices found to be within the constitutional authority of a state, legislators cannot be deemed unreasonable in enacting. . . . [S]ome other tests . . . must surely be guiding the Court than the absence of a rational justification for the legislation. But I know of no other test which this Court is authorized to apply in nullifying legislation. . . .

The uncontrollable power wielded by this Court brings it very close to the most sensitive areas of public affairs. As appeal from legislation to adjudication becomes more frequent, and its consequences more far-reaching, judicial self-restraint becomes more and not less important, lest we unwarrantably enter social and political domains wholly outside our concern. . . .

Of course patriotism can not be enforced by the flag salute. But neither can the liberal spirit be enforced by judicial invalidation of illiberal legislation. Our constant preoccupation with the constitutionality of legislation rather than with its wisdom tends to preoccupation of the American mind with a false value. The tendency of focussing attention on constitutionality is to make constitutionality synonymous with wisdom, to regard a law as all right if it is constitutional. Such an attitude is a great enemy of liberalism. Particularly in legislation affecting freedom of thought and freedom of speech much which should offend a free-spirited society is constitutional. Reliance for the most precious interests of civilization, therefore, must be found outside of their vindication in courts of law. Only a persistent positive translation of the faith of a free society into the convictions and habits and actions of a community is the ultimate reliance against unabated temptations to fetter the human spirit.

Several aspects of the Supreme Court opinions in *Barnette* deserve special emphasis:

1. Jackson's majority opinion proceeded on a ground never raised or argued by the parties, which, in fact, had never been considered in any of the previous flag-salute cases. Jackson invoked a freedom of *political* conscience to hold that nobody could be required to participate in the flag-salute ceremony, whereas all previous discussion had turned on whether Jehovah's Witnesses could claim a *religious* exemption from an otherwise valid requirement. This rendered irrelevant all the briefs filed in the present case, as well as both opinions in *Gobitis*.

2. Since Frankfurter's *Gobitis* opinion was now irrelevant, most of Jackson's attack on that opinion was similarly beside the point. Certainly none of Frankfurter's arguments against a special exemption needed refutation. At least the second and third "grounds" singled out by Jackson did not even deal with the religious freedom issue, but were directed at the substantive due process question of *reasonableness*.

3. Despite their satisfaction with Jackson's rationale, Justices Black, Douglas, and Murphy felt impelled to argue and decide the religious freedom issue, so as to underscore what the Court had done in the license tax cases (see p. 31). At this time, there clearly were at least five justices committed to the repudiation of the traditional religious freedom rule and the substitution of some sort of interest-weighing standard akin to the "clear and present danger" test.

4. Justice Frankfurter was in substantial agreement with Jackson's freedom of thought argument, merely objecting to its application in these circumstances. ("Saluting the flag suppresses no belief. . . .") Most of his fire was directed at the new religious freedom standard set out in the concurring opinions, which he considered not only mistaken but downright dangerous.

### Impact: The Public Reacts, Quietly

Virtually the only effect of the Supreme Court decision and mandate in West Virginia was to make an already existing situation permanent. The flag-salute regulation had been suspended throughout the state since October, 1942; all Witness children were already back in school. While only the West Virginia flag regulation was directly involved in *Barnette*, that decision did establish the constitutional invalidity of every state or local compulsory flag-salute rule in the United States. Official compliance was substantial, though not immediately complete. No great rush was on to repeal or amend the various flag-salute statutes; only New Jersey and Oklahoma moved in this direction. Most states were content to apply the same statutes in a new manner; after all, none of them demanded in so many words that pupils must salute. In the next several years the attorneys general of Massachusetts and Colorado cited *Barnette* in ruling that the salute could not be compelled under those states' flag laws. Other school officials reached the same conclusion unaided. In Minersville, Lillian and William Gobitis, the original expellees, were beyond the compulsory school age. But the Minersville school board moved promptly, if unenthusiastically, to readmit three other Gobitis children it had expelled in 1941 and 1942.

There was some local recalcitrance, of course. Reports of post-*Barnette* expulsions came from Maryland, Oregon, and Colorado; probably several others did not reach public notice. On the whole, though, school authorities conformed to the ruling. In most areas enthusiasm for the compulsory salute showed a marked decline after mid-1942. Many schools gave up the fight while they were still winning. One factor may have been continued pressure from the Department of Justice. Aside from pushing its interpretation of Public Law 623, the Civil Rights Section had pressed the District Court decision in *Barnette* on the local school boards as an additional reason for suspending operation of their flag-salute regulations. It seems reasonable that this pressure was intensified after the Supreme Court decision. Another important factor was simple weariness. The flag salute was pretty well worn out as an issue; it must have been especially tiresome in the face of the Witnesses' supreme stubbornness.

With the fall of the compulsory flag salute, the collapse of more refined legal reprisals based on it was inevitable. In *Taylor* v. *Mississippi* (1943), decided on the same day as *Barnette,* the Supreme Court unanimously invalidated Mississippi's new flag-sedition law as applied to Jehovah's Witnesses. If "stubborn refusal" to salute the flag was constitutionally protected, the Court reasoned, mere advocacy of such behavior must be similarly immune. Three months later, in *Pendley* v. *State* (1943), the Oklahoma Court of Criminal Appeals threw out convictions of Witness parents and teachers for "hindering" the flag ceremony. State Appellate Courts in Pennsylvania and Colorado upset school-law convictions based on pre-*Barnette* expulsions. In the California case of *Cory* v. *Cory* (1945), the *Barnette* ruling figured in a divorce case. The trial court had awarded the divorce to the husband (clearly the more "guilty" party) and given him most of the community property and custody of the children after learning of the nonsaluting views of the mother, a Witness. The Appellate Court cited *Barnette* in reversing all these dispositions.

Public and private persecution of Jehovah's Witnesses at the local level had died down considerably by late 1942. This resulted partly from increased activity by the Justice Department and partly from public preoccupation with more positive contributions to the war effort. The *Barnette* decision had very little effect one way or another.

Press comment on *Barnette* was almost wholly favorable. Of eleven law review articles taking a definite position, nine were highly commendatory.

Editorials in the big-circulation newspapers ran about two to one in favor. Magazine comment—general circulation, Catholic, Protestant—unanimously applauded the decision. A few writers suggested that the Supreme Court could have saved itself and everybody much strain by deciding the issue right in 1940. Dissenting views were also voiced. The St. Louis *Globe-Democrat* expressed bewilderment as to why "disdain of the United States flag is not a punishable offense." To a representative of the Patriotic Order of the Sons of America, *Barnette* meant "less respect for the Flag and greater power for minority groups on questions of loyalty. . . ." But the dominant feeling was relief that the issue was finally settled and settled fairly.

### Epilogue: A More Tolerant Nation, A More Mellowed Sect

*Barnette* settled the flag-salute controversy, apparently permanently; it is unclear how much more it accomplished. Jackson's "political conscience" doctrine has not figured in any later decision; it was flatly ignored in *American Communications Association* v. *Douds* (1950), which upheld the Taft-Hartley noncommunist affidavit requirement. What of the new religious-freedom position set forth in the concurring opinions and clearly adhered to in 1943 by a majority of the Court? Interestingly enough, while the Court's break with the old rule is clear, it has never produced a majority opinion clearly setting forth the standard now being applied. Indeed, from 1945 to 1961, the Court managed, despite a host of opportunities, to avoid writing any opinions in religious-freedom cases. Some clues can be drawn, however, from *Braunfeld* v. *Brown* (1961), in which a six-justice majority upheld the state Sunday laws against a religious freedom challenge by a firm of Orthodox Jews (see p. 297). The opinions indicate that the justices, Frankfurter included, are firmly committed to some sort of interest-weighing approach to religious freedom, probably a diluted version of the standard proposed by the Bill of Rights Committee. It is also clear, however, that they are trying to minimize the effects of their break with tradition by indulging a fairly strong benefit of the doubt in favor of the state. The extreme "clear and present danger" formula advanced in the Black-Douglas concurrence has not been mentioned since 1944. While religious freedom remains in a "preferred position," it is vulnerable to most reasonable regulations. It remains to be seen whether the Supreme Court ever will invalidate any regulation, other than the compulsory salute, that would not have been invalid under the traditional rule.

What of Jehovah's Witnesses? Since 1943 they have settled down to a quieter existence. Sporadic violence has occurred, and they have had to carry more local ordinances to the Supreme Court, usually winning. For example, *Saia* v. *New York* (1947) upset a discretionary permit requirement for operation of sound trucks, while *Niemotko* v. *Maryland* (1951) and *Fowler* v. *Rhode Island* (1953) invalidated similar ordinances governing religious meetings in public parks. On the other hand *Poulos* v. *New Hampshire* (1953) went against a Witness on the narrow ground that he had failed to exhaust his administrative remedies. The Witnesses' immunity from the flag salute and their right to pamphleteer without undue interference are pretty well established and generally respected by local authority. The one area in which their triumph is less than complete is the draft; here the Witnesses have made concessions of their own. While draft boards and courts recognized the ministerial status of full-time Witness pamphleteers, they refused to extend the classification to part-time workers. As a result, some 4,120 Witnesses went to jail during World War II rather than accept any lesser form of exemption. Since 1950, however, the Witnesses have shown increasing willingness to accept ordinary conscientious-objector status instead of ministerial exemption, where the latter has been denied. Areas of conflict between Jehovah's Witnesses and their legal environment continue to shrink.

The Witnesses themselves have mellowed in recent years. New converts and new generations among the old faithful tend to be less alienated and to lean more toward "respectability." No longer is the United States Government denounced regularly as an agent of Satan. Even the Witnesses' jibes at the Catholic Church lack their old sting. Although they still look for the imminent end of the world, Jehovah's Witnesses now appear to be well equipped for a long stay.

### Table of Cases, in Order of Citation in the Text

*West Virginia State Board of Education* v. *Barnette*, 319 U.S. 624 (1943).
*Lovell* v. *Griffin*, 303 U.S. 444 (1938).
*Schneider* v. *Irvington*, 308 U.S. 147 (1939).
*Minersville School District* v. *Gobitis*, 310 U.S. 586 (1940).
*Cox* v. *New Hampshire*, 312 U.S. 569 (1941).
*Chaplinsky* v. *New Hampshire*, 315 U.S. 568 (1942).
*State* v. *Smith*, 155 Kan. 588, 127 P(2d) 518 (1942).
*Bolling* v. *Superior Court*, 16 Wash.(2d) 373, 133 P(2d) 803 (1943).
*Jones* v. *Opelika*, 316 U.S. 584 (1942), *vacated*, 319 U.S. 103 (1943).
*Murdock* v. *Pennsylvania*, 319 U.S. 105 (1943).
*Stromberg* v. *California*, 283 U.S. 259 (1931).
*Taylor* v. *Mississippi*, 319 U.S. 583 (1943).
*Pendley* v. *State*, 77 Okla. Cr. 259, 141 P(2d) 118 (1943).
*Cory* v. *Cory*, 70 Cal. App.(2d) 563, 161 P(2d) 385 (1945).
*American Communications Assoc.* v. *Douds*, 339 U.S. 382 (1950).
*Braunfeld* v. *Brown*, 366 U.S. 599 (1961).

*Saia* v. *New York,* 334 U.S. 558 (1947).
*Niemotko* v. *Maryland,* 340 U.S. 268 (1951).
*Fowler* v. *Rhode Island,* 345 U.S. 67 (1953).
*Poulos* v. *New Hampshire,* 345 U.S. 395 (1953).

### Sources

Primary sources for *West Virginia State Board of Education* v. *Barnette* are the briefs filed in the District Court (on file there) and the Supreme Court (in its library and on microfilm in most large law school libraries), and the fragmentary record of the oral argument preserved in 11 *U.S. Law Week* 3,279 (1943). Many individuals involved in the *Barnette* litigation have consented to be interviewed: notably Walter Barnette; Lucy, David, and Louellan McClure; W. W. Trent; Horace S. Meldahl; Hayden Covington; and William G. Fennell. The largest single fund of primary information on the flag-salute controversy is contained in the voluminous *American Civil Liberties Union Archives,* on file in the Princeton University Library and on microfilm in the New York Public Library. The Department of Justice has a thirty-eight-folder file of raw data on Jehovah's Witnesses and their troubles, which is not yet generally available to public inspection. The writer made a thorough search of law reviews, leading newspapers, and other periodicals for comment on the flag-salute cases and further information on anti-Witness persecution. For Public Law 623, see H.J.R. 303, 36 U.S.C. § 172 (Supp. 1942). A copy of the Rotnem memorandum on this subject is attached as an appendix to Covington's District Court brief in *Barnette;* another copy was furnished this writer by the Civil Rights Section.

There is a wealth of secondary material on the flag-salute controversy, only a few choice samples of which can be listed here. On the activities of patriotic organizations, see Bessie L. Pierce, *Citizens' Organizations and the Civic Training of Youth* (New York: Scribner's, 1935). On Jehovah's Witnesses, see Joseph F. Rutherford, *Enemies* (Brooklyn: Watchtower Society, 1937); Herbert Stroup, *The Jehovah's Witnesses* (New York: Columbia University Press, 1945); Richard Harris, "Reporter at Large: I'd Like to Talk to You for a Minute," *New Yorker* (June 15, 1956), p. 72. On the Civil Rights Section, see Robert K. Carr, *Federal Protection of Civil Rights: Quest for a Sword* (Ithaca: Cornell University Press, 1947). For a semiofficial expression of the Section's views on the Witnesses' flag-salute troubles, see Victor Rotnem and F. G. Folsem, Jr., "Recent Restrictions upon Religious Liberty," 38 *American Political Science Review* 1,053 (1942). For a book-length treatment of the flag-salute controversy as a whole, see this writer's *Render unto Caesar: The Flag Salute Controversy* (Chicago: University of Chicago Press, 1962).

# 2

## INDUSTRIAL RELATIONS

# The Portal-to-Portal Pay Case

## Richard E. Morgan

CHIEF JUSTICE STONE suffered a cerebral hemorrhage while presiding over the Court on April 22, 1946, and died later that day. President Truman nominated Fred M. Vinson of Kentucky for the post. Vinson was a close personal friend of the President with unique experience in all three branches of the Federal Government. Long a member of the House of Representatives and its pre-eminent expert in the drafting of tax legislation, he was appointed to the important Court of Appeals for the District of Columbia in 1938. During the war he was drafted by President Roosevelt for the posts of Director of Economic Stabilization and of War Mobilization and Reconversion. President Truman made him Secretary of the Treasury in 1945, and from that post he moved to the Supreme Court.

Associate Justice Jackson was at this time on leave from the Court, concluding a year's service as American chief prosecutor at the Nuremburg trial of war criminals. He had been considered for the Chief Justiceship in 1941, when it went to Stone, and had again been a candidate in 1946. Three days after he had been passed over for the second time, he issued from Nuremburg a shocking and bitter attack on his colleague Justice Black, whom he apparently blamed for his failure to secure the appointment. He asserted that Black's alleged opposition went back to a 1945 case, in which Black's law partner of two decades earlier had appeared as counsel. Jackson had questioned the propriety of Black's participation in the decision, but Black had nevertheless cast the deciding vote in a five-to-four decision in favor of his former partner's client. Black refused to reply to this public attack.

The case that Jackson referred to was *Jewell Ridge Coal*

*Co.* v. *Local No. 6167, United Mine Workers,* in which the coal miners were claiming that they should be paid for the time spent underground traveling from the portal of the mine to the working face where they began to dig coal, and similarly for the return journey to the mine portal. This was no profound constitutional issue such as the Court had considered in the flag-salute cases. Here was only a problem of statutory construction; specifically, what had Congress meant by the word "work" in the Fair Labor Standards Act of 1938? This case was thus typical of the economic controversies which faced the Court of the 1940's. Basic questions of congressional power over the economy had been settled. The Court only had to determine how far Congress had meant to go in its statutes. Nevertheless, these issues of statutory interpretation could be of major significance to the country.

The conclusive "portal-to-portal" decision did not come until 1946, and it is the focus of this study. It was decided on the same day, June 10, that Jackson issued his blast from Nuremburg. He was, of course, not a participant in the decision, and the Chief Justice's chair was vacant, since Vinson's nomination was not confirmed until ten days later. There was one member of the Court who was new since 1943: The conservative Roberts had resigned in 1945, and President Truman had replaced him by one of his Senate colleagues, Harold H. Burton of Ohio, a Republican—the first Republican to join the Court since the Hoover administration.

# THE DATE was December 5, 1946, the scene the luxurious Starlight Roof of the Waldorf Astoria. Seated comfortably around that large room, the audience listened quietly as the principal speaker of the evening approached his peroration. This attention was justified for the speaker was delivering a warning of impending disaster. The listeners were members of the National Association of Manufacturers, and the object of their attention was Raymond S. Smethurst, General Counsel of that organization.

Smethurst announced that an "invisible bankruptcy" was stalking American industry in the form of portal-to-portal pay. According to a United States Supreme Court decision the preceding spring in the case of *Anderson* v. *Mt. Clemens Pottery Co.,* employers were now required to pay employees for the time they spent (on company property) walking to and from their places of work and in preparing to begin actual production. Moreover, Smethurst explained, the Court had given its holding retroactive effect. Employees had the right to collect back pay for such activities which they had performed in the past, plus damages. Six months had elapsed since the Court had handed down its ruling, and employees had filed hundreds of suits to recover gigantic sums from their bosses; the total amount demanded in these suits was in the billions. Smethurst declared that employers must strike back and destroy this menace or be destroyed themselves. The audience, by its applause, obviously agreed. An NAM spokesman later said that the *Mt. Clemens* decision "will have a tremendous effect on business activity, on the possible liquidation of businesses. . . . Two companies in New England . . . were forced to close down because their assets were not sufficient to cover bonds which had to be posted in connection with litigations."

The deep concern of those who gathered in New York that December evening mirrored fairly the reaction of the American business community to the issue of "portal pay" (a shorthand phrase describing the holding in the *Mt. Clemens* case). A representative of the United States Chamber of Commerce called for Congress to investigate the dark and alien forces which must be behind portal pay, for "it is passing strange that *legitimate* trade unions will bring legal actions that threaten to bankrupt the firms or even entire segments of industries that provide jobs for their members." Probusiness newspapers, trade magazines, and prominent industrialists joined voices in lamenting the Supreme Court's action, and in prophesying disaster unless the effect of the decision could somehow be undone. *Newsweek* lamented that

> Portal-pay decisions upholding union . . . demands could ruin many employers big and little. The average of $4,000 a worker demanded from Ford, for example, would mean a total of $2,800,000,000 if similar claims were levied against the whole industry.

The "fear psychology" reflected in these statements was encouraged by the spirit of the times; 1946 had been a year of mounting labor-management tension. Prices had begun to spiral, and many grievances and hostilities suppressed during the war forced their way to the surface, animating the labor-management dialogue. Newspaper headlines had recorded the bitter controversy concerning the trial of John L. Lewis for contempt of court after he defied an injunction forbidding a strike by soft-coal miners. A paralyzing rail strike had only been averted by threat of Government seizure. As one observer later remarked, "A fury of anti-labor feeling swept the country. . . ." Many types of consumer goods were in short supply, and economic frustration, in one form or another, had darkened the days of almost every American. In this super-charged atmosphere the Court's decision could not help but touch off a kind of "limited war" between employer and employee groups. Many lawyers, following the time-honored practice of asking far more than they expected to get, filed suits demanding huge recoveries. As the sums grew more astronomical, fear and hostility grew more intense and widespread. By late 1946 a showdown seemed to be approaching.

To appreciate all that was involved in the dispute, it is necessary to go back eight years from December, 1946, and to examine the genesis of the national Fair Labor Standards Act (FLSA) of 1938—for it was on an interpretation of this Act that the Supreme Court based its decision in the *Mt. Comens* case.

### What Is Work? A Study in "Legislative Oversight"

The FLSA of 1938 was the last major piece of social legislation passed under Franklin Roosevelt's New Deal. It was enacted only after months of bitter wrangling between the White House and Capitol Hill.

The portal-pay controversy was the result of ambiguities in the wording of this statute. The Act aimed at achieving certain general social goals toward which reform liberals and progressives had struggled for over half a century—but had been thwarted either by an orthodox Supreme Court, or by a conservative Congressional majority. The Act was intended to eliminate child labor, put a floor under wages, and make sure that any employer who worked his employees longer than the socially desirable forty-hour week would pay a premium (time-and-a-half) for doing so.

The original bill was drafted in the Department of Labor by the Departmental Solicitor, Gerard Reilly, and his assistant, Rufus G. Poole. Outside aid came from Robert Jackson, then Assistant Attorney General, and that roving legislative craftsman, Benjamin Cohen. This draft was rewritten at least once in each House of Congress and again in a conference committee (each alteration was accomplished under the pressure of time and amid a welter of conflicting and stridently voiced claims). Emotions ran high, and various objections were raised concerning the principles of the proposed bill. However, at no point did anyone think of stating what was meant by the simple word "work." The debates and hearings on various drafts of the bill were concerned with "great questions" about the desirability of the measure—about its constitutionality and compatibility with "the American way of life." The Congressmen, Senators, interest-group representatives, and Roosevelt Administration bureaucrats apparently assumed that they knew what work was, and that for statutory purposes no more precise definition was required than the meaning that word conveyed in common parlance. As is often the case, the problem of interpretation which arose after the passage of the Act could not be resolved simply by an appeal to the "intent of Congress." Congress had no intent because it did not consider and resolve the problem specifically.

The absence of a definition of work was far from the only ambiguity of the Act. While it is unsophisticated to expect perfect clarity from our national legislature, the level of ambiguity and generality of the FLSA was extreme. Senator David I. Walsh, a Democrat of Massachusetts, sensed this dilemma. In a speech to the Senate, he lamented the absence of more precise standards by which the Act might be administered. But he went on to point out that the "alternative [might be] no action, and leaving those many millions of wage earners to a continuance of past exploitation. . . . I pray that the bill may be administered with the care and caution . . . of a physician and not with the club of a policeman."

### Administrative Attempts at Definition

As Senator Walsh had indicated, the delicate task of resolving the problems created by the Act devolved first upon the executive agency charged with its administration. In the Act, Congress had provided for a new agency within the Department of Labor—the Wage and Hour Division. This Division was to be headed by a single Administrator vested with the responsibility of implementing the FLSA. Difficulty arose, however, as to the authority which should be available to this official in carrying out his mandate under the law.

New Deal backers of the FLSA had wanted an Administrator capable, if necessary, of laying down comprehensive sets of rules which would have the force of law, and that could be relied on in the courts as having created legal rights and obligations. By 1938, however, Congress was becoming alarmed at the power of "New Deal" executive agencies. As a result, rule-making power was denied the administrator, and the new Division was restricted to issuing advisory opinions as to the meaning of the Act.

Despite this handicap, the Wage and Hour Division did make an attempt to define "work," through a general advisory opinion and several *ad hoc* recommendations issued between 1939 and 1942.

On May 3, 1939, the Administrator issued *Interpretive Bulletin No. 13*— a document that warrants quotation at some length:

> 2. The Act contains no express guide as to the manner of computing hours of work and reasonable rules must be adopted for purposes of enforcement of the wage and hour standards. As a general rule, hours worked will include (1) all time during which an employee is required to be on duty or to be on the employer's premises or to be at a prescribed workplace, and (2) all time during which an employee is suffered or permitted to work whether or not he is required to do so.

And a few passages later:

> 9. The problem of travel time, in relation to hours worked, arises in a great variety of situations and no precise mathematical formula will provide the answer in every case. The question is often one of degree; if the time spent by an employee in traveling is reasonably to be described as "all in a day's work," such time should be considered hours worked under the Act.

And still later:

> 12. If a crew of workers is required to report for work at a designated place at a specific hour and all the employees are then driven to the place where they are to perform work, the time spent in riding to such a place should be considered hours worked. Similarly, the time spent returning from the place at the close of the day's work should be considered hours worked.

This definition of work as including travel time in some cases was announced when the momentum of the New Deal was not yet spent, and when the business community was only beginning to recover from the decline in prestige it had suffered between 1929 and 1937. Although management's lawyers were well aware of the position taken by the Administrator, there is no evidence that they viewed it as an immediate threat. *The National Association of Manufacturers Law Digest* made only passing reference to the issuance of the Bulletin and did not choose to elaborate on its possible implications. If the businessmen who stood to lose under the terms of *Interpretive Bulletin No. 13* suspected any incipient danger to their treasuries, they uncharacteristically kept their fears to themselves. Since no one actually lost money at that time because of the advisory opinion, it made no deep impression on the corporation lawyers. Harvey M. Crow, now Associate General Counsel of the NAM, recalls that his organization's legal staff saw certain "dangers" in the Bulletin, but felt it wise not to specify these dangers in print.

If management was slow in detecting the implications of the Administrator's position, the Congress of Industrial Organizations and its General Counsel, Lee Pressman, were not. Early in 1940 Pressman was approached by an officer of the Mine, Mill and Smelter Workers of America, CIO, who suggested that workers in his union who were engaged in underground metal mining were entitled under the terms of *Interpretive Bulletin No. 13* to overtime pay that was presently being denied them. By mid-1940 the CIO (on behalf of the member union) had petitioned the Administrator for a determination of what constituted compensable work in the underground metal mines. In copper, iron, and lead mines the wages of the miners were computed from the time they reached the "mining face" until they left it. The face might be miles underground, and the trip from the mine portal (on company property) to the face might be long and hazardous. The mine owners, however, did not consider the trips as work, and under the "custom of the industry" miners were not paid for the time involved. In March, 1941, the Administrator issued an opinion holding that the time spent by miners in such trips, provided that the miners worked a forty-hour week at the face, was compensable overtime work under the FLSA.

While the general statements of 1939 had gone unnoticed, the opinion in the metal mining case drew the fire of that sector of the business community most immediately involved—the mining industry. The owners and operators of the metal mines refused to settle the issue with their unions on the basis of the Administrator's opinion and rushed a test case to the courts.

Meanwhile, the metal mining opinion had not gone unnoticed by the coal miners and their union leaders. In the coal industry existing contracts, originally negotiated by the United Mine Workers and the coal companies, provided only for face-to-face pay. Despite these contracts the UMW saw no reason for distinguishing travel in coal mines from travel in metal mines, where the employee-employer relationship was governed by custom, not by contract. UMW leaders argued that if the FLSA had vested rights in employees to certain kinds of overtime pay, then a contract could not destroy these rights any more than a custom could. The coal companies, not surprisingly, found such reasoning unpersuasive. They refused to concede to union demands for travel pay, and the UMW then turned to the courts to vindicate its members' rights. With the commencement of the metal mining and coal mining litigation, the portal-pay controversy moved from its administrative phase to its judicial phase.

### Judicial Attempts at Definition

When the metal mining case (*Tennessee Coal, Iron and Rr. Co.* v. *Muscoda Local No. 123*) and the coal mining case (*Jewell Ridge Coal Corp.* v. *Local No. 6167, UMW*) were decided by the Supreme Court in 1944 and 1945, respectively, they were regarded as sweeping victories for the broad definition of work advocated by organized labor and by the Wage and Hour administrator. In the *Muscoda* case Justice Frank Murphy, who had earned the enmity of the business community as a prolabor governor of Michigan during the 1930's, declared (for a Court divided seven to two) that:

> This compulsory travel [from the mine portal to the working face] occurs entirely on petitioners' property and is at all times under their strict control and supervision. Such travel, furthermore, is not primarily undertaken for the convenience of the miners and bears no relation whatever to their needs or to the distance between their homes and the mines. Rather the travel time is spent for the benefit of petitioners and their ore mining operations. . . . [This] is a fossorial activity bearing all the indicia of hard labor.

As to the question of whether the "immemorial custom of the industry" barred recovery by the miners (as dissenting Justice Roberts and Chief Justice Stone felt it did) the Court majority declared that: "The Fair Labor Standards Act was not designed to codify or perpetuate those customs and contracts which allow an employer to claim all of an employee's time while compensating him for only part of it."

The most casual reading of the *Muscoda* opinion reveals that the Court had, by its dicta concerning contracts, practically decided the *Jewell Ridge* case in advance. The existence of current contracts was the only factor differentiating the coal mining from the metal mining situation. Thus, a year later, Justice Murphy, now speaking for a Court divided five to four, brushed aside the coal industry's arguments with an impatient reference to the *Muscoda* case:

> *In Tennessee Coal Co.* v. *Muscoda Local,* 321 U.S. 590, this Court held that underground travel in iron ore mines constituted work and hence was included in the compensable work week within the meaning of Section 7 (a) of the Fair Labor Standards Act of 1938, 52 Stat. 1060, 1063, 29 U.S.C. Sec 207(a). The sole issue in this case is whether any different result must be reached as regards underground travel in bituminous coal mines.

The Court went on to agree with UMW arguments that contracts could not nullify vested rights and concluded that a result different from that in the *Muscoda* case was not warranted.

In dissent Justice Jackson (joined by Chief Justice Stone, Justice Roberts, and Justice Frankfurter) protested vigorously against any diminution of contractual rights in what he regarded as the absence of any clear legislative intent to accomplish that effect. However, Justice Murphy and his majority brethren remained unmoved by such appeals to the sanctity of contracts.

With these mining decisions the first real blood was drawn in the portal-pay struggle. But while rumblings from the corporate community increased, the businesses actually affected represented only a limited segment of American industry. More was necessary to engage the business community at large. Pressman and the other CIO lawyers had achieved their immediate goal of gaining portal-to-portal pay for miners, and they had no plans to push for an extension of the principle into other industries. Another case, however, with the potential to effect just such an extension was making its way to the Supreme Court—a case that could make portal pay the law not only for underground mines but for all types of industrial situations—the case of *Anderson* v. *Mt. Clemens Pottery Co.*

### "Great Oaks from Little Acorns . . ."

The small city of Mount Clemens, Michigan, is situated atop a natural bluff overlooking the Clinton River some twenty miles northeast of Detroit. In the nineteenth century it was famous as the "Spa of Michigan," and the mineral waters from its many springs were reputed to possess great curative powers. In the 1940's Mount Clemens developed another attraction—gambling. Detroit was "closed down," but the satellite town above the Clinton was wide open. The air still smelled of sulphur from the springs, but more visitors came to take a chance than to take the cure. Before World War II industry played a small part in the life of Mount Clemens, but among the few factories on the outskirts of town there was a sizable one which made dishes.

As of 1941 the Mt. Clemens Pottery Company (a subsidiary of S. S. Kresge) was the largest manufacturer of dinnerware pottery in the United States, employing between 1,000 and 1,200 workers. During the winter of 1940–41 relations between the workers (represented by Local 1083, United Pottery Workers of America, CIO) and the Pottery Company management steadily deteriorated. The union had failed to achieve satisfactory concessions on a series of grievances concerning working conditions, and a strike was called. Working conditions at the plant were almost medieval; wages were substandard even for a traditionally low-wage resort town like Mount Clemens; and on top of that, the employees were required to purchase from the company certain equipment used for making the pottery. (Company markups on this equipment often ran to 30 per cent.) Nor, it seems, were the law-enforcement agencies in Mount Clemens exactly neutral regarding labor and management. The place was a tight "company town," and rumors of a lockout began to circulate. CIO leaders were appalled at the plight of the pottery workers and were convinced that only if the workers could get into court could their situation be improved. But no local lawyer would handle the case. The workers' cause was unpopular in northern Michigan, and they lacked the funds for court expenses.

At this point a CIO official, August Scholle, working in the Midwest, recalled a lawyer he knew named Edward Lamb. They had been friends in Toledo, Ohio, before Scholle joined the CIO, and Lamb continued to practice law there. Today, Lamb is a self-made millionaire whose far-flung holdings (known as Lamb Enterprises) are directed from his offices in Toledo's Lamb Building. His social consciousness and identification with workingmen, however, is still as acute as on that day in 1941, when Scholle asked him, as a personal favor, to go to Mount Clemens, take stock of the situation, and see if something could be done for the workers and their besieged local union. Lamb agreed to go and arrived in Mount Clemens shortly thereafter to find himself in the middle of a labor dispute more bitter than any he had ever experienced. "That little resort town," Lamb recalls, "was worse than anything I ever saw—and I saw the steel towns under martial law during the thirties."

In addition to other grievances, Lamb discovered that the pottery workers were not paid for almost one hour each day spent on the premises and recorded on their timecards. This suggested to Lamb an especially promising avenue for judicial attack. Perhaps the national Fair Labor Standards Act could be invoked to secure compensation for the hours lost. To take the case to the State Court in Mount Clemens, Lamb reasoned, would be tactical folly. His best course was to get into a Federal District Court, and out of the antilabor atmosphere of Mount Clemens. No money was available to pay costs, but Lamb was so angered by working conditions at the Pottery that he covered expenses from his own pocket. Working quietly, and at night, Lamb visited pottery workers in their homes to gather evidence for a suit against the company. When a representative sample of the workers had been contacted, he shifted his base of operations from Mount Clemens to the Federal Court in Detroit.

On April 16, 1941, Lamb filed a complaint in the District Court of the United States for the Eastern District of Michigan, Southern Division, before Judge Frank Picard in the name of one Steve Anderson, and all other employees of the Mt. Clemens Pottery Company who were "similarly situated." Judge Picard, who received the complaint papers, possessed one of the most colorful backgrounds of all the Federal judges. Born into a famous family of high-wire artists, the Judge had been a star circus performer before attending law school—key man of the celebrated "Flying Picards." His pre-judicial career had left Picard with a sympathy toward the problems of organized labor that was to prove important in the litigation. His first action in the case, however, caused trouble for Lamb. Picard held that Lamb could not represent all the pottery workers in a "class action," but would have to obtain the express consent of every worker he wished to represent. Many pottery workers proved reluctant to sign the lists, circulated by the local union, which would make them parties to the suit. Mount Clemens was alive with rumors of company reprisals awaiting those who signed—many withdrew their names after a few days or even hours. Finally, however, a sizable list was amassed, and Lamb was ready to proceed with the trial.

The employees' claim was simple enough. At the Mt. Clemens Pottery Company, time clocks were located immediately inside the gates, and up to three hundred yards away from the places where workers performed their assigned duties. An employee's pay was computed from fourteen minutes after he punched in at the time clock, until fourteen minutes before he punched out at noon. The same procedure of automatic subtraction was followed when the employee returned from his lunch period, and when he punched out at the end of the day. In short the employees were not compensated for fifty-six minutes a day shown on their timecards. The employees arrived and left the plant so as to put in a normal forty-hour week, exclusive of the uncompensated fifty-six minutes each day. Management argued that employees had no right to overtime pay since the additional fifty-six minutes were not spent in producing pottery. This time, management asserted, was not compensable under the FLSA.

Edward Lamb asked Judge Picard to determine, first, whether the Mt. Clemens employees were automatically entitled to compensation for *all* time shown on their timecards. Should Picard decide that the employees were not so entitled, Lamb asked, second, that the Judge determine if any *parts* of the extra fifty-six minutes per day were compensable—for example, the time workers spent in walking to machines and readying them for operation.

Frank E. Cooper, of Detroit, and Bert V. Nunneley, of Mt. Clemens, had been retained by the Kresge Company to defend the Pottery management. They replied that the employees did nothing directly productive during the uncompensated time, and that even if some part of the time were spent in activities compensable under the FLSA, the employees must prove the *exact* extent of such partial work. Existing case law interpreting the FLSA supported the Pottery lawyers' claim that a presumptive showing by the employees that some work had taken place was insufficient to warrant relief under Section 7(a). In the absence of detailed records, kept by the employer, such a burden of proof was almost impossible for the employees to fulfill.

The management case, resting squarely on precedent, seemed impressive. The workers could only estimate the time spent in performing various specific tasks in the uncompensated fifty-six minutes; the argument that all time shown on the time clocks was automatically compensable as work, appeared, to Lamb, the strongest reed on which he could lean. The main thrust of his argument in the District Court was at that point.

During the summer and fall of 1941, charges and countercharges were traded in a complicated series of motions for dismissal and summary judgment. The management lawyers were frank about their tactics—they meant to delay and prolong the trial by every available means on the theory that Lamb, the workers, or both would soon give up. As the end of the year approached, Lamb decided to secure a detailed investigation of work conditions at the Pottery. On December 2, 1941, he submitted to Picard a motion calling for the appointment of a special master to carefully investigate the facts of the case, hold any hearings necessary, and report to the District Court both as to questions of law and fact. The Pottery lawyers opposed the motion, but on January 28, 1942, Judge Picard appointed Donald L. Quaife, as Special Master to ". . . expeditiously conduct . . . hearings and make his report including his findings of fact and conclusions of law thereon to this Court by the 1st day of April, 1942."

Mr. Quaife missed his target date by almost one year. He began hearings promptly on February 9, 1942, but the interrogation of witnesses dragged on through thirty volumes of typewritten transcript. Finally, on March 23, 1943, Quaife submitted the report of his findings and conclusions to Judge Picard.

The general outline of arguments presented before the Special Master is noted here.

Cooper and Nunneley continued to insist that, even if some strange kind of nonproductive work did take place, it was up to the employees to prove conclusively the exact extent of such work. Lamb argued that since the Pottery management maintained no records of the time spent by the workers in incidental activities, the court should make a reasonable estimate of the amount of back overtime pay due the employees, provided a presumptive showing could be made that some compensable work had taken place.

To make such a presumptive showing, a steady stream of Pottery employees were paraded before the Special Master to testify as to the minutes and fractions of minutes spent each day in such activities as opening windows, sharpening tools, and walking to and from the Pottery gate.

In the report finally submitted to Judge Picard, the Master found no trouble in concluding that the plaintiffs' claim to compensation for all time shown on the timecards was without merit. With respect to the claim of partial compensability Quaife had only slightly more difficulty. He was persuaded that some work might have taken place, but (following the argument of the defense) he saw the burden of exact proof as resting on the employees:

> 6. Plaintiffs have the burden of proof to show that they spent time in their employment which the company did not give credit for.
>
> 7. Plaintiffs have not established work done by them which the company did not credit them for, with the possible exception of preliminary work.
>
> 8. A computation of the time spent in preliminary work by each employee each week and not credited to him by the company cannot be made except upon a speculative basis, and accordingly forms no basis for recovery of overtime pay.

This appeared to presage a complete victory for the Pottery management, but Judge Picard, who had evinced sympathy for the Mt. Clemens workers throughout the proceedings, found the Master's report disturbing. He was well aware of his common-law obligation to accept a Master's report in its entirety, unless it contained a clear error of fact or law, and that he could not properly substitute his own judgments or opinions for those of a Special Master. Despite this, Picard felt that the report, in this case, contained an error of fact of sufficient magnitude to warrant correction by the court. Consequently, on June 30, 1943, Picard handed down a decision in which the Master's report was substantially altered. The Judge held that seven of the uncompensated fourteen minutes in the morning, and nine of the fourteen minutes at the return from lunch, must certainly have been used by the employees for *actual productive* work, and hence represented compensable overtime. It should be emphasized that this decision, while in favor of the employees in the sense that an award was made to them, avoided the really significant problem presented by the case. Judge Picard did not advance any new definition of work, or alter in any way the burden of proof which rested on the employees. He simply stated his conclusion that the production of pottery, which everyone agreed was work, had occupied seven of the fourteen uncompensated minutes in the morning, and nine of the uncompensated fourteen minutes at the conclusion of the lunch period. The cost of this judgment to the Pottery management might have run to several hundred thousand dollars.

The Mt. Clemens Pottery Company, however, was not willing to let the case go at that. The Pottery lawyers regarded Judge Picard's substitution of his personal view of the facts for that of the Master as both morally and legally vulnerable. The case was appealed to the United States Circuit Court of Appeals for the Sixth Circuit.

The argument of both sides, before the Court of Appeals, was directed largely to the propriety of Judge Picard's alteration of the Master's report. Circuit Judges Xen Hicks, Elwood Hamilton, and John Martin, confining themselves to this point, found themselves persuaded by the arguments against Picard's action as set forth by Cooper and Nunneley. On May 21, 1945, Circuit Judge Martin, writing for a unanimous court held that:

> There was abundant substantial evidence to support the findings of the special Master. . . . The arbitrary formula applied by the district judge, in lieu of acceptance of the master's finding, produced a judgment based upon surmise and conjecture, which cannot be sustained.

The judgment of the District Court was reversed and the case dismissed. Judge Martin also took advantage of the occasion to remark that:

> The burden rested on each of the plaintiffs here to prove by a preponderance of evidence that he did not receive the wages he was entitled to receive under the Fair Labor Standards Act. . . . It does not suffice for the employee to base his right to recovery on a mere estimated average of overtime worked.

In the face of this declaration, Edward Lamb and the local union of pottery workers (as the real sponsors of the litigation) had to decide whether to attempt to carry the case to the Supreme Court, or to cut their losses and save the cost of "cert papers." Whatever doubt there might have been at this juncture was eliminated, however, when the CIO decided to take a hand in the case. The CIO had carefully watched the development of a judicial definition of work in the metal mining and coal mining cases and now decided that the *Mt. Clemens* case was worth taking to the Supreme Court.

Lee Pressman "discovered" the *Mt. Clemens* case immediately after the Court of Appeals ruling, and he hastened to discuss the potential of the case with CIO President Philip Murray. Both men were struck and excited by the possibility of achieving a definition of work which would extend the portal-to-portal principle of the mining decisions to other areas of industry. Pressman and Murray reasoned that such a definition, coming from the Supreme Court, would provide a powerful weapon which organized labor could employ in collective bargaining. World War II wage controls were to end in the coming year (1946), and the CIO wanted to be at maximum bargaining strength for the crucial round of contract negotiations which would come with the removal of governmental wage ceilings. The CIO leaders realized that a favorable decision in the *Mt. Clemens* case would add to their strength. Union negotiators would be in a position to insist that employers grant concessions on wage rates and working conditions or face court action for vast sums in retroactive pay due their employees. Thereupon, Pressman raised his sights from portal pay in mines to portal pay for American workers generally.

On August 20, 1945, Pressman joined Edward Lamb in filing a petition for certiorari, asking the Supreme Court to review the findings of the Court of Appeals. On October 15, 1945, the petition was granted.

In the brief submitted to the Court, Lamb did not confine himself to a narrow common-law argument in justification of Judge Picard's decision. He referred to the major questions which had emerged at this stage of the litigation: whether work included walking time and make-ready time, and what standard of proof should be required of employees seeking to recover overtime and damages under the FLSA. In addition, attention was devoted to the argument, carried over from the trial phase of the case, that all time shown on timecards should be automatically compensable.

Cooper and Nunneley, in a long brief which drew extensively from the record of the hearings before the Master, stuck with their successful Court of Appeals argument that, since the Master's report showed no "clear error," Judge Picard went beyond his power in disregarding it.

One *amicus curiae* brief was submitted in support of Lamb's position by the Solicitor General of the United States on behalf of the Wage and Hour Division. Nothing new was added by the brief, which simply set forth Lamb's arguments in a shortened form. This document is interesting, however, in that it revealed that L. Metcalfe Walling, the Administrator, was still ready to support the principles of *Interpretive Bulletin No. 13* in open court.

The *Mt. Clemens* case was argued before the Supreme Court on January 29, 1946, and the decision of the Court was announced on June 10, 1946.

---

### *ANDERSON* v. *MT. CLEMENS POTTERY CO.*
#### 328 U.S. 680 (1945)

Mr. Justice Murphy delivered the opinion of the Court.

The Mt. Clemens Pottery Company, the respondent, employs approximately 1,200 persons. . . . Working time is calculated by respondent on the basis of the time cards punched by the clocks. Compensable working time extends from the succeeding even quarter hour after employees punch in to the quarter hour immediately preceding the time when they punch out.

Thus an employee who punches in at 6:46 A.M., punches out at 12:14 P.M., punches in again at 12:46 P.M., and finally punches out at 4:14 P.M. is credited with having worked the 8 hours between 7 A.M. and 12 noon and between 1 P.M. and 4 P.M.—a total of 56 minutes less than the time recorded by the time clocks.

Seven employees and their local union, on behalf of themselves and others similarly situated, brought this suit under § 16(b) of the Fair Labor Standards Act . . . alleging that the foregoing method of computation did not accurately reflect all the time actually worked and that they were thereby deprived of the proper overtime compensation guaranteed them by § 7(a) of the Act. . . .

The District Court referred the case to a Special Master. After hearing testimony and making findings, the Master recommended that the case be dismissed since the complaining employees "have not established by a fair preponderance of evidence" a violation of the Act by respondent. . . .

[The District Court altered the Master's Report slightly in favor of the workers; however, the Court of Appeals reversed the District Court and upheld the Master's Report in its original form.]

But we believe that the Circuit Court of Appeals, as well as the master, imposed upon the employees an improper standard of proof, a standard that has the practical effect of impairing many of the benefits of the Fair Labor Standards Act. An employee who brings suit under § 16 (b) of the Act for unpaid minimum wages or unpaid overtime compensation, together with liquidated damages, has the burden of proving that he performed work for which he was not properly compensated. The remedial nature of this statute and the great public policy which it embodies, however, militate against making that bur-

den an impossible hurdle for the employee. Due regard must be given to the fact that it is the employer who has the duty under § 11(c) of the Act . . . to keep proper records of wages, hours and other conditions and practices of employment and who is in a position to know and to produce the most probative facts concerning the nature and amount of work performed. Employees seldom keep such records themselves; even if they do, the records may be and frequently are untrustworthy. It is in this setting that a proper and fair standard must be erected for the employee to meet in carrying out his burden of proof.

When the employer has kept proper and accurate records the employee may easily discharge his burden by securing the production of those records. But where the employer's records are inaccurate or inadequate and the employee cannot offer convincing substitutes a more difficult problem arises. The solution, however, is not to penalize the employee by denying him any recovery on the ground that he is unable to prove the precise extent of uncompensated work. Such a result would place a premium on an employer's failure to keep proper records in conformity with his statutory duty; it would allow the employer to keep the benefits of an employee's labors without paying due compensation as contemplated by the Fair Labor Standards Act. In such a situation we hold that an employee has carried out his burden if he proves that he has in fact performed work for which he was improperly compensated and if he produces sufficient evidence to show the amount and extent of that work as a matter of just and reasonable inference. The burden then shifts to the employer to come forward with evidence of the precise amount of work performed or with evidence to negative the reasonableness of the inference to be drawn from the employee's evidence. If the employer fails to produce such evidence, the court may then award damages to the employee, even though the result be only approximate. See note, 43 Col. L. Rev. 355.

The employer cannot be heard to complain that the damages lack the exactness and precision of measurement that would be possible had he kept records in accordance with the requirements of § 11(c) of the Act. And even where the lack of accurate records grows out of a bona fide mistake as to whether certain activities or nonactivities constitute work, the employer, having received the benefits of such work, cannot object to the payment for the work on the most accurate basis possible under the circumstances. Nor is such a result to be condemned by the rule that precludes the recovery of uncertain and speculative damages. That rule applies only to situations where the fact of damage is itself uncertain. But here we are assuming that the employee has proved that he has performed work and has not been paid in accordance with the statute. The damage is therefore certain. The uncertainty lies only in the amount of damages arising from the statutory violation by the employer. In such a case "it would be a perversion of fundamental principles of justice to deny all relief to the injured person, and thereby relieve the wrongdoer from making any amend for his acts. . . ."

We therefore turn to the facts of this case to determine what the petitioning employees have proved. . . .

The employees did prove . . . that it was necessary for them to be on the premises for some time prior and subsequent to the scheduled working hours. The employer required them to punch in, walk to their work benches and perform preliminary duties during the fourteen-minute periods preceding productive work; the same activities in reverse occurred in the fourteen-minute periods subsequent to the completion of productive work. Since the statutory workweek includes all time during which an employee is necessarily required to be on the employer's premises, on duty or at a prescribed workplace, the time spent in these activities must be accorded appropriate compensation.

The time necessarily spent by the employees in walking to work on the employer's premises, following the punching of the time clocks, was working time within the scope of § 7 (a). . . .

Such time was under the complete control of the employer, being dependent solely upon the physical arrangements which the employer made in the factory. Those arrangements in this case compelled the employees to spend an estimated two to twelve minutes daily, if not more, in walking on the premises. Without such walking on the part of the employees, the productive aims of the employer could not have been achieved. The employees' convenience and necessity, moreover, bore no relation whatever to this walking time; they walked on the employer's premises only because they were compelled to do so by the necessities of the employer's business. In that respect the walking time differed vitally from the time spent in traveling from workers' homes to the factory. . . .

We do not, of course, preclude the application of a *de minimis* rule where the minimum walking time is such as to be negligible. . . .

Thus we remand the case for the determination of the amount of walking time involved and the amount of preliminary activities performed, giving due consideration to the *de minimis* doctrine and calculating the resulting damages under the Act. We have considered the other points raised by the petitioners but find no errors.

*Reversed and remanded. . . .*

MR. JUSTICE BURTON dissenting, with whom MR. JUSTICE FRANKFURTER concurs.

The opinion of the Court in this case has gone far toward affirming the Circuit Court of Appeals. I believe it should go the rest of the way. . . .

The Master determined that the time spent in walking from the time clocks to the places of work was not compensable working time in view of the established custom in the industry and in the plant. Moreover, the employees were free to take whatever course through the plant they desired and to stop off at any point to talk with other employees or to do whatever else they liked. Some workers came to the time clocks as late as one minute before the time to reach their place of productive work. The so-called "preliminary activities" are identified in this case as those of "putting on aprons and overalls, removing shirts, taping or greasing arms, putting on finger cots, preparing the equipment for productive work, turning on switches for lights and machinery, opening windows and assembling and sharpening tools." The master found that the employees had not offered proof of the time used for these purposes with sufficient degree of reliability or accuracy for it to become the basis for recovery of overtime compensation. The employer would have still greater difficulty in keeping an accurate record of the time spent by each employee in such activities. These activities are of such a nature that the knowledge of them and the time spent in doing them rests particularly with the employees themselves. Such activities are of quite a different character from those made the basis of compensable time in the coal mine portal-to-portal cases. . . .

While conditions vary widely and there may be cases where time records of "preliminary activities" or "walking time" may be appropriate, yet here we have a case where the obvious, long-established and simple way to compensate an employee for such activities is to recognize those activities in the rate of pay for the particular job. These items are appropriate for consideration in collective bargaining.

To sustain the position of the Court in requiring these additional moments to be recorded and computed as overtime, it is necessary to hold that Congress, in using the word "workweek," meant to give that word a statutory meaning different from its commonly understood reference to the working hours between "starting" and "quitting" time—or from "whistle to whistle." There is no evidence that Congress meant to redefine this common term and to set aside long-established contracts or customs which had absorbed in the rate of pay of the respective jobs recognition of whatever preliminary activities might be required of the worker by that particular job. . . .

For these reasons, I believe that the judgment of the Court of Appeals should be affirmed.

---

The die was cast, however, and the judicial phase of the battle over portal pay had resulted in a victory for what may be described as the "labor position." The implications of the *Mt. Clemens* case were vast. Heretofore, the principle of portal-to-portal pay had been limited in its application to underground mines. Now the Supreme Court, in a single stroke, had extended that principle across the board. The Mt. Clemens Pottery works was typical of plants all over the country in which American industrial workers performed their duties. If portal pay was law for Mt. Clemens Pottery, the conclusion was inescapable that portal pay was the law generally. All industrial workers, it appeared, were legally entitled to such compensation provided that they were able to make a presumptive showing that some uncompensated work (under the Supreme Court's new definition of that term) either had taken or was taking place.

The portal-pay controversy, however, was far from finished. The problem of what constituted work, which was originally the consequence of a Congressional lack of precision, was now to come full circle; the most bitterly fought phase of the struggle over portal pay came, in 1947, in the halls of Congress.

### The Congressional Climax

At first, the decision in the *Mt. Clemens* case was hardly noticed in the press. While the *Muscoda* and *Jewell Ridge* litigations had been highly publicized, little attention had been paid to the pottery case as it worked its way up to the Supreme Court. When the case had come before the High Court, no business groups had submitted *amicus curiae* briefs in support of the management position as they had done in the *Muscoda* and *Jewell Ridge* cases. The corporate community seemed unaware that this little package could contain judicial dynamite.

Organized labor, as it had done after the issuance of *Interpretive Bulletin No. 13,* moved swiftly to seize the initiative. The CIO, which had been pushing for a broad definition of work since 1939, lost no time in advising the leadership of its member unions of the *Mt. Clemens* decision, and of the rights thereby conferred on employees. Most important, however, the CIO encouraged the local leaders to sponsor legal actions aimed at recovering back overtime pay for their employees. In courthouses across the land suits were filed by employees demanding, from their employers, retroactive overtime pay for travel time and make-ready activities, and equal amounts (to the total retroactive overtime pay due) in liquidated damages under Section 16(b) of the FLSA. By December 9, 1946, the first of a series of articles appeared in the New York *Times,* listing major corporations being sued. A month later *Time* magazine stated, "the suits came so fast that newspapers ran lists of companies sued in long columns, like disaster victims—which they well might be."

The more conservative American Federation of Labor disapproved of bringing suits and advised its member unions that they should seek to have portal-pay clauses inserted in their next contract without resorting to court action to recover back overtime pay due employees. But the CIO (while it also looked on the *Mt. Clemens* decision primarily as a weapon to be used against management in collective bargaining) continued to encourage suits on the theory that the more pressure on management the better for success at the bargaining table. The CIO monthly publication *Economic Outlook* announced:

> The unions are not responsible for the accumulation of the workers' retroactive legal claims. . . . The piling up of workers' claims to back pay for "portal-to-portal" time arose from the law itself, and in large part from the failure of employers to comply with administrative rulings and court decisions that for some years have been indicating that "make-ready time" . . . should be paid for under the Fair Labor Standards Act. . . .
>
> Under the law, the workers' claims exist regardless of union policy about pushing them. . . .
>
> With profits and living costs at record-breaking levels, it is natural that workers should seek money to which they have a legal right. Wage earners have received a raw deal which has undermined family welfare and national safety.

With CIO locals thus "unleashed," more and more employers found themselves named as defendants in actions under the overtime provisions of the Fair Labor Standards Act.

Unions themselves did not bring these suits. The parties of record were individual workers. It was clear, however, the unions supplied the initiative to begin the suits, and "sponsored" the litigations in every sense of the word. The typical pattern was for the local union leadership to select certain of its members to serve as the parties of record and then to obtain legal counsel to serve these parties. This done, the local union leaders, along with the lawyers they had selected, would plot the strategy by which the case was to be argued, and decide on the amount of back overtime pay and damages to be demanded from the employer. The United Steelworkers of America, CIO, actually published and circulated a "field manual" on the subject, which outlined each step the local union should follow in instigating a portal-to-portal suit.

These hasty suits were to prove a major tactical blunder on the part of organized labor. The amounts demanded of employers were staggering. These huge sums, combined with the slight flavor of a "labor conspiracy" which surrounded the suits, moved business opinion from unconcern over the *Mt. Clemens* decision in June, 1946, to distress by September, and finally to something near hysteria by the end of the year. More cool-headed observers were quick to point out that the final awards in these cases would certainly not come close to the amounts employees were demanding. Many of the claims rested on little except wishful thinking, and the plaintiffs could never have made even the presumptive showing of "work performed," required by the *Mt. Clemens* decision. Nevertheless, management did stand to lose substantial sums, and the corporate community came to appreciate that it had lost an important battle in the courts. Business leaders began to fear that organized labor, like a wolf pack, was moving in for the kill.

On December 18 the New York *Times* announced, in its financial section, that executives all over the country "are confused and uncertain about the portal-to-portal pay decision of the United States Supreme Court." That same week *Time* proclaimed:

> Dazed by such astronomical sums, businessmen feel that they are being unfairly penalized, that the Wages & Hours Act was not intended to cover such cases. As the suits piled up, they fervently hoped that one of the first things Congress does is to find a way to keep them from losing their shirts.

Before the month was out *Newsweek, U.S. News,* and *Business Week* had called on the new 80th Congress to right the wrong done by the Supreme Court when, as *Newsweek* put it, the Court had assumed the "role of Santa Claus to labor unions."

Indeed, the removal of the battle to the Congressional arena was the obvious next move of the opponents of portal pay. Beginning in 1937, the business community had become increasingly alienated from the Supreme Court—which during the first three decades of the twentieth century had seemed to stand as the bulwark of laissez-faire conservatism against the onslaughts of radicals who demanded governmental intervention in the economy. In 1938 Frank J. Hogan, President of the American Bar Association (an organization that fully mirrored the conservatism of American business in the 1930's), gave voice to this growing disaffection with the Supreme Court:

> Again and again the Court turned aside from what had long been looked upon as "established" principles of constitutional law. . . . The day must come when the future chroniclers of our judicial history [will record] unstinted praise to the rugged sturdiness of McReynolds and Butler, shown in their courageous efforts to preserve landmark after landmark of the law. . . .

Mr. Hogan also had some advice about what the American people should do now that the Court had abandoned the true way—advice which was to be tested by the business community in the struggle over portal pay:

> The American people must look to the legislative [branch of government] rather than the judiciary for the preservation of those liberties which can be preserved only by observance of limitations upon the exercise of [governmental] power. . . .

If the business community had lost its old friend, the Federal judiciary, it had certainly gained a new one in the Republican Congress elected in the autumn of 1946. Hugo Black and Frank Murphy might scourge business from the bench of the Supreme Court, but Bob Taft and Joe Martin presided over probusiness majorities in the Chambers across Capitol Plaza.

On December 24, 1946, the New York *Times* reported the launching of a counterattack in Congress by the business community. "The United States Chamber of Commerce took the lead in the business drive with plans to poll its membership on a series of proposed amendments to the law (FLSA)." As the *New Republic* put it on January 6, "The highest-paid corporation lawyers in the country have converged upon Washington to prepare a common defense against labor's billion-dollar claims for retroactive portal-to-portal wages." The Congressional phase of the portal-pay battle was under way. Business leaders were confident that in Congress they would be able to assert their claims more successfully than when the problem of defining work had rested principally with the Wage and Hour Division, or with the courts.

### About the 80th Congress

In order to understand the Congressional phase of the portal-pay controversy, it is necessary to realize that Congress itself is always much more than a passive register of the forces brought to bear upon it. The 80th Congress was, in a sense, the arena of battle, but it was also to become a participant in the struggle with its own particular goal.

Most Republican Congressmen and Senators shared the desire of businessmen to eliminate portal-to-portal pay, and many conservative Democrats also saw eye-to-eye with the representatives of the business community on what should be done about the *Mt. Clemens* decision. Beyond this, however, the 80th Congress (or at least its Republican majority) was seized by the conviction that its special historical mission was to re-establish the primacy of Congress over the other organs of the national government. After having been somewhat muted during the New Deal and the war years, Congressional voices demanded, in 1947, supremacy for the "true representatives of the people." As Republican leader Joe Martin put it in his memoirs:

> When I first became Speaker, in January 1947, early in the Eightieth Congress, the Republicans had been through twelve years of Franklin Roosevelt and nearly two years of Harry Truman. Now that we were at last in control of both houses we were determined that Congress should be a much stronger, more independent force that it had been since 1933.
>
> "Our American concept of government," I told the House in my first address as Speaker, "rests upon the idea of a dominant Congress. Congress is the people's special instrument of control over their government. . . . This nation can remain free only through a strong, vigorous Congress . . . which will protect the liberties of the people and not delegate

THE JUDGE AND THE GENII

its fundamental powers either to the executive or to arrogant bureaucrats."

These words fairly captured, I believe, the attitude of the Eightieth Congress.

Congressmen and Senators bitterly resented any diminution, actual or imagined, of the authority of Congress. The Supreme Court, as it presumed to pronounce upon the "intent of Congress," was a prime offender in this regard.

Thus, the particular goal of the majority of the 80th Congress in the portal-pay struggle was to assert Congressional supremacy over the Supreme Court—to inform the Court, in no uncertain terms, that it was to conduct itself in the future in such a way as to avoid "usurping the legislative function." Fresh from a victory at the polls, the Republican majority of the 80th Congress seemed to be in an excellent tactical position to engage in "Congressional imperialism" at the same time it came to the aid of the business community.

### The Battle Is Joined

During the opening days of the First Session of the 80th Congress, the portal-pay issue was obscured by the free-for-all over the seating of Senator Theodore Bilbo of Mississippi. The issue presented by the *Mt. Clemens* decision, however, lay like a submerged log, just below the surface of Congressional activities that were reported daily in the press. During the first two weeks of January, 1947, both *Time* and *U.S. News* were careful to remind their readers that bills for the relief of business were in preparation on Capitol Hill. Before the month was out three such bills had been introduced in the House and two in the Senate.

### In the House

The first bill introduced in the House, aimed at nullifying the effects of the *Mt. Clemens* decision, was a legislative broadside directed at the FLSA that bore the imprimatur of Representative Clare Hoffman (R., Michigan). It was referred to the House Committee on Education and Labor, but became lost in the welter of activity in that Committee which presaged the Taft-Hartley Act of 1947. The bill had been very extreme, and its inability to draw support probably resulted from the fact that, while many Congressmen wanted to weaken the FLSA, very few wanted to murder it publicly. One commentator remarked that it was an "Alice in Wonderland bill, disposing of all troubles with a casual 'off with their heads.' . . ."

Another portal-pay bill was introduced as a House Joint Resolution, and was sponsored by Representative Harold Knutson (R., Minnesota). In a few short sentences this resolution sought to eliminate the portal-pay problem by withdrawing, from state and Federal courts, jurisdiction over cases arising under Section 7(a) of the FLSA that were concerned with overtime pay. This resolution was referred to the Committee on the Judiciary, but was never acted upon in any way.

A third House bill aimed at reversing the *Mt. Clemens* decision was introduced by Representative John W. Gwynne (R., Iowa) and was also referred to the Committee on the Judiciary. For years Congressman Gwynne had been introducing bills which sought to tinker with the Federal judicial system. In the 79th Congress he had attempted to secure passage of a bill which would have limited the ability of employees to sue their employers under the FLSA because he felt the courts were not interpreting the Act in accordance with the intent of Congress. In the 80th Congress his efforts were crowned with success. It was the Gwynne bill, rewritten in a "clean" form, that was eventually passed by both Houses; with only a few minor changes, it became the Portal-to-Portal Act of 1947.

This bill, H.R. 584, attacked portal pay in two ways: first, it provided that travel and make-ready time was not and never had been work under the FLSA; second, it provided that no court, state or Federal, was to entertain suits for portal pay under the FLSA—regardless of whether the suits had been instituted before or after the passage of the bill. The first provision alone was enough to wipe out the suits; the second was actually a "punishment" of the courts for misbehavior.

The hearing on H.R. 584 opened on February 3, 1947, before Subcommittee No. 2 of the Committee on the Judiciary. Besides its Chairman, Representative Gwynne, the Subcommittee was made up of Representatives Angier L. Goodwin (R., Massachusetts), Kenneth B. Keating (R., New York), Francis E. Walter (D., Pennsylvania), Joseph R. Bryson (D., South Carolina), and Thomas J. Lane (D., Massachusetts). Businessman after businessman made his way to the witness chair and proclaimed that the fate of the Republic hung in the balance. The first witness, Milton Smith, Assistant General Counsel of the Chamber of Commerce of the United States, asserted that it was "vital to the public interest that this law [the FLSA] be revised so as to remove its uncertainties and inequities and to make definite the areas of its applicability." The dissatisfaction of business leaders with the Supreme Court found a voice in James P. Rogers, secretary of an association of lumber companies, who insisted, in tortured syntax, that "the *Jewell Ridge* case is the really bad case, it is not the *Mount Clemens* case, so far as the doctrine of law . . . announced that it is so bad . . . it illustrates that this is a creeping thing." Other business witnesses joined their voices in a chorus predicting the immediate disintegration of the nation's economy if the Gwynne bill were not adopted.

The brunt of the opposition to the Gwynne bill fell on a few representatives of the CIO. The closest they came to a counterattack was the appearance before the Subcommittee of David J. McDonald, Secretary-Treasurer of the United Steelworkers of America, CIO, who vigorously opposed H.R. 584. Fortified by his theatrical training at the Carnegie Institute of Technology

Drama School, McDonald painted for the Subcommittee a Dantesque picture of an employee on his way to work in a steel mill:

> He is walking across steel plates, usually covered with grease. . . .
> White [hot] bars are passing underneath him. The heat is beating upon
> him from these bars. . . . As he approaches the open hearths them-
> selves, perhaps he has passed through three or four mills. Perhaps he has
> gone outside in the process . . . into the cold again [in the winter] or in
> summertime, into the heat. Then he repeats the process, in and out of the
> mill. All the time he is encountering these physical dangers, and all the
> time he is under the supervision of the company.

If the Subcommittee was impressed by McDonald's performance, the impression did not last long. Lee Pressman, who followed McDonald to the witness chair, was unable to evoke any favorable response from the Congressmen to his careful legal arguments in support of the *Mt. Clemens* decision. Irving Richter, National Legislative Counsel of the United Auto Workers, CIO, and the last of the labor witnesses to appear before the Subcommittee, was moved to exclaim, "There seems to be a race on to see which member of Congress can break the tape with the first bill that would meet the requirements of the National Association of Manufacturers." Actually, the labor representatives never stood a chance of success. The vast amounts involved in the suits, and the hostile public opinion (helped along by a business public relations campaign) that the suits had created, made it impossible to argue effectively in Congress for portal-to-portal pay. One of the labor representatives, who appeared before Subcommittee No. 2, later remarked that although he had believed in the rectitude of his general position, he had felt utterly absurd in defending portal-pay suits that "ran into sums of money bigger than the national debt."

The Subcommittee was not in the least disturbed by the fact that the Gwynne bill "overruled" a Supreme Court decision. Almost every probusiness witness reminded the Congressmen that the Court had not read the FLSA in the light of the "clear" intent of Congress, and a mood of Congressional truculence prevailed during the hearings. It was simply assumed, throughout the course of the hearings before Subcommittee No. 2, that it was perfectly proper for the Congress to "reverse" the Supreme Court; no one bothered mentioning a precedent for such action—although precedents did exist that could have been pressed into service had anyone felt them necessary.

The Subcommittee was somewhat concerned, at first, about the constitutionality of the Gwynne bill to the extent that it *retroactively* deprived individuals of rights that the courts had held to have been vested in them by the FLSA. The Fifth Amendment bars deprivations of property rights without due process of law. However, Raymond S. Smethurst, Counsel of the NAM, hastened to assure the Congressmen that they need have no fears on this score: "It is apparent that Congress may withdraw entirely the right of the courts to proceed with suits based upon rights created by Federal statute, and this power tends as to all pending cases even though cognizable when commenced." To prove this point Smethurst, James P. Rogers, and others, submitted lengthy briefs in support of retroactive deprivations of property rights.

The hearings concluded on February 10, 1947, and on February 26, 1947, a rewritten or "clean" version of the Gwynne bill was reported out by the Committee on the Judiciary as H.R. 2157. The bill was brought to the floor of the House on February 28 and was debated and passed (345 to 56) the same day. Although a small group of Congressmen did come forward to oppose the bill, they did so on the grounds of justice for employees, not because of the attack on the Supreme Court that the bill contained. The tone of this opposition was set by the venerable Chicago Democrat, Adolph Sabath, who held that "most of these actions [portal-pay suits] have been entered into, not only in good faith but under great justification, against employers always ready and willing to chisel a little free work from the men and women who work for them."

### In the Senate

In early January, 1947, two bills were introduced in the Senate to deal with the problems raised by the *Mt. Clemens* decision. The first bill, S. 49, sponsored by Senator Homer Capehart (R., Indiana), was an extreme measure much like the Gwynne bill, and it was promptly shelved. The second bill, S. 70, was more moderate than either S. 49 or the Gwynne bill and sought to solve the portal-pay problem by redefining the intent of Congress without tampering with the jurisdiction of the courts. S. 70 was introduced by Senator Alexander Wiley (R., Wisconsin), who was then Chairman of the Senate Committee on the Judiciary.

Hearings on S. 70 opened on January 15, 1947, before a Subcommittee of the Committee on the Judiciary, which consisted of Senator Forrest C. Donnell (R., Missouri) as Chairman, Senator John Sherman Cooper (R., Kentucky), and Senator James O. Eastland (D., Mississippi). Representatives of the business community gave the same testimony and submitted the same documents before this body which they were to present a few weeks later before the House Subcommittee. William C. Chandler, a New York corporation lawyer, told the Senators:

> It seems to me that Congress, having plenary power to legislate, being of equal dignity in its field to the Supreme Court, if the Court interpreted an act of Congress in the way Congress had not intended it to be interpreted, then it should have the right to place its own interpretation on the Act. . . .

After the close of the hearings on January 30, 1947, S. 70 was modified slightly, and on February 26, 1947, was reported out favorably by the full Committee on the Judiciary.

Before S. 70 could come to the Senate floor, however, the Gwynne bill was passed in the House and referred to the Judiciary Committee. S. 70 was then sent back to the Committee to be "harmonized" with the Gwynne bill. On March 10, 1947, the product of this melding process was reported out. The moderate S. 70 had almost disappeared, and it was an only slightly altered Gwynne bill that went before the Senate.

The original version of S. 70 seems to have provoked little opposition, but the new H.R. 2157 caused some trouble. Five members of the Judiciary Committee issued a minority report that condemned the bill as an attempt to wreck the FLSA; and in contrast to the situation in the House several members of the Senate were willing to oppose this "tough" bill not only on the grounds that it was unfair to labor, but also that it constituted an improper invasion of the domain of the Judicial Branch of Government. This was the high point of "Lib-Lab" opposition to the Gwynne bill.

Senators McCarran (D., Nevada) and McGrath (D., Rhode Island) led the attack on the bill as unjust to labor, and urged, on the Senate floor, the adoption of a substitute bill they had prepared. The pro-Court opposition to the bill was led by the Minority Leader, Senator Alben Barkley, who deplored the action as "a declaration of no confidence in the courts of the United States." Senator Ernest McFarland delivered a scathing attack on the constitutionality of the proposed act, and Republican Senator Charles Tobey of New Hampshire gave the opposition a bipartisan flavor by decrying the anti-Supreme Court aspects of the bill.

As in the House, however, the backers of a "hard" portal-pay bill finally had the votes to pass it. The McCarran-McGrath Amendment was overwhelmingly defeated, and the bill, including the section withdrawing jurisdiction from the courts, was passed by the Senate on March 21, 1947, by a vote of 64 to 24.

From the beginning the bill had been backed by a strong coalition of Republicans and Southern Democrats. This portal-pay majority was, in fact, the continuing and cohesive conservative coalition that dominated the 80th Congress during 1947 and 1948. The roll-call votes on the Gwynne bill bear a marked resemblance to the votes on H.R. 3020—the bill that became the Taft-Hartley Act of 1947. Given this coalition (which may fairly be called the most probusiness and anti-Court in recent American history), and given the public hostility engendered by the recklessness of small-time lawyers and union officials, organized labor was foredoomed in its defense of the *Mt. Clemens* decision and of the judicial definition of work. Congress passed an extreme bill that sought to relieve the business community of the threat of portal pay—and also sought to teach the Supreme Court a lesson. The "preamble" to the Gwynne bill, as finally passed, was one of the harshest statutory rebukes ever directed to the Court:

> Section 1.   (a) The Congress hereby finds that the Fair Labor Standards Act of 1938, as amended, has been interpreted judicially in disregard of long-established customs, practices, and contracts between employers and employees, thereby creating wholly unexpected liabilities, immense in amount and retroactive in operation, upon employers with the result that, if said act as so interpreted were permitted to stand, (1) payment of such liabilities would bring about financial ruin of many employers and seriously impair the capital resources of many others thereby resulting in the reduction of industrial operations, halting of expansion and develop-ment, curtailing employment and the earning power of employers; (2) the credit of many employers would be seriously impaired; (3) there would be created both an extended and continuous uncertainty on the part of industry; . . . (4) employees would receive windfall payments [and] . . . champertous practices would be encouraged. . . .[1]
>     (b) It is hereby declared to be the policy of Congress in order to meet the existing emergency and to correct existing evils (1) to relieve and protect interstate commerce from practices which burden and obstruct it; (2) to protect the right of collective bargaining; and (3) to define and limit the jurisdiction of the courts.

On May 14, 1947, President Truman signed this bill into law as the Portal-to-Portal Act of 1947. However, evidence indicates that the President did so regretfully. In his message to Congress conveying his approval of the bill Truman began by stating that "in the interests of the economic stability of our Nation, it is essential to clarify this matter [the right of employees to portal pay] by statute." But within a few paragraphs Truman made clear his distaste for this particular statute.

> I am aware that this Act introduces new and possibly ambiguous lan-guage, the effects of which can be accurately measured only after inter-pretation by the courts. I have therefore instructed the Secretary of Labor to keep me currently informed as to the effects of this Act upon the preservation of wage-and-hour standards. If those effects prove to be detrimental to the maintenance of fair labor standards of our workers, I shall request the Congress to take prompt remedial action.

Partisans of portal pay might have had a powerful (possibly decisive) ally in the President if Truman's hand had not been forced by snowballing portal-pay suits. As it was, aroused public opinion (and the very real drag that the

---

[1] A champertous practice is an arrangement whereby an unethical lawyer drums up business by taking a case for no set fee, but rather for a percentage of any recovery awarded if the suit is successful.

suits promised to have on the national economy) prompted the President to let the bill pass with a stern warning. Thus, the Act went on the books, and the issue of portal-to-portal pay ceased to exist as such.

### The Mt. Clemens Workers

And what of the Mt. Clemens pottery workers? In all the nation-wide excitement, in all the tumult and shouting, what happened to Edward Lamb and Steve Anderson?

One irony of the portal-pay controversy is that the *Mt. Clemens* case, after having been sent back to the District Court for final disposition in the light of the Supreme Court decision, was dismissed on the grounds of the common-law rule that the law does not concern itself with trifles. Judge Picard held that, using the standards supplied by the Supreme Court, he could not find that the workers at the Mt. Clemens Pottery had been uncompensated for any amount of travel time or make-ready time sufficient to warrant a remedy at law. Thus it was that the litigation that had opened the way for several billion dollars worth of suits by employees against their employers left the lawyer and workers who had begun it with only bills for six years of struggle in the courts. Picard's decision could have been appealed, but in the face of the new Portal-to-Portal Act, the CIO, the workers, and Edward Lamb decided to cut their losses and quit.

## Portal Pay and Pluralistic Politics

As is usual in the American political process, none of the major institutional or interest-group participants in the struggle over portal pay was either completely victorious or completely defeated. The pattern of gains and losses that resulted from the controversy illustrates nicely the "nonabsolute" nature of pluralistic politics in the United States, and it also reveals the delicate, often hostile, relationship that exists between Congress—which makes law—and the Supreme Court—which must make sense out of law.

At first glance, it might seem that the business community won a total victory with the passage of a strongly worded statute that nullified the *Mt. Clemens* decision and censured the Supreme Court. The numerous portal-pay suits then pending were wiped out, and all possibility of future actions by employees seeking portal pay was foreclosed. But when one looks beyond these admitted gains, this initial judgment must be seriously amended.

During the period between the decision in the *Mt. Clemens* case and the enactment of the Portal-to-Portal Act of 1947 (June, 1946 to May, 1947) many business organizations negotiated settlements with their employees on the issue of accrued portal pay. In October, 1946, for instance, the Dow Chemical Company arrived at an agreement with its union that cost the company $3,970,000 in retroactive overtime pay for travel and make-ready activities.

In addition to such negotiated settlements, the issue of portal-to-portal pay certainly influenced the course of collective bargaining in the year during which the Mt. Clemens decision remained in effect. It must be remembered that the main objective of organized labor with regard to the *Mt. Clemens* decision was never to obtain windfall awards for employees, but rather to use the issue of portal pay as a lever with which to extract concessions from management in bargaining over the terms of new contracts. The eleven months between June, 1946, and May, 1947, saw labor-management contracts signed in industries such as steel and textiles. Wartime controls were gone and many important concessions were wrested from management during that time. While it would be absurd to credit this labor success to the pressure of portal-pay suits alone, their effect cannot be discounted. From 1947 onward, almost all labor contracts included provisions providing for portal pay.

Thus the bill finally passed by Congress, although tailored to business specifications, could not recover for corporate treasuries what they had already lost in negotiated settlements for back overtime pay and in contract concessions. The mills of American politics grind slowly, and because they do, no remedy was available soon enough to keep business from losing a good deal as a result of the *Mt. Clemens* decision.

When Congress disallowed portal-to-portal pay, not only was a potent collective-bargaining weapon denied to union leaders, but a certain psychological advantage was given to management. Having been so successful in Congress once, business could trade, for a short time at least, on the expectation that it might be successful again on other issues. Management could foster the impression that Congress sat on its side of the bargaining table.

These were significant losses, and the CIO was painfully aware that it had taken a drubbing on Capitol Hill. Yet the gains won before the passage of the Act remained undisturbed. The American national government is made up of separated institutions sharing power; what one institution (such as the Supreme Court) does, another institution (such as Congress) cannot completely undo.

### The 80th Congress

The probusiness majority of the 80th Congress was quite able to pass a bill that was attractive to the business community. A small minority of prolabor Congressmen and Senators were beaten down time after time, and the proponents of a "hard" portal-pay bill were rarely forced to compromise.

Speaker Martin's Republicans were much less successful, however, in achieving their own particular goal—the assertion of Congressional supremacy over the Supreme Court. The Court was verbally chastized in the Portal-to-Portal Act, and its jurisdiction (along with that of all other courts) was curtailed in a minor way. Various writers and publications took the opportunity to twit and reprove the Court. With flowing condescension *Collier's* requested:

> On the big bench from now on, couldn't we have a little more discretion, a little more care in the use of language, a little more calculation of the possible consequences of such things as this [portal pay]? Supreme Court failure to stick severely to the subject under discussion can be calamitous to the whole country, and in this affair it almost was.

Additionally, the Act set another precedent for Congressional "reversal" of Supreme Court decisions and was cited in later years by various groups urging Congress to overturn holdings of the Court that they found obnoxious. This was the "punishment" meted out to the Court, and ultimately it proved slight.

In fact, a much wider range of "Court-curbing" tactics was available to Congress by virtue of its power over the judiciary set forth in Article II, Sec. 1, of the Constitution. Legally, a much greater limitation of jurisdiction could have been imposed on the Court. Politically, however, the Congressional majority had gone as far as it felt it could. The storm of public protest that had greeted Roosevelt's "Court Plan" a decade before was ample warning that more justification than just the *Mt. Clemens* decision would be needed for the public to accept an all-out attack upon the independence of the judiciary. Such increased justification might, perhaps, have been supplied by the Court in the year following the passage of the Act, but it never was. Without a Congressional follow-up, the stinging language of the Portal-to-Portal Act was ineffectual. When the extreme "congressional imperialism" of the 80th Congress ended with the election of 1948, the Supreme Court emerged with its powers virtually undisturbed, ready to assert its role as a coordinate branch of government. Viewed from the perspective of 1963, the Portal-to-Portal Act appears as an only marginally successful attempt by Congress to subdue what it then regarded (and would come to regard again) as an errant Supreme Court.

### The Supreme Court

Did the Supreme Court deliberately avoid provoking Congress in the year after the passage of the Act and thus facilitate its "escape?" Ultimately, this must remain an open question, but circumstantial evidence suggests at least the possibility that some members of the Court subordinated strong views about the desirability of portal pay to a concern for preserving the Court's independence vis-à-vis the Congress.

Two real questions existed as to the constitutionality of the Portal-to-Portal Act of 1947. First, it constituted a possible deprivation of vested property rights in violation of the due process clause of the Fifth Amendment. Second, it restricted the jurisdiction of both state and Federal courts and denied any forum to certain claims arising under the FLSA. Although Congress has plenary power over the appellate jurisdiction of the Supreme Court, it is questionable whether Congress can prevent a particular claim from being made in any court at any time. This aspect of the Act was also suspect under the due process injunction of Amendment Five.

The Act was challenged at once in numerous Federal district court proceedings, and by early 1948 several of these cases had been decided and reviewed by courts of appeal. In no instance was the statute actually declared unconstitutional, but the grounds on which judges upheld it were confused and contradictory. Articles appeared in law reviews suggesting that the Supreme Court should resolve these questions, and a petition for a writ of certiorari was presented to the Court requesting that it hear a case involving the constitutionality of the Act. The petition was denied. The questions went unanswered.

What conclusions can one draw from the Court's refusal? Only this: all five justices who made up the *Mt. Clemens* majority were still on the Court when the petition for certiorari was denied; since it takes four affirmative votes to grant certiorari, it is obvious that at least two proportal-pay justices felt, for one reason or another, that it would be ill-advised to reopen the question by passing upon the Portal-to-Portal Act. More than this we cannot know. However, speculation as to the motives of Supreme Court justices is often the lot of constitutional lawyers and political scientists. The "political" explanation for the Court's action in this instance is a fascinating one—deserving of consideration if not uncritical acceptance.

### Political Actors and Political Style

Viewed from the perspective of 1963, the struggle chronicled here may appear as just one of the many instances since the close of World War II in which labor and management have squared off against one another. The highly political context in which the issue of portal pay was decided does not seem at all novel to us. Mid-twentieth-century Americans are used to seeing the great economic questions of their society decided through the operation of the political process—used to seeing judges, union leaders, corporation managers, trade association lawyers, Congressmen, Federal bureau chiefs, and Presidents of the United States taking sides against one another to fight out some question of who shall get what in the American economy.

This very quality of sameness, however, makes the story of portal pay worth telling. The politico-economic issues changed with bewildering rapidity during the 1940's and 1950's, but the styles of the combatants remained the same. Whether the battle was over the Taft-Hartley Act in 1947 or the minimum wage in 1961, over President Truman's seizure of the steel mills in 1952 or the Landrum-Griffin Act in 1959, the same institutional actors who appeared in the portal-pay case came forward to defend their interests. Personnel may change in Congress, in the offices of the NAM, or in the White House, but the character of these institutions persists. Conflict between these particular actors has raged for several decades past, and will, in all probability, rage for decades hence. By recalling the various political styles so clearly revealed in this one battle from the 1940's, the student may, perhaps, better understand the unfolding politico-economic struggles of the 1960's.

### Table of Cases, in Order of Citation in the Text

*Anderson* v. *Mt. Clemens Pottery Co.,* 328 U.S. 680 (1945).
*Tennessee Coal Co.* v. *Muscoda Local,* 321 U.S. 590 (1944).
*Jewell Ridge Coal Corp.* v. *Local No. 6167, UMW,* 325 U.S. 161 (1945).
*Anderson* v. *Mt. Clemens Pottery Co.,* 60 F. Supp. 146 (1942).
*Mt. Clemens Pottery Co.* v. *Anderson,* 149 F. 2d 461 (1944).

### Sources

In making this study of the portal-pay controversy I have relied primarily on official documents and newspapers to provide a skeleton for the narrative and on personal interviews to enrich and deepen the picture presented by the printed "record." For the judicial phase of the controversy, official court reports were supplemented by a copy of the trial record and the Special Master's Report owned by the Columbia University Law Library. For the Congressional phase of the dispute the *Congressional Record,* committee reports, and transcripts of hearings were drawn upon. My use of the New York *Times'* columns is evident throughout, and in order to provide a wide sampling of editorial comment on portal pay a large number of popular periodicals were searched. In addition certain specialized publications such as trade association journals and union newsletters were examined. My principal debt, however, is to Lee Pressman, formerly of the CIO, to Harvey M. Crow of the NAM, and to Edward Lamb; each man read an earlier draft of this study and discussed with me his participation in, and impressions of, the portal-pay case.

# 3

## CRUEL AND UNUSUAL PUNISHMENT

# The Electric-Chair Case

## Barrett Prettyman, Jr.

CHIEF JUSTICE VINSON in his first term on the Court did not succeed in reducing the rate of disagreement in the Court's decisions. In fact, only 36 per cent of the Court's major cases decided by full opinion were unanimous, and 26 of the split decisions were by a 5 to 4 vote. One of these 5 to 4 decisions occurred in the case with which we are here concerned.

With the *Willie Francis* case we look for the first time at the problem of the Supreme Court's peculiar responsibility in the administration of the American system of criminal justice. The guarantee of a fair trial is one of the basic protections in a government of laws, and the Constitution has an entire battery of provisions incorporating Anglo-Saxon standards of trial procedure. Most of these guarantees are found in the Bill of Rights, from the Fourth through the Eighth Amendments. The provisions appearing there include the guarantee of due process of law, the right to indictment by grand jury and trial by jury, freedom from self-incrimination or unreasonable searches and seizures, and the prohibition against excessive bail and cruel and unusual punishment.

Obviously these guarantees are to be enforced in federal criminal prosecutions, but the Supreme Court held as early as 1833 that the Bill of Rights did not apply to the states. The post-Civil War period, however, saw the ratification of the Fourteenth Amendment, with a due process clause adopted specifically to cover the states: "nor shall any state deprive any person of life, liberty, or property, without due process of law. . . ."

Since 1884 the Supreme Court has been torn between two

possible interpretations of this language so far as it applies to state criminal prosecutions. The first is that the Fourteenth Amendment gathers up all the procedural protections of the Fourth through the Eighth Amendments and makes them applicable also to the states. The second is that the standard of due process is a flexible one that is not spelled out elsewhere in the Constitution and that requires the Supreme Court itself to determine what procedures will meet the tests of a system of "ordered liberty." In the *Willie Francis* case the Supreme Court had to assume the burden of divining what was due process in a startlingly unusual set of circumstances.

THE BOY in the cell looked older than seventeen, but seventeen he was. He appeared lanky and angular, with his 150 pounds stretched out over a five-foot, ten-inch frame. His feet and hands were big, out of proportion to the rest of him.

His name was Willie Francis; everyone knew him as Willie. The newspapers said he was an illiterate Negro. As a matter of fact, he could read and write, and he thought clearly, if not entirely in an organized manner. But he suffered from one defect that caused him untold agony. He stuttered.

It was May 2, 1946—a Thursday night. Outside, the townfolk were thinking ahead to the weekend and listening to the radio news of Mr. Justice Jackson's cross-examination of the Nazi war criminals in Nuremberg. Willie was thinking ahead to the weekend too, but he wasn't interested in news from abroad. His was a tight little world—no longer, no broader, no higher than his cell.

Gilbert Ozeene padded up to the cell and looked through, but Willie, standing at the barred window, hardly noticed. Ozeene was sheriff of Iberia Parish, an oddly shaped Louisiana "county" fronting on Vermillion Bay, just off the Gulf of Mexico. The sheriff asked if Willie wanted anything to eat or drink. Willie looked away from the window and nodded. He said he wanted something good to eat.

The sheriff went out and bought the best steak he could find and some ice cream and cake. Willie took the food gratefully and sat on the cot with the tin plate balanced on his knees. He solemnly ate every bit of the food, staring at it and thinking about it to keep his mind away from the weekend that wouldn't happen. For on Friday, May 3, between the hours of noon and 3:00 P.M., Willie Francis was to be electrocuted.

Adapted from *Death and the Supreme Court*, Chapter 3 ("If at First"), © 1961, by Barrett Prettyman, Jr., by permission of Harcourt, Brace & World, Inc.

Certainly, at this point, neither Willie nor his lawyers could have foreseen that his case would become a *cause célèbre* in the Supreme Court of the United States. For his trial was over, the time for filing an appeal had elapsed, and no new legal maneuvering was contemplated on his behalf. An appreciation of what occurred next requires a brief critique of procedure in criminal cases in general, and of capital cases in particular, before the nation's highest Court.

Criminal cases reach the Supreme Court from two sources: the state and Federal courts. Since the Supreme Court has general supervisory jurisdiction over all Federal courts, it can and does reverse Federal convictions not only for violation of constitutional rights but also for other substantive deficiencies and even where the lower tribunals have failed to follow certain procedural rules. But cases coming from state courts are governed by more restrictive standards. The Supreme Court's jurisdiction in such cases can be invoked only when the Federal Constitution has been violated. The result is that the Court is forced to leave standing many state convictions which would have been reversed if they had arisen in the Federal courts, but which do not involve errors of constitutional proportions.

### The Rapid Growth of the Criminal Docket

Surprisingly, no statistics are kept that show the number of criminal cases filed in the Supreme Court each term. However, beginning in 1947, all cases accompanied by motions for leave to proceed *in forma pauperis*—that is, applications by indigents for permission to file for review without payment of court costs—have been tabulated by the Court on a separate "miscellaneous" docket, and since most of these indigent cases are criminal in nature, some concept of the Court's business in criminal matters can be gleaned from this docket. As contrasted with the Court's regular "appellate" and "original" dockets, which have appreciated in size rather slowly (a rise of less than 15 per cent over the last fourteen years) the "miscellaneous" docket has more than doubled during the same period. Over 1,000 cases were filed during the 1960–61 term of Court.

The Supreme Court today hears and decides less than 2 per cent of the cases on its miscellaneous docket. This is a smaller percentage than it heard and decided from the same docket at the time of the *Willie Francis* case, and it is also a smaller percentage than it hears and decides from its regular appellate docket today. Since the number of defendants prosecuted each year in this country has remained remarkably constant despite a rapid growth in population, the question arises as to why criminal applications to the Supreme Court have increased so markedly in recent years.

The answer seems to lie in the fact that the Court, in those cases it has chosen to review, has greatly broadened the rights of defendants, both substantively and procedurally, through a more liberal interpretation of the due process clause of the Fourteenth Amendment. Whereas in the 1930's only a confession coerced by physical brutality ran afoul of due process, today psychological pressures or an incommunicado detention that merely provides an opportunity for coercion may invalidate a confession. Whereas in the 1930's the states were free to regulate criminal appellate procedures as they saw fit, today they must accord indigent defendants the same privileges as are granted to defendants who pay their way, on the theory that a citizen cannot be discriminated against because of lack of funds.

The result of this broadening protection has been twofold. First, a convicted felon has nothing to lose (not even money) by taking his case all the way to the High Court and, second, the Court's rulings have given hope, where previously there was none, that some constitutional error may have permeated the felon's trial.

The Court's responsibility as these applications pour in at a greater rate each term is complicated by the fact that many *in forma pauperis* petitions are in the defendant's own handwriting—barely legible, ungrammatical, and wild in their accusations. The mere logistics of sorting through this mass of literature and uncovering the one case in many that merits review are awesome indeed, and the Court is constantly haunted by the fear that time and patience may suspend just at the wrong moment.

With a single exception, the crime itself seems to play little part in whether the Court will hear and decide a given case. Thus, the Court recently refused to review convictions carrying life sentences during the same term that it heard and reversed a conviction for loitering and disorderly conduct involving a twenty-dollar fine. By such action the Court attempts to make clear that an accused is entitled to constitutional protection regardless of the nature of his crime, and a violation of rights in an insignificant misdemeanor case is no more to be countenanced than if it had occurred during prosecution for a serious felony.

The single exception to this attitude toward the crime is directed to the capital offense. Since capital cases first began coming to the Court, the justices have recognized that because a mistake cannot be remedied once the defendant has gone to his death, special rules apply when life is at stake. Not only will the Court give particular, meticulous attention to each death case, but both the state and Federal courts will be kept to a rigid standard of fairness, additional safeguards will apply, and substantial doubts will be resolved in favor of the accused. For example, the Court has ruled that an accused in a first-degree murder case must be represented by counsel at trial, even though the Court has not yet held that the Constitution requires the same accused to be represented when on trial for lesser offenses.

When a matter involving the death sentence arrives at the Court, the label "capital case" is printed in red on the outside cover of the file. This is the only type of case coming to the Court that receives a designation all its own. If the case is *in forma pauperis,* so that only one set of papers has been filed instead of the usual forty, the set is circulated among all nine justices, accompanied by a memorandum prepared by one of the Chief Justice's law clerks. The file receives each justice's careful attention, and when he is through with it, he initials a check-off sheet stapled to the file and sends the papers on to the next of his brethren.

Again, no statistics are regularly kept in regard to the Court's treatment of capital offenses. However, a case-by-case study of a recent term's work reveals that of the 2,178 cases the Court was asked to review, 42 involved the death penalty. The Court refused to hear argument in 29, returned 2 to the lower courts for further hearings, listened to argument in 11 (6 of which were subsequently dismissed because the facts of record did not support the alleged grounds of appeal), and reversed 5. Thus, while it can be generalized that it is far easier for a condemned man to have his case heard than for the average litigant (whose chances are one in twenty), the fact remains that out of every four condemned men, only one receives a Supreme Court hearing. Death, for all the attention its presence commands, did not have in 1946, and does not have today, any guaranteed admission to our highest Court. It was against this background that the *Willie Francis* case developed.

### Five Shots from a Fifteen-Year-Old

Sitting in his cell on May 2, 1946, eating his steak, Willie remembered what a stir had been created in St. Martinville back in November, 1944, when Andrew Thomas had been found murdered. Willie was only fifteen at the time. St. Martinville, with its population of about 4,000, was eight miles due north of New Iberia and over the line in St. Martin Parish. Andrew Thomas was a popular St. Martinville druggist who lived on the main highway. He had come home from work one night and parked his car. As he stepped away from the garage, he was shot five times by someone standing in the shadows. One bullet crashed through his right eye, two more entered under his right armpit, and the last two struck the center of his back as he spun around. When the police found him stretched out in the driveway, a watch and a wallet containing four dollars were missing.

Harold Resweber, Sheriff of St. Martin Parish, working closely with the state police, searched fruitlessly for months, following up every possible thread that might lead to the killer. A neighbor of Thomas said the shots had wakened her, and she had seen a car parked in front of Thomas' house with its lights on, but no trace of the car could be found. Resweber's one break came when a city employee, clearing away the tall grass a short distance from Thomas' house, found a pistol that had been stolen from the car of one of Resweber's deputies a few months before.

In the meantime an unrelated search had been going on in Port Arthur, Texas, 200 miles southwest of St. Martinville. The chief of police of Port Arthur and several of his men were waiting at a railroad station to meet a man they suspected of carrying illegal narcotics. When the man alighted from the train, the police followed him. The man saw them, dropped his suitcase, and ran. As the police approached the suitcase, they saw a second man, a Negro, crouched under a nearby tree. Thinking the Negro might be an accomplice of the dope peddler, they picked him up and took him in for questioning.

The Negro identified himself as Willie Francis of St. Martinville, Louisiana. In his pocket was a wallet that had belonged to Andrew Thomas. After a brief interrogation Willie stammered out a confession that he had assaulted and robbed an elderly man in a Port Arthur apartment just a few days before. And in his confession Willie also admitted that months ago he had killed and robbed Andrew Thomas in St. Martinville.

The Port Arthur police had heard of the Thomas murder. While Willie's confession was being reduced to paper for him to sign, the chief of police was calling Sheriff Resweber of St. Martin Parish to tell him that Thomas' killer was in custody.

Resweber immediately drove to Port Arthur with several deputies. Because of the more serious nature of the St. Martinville crime, the Port Arthur police gave up their custody of Willie, retaining only a warrant against him in case he was later released, and turned him over to Resweber. Resweber and his deputies, with Willie in tow, began the return trip to St. Martinville.

On the way back, Willie confessed again. He said he had waited two or three hours for Thomas, whom he knew slightly, and had shot him five times with a pistol stolen from a deputy sheriff's car. He pointed out to Resweber the grassy area where he had thrown the pistol after the shooting. It was the same spot where the deputy's pistol had already been found. Willie told Resweber he had taken Thomas' watch to a jewelry store in New Iberia and sold it for five dollars. Willie also gave the sheriff the names of two Negroes who he said were implicated in the crime.

Resweber began checking out the details of the story. He could find no Negroes with the names Willie had given him, and he concluded that this part of the story was fictitious. The pistol was sent to the Federal Bureau of Investigation in Washington along with a bullet recovered from Thomas' body, but the package was lost in the mails and never recovered. Resweber took Willie to the jewelry store in New Iberia where the watch had been sold, but the jeweler could not remember Willie or the watch. Several days later, however, the jeweler found among his bric-a-brac a watchcase with the murdered man's initials on the back.

The deputy's pistol had been encased in a holster at the time it was stolen, and Resweber kept pressing Willie as to what he had done with the holster. Finally, a few weeks before his trial, Willie led Resweber to a railroad culvert behind Thomas' house where he said he had tossed it. Working with hoes, Resweber's men dug out all of the accumulated dirt under the culvert and discovered a holster with the same leafy design as that owned by the deputy. The case against Willie Francis was complete.

His trial for murder lasted three days. Since no one had witnessed the crime and the pistol had been lost in the mails, the state's evidence consisted almost entirely of Willie's two confessions—the written one signed in Texas and the oral one given to Sheriff Resweber. A dozen witnesses appeared for the prosecution to testify as to the voluntary nature of these confessions. Willie's two court-appointed attorneys called no witnesses in his behalf. The neighbor who had seen the car parked in front of Thomas' house did not testify. No transcript of the trial was taken, no request for a change of venue (site of trial) entered, no motion for a new trial made, and no appeal filed. Just a week after his indictment, a jury found Willie Francis guilty of murder. The next day he was sentenced to death by electrocution, and five months later Governor James H. Davis signed a mandatory death warrant, calling for Willie's execution on Friday, May 3, 1946, between the hours of noon and 3 P.M.

### "Good-By, Willie"

Sheriff Resweber was not taking any chances on mob rule. He transferred custody of Willie over to his friend Sheriff Ozeene for safekeeping in the New Iberia jail until the day of the execution. Now it was already May 2, and Willie was eating his last meal. Sheriff Ozeene came by to say good night, and the two men chatted briefly on either side of the bars. Willie ended the conversation by saying he guessed he was ready to die. When Ozeene left, Willie lay down on the hard cot and slept fitfully.

In the morning the sheriff and several of his deputies came to Willie's cell and told him it was time to go back to St. Martinville for the electrocution. As they left, Sheriff Ozeene noticed some writing laboriously etched on the cell wall. It read: "I kill Andrew Thomas and today he is lying in a grave and I am not a killer but I wonder where I am going to be lying and in what kind of grave I don't know."

The men drove mostly in silence during the eight-mile trip to the St. Martin Parish jail in St. Martinville. Willie, handcuffed in the back seat of the sedan, looked through the windows at the familiar sights, but said very little. He and his brothers had been raised in this area. Willie had left school early to work at odd jobs—in a food products plant, a garage, and at various places around town. He had been in a few scrapes during his early teens, but nothing serious until the Thomas affair. He had liked St. Martinville. Now as the sedan swung around the courthouse square where Willie had often played as a child and pulled up in front of the town's main building, which served the parish as both courthouse and jail, Willie seemed hardly conscious of his surroundings. He was ushered inside, where Sheriff Resweber took charge and led him into a small cell, indistinguishable from the one he had occupied in New Iberia for the last seven months.

Unlike some states, Louisiana in 1946 executed its citizens "on the spot." Instead of transporting condemned criminals to a central prison where a permanent death cell was maintained, Louisiana sent its equipment around the state, executing criminals in the various jails where they happened to be held. The portable, hardwood electric chair was carried from town to town in a truck operated out of the Louisiana State Penitentiary at Angola.

The truck had arrived in St. Martinville the night before and now stood parked at the side of the courthouse with the electric chair still inside. The chair had already been tested by the penitentiary's chief electrician and found to be in perfect working order. As was his custom, the chief electrician intended to remain at Angola and send an assistant to take charge of the actual electrocution. In this instance the assistant would be a prison inmate, Vincent Venezia. The man actually in charge of the chair would be Captain E. Foster, a regular member of the penitentiary staff. Normally, the warden of the penitentiary accompanied the portable electric chair on its rounds. On this occasion, however, he stayed behind to entertain Governor Davis, who happened to be calling at his home in Angola.

The inmate, Venezia, arrived at St. Martinville shortly after 8:30 A.M. He joined Captain Foster at the truck, and the two of them, assisted by courthouse personnel, began unloading the portable electric chair and a large panel of switches and wires. The chair and panel were carried into the courthouse and placed in a kind of anteroom—almost a hallway— where the execution would take place. The room was bare, with cells ranged around it and emptying into it on three sides. The chair was placed in the middle of the room and the instrument panel laid nearby. The chair was so heavy that it did not have to be screwed into the floor. Venezia began attaching the wire leading from the chair to the panel and then ran several wires from the panel out through the window and on to the lawn. He went outside and attached these wires to the penitentiary truck, which carried its own generator, serving electric current directly to the chair inside the courthouse.

When he had completed the rather complicated wiring procedures, Venezia set the generator voltage at 2,500 and tested his ammeters, A.C. and D.C. He ran the generator for about five minutes to make certain that everything was in working order. It was 11 A.M. before he and Captain Foster were able to relax and enjoy a smoke.

While Willie was being prepared, his father arrived at the jail in a hearse carrying a wooden coffin. The coffin was unloaded and carried inside, where it would be ready as soon as Willie had been pronounced dead by the coroner. A man across the street from the courthouse saw the father "walk frantically and stupidly around like a drunk man." Several curious bystanders began to gather about the courthouse square.

Just before noon, the Rev. L. Maurice Rousseve, the chaplain who would officiate at the execution, arrived at the courthouse and was immediately ushered into Willie's cell. He spoke in soft tones, and Willie stuttered back a few words. The priest decided that the boy was resigned to his fate.

Precisely at noon Sheriff Resweber and his deputies opened the cell door and told Willie it was time. Willie got shakily to his feet, looked once at Rev. Rousseve, and walked out. The small group moved self-consciously to the nearby anteroom, which had been converted into an execution chamber. About a dozen men were present, only a few of whom Willie knew. Four of them had been appointed by Sheriff Resweber as official witnesses of the execution. Captain Foster, in charge of the chair, stood in the center to supervise the preparations, while Venezia waited outside by the truck. Sheriff Ozeene, Sheriff Resweber, a few of their deputies, and a state police captain milled about inside, seeing to last-minute details. Two Negro priests watched uncomfortably. The coroner of St. Martin Parish, the same man who had performed an autopsy on the murdered man, waited off to one side to pronounce Willie dead. Another doctor was also present, as required by law.

The condemned boy and Rev. Rousseve entered the anteroom close together. Willie surveyed the chair, oblivious of the curious stares of the onlookers. He was led to the chair and seated. Deputies began strapping down his arms and legs. It took a few minutes to make sure the straps were secure.

Captain Foster placed gauze dipped in salt water around Willie's head to help speed the electric current. Electrodes were attached to Willie's left leg and to his head over the gauze. Wires were connected. Finally, Captain Foster walked to the window and signaled to Venezia that everything was ready to go. Venezia had the generator going, and his gauge checked out. By now, a large crowd had gathered around the truck, some drawn by the deafening roar of the generator and others by their knowledge of the event scheduled to take place inside.

In the jail Rev. Rousseve stepped up to the electric chair and administered the last rites of the church to Willie. He held up a cross, and Willie kissed it. The priest stepped back, and Sheriff Resweber leaned close to the boy to ask if he had anything to say. Willie remained silent, staring straight ahead. The sheriff took a black hood and placed it over Willie's head, covering his eyes but leaving his mouth free, with a small slit at nose level to allow him to breathe.

The sheriff stepped back and nodded to Captain Foster. The captain checked the dial on his instrument panel once more—it registered at the proper level—and in a quiet voice that seemed unconscionably loud in the complete silence of the crowded room, said, "Good-by, Willie."

### The Reprieve that No One Sought

Willie did not answer, and Captain Foster, with a quick downward motion, threw the switch. For a fraction of a second, nothing happened. Then Willie jumped. He strained against the straps. He groaned. But even those who were witnessing their first execution knew something was wrong. Willie's body, though arched, was obviously not at the point of death. Captain Foster, all in one motion, frantically threw the switch off and then on again. Those closest to Willie heard him strain out the words, "Let me breathe." Captain Foster yelled out the window, exhorting Venezia to give him more juice. The startled Venezia yelled back that he was giving him all he had. His gauge showed that electricity was being generated, and he could not understand what the difficulty was.

Only a few seconds had passed, and yet the horrified spectators inside the jail felt as if they had stood transfixed for minutes. As they stared at Willie, they saw his lips puff out and swell like those of a pilot undergoing the stress of supersonic speeds. His body tensed and stretched in such catatonic movements that the chair, which had not been anchored to the floor, suddenly shifted, sliding a fraction of an inch along the floor.

"Take it off. Let me breathe." The agonizing words sputtered out. They roused Sheriff Resweber to action. He signaled to Captain Foster, who by now knew that his apparatus would not kill Willie Francis. He threw the switch back into an upright position. All in all, about two minutes had now passed since the switch had been thrown, and some of those present realized they had hardly breathed during the entire period.

The hood was lifted from Willie's head, the electrodes were removed and the straps unbuckled all around. Although obviously shaken, Willie was able to get to his feet by himself. He was taken by Sheriff Ozeene into an adjoining room, where they were joined by the coroner.

Ozeene asked Willie if he was hurt. Willie said no, but that the electricity had "tickled" him. The coroner, listening to Willie's chest through his stethoscope, heard a fast heart beat but otherwise no unusual symptoms. He said nothing to Willie, and Willie did not speak to him. When the coroner had gone, Ozeene asked Willie if he wanted any water, but the boy, sitting hunched over on a cot, shook his head. Rev. Rousseve entered the room and stayed about twenty minutes.

In the meantime Sheriff Resweber had taken Captain Foster to his office in another part of the jail, and Foster was placing a call to the warden's home in Angola. The warden answered and, as soon as he learned the nature of the call, said he would let Foster speak directly to Governor Davis. The Governor listened patiently to Foster's explanation of what had happened, decided that a reprieve from an immediate second attempt at electrocution was in order, and told Foster to take Willie back to the New Iberia jail. The Governor and the warden agreed that another date should be set at once, but when the Governor started to fix the following Saturday, May 11, for the new attempt, the warden informed him that another execution was scheduled for Leesville on that day, and he could not handle two at one time. The Governor therefore moved the date back one day to Friday, May 10, and personally wrote out a temporary reprieve and a second death warrant.

Captain Foster returned to the room where Willie was resting and told Ozeene of the Governor's decision. Ozeene and his deputies took Willie out of the cell and into the hallway where Sheriff Resweber was waiting to ask how his prisoner was doing. Willie said simply, "The Lord was with me that time," and the group moved quickly out into the sunlight. The waiting townspeople, excited by those mysterious signals from Foster to Venezia, were astonished to see the man who supposedly had just been electrocuted come striding out between two deputies. He was hustled into the sedan, which roared away, heading north from the courthouse square.

Willie was driven the eight miles back to New Iberia and placed in the same cell he had occupied the night before—the cell he had thought he would never see again. Though nervous and shaken, he ate a full lunch. Ozeene checked on him at five and again at seven o'clock that evening, but by then, the story of what had happened at St. Martinville had reached the press, and reporters were arriving to take pictures. When they left, Willie tried to sleep, but that night and for two nights thereafter he was extremely nervous, starting up in his sleep and breaking out into sudden swaths of perspiration. Then he became calmer and settled back into the routine life of the jail.

### Two Young Attorneys Enter the Case

The miracle that saved Willie Francis from death caught the public's imagination. The story was featured all across the country, and letters began pouring in, commiserating with Willie and admonishing the Governor not to send the boy through this experience again. Willie read all the letters delivered to his cell and even tried to answer most of them. It was a good way to pass time.

Willie's father was a farmer who eked out the family income on poor and uncharitable land. He began asking where he could find a lawyer to help his son. A friend advised him to see Bertrand de Blanc, a thirty-five-year-old graduate of the Louisiana State Law School who had just returned from three years in the service and had hung out his shingle next to the jail. The father went to see the lawyer and explained to him his impoverished circumstances, but de Blanc said he would do what he could. His first task, he knew, was to delay the new execution date so that he could file appropriate papers in court. He accomplished this task when the state's Lieutenant Governor, acting during the Governor's absence, issued a thirty-day stay of execution.

De Blanc now had to face up to the legal problems confronting him. Two methods of proceeding were open. He could go to the courts, or he could appeal to the Governor and the State Board of Pardons.

The route through the courts was beset with difficulties. His argument against another attempt at an execution would have to be based upon some principle recognized in the law. Since there had been no appeal from the conviction, he felt he could not raise at this late stage a number of issues relating to the trial itself, but instead would have to argue that regardless of whether or not the conviction had been valid originally, the unsuccessful attempt at electrocution violated the defendant's constitutional rights and vitiated either the conviction itself or at least the sentence of death. This would require some legal tightrope walking, and he doubted whether the Louisiana courts would listen to him.

His route by way of the Governor and the Board of Pardons was more inviting. The argument here could be based upon more equitable grounds. The Board and the Governor had discretion to commute a sentence for whatever reasons they deemed sufficient and were not required to hold either the conviction or the original sentence illegal, void, or in any way deficient. De Blanc felt that regardless of the obstacles in the way of a strict legal argument, the equities were certainly with him.

Nevertheless, he decided to proceed first through the Louisiana courts. His reasoning was that after the courts turned him down, the choice would lie squarely in the hands of the Executive Branch, and the Board and Governor could not then avoid their duty by arguing that de Blanc should first pursue other remedies. Therefore, he petitioned for a writ of habeas corpus in the same court that had convicted Willie. He argued that the state and Federal Constitutions had been violated in two respects. First, Willie had once been put in jeopardy of losing his life, and to attempt to electrocute him again would constitute double jeopardy. Second, to put Willie back in the chair after his agonizing experience would be such cruel and unusual punishment as to violate due process of law. The trial court denied the petition.

De Blanc immediately filed papers in the Louisiana Supreme Court. Because the case was so unique, he was not certain precisely which method of appeal he should follow, so he filed four different writs (certiorari, mandamus, prohibition, and habeas corpus) just to make sure. The Louisiana Supreme Court, without a hearing, denied all four of them; the court concluded that it had no authority to act. Since the trial and the sentencing had been entirely regular, there was nothing the appellate court could do simply because something had gone wrong with the execution. The only authority to grant a pardon or commute a sentence was vested in the Governor, who, in turn, could act only upon recommendation of the Board of Pardons.

The case now was in the position de Blanc had anticipated. The courts had placed the responsibility squarely in the laps of the Board and Governor. With only a week left before the execution, de Blanc requested a special meeting of the Board of Pardons in New Orleans. At the same time, however, he looked ahead to a possible denial by the Board of his plea for clemency, in which event only one course remained open—an appeal to the

United States Supreme Court. Through a friend, he contacted a Washington attorney, J. Skelly Wright, and asked him to prepare appropriate papers in the event that resort to the Supreme Court became necessary.

Wright (who years later was to be appointed to the United States District Court and then to the Court of Appeals) was the same age as de Blanc, thirty-five, and was also a native Louisianian, although he practiced law in the nation's capital. A graduate in philosophy and law from Loyola University in New Orleans, he had become a member of the bar at twenty-three, entered the United States Attorney's Office, and begun handling all types of civil and criminal cases for the United States, including the trial of some of the Louisiana scandal cases of 1940 and the sabotage cases of 1941. He had entered the coast guard in 1942, completed a tour of duty on a sub-chaser, and then been assigned to Europe for work in connection with the transportation of material to the Continent. After two-and-one-half years in service, he had returned to the United States Attorney's Office as first assistant and had prosecuted a number of war-fraud cases. He resigned in May, 1946, to enter private practice in Washington, and this is where de Blanc found him. Wright said he would be happy to prepare the necessary papers for the Supreme Court.

An extensive correspondence developed between de Blanc and Wright, as they attempted to coordinate their efforts. De Blanc was informed by the Lieutenant Governor that if a petition were filed in the United States Supreme Court prior to the Board of Pardons hearing in New Orleans, the Board would not act until the Supreme Court disposed of the case. Therefore, de Blanc requested Wright not to file his petition in the Supreme Court until the Board reached its decision.

### Impassioned Pleas to the Board of Pardons

On May 31, 1946, one week before the new date of execution, the Board of Pardons met in New Orleans. Captain Foster and Venezia, the inmate, both gave their stories. They told of setting up the chair, of testing it, and of their attempts at electrocution. Although Foster was not an electrician and Venezia had not been present in the jail, both gave their opinion that no electricity could have passed through Willie's body. They pointed out that the chair had never failed to operate before or since May 3, and that, in fact, it had been used successfully the following day in another part of the state. Venezia said that he had carefully investigated the chair after the mishap and discovered a loose wire running from the panel to the truck. In his opinion the electricity generated by the truck had run directly into the ground and failed to reach Willie. Foster agreed. He said Willie's protruding lips could have been caused by the hood being fastened too tightly around his head, and the chair could have shifted simply as the result of Willie moving his feet.

Sheriffs Resweber and Ozeene explained briefly the history of Thomas' murder and Willie's arrest, and the coroner told of his examination of Willie after the attempted execution. The warden related the phone call that resulted in the reprieve. He also said he had received a letter from the general manager of the Texas prison system, telling of an execution that had failed in Texas in 1938. On that occasion, one John Vaughn was led to the electric chair and strapped into place. The electrical system, however, totally failed to function. The Governor granted two successive reprieves, and one court granted a restraining order against a further attempt, but the judge who had originally sentenced Vaughn dissolved the restraining order, and Vaughn was subsequently electrocuted.

The District Attorney who had prosecuted Willie's case summed up his position before the Board: "How can we expect [juries] to convict men to pay their debts to society when, afterward, what they have done is undone by another authority of law having the power to do so." And he warned the Board,

> There is another side to this case. I don't want to refer to an unpleasant question, but those are facts that happen. We have repeatedly known in the past, unfortunately, of lynchings going on after crimes are committed. The only way and safest way to keep that from happening is to bring to justice and punish, according to each case, the guilty party. Society looks to us to do our duty, and I know that you gentlemen are not going to be carried away by sentiment in this case and that you are going to carry the law as far as it is possible to do so.

Several persons appeared on Willie's behalf. Perhaps the most effective was a white priest who belonged to a religious order called "The Holy Ghost Fathers" and who had prepared Willie for the execution during his seven months in the New Iberia jail. There was also a message from the boy's bishop, who wrote: "The torture of mind and body through which Willie Francis, St. Martinville negro, has already passed entitles him in my humble opinion to reprieve and commutation of sentence. It would be most unfortunate if the impression were created that there is no justice or mercy for a negro in Louisiana."

De Blanc made a detailed and eloquent statement on Willie's behalf. He presented six affidavits from witnesses who had seen Willie when the switch was thrown and who thought that electricity had swept through his body. As de Blanc summed it up, "Everything was done to electrocute this boy up to and including the pulling of the switch and the passing of electricity into his body. He died mentally; his body still exists, but through no fault of his." De Blanc said this was the first time in Louisiana history that a boy as young as fifteen had committed a homicide for which he had been given the death penalty. And he added,

> The main point which I wish to stress, gentlemen, is that no man should go to the chair twice. No man should suffer impending death twice. The

voice of humanity and justice cries out against such an outrage. You men who compose this Honorable Body are just and sincere, and I know that you will be guided only by the hand of justice. I am not asking that this boy be set free. I am only asking that his sentence be commuted from death to life imprisonment in the State Penitentiary. Is that too much to ask for a boy who has gone through the mental and physical torture that he has?

De Blanc then cited several unique cases of his own to support his position that justice required a commutation. The first was that of John Lee of Dorset, England, in the year 1889. Lee was placed on the scaffold three times, and each time the trap failed to operate, despite the fact that when he was removed from the scaffold, his weight in sand operated the trap perfectly. After the third try, Lee was reprieved by the Home Secretary.

The second case was that of Shadrach, Meshach, and Abednego, cast into the fiery furnace by King Nebuchadnezzar for refusing to bow down to a golden statue. When the flames failed to burn them, they were pardoned and allowed to go their way. The third case was also from the Old Testament. Daniel, refusing to obey King Darius' edict against petitioning anyone but the king, was cast into the den of lions, and the den was sealed with the king's ring. The next day Daniel was found alive and unharmed. This was considered divine intervention, and he was pardoned.

Then there was the strange case of Will Purvis, sentenced by the State of Mississippi to be hanged on February 7, 1894. Something went wrong, Purvis was not killed, and when the sheriff immediately attempted to hang him again, the crowd witnessing the event opposed it, and the condemned man was returned to jail. The Governor refused to commute the sentence, and three appeals to the courts failed. A mob then rescued Purvis from jail, and he lived for some time with relatives and friends. A new governor agreed to commute his sentence to life imprisonment if he surrendered, and two years later he was pardoned altogether when the state's star witness said he could have been mistaken in his identification of Purvis. Years afterward, another man confessed to the crime, and the Mississippi legislature voted Purvis $5,000 as indemnity for the agony of his earlier years.

Finally, de Blanc cited the peculiar circumstances surrounding the case of Lonnie Eaton, another Louisiana Negro, convicted of killing a white man in December, 1917, and sentenced to be hanged. Some time after the date of the hanging, the sheriff wrote the governor that he had been "so rushed with work" that he had forgotten to hang Eaton. The Governor promptly signed a commutation of Eaton's sentence from death to life imprisonment.

### "I Would Not Want the Stain of His Blood on My Hands"
De Blanc paused in his recitation and surveyed the impassive faces before him. In a gentler tone he reminded them of Willie's fine prison record, and

he ventured, "I'd stake my reputation that he would make a model convict at the State Penitentiary." He pointed out that Willie's conviction rested almost entirely on his own confessions, and he argued the unreliability of such confessions, citing a number of instances in which persons had confessed to crimes they had not in fact committed.

Suddenly, in the midst of this argument, de Blanc reached into his briefcase, took out a picture, and held it up before the Board. It showed Willie strapped in the electric chair. Where it had come from was something of a mystery, since no one remembered it having been taken during the excitement and confusion of the attempted execution. Some thought the Rev. Rousseve must have snapped it and others a police photographer; in any case, there it was, and it served as a grim reminder of what had occurred and of the serious business before the Board. Pointing to the picture and waving it before the members, de Blanc admonished them:

> Look at him strapped to the chair of death, the chair that had already claimed twenty-three victims, the chair that was later to claim another victim. What chance did he think he had of surviving? Look at him, gentlemen, a beaten animal; do you think there was any hope within that brain? Here you see the picture of a human being facing death, a boy on the threshold of eternity, a picture that speaks a thousand words. Here is a boy who, were it not for a quirk of fate, was about to plunge headlong into the dark abyss of death. What thoughts ran through his mind? Is there any belligerency in that bowed head? Is there anything but humility in those dark features? Is this not a picture of total resignation?

De Blanc abruptly changed his tone.

> Gentlemen, I have traveled throughout southern Louisiana since the attempted electrocution on May 3rd, and I can say with certainty that public opinion is against this boy being electrocuted again. If this boy goes back to the chair, they will say that the one and only reason is to satisfy the bestial lust for blood, to satisfy this cry for revenge. If he goes back to the chair they will say that it is nothing short of murder.
>
> People all over America have written to me expressing their sincere belief that it was the hand of God that stopped the electrocution. They have expressed their horror and disgust at a second attempt. I say in all sincerity that I believe that Willie Francis was not killed because it was not meant that he should be killed, that there was some reason, perhaps not explainable, but still there was a reason in the design of Fate that this boy should live. Fate acts in strange ways. I, for one, would want no part in his re-execution. When I meet my God face to face, I would not want the stain of his blood on my hands.

Then, in ringing tones, he concluded: "You, gentlemen, are the heart and soul of the State of Louisiana in this case. Men and women everywhere are asking: What will Louisiana do in this case? Will they return this boy to the chair? Will Louisiana be fair to this Negro? A boy's life is in your hands. I have done my duty. All remedies have been exhausted—the case is in your hands."

The Board, to a man, was unmoved by the plea. Three days after the hearing de Blanc wired Wright in Washington: "Board refused to commute sentence. File petition and wire me." Wright was prepared with his petition asking the Supreme Court to hear the case, and he filed it the next day. Because Willie was to be electrocuted in three days, the Court immediately issued a stay of execution until it could decide whether to hear the case. Governor Davis was also issuing a reprieve "until further order" so that Willie would have time to take his case to the High Court.

### An Unparalleled Error Leads to More Work

But on Monday, June 10, Wright received sad news from the clerk of the Court. Wright wired de Blanc, "Supreme Court denied writ Francis case today." And he wrote de Blanc the same day that he was "consoled by the fact that we did everything in our power to be of assistance." De Blanc told Willie's parents that the Supreme Court had refused to hear the case and then visited Willie in jail to explain that all avenues had been covered; there seemed to be no further hope and nowhere else to turn. Willie was badly shaken, as was de Blanc. For a long while the youngster sat quietly with his attorney, his mind filled not with the unknown, as before, but rather with a vivid awareness of the horrible experience he had already undergone and would have to undergo again. After a while he rallied and told de Blanc he would see the reporters who were clamoring to obtain a statement from him. He told them, "I'm praying harder than ever. Got myself a new prayer book. All I can do is wait." The Governor, in the meantime, prepared to set a new date for the execution.

The next day, Tuesday the 11th, an occurrence virtually unparalleled in Supreme Court history came to light. A horrified clerk at the Supreme Court discovered that a terrible error had been made. Owing to a clerical mistake, the Willie Francis case had been designated "denied" instead of "granted." The Court had, in fact, decided to hear Willie's case, and Mr. Justice Black had even ordered that "execution and enforcement of the sentence of death imposed upon petitioner, Willie Francis . . . be, and the same is hereby, stayed pending further order of this Court."

As soon as he had discovered his mistake and had discussed it with the Chief Justice, the clerk phoned Wright and Governor Davis and notified reporters. Wright immediately called de Blanc, even as the news services were sending the story out over the wires. By the time de Blanc reached the jail with candy, cigarettes, and magazines for his client, reporters were already converging on the scene, and they were soon allowed to talk to Willie. They found him sitting on the cot of his cell, chewing a nickel candy bar. Asked for his reaction to the news, Willie said, "That's funny, sort of. I was expecting good news yesterday, and I got bad. And now when I'm expecting bad news, it's good." He smiled. "I feel pretty good."

The reporters pressed him as to whether he would be content with life imprisonment if he were lucky enough to have the death sentence commuted. On this point Willie was adamant. "A life in prison would be a lot better than that chair."

The Supreme Court had acted at the very end of its term, so that oral argument in the case of *Louisiana* ex rel. *Francis* v. *Resweber* could not be heard until the following fall. Willie Francis waited. The public furor over his predicament died down; his mail lessened to a few miscellaneous notes. A magazine, the *World's Messenger,* had established a "Willie Francis Defense Fund" which still drew a little money, from ten cents to five dollars, from each of dozens of contributors around the country, but on the whole the public lost interest.

The work of the lawyers, however, went on. De Blanc and Wright finished their brief, and filed it with the Court. In addition to the arguments already advanced by de Blanc, Wright added two additional ones so that every possible avenue of escape would be probed. He argued that Willie had been denied equal protection of the law—that is, he had been treated differently by the state from its other citizens—because he was not put to death mercifully, but instead had to face two electrocutions. Wright also argued that Willie's trial had been such "a farce and a travesty" that even though there had been no appeal, the Supreme Court could now recognize a denial of due process.

But his chief argument remained the one based on the Eighth Amendment, which provides succinctly: "Excessive bail shall not be required, nor excessive fines imposed, nor cruel and unusual punishments inflicted." What are "cruel and unusual punishments"? Only a half-dozen times in its history had the Supreme Court attempted to deal with this provision, which originated in an Act of Parliament of 1688. The Court had clearly established that an electrocution properly carried out was not in itself such a cruel and unusual punishment as to violate the Constitution, but beyond that, little had been decided which aided Wright in his argument. He could only reason from logic that for the State of Louisiana to put a defendant through the agonies of electrocution not once, but twice, was so cruel, so unusual, that the Constitution prohibited it.

Up to the time of the argument, the two lawyers were thinking of new ideas and reviewing old ones. At one point de Blanc wired Wright, "To counteract any possible suppositions on the part of the Court that it is impossible to survive electrocution, it has been suggested to me that the citation of actual certified hospital cases on file of workmen on high-powered lines who have been electrocuted and have survived might prove important." And Wright, for his part, was obtaining historical materials from such sources as the New York State Library and asking friends at law schools to look into background documents dating back to Magna Carta that dealt with the "double jeopardy" and "cruel and unusual punishment" clauses.

### The Brooding Justices Listen to Argument

The day of the argument was a chill November 18, 1946. De Blanc flew to Washington to sit at the counsel table, but Wright made the oral presentation. He looked short, standing at the large lectern, though his heavy build lent conviction and strength to his appearance.

He was confronted by legal difficulties that the laymen present could not very well appreciate. The so-called double jeopardy clause of the Fifth Amendment and the cruel and unusual punishment clause of the Eighth Amendment are not prohibitions directly against the states, but only against the Federal government. Through a long process of interpretation, the Supreme Court had ruled that certain prohibitions in the Bill of Rights, though not directly binding on the states, are so involved with our fundamental concept of justice that they are part of that due process of law that every state, as well as the Federal government, must provide its citizens. Therefore, Wright's job was to convince the Court not only that a second electrocution would constitute double jeopardy and cruel and unusual punishment but that these prohibitions were a part of due process.

He realized that even if he had little precedent to go on, the factual situation was to his advantage. And so he drilled home the facts of the case—the long ordeal of preparing for death, the final hours, the horror of being put into the chair, the hood and straps and electrodes and wires, the final rites, and then the moment of truth itself. Yet when he began to show from the affidavits of eyewitnesses that some electricity must have reached the condemned man's body, Chief Justice Fred M. Vinson stopped him. Those affidavits, he said, were not officially part of the record and could not be relied on. Wright tried to explain that since no hearing had been ordered in the state courts, he had been given no opportunity to create a record, and he was forced to rely on the affidavits whether officially admitted into evidence or not. Moreover, if there was any question about the facts as recited in the affidavits, the Court should at least send the case back for a factual hearing into just what did occur at the execution.

Several of the justices asked Wright what would happen if they reversed the case. They were concerned because of the statement in the Louisiana Attorney General's brief that utter confusion would result, since state officials lacked authority to impose another sentence. Francis might be held in jail indefinitely simply because the legislature had never dealt with this situation. But Wright told the Court that the solution to the problem of imposing a sentence less than death could be left to the discretion of the state; he was sure the officials would find a way once the Court ruled that the death penalty in this case was unconstitutional.

The state's case was presented by L. O. Pecot, the man who had prosecuted Willie in the trial court, and Michael E. Culligan, an Assistant Attorney General of the state. They argued that the Supreme Court had no jurisdiction in the case. The Louisiana courts had ruled that as a matter of state law, they could do nothing; the Supreme Court could not now rule that they must. Sending the case back would be a futile gesture since sole discretion to commute a sentence lay with the Board of Pardons and the Governor, whom the Supreme Court could not direct to act.

It was a quiet though dramatic argument on both sides. The justices seemed unusually subdued, perhaps under the impact of the terrible events which had already befallen Willie and the possibility that those events would be repeated if the Court failed to intervene. The spirit of the Court was almost sullen, and the justices, straight-backed or bent forward, looked like brooding Rodin figures, black-robed and black of mood, almost resentful that this insoluble problem had been put before them.

The argument completed, the critical decision-making process began. Each "decision" Monday after the Willie Francis argument Wright checked with the clerk of the Court as to whether the justices had reached a result. And each Monday he wired de Blanc, who waited in his office until he had received the news that as yet nothing had come down.

The opinions in the Willie Francis case were rendered on January 13, 1947, just two months after the oral argument and over two years after the murder of Andrew Thomas. There was no "opinion of the Court"—that is, a majority of the Court could not agree on any single opinion. Instead, Chief Justice Vinson and Justices Hugo L. Black and Jackson (who had returned from Nuremberg only a few months before the argument) joined in an opinion by Mr. Justice Stanley F. Reed; Justices William O. Douglas, Frank Murphy, and Wiley Rutledge joined a dissenting opinion by Mr. Justice Harold H. Burton; and the ninth and deciding vote was cast by Mr. Justice Felix Frankfurter, who joined in neither of the other opinions but wrote one of his own.

---

*LOUISIANA* ex rel. *FRANCIS* v. *RESWEBER, SHERIFF,* et al.
329 U.S. 459 (1947)

MR. JUSTICE REED announced the judgment of the Court in an opinion in which THE CHIEF JUSTICE, MR. JUSTICE BLACK and MR. JUSTICE JACKSON join.

. . . By the applications [to the Louisiana courts] petitioner claimed the protection of the due process clause of the Fourteenth Amendment on the ground that an execution under the circumstances detailed would deny due process to him because of the double jeopardy provision of the Fifth Amendment and the cruel and unusual punishment provision of the Eighth Amendment.[1] These federal constitutional protections, petitioner claimed, would be denied because he had once gone through the difficult preparation for execution and had once received through his body a current of electricity intended to cause death. The Supreme Court of Louisiana denied the applications on the ground of a lack of any basis for judicial relief. That is, the state court concluded there was no violation of state or national law alleged in the various applications. It spoke of the fact that no "current of sufficient intensity to cause death" passed through petitioner's body. It referred specifically to the fact that the applications of petitioner invoked the provisions of the Louisiana Constitution against cruel and inhuman punishments and putting one in jeopardy of life or liberty twice for the same offense. We granted certiorari on a petition, setting forth the aforementioned contentions, to consider the alleged violations of rights under the Federal Constitution in the unusual circumstances of this case. . . . So far as we are aware, this case is without precedent in any court.

To determine whether or not the execution of the petitioner may fairly take place after the experience through which he passed, we shall examine the circumstances under the assumption, but without so deciding, that violation of the principles of the Fifth and Eighth Amendments, as to double

jeopardy and cruel and unusual punishment, would be violative of the due process clause of the Fourteenth Amendment. . . . As nothing has been brought to our attention to suggest the contrary, we must and do assume that the state officials carried out their duties under the death warrant in a careful and humane manner. Accidents happen for which no man is to blame. We turn to the question as to whether the proposed enforcement of the criminal law of the state is offensive to any constitutional requirements to which reference has been made.

*First.* Our minds rebel against permitting the same sovereignty to punish an accused twice for the same offense. . . . But where the accused successfully seeks review of a conviction, there is no double jeopardy upon a new trial. . . . Even where a state obtains a new trial after conviction because of errors, while an accused may be placed on trial a second time, it is not the sort of hardship to the accused that is forbidden by the Fourteenth Amendment. *Palko* v. *Connecticut* (302 U.S. 319, 328. . . . As this is a prosecution under state law, so far as double jeopardy is concerned, the *Palko* case is decisive. For we see no difference from a constitutional point of view between a new trial for error of law at the instance of the state that results in a death sentence instead of imprisonment for life and an execution that follows a failure of equipment. When an accident, with no suggestion of malevolence, prevents the consummation of a sentence, the state's subsequent course in the administration of its criminal law is not affected on that account by any requirement of due process under the Fourteenth Amendment. We find no double jeopardy here which can be said to amount to a denial of federal due process in the proposed execution.

*Second.* We find nothing in what

---

[1] Fifth Amendment: ". . . nor shall any person be subject for the same offence to be twice put in jeopardy of life or limb; . . ."

Eighth Amendment: "Excessive bail shall not be required, nor excessive fines imposed, nor cruel and unusual punishments inflicted."

took place here which amounts to cruel and unusual punishment in the constitutional sense. The case before us does not call for an examination into any punishments except that of death. . . . The traditional humanity of modern Anglo-American law forbids the infliction of unnecessary pain in the execution of the death sentence. Prohibition against the wanton infliction of pain has come into our law from the Bill of Rights of 1688. The identical words appear in our Eighth Amendment. The Fourteenth would prohibit by its due process clause execution by a state in a cruel manner. . . .

Petitioner's suggestion is that because he once underwent the psychological strain of preparation for electrocution, now to require him to undergo this preparation again subjects him to a lingering or cruel and unusual punishment. Even the fact that petitioner has already been subjected to a current of electricity does not make his subsequent execution any more cruel in the constitutional sense than any other execution. The cruelty against which the Constitution protects a convicted man is cruelty inherent in the method of punishment, not the necessary suffering involved in any method employed to extinguish life humanely. The fact that an unforeseeable accident prevented the prompt consummation of the sentence cannot, it seems to us, add an element of cruelty to a subsequent execution. There is no purpose to inflict unnecessary pain nor any unnecessary pain involved in the proposed execution. The situation of the unfortunate victim of this accident is just as though he had suffered the identical amount of mental anguish and physical pain in any other occurrence, such as, for example, a fire in the cell block. We cannot agree that the hardship imposed upon the petitioner rises to that level of hardship denounced as denial of due process because of cruelty.

*Third.* The Supreme Court of Louisiana also rejected petitioner's contention that death inflicted after his prior sufferings would deny him the equal protection of the laws, guaranteed by the Fourteenth Amendment. This suggestion in so far as it differs from the due process argument is based on the idea that execution, after an attempt at execution has failed, would be a more severe punishment than is imposed upon others guilty of a like offense. That is, since others do not go through the strain of preparation for execution a second time or have not experienced a non-lethal current in a prior attempt at execution, as petitioner did, to compel petitioner to submit to execution after these prior experiences denies to him equal protection. Equal protection does not protect a prisoner against even illegal acts of officers in charge of him, much less against accidents during his detention for execution. . . . Laws cannot prevent accidents nor can a law equally protect all against them. So long as the law applies to all alike, the requirements of equal protection are met. We have no right to assume that Louisiana singled out Francis for a treatment other than that which has been or would generally be applied.

*Fourth.* . . . Nothing is before us upon which a ruling can be predicated as to alleged denial of federal constitutional rights during petitioner's trial. . . .

*Affirmed.*

MR. JUSTICE FRANKFURTER, concurring.

When four members of the Court find that a State has denied to a person the due process which the Fourteenth Amendment safeguards, it seems to me important to be explicit regarding the criteria by which the State's duty of obedience to the Constitution must be judged. Particularly is this so when life is at stake.

Until July 28, 1868, when the Fourteenth Amendment was ratified, the Constitution of the United States left the States free to carry out their own notions of criminal justice, except insofar as they were limited by article I, § 10 of the Constitution which declares: "No State shall . . . pass any Bill of Attainder, [or] ex post facto Law . . ." The Fourteenth Amendment placed no specific restraints upon the States in the formulation or the administration of their criminal law. It restricted the freedom of the States generally, so that States thereafter could not "abridge the privileges or immunities of citizens of the United States," or "deprive any person of life, liberty, or property, without due process of law," or "deny to any person within its jurisdiction the equal protection of the laws."

These are broad, inexplicit clauses of the Constitution, unlike specific provisions of the first eight amendments formulated by the Founders to guard against recurrence of well-defined historic grievances. But broad as these clauses are, they are not generalities of empty vagueness. They are circumscribed partly by history and partly by the problems of government, large and dynamic though they be, with which they are concerned. The "privileges or immunities of citizens of the United States" concern the dual citizenship under our federal system. The safeguards of "due process of law" and "the equal protection of the laws" summarize the meaning of the struggle for freedom of English-speaking peoples. They run back to Magna Carta but contemplate no less advances in the conceptions of justice and freedom by a progressive society. . . .

When, shortly after its adoption, the Fourteenth Amendment came before this Court for construction, it was urged that the "privileges or immunities of citizens of the United States" which were not to be abridged by any State were the privileges and immunities which citizens theretofore enjoyed under the Constitution. If that view had prevailed, the Privileges or Immunities Clause of the Fourteenth Amendment would have placed upon the States the limitations which the specific articles of the first eight amendments had theretofore placed upon the agencies of the national government. After the fullest consideration that view was rejected. The rejection has the authority that comes from contemporaneous knowledge of the purposes of the Fourteenth Amendment. . . . The notion that the Privileges or Immunities Clause of the Fourteenth Amendment absorbed, as it is called, the provisions of the Bill of Rights that limit the Federal Government has never been given countenance by this Court.

Not until recently was it suggested that the Due Process Clause of the Fourteenth Amendment was merely a compendious reference to the Bill of Rights whereby the States were now restricted in devising and enforcing their penal code precisely as is the Federal Government by the first eight amendments. On this view, the States would be confined in the enforcement of their criminal codes by those views for safeguarding the rights of the individual which were deemed necessary in the eighteenth century. Some of these safeguards have perduring validity. Some grew out of transient experience or formulated remedies which time might well improve. The Fourteenth Amendment did not mean to imprison the States into the limited experience of the eighteenth century. It did mean to withdraw from the States the right to act in ways that are offensive to a decent respect for the dignity of man, and heedless of his freedom.

These are very broad terms by which to accommodate freedom and authority. As has been suggested from time to time, they may be too large to serve as the basis for adjudication, in that they allow much room for individual notions of policy. That is not our concern. The fact is that the duty of such adjudication on a basis no less narrow has been committed to this Court.

In an impressive body of decisions this Court has decided that the Due Process Clause of the Fourteenth Amendment expresses a demand for civilized standards which are not defined by the specifically enumerated guarantees of the Bill of Rights. They neither contain the particularities of the first eight amendments nor are they confined to them. That due process of law has its own independent function has been illustrated in numerous decisions, and has been expounded in the opinions of the Court which have canvassed the matter most thoroughly. . . . Insofar as due process under the Fourteenth Amendment requires the States to observe any of the immunities "that are valid as against the federal government by force of the specific pledges of particular amendments," it does so because they "have been found to be implicit in the concept of ordered liberty, and thus, through the Fourteenth Amendment, become valid as against the states." *Palko* v. *Connecticut,* supra, at 324–25.

The Federal Bill of Rights requires that prosecutions for federal crimes be initiated by a grand jury and tried by a petty jury; it protects an accused from being a witness against himself. The States are free to consult their own conceptions of policy in dispensing with the grand jury, in modifying or abolishing the petty jury, in withholding the privilege against self-crimination. . . . In short, the Due Process Clause of the Fourteenth Amendment did not withdraw the freedom of a State to enforce its own notions of fairness in the administration of criminal justice unless, as it was put for the Court by Mr. Justice Cardozo, "in so doing it offends some principle of justice so rooted in the traditions and conscience of our people as to be ranked as fundamental. . . ."

A State may offend such a principle of justice by brutal subjection of an individual to successive retrials on a charge on which he has been acquitted. Such conduct by a State might be a denial of due process, but not because the protection against double jeopardy in a federal prosecution against which the Fifth Amendment safeguards limits a State. . . . Again, a State may be found to deny a person due process by treating even one guilty of crime in a manner that violates standards of decency more or less universally accepted though not when it treats him by a mode about which opinion is fairly divided. But the penological policy of a State is not to be tested by the scope of the Eighth Amendment and is not involved in the controversy which is necessarily evoked by that Amendment as to the historic meaning of "cruel and unusual punishment. . . ."

Once we are explicit in stating the problem before us in terms defined by an unbroken series of decisions, we cannot escape acknowledging that it involves the application of standards of fairness and justice very broadly conceived. They are not the application of merely personal standards but the impersonal standards of society which alone judges, as the organs of Law, are empowered to enforce. When the standards for judicial judgment are not narrower than "immutable principles of justice which inhere in the very idea of free government," *Holden* v. *Hardy,* 169 U.S. 366, 389, "fundamental principles of liberty and justice which lie at the base of all our civil and political institutions," *Hebert* v. *Louisiana,* 272 U.S. 312, 316, "immunities . . . implicit in the concept of ordered liberty," *Palko* v. *Con-*

*necticut,* supra, at 324–25, great tolerance toward a State's conduct is demanded of this Court. . . .

I cannot bring myself to believe that for Louisiana to leave to executive clemency, rather than to require, mitigation of a sentence of death duly pronounced upon conviction for murder because a first attempt to carry it out was an innocent misadventure, offends a principle of justice "rooted in the traditions and conscience of our people. . . ." Short of the compulsion of such a principle, this Court must abstain from interference with State action no matter how strong one's personal feeling of revulsion against a State's insistence on its pound of flesh. One must be on guard against finding in personal disapproval a reflection of more or less prevailing condemnation. Strongly drawn as I am to some of the sentiments expressed by my brother BURTON, I cannot rid myself of the conviction that were I to hold that Louisiana would transgress the Due Process Clause if the State were allowed, in the precise circumstances before us, to carry out the death sentence, I would be enforcing my private view rather than that consensus of society's opinion which, for purposes of due process, is the standard enjoined by the Constitution.

The fact that I reach this conclusion does not mean that a hypothetical situation, which assumes a series of abortive attempts at electrocution or even a single, cruelly willful attempt, would not raise different questions. . . .

MR. JUSTICE BURTON, with whom MR. JUSTICE DOUGLAS, MR. JUSTICE MURPHY and MR. JUSTICE RUTLEDGE concur, dissenting. . . .

We believe that the unusual facts before us require that the judgment of the Supreme Court of Louisiana be vacated and that this cause be re-manded for further proceedings not inconsistent with this opinion. Those proceedings should include the determination of certain material facts not previously determined, including the extent, if any, to which electric current was applied to the relator during his attempted electrocution on May 3, 1946. Where life is to be taken, there must be no avoidable error of law or uncertainty of fact. . . .

[The Fourteenth] Amendment provides: "nor shall any State deprive any person of life, liberty, or property, without due process of law; . . . ." When this was adopted in 1868, there long had been imbedded deeply in the standards of this nation a revulsion against subjecting guilty persons to torture culminating in death. Preconstitutional American history reeked with cruel punishment to such an extent that, in 1791, the Eighth Amendment to the Constitution of the United States expressly imposed upon federal agencies a mandate that "Excessive bail shall not be required, nor excessive fines imposed, nor cruel and unusual punishments inflicted." Louisiana and many other states have adopted like constitutional provisions. See Section 12 of Article I of the Constitution of Louisiana (1921).

The capital case before us presents an instance of the violation of constitutional due process that is more clear than would be presented by many lesser punishments prohibited by the Eighth Amendment or its state counterparts. Taking human life by unnecessarily cruel means shocks the most fundamental instincts of civilized man. It should not be possible under the constitutional procedure of a self-governing people. Abhorrence, of the cruelty of ancient forms of capital punishment has increased steadily until, today, some states have prohibited capital punishment altogether. It is unthinkable that any state legislature in modern times would enact a statute expressly authorizing capital punishment by repeated applications of an electric current separated by intervals of days or hours until finally death shall result. The Legislature of Louisiana did not do so. The Supreme Court of Louisiana did not say that it did. The Supreme Court of Louisiana said merely that the pending petitions for relief in this case presented an executive rather than a judicial question and, by that mistake of law, it precluded itself from discussing the constitutional issue before us.

In determining whether the proposed procedure is unconstitutional, we must measure it against a lawful electrocution. The contrast is that between instantaneous death and death by installments—caused by electric shocks administered after one or more intervening periods of complete consciousness of the victim. Electrocution, when instantaneous, *can* be inflicted by a state in conformity with due process of law *In re Kemmler*, 136 U.S. 436. The Supreme Court of Louisiana has held that electrocution, in the manner prescribed in its statute, is more humane than hanging. . . .

The all-important consideration is that the execution shall be so instantaneous and substantially painless that the punishment shall be reduced, as nearly as possible, to no more than that of death itself. Electrocution has been approved only in a form that eliminates suffering.

The Louisiana statute makes this clear. It provides that:

"Every sentence of death imposed in this State shall be by electrocution; that is, causing to pass through the body of the person convicted a current of electricity of sufficient intensity to cause death, and the application and continuance of such current through the body of the person convicted until such person is dead. . . ."

It does not provide for electrocution by interrupted or repeated applications of electric current at intervals of several days or even minutes. It does not provide for the application of electric current of an intensity less than that sufficient to cause death. It prescribes expressly and solely for the application of a current of sufficient intensity to cause death and for the *continuance* of that application until death results. Prescribing capital punishment, it should be construed strictly. There can be no implied provision for a second, third or multiple application of the current. There is no statutory or judicial precedent upholding a delayed process of electrocution.

These considerations were emphasized in *In re Kemmler,* supra, when an early New York statute authorizing electrocution was attacked as violative of the due process clause of the Fourteenth Amendment because prescribing a cruel and unusual punishment. In upholding that statute, this Court stressed the fact that the electric current was to cause instantaneous death. Like the Louisiana statute before us, that statute called expressly for the continued application of a sufficient electric current to cause death. It was the resulting "instantaneous" and "painless" death that was referred to as "humane". . . .

If the state officials deliberately and intentionally had placed the relator in the electric chair five times and, each time, had applied electric current to his body in a manner not sufficient, until the final time, to kill him, such a form of torture would rival that of burning at the stake. Although the failure of the first attempt, in the present case, was unintended, the reapplication of the electric current will be intentional. How many deliberate and intentional reapplications of electric current does it take to produce a cruel, unusual and unconstitutional punishment? While five applications would be more cruel and unusual than one, the uniqueness of the present case demonstrates that, today, two separated applications are sufficiently "cruel and unusual" to be prohibited. If five attempts would be "cruel and unusual," it would be difficult to draw the line between two, three, four and five. It is not difficult, however, as we here contend, to draw the line between the one continuous application prescribed by statute and any other application of the current.

Lack of intent that the first application be less than fatal is not material. The intent of the executioner cannot lessen the torture or excuse the result. It was the statutory duty of the state officials to make sure that there was no failure. . . .

Executive clemency provides a common means of avoiding unconstitutional or otherwise questionable executions. When, however, the unconstitutionality of proposed executive procedure is brought before this Court, as in this case, we should apply the constitutional protection. In this case, final recourse is had to the high trusteeship vested in this Court by the people of the United States over the constitutional process by which their own lives may be taken.

In determining whether a case of cruel and unusual punishment constitutes a violation of due process of law, each case must turn upon its particular facts. The record in this case is not limited to an instance where a prisoner was placed in the electric chair and released before being subjected to the electric current. It presents more than a case of mental anguish, however severe such a case might be. The petition to the Supreme Court of Louisiana expressly states that a current of electricity was caused to pass through the body of the relator. This allegation was denied in the answer and no evidence was presented by either side. The Supreme Court of Louisiana thereupon undertook to decide the case on the pleadings. It said:

"Our conclusion is that the complaint made by the relator is a matter over which the courts have no authority. Inasmuch as the proceedings had in the district court, up to and including the pronouncing of the sentence of death, were entirely regular, we have no authority to set aside the sentence and release the relator from the sheriff's custody. . . ."

This statement assumed that the relief sought in the Supreme Court of Louisiana was only a review of the judicial proceedings in the lower state courts prior to the passing of sentence upon the relator on September 14, 1945. On the contrary, the issue raised there and here primarily concerns the action of state officials on and after May 3, 1946, in connection with their past and proposed attempts to electrocute the relator. This issue properly presents a federal constitutional question based on the impending deprivation of the life of the relator by executive officials of the State of Louisiana in a manner alleged to be a violation of the due process of law guaranteed by the Fourteenth Amendment. The refusal of the writs necessarily denied the constitutional protection prayed for. In ruling against the relator on the pleadings, in the absence of further evidence, the Supreme Court of Louisiana must be taken to have acted upon the allegations of fact most favorable to the relator. The petition contains the unequivocal allegation that the official electrocutioner "turned on the switch and a current of electricity was caused to pass through the body of relator, all in the presence of the official witnesses." This allegation must be read in the light of the Louisiana statute which authorized the electrocutioner to apply to the body of the relator only such an electric current as was of "sufficient intensity to cause death." On that record, denial of relief means that the proposed repeated, and at least second, application to the relator of an electric current sufficient to cause death is not, under present circumstances, a cruel and unusual punishment violative of due process of law. It exceeds any punishment prescribed by law. There is no precedent for it. What then is it, if it be not cruel, unusual and unlawful? In spite of the constitutional issue thus raised, the Supreme Court of Louisiana treated it as an executive question not subject to judicial review. We believe that if the facts are as alleged by the relator the proposed action is unconstitutional. We believe also that the Supreme Court of Louisiana should provide for the determination of the facts and then proceed in a manner not inconsistent with this opinion. . . .

The remand of this cause to the Supreme Court of Louisiana in the manner indicated would not mean that the relator necessarily is entitled to a complete release. It would mean merely that the courts of Louisiana must examine the facts, both as to the actual nature of the punishment already inflicted and that proposed to be inflicted and, if the proposed punishment amounts to a violation of due process of law under the Constitution of the United States, then the State must find some means of disposing of this case that will not violate that Constitution. . . .

---

## Two Surprise Votes and One Maverick

Thus, by a vote of five to four, the Supreme Court turned down Willie's plea.

Mr. Justice Reed could have decided simply that the double jeopardy and cruel and unusual punishment clauses are not binding on the states. Such a ruling, however, would have established a precedent in cases involving unrelated and as-yet-unforeseeable facts. In a case which, because of the admittedly unprecedented facts, would be unlikely to recur, it was safer to proceed as he did, by assuming without deciding that double jeopardy and cruel and unusual punishment would both violate due process.

The cruel and unusual punishment argument obviously gave Reed some difficulty. The key to the solution insofar as he was concerned seems to have been the word "accident," which he repeated several times. Virtually all of the criminal cases coming before the Supreme Court involve some element of purposeful action taken by the police, the prosecutor, the trial judge, or the jury: someone, somewhere, has deliberately made a decision which affects the rights of the defendant. But here, no one had deliberately caused Francis the anguish he undoubtedly suffered. The faulty electric chair seemed an act of God.

It surely came as a surprise to many that Mr. Justice Black joined in Reed's opinion. Black is often described as a "liberal" and a "leading member of the civil rights bloc." His vote in this case shows how misleading labels can be when it comes to judging judges.

Unlike some of his brethren, Black does not believe that the rights in the Bill of Rights—which he broadly interprets to include all provisions in the Constitution and the amendments which protect individual liberty—can be abridged when outweighed by the public interest. The Bill of Rights, to Black, contains absolute prohibitions. Free speech means that speech must be free, and not simply free when there is no clear and present danger of substantive evil. The purpose of the Bill of Rights was to withdraw from government all power to act in certain areas.

Nevertheless, Black has recognized that some language in the first ten amendments is less precise, less definite, and more equivocal than in others. One of the least precise of all the amendments is that prohibiting the infliction of "cruel and unusual punishments." Faced with this obscure language, and unwilling to adopt the view that that which shocks the conscience of civilized man must of necessity be unconstitutional, Black could not bring himself to vote with the dissenters.

If it was surprising to find Black voting with Reed, it was just as unusual to discover Mr. Justice Burton writing for Douglas, Murphy, and Rutledge. Burton, a quiet, sensitive but utterly detached judge, was normally identified with the more "conservative" element of the Court. A former mayor of Cleveland and United States senator, he was precise and undramatic, but sometimes extraordinarily effective. His dissent in the *Willie Francis* case persuasively built fact upon fact and premise upon premise until the whole piece conveyed a strange and exciting depth of conviction. For Burton, the all-important consideration was that an execution be instantaneous, and in support of his thesis that Francis had actually received—or at least was entitled to prove that he received—electricity during the first attempt, Burton quoted the very affidavits which Chief Justice Vinson had chastised Wright for citing during oral argument.

Mr. Justice Frankfurter's opinion, joined in by no other justice and yet decisive in the result, must have been torn from the soul. For Frankfurter is an avowed opponent of capital punishment. He opposes it not only on intellectual grounds but on grounds of conscience, morality, and personal revulsion. He abhors the sensationalism accompanying a death case, the subjection of human beings to the agonies involved in preparing for death, and the taking of life itself. And so his opinion stands as a personal monument to judgment over feeling.

His long argument that the "double jeopardy" and "cruel and unusual punishment" clauses are not intrinsically binding on the states was surely his answer to Mr. Justice Black's view that the prohibitions against the states are specific and enumerated. Although quick to point out that he might rule differently if there had been a series of abortive attempts at electrocution, Frankfurter nevertheless concluded, as he did in an increasing number of criminal cases in later years, that the state must be left to its own devices.

The vagaries of fate which had plagued Willie and his lawyers from the beginning were still operative. When Wright called the Supreme Court on the day these decisions came down, he was told that the Louisiana court had been "reversed." Fortunately, he checked back before spreading the news and found that, once again, someone had made a mistake. The Louisiana court was in fact affirmed, and Wright had lost the case. The mistake, however, led Wright to a more careful reading of the justices' texts, and he came to the conclusion that what Burton had written had at one point been a majority opinion. He pointed out to the press that certain language in the Burton opinion sounded very much like a majority order. (For example, "We believe that the unusual facts before us require that the judgment of the Supreme Court of Louisiana be vacated and that this cause be remanded for further proceedings not inconsistent with this opinion," and, later, "We believe also that the Supreme Court of Louisiana should provide for the determination of the facts and then proceed in a matter not inconsistent with this opinion.") To lawyers, this was strange language for a dissent. It was Wright's idea that perhaps Mr. Justice Jackson had changed his vote—and the result—at the last minute. While this is pure conjecture, it is not incompatible with Jackson's independent nature, instilled from childhood.

Jackson grew up a Democrat in a Republican county of New York. He clerked in a law office while still in high school despite his father's hearty disapproval of law as a career. He never went to college and began the actual practice of law after one year of law school and while only twenty-one years of age. He had a flair for the law and was a quick success at the bar. After many years of practice, his acquaintanceship with Franklin Roosevelt ripened into friendship and finally into government posts. Jackson was perhaps the finest solicitor general the country has had. He moved from there to the attorney generalship and then to the Supreme Court. Less than a year before the decision in the Francis case, he had been engaged in the now famous feud with Mr. Justice Black.

Jackson constantly worried about the Court's habit of telling the states how to conduct their criminal procedures, and in his beautiful prose style— pungent, witty, and incisive—he did not hesitate to communicate his fears to his brethren. Even a practical awareness that police and local officials were often overzealous did not dissuade him from a dislike of what he once called "interferences with states' rights under the vague and ambiguous mandate of the Fourteenth Amendment." It would not have been unlike Jackson to vote originally against a second electrocution and then, when the opinions were in cold print, to change his vote in favor of leaving Louisiana to its own devices.

### "Death and Me Is Old Neighbors"

Sheriff Ozeene brought Willie the news of the Supreme Court's decision and found the boy standing at the window of his cell, looking out at the bleak winter scene. Willie listened and then sat down hard on the cot, got up again, and walked up and down the cell. "It's the same thing again," he stammered. "It's the same thing all over again. I got to start worrying again."

Once again the reporters descended on New Iberia to interview the jail's most celebrated inmate. They were ushered in and found Willie singularly cool and composed. He told them he was "right interested to find out if I can die like the man I thought I was." He leaned back against the damp wall of the cell. "I always sort of wondered if I was a brave man. Now I guess I'm gonna find out. And I'm going to find out the hard way, boss, so there won't be no doubt in my mind when I leave. A lot of men never find out. A lot of men die still wondering if they was the men they thought they was."

The reporters told Willie that Governor Davis had just announced he would sign a new death warrant as soon as the mandate from the Supreme Court arrived. Willie smiled. "Death and me is old neighbors," he said, stuttering on the word "neighbors." "But remember this, I'm a closer neighbor of the Lord."

De Blanc told the reporters that Willie "is a lot calmer than he was last May when he walked away from the chair." The attorney shook his head. "He's amazing. And he's still got a chance, since the Supreme Court ruling against him was only five to four. We're filing for another hearing as soon as possible." Willie was not so sure. He prophesied: "This time it'll be different. That electric chair is going to work."

In Washington, Wright was filing a petition for rehearing in the Supreme Court. In it, he pointed out an interesting fact that had escaped notice until then. Prior to Willie's attempted execution, Louisiana law laid down no specific qualifications for the operator of an electric chair. Two months after Willie's experience, however, the Louisiana legislature changed the statute to require that the operator of the electric chair be "a competent electrician who shall not have been previously convicted of a felony." This was an admission by the State of Louisiana, argued Wright, that the attempt to electrocute Willie had been carried out incompetently. This was particularly important in view of Justice Reed's opinion "that the state officials carried out their duties under the death warrant in a careful and humane manner."

The Supreme Court, however, denied Wright's petition for rehearing and his supplemental petition for rehearing and vacated the stay of execution which it had previously entered. Almost immediately de Blanc requested a second hearing before the Board of Pardons in Louisiana. For the first time in any pleading, he alleged that "at least one" of those who acted as officials in conducting the electrocution "was thoroughly intoxicated." De Blanc hoped that the close vote in the Supreme Court, the expression of personal distaste by the justices, the nation-wide attention focused on the case, and his new allegation in regard to intoxication would all combine to sway the Board of Pardons. He was greatly disappointed when the Board once again unanimously rejected his pleas.

### The Switch Is Thrown Again

Time was now a critical factor, with the end of April approaching and a new execution date set for Friday, May 9, 1947. At one point, Sheriff Resweber later told reporters, Willie threatened to kill himself with a razor smuggled into his cell in a Bible. De Blanc persisted in his efforts; he filed, instead of habeas corpus in a Federal court, a motion for a new trial and a motion in arrest of judgment in the trial court of the state. By the time the trial court and the Louisiana Supreme Court had denied his motions, it was May 7, with only two days to go.

De Blanc flew to Washington. He and Wright filed in the Supreme Court not only a petition for a writ of certiorari, the traditional method of requesting the Court to hear a case, but also an original petition for a writ of habeas corpus. This is the writ issued by a judge directing a jailer to produce the prisoner and state the reason for his being held; it is the traditional method of testing the legality of someone's detention. Normally, habeas corpus is filed first in a Federal District Court and then appealed up to the Supreme Court, but there was no longer time for any such procedure. The ground for their petitions was that they had discovered new evidence. The "newly discovered evidence" was an affidavit signed by a former city judge of New Iberia. On the basis of this affidavit, Willie's lawyers alleged that

> On the day so appointed for [Francis'] execution, [Francis] was placed in an electric chair, that at the time, the executioner and other persons connected with carrying out the execution were so drunk that it was impossible for them to have known what they were doing, that the scene was a disgraceful and inhuman exhibition, that as soon as the switch controlling the current was taken off, the drunken executioner cursed Willie Francis and told him that he would be back to finish electrocuting him and if the electricity did not kill him, he would kill him with a rock. [Francis] also alleges upon information and belief that the executioner was actuated by sadistic impulses and either willfully, deliberately and intentionally applied less than a minimal lethal current, for the purpose of torturing [Francis], or acted with such wanton, reckless and inhuman indifference to the probability of inflicting excruciating and unnecessary pain upon [Francis] that in fact less than a minimal lethal current of electricity passed through the body of [Francis]; and that as a consequence of the premises, [Francis] was cruelly, inhumanly, and excruciatingly tortured. The punishment thus inflicted upon [Francis] was cruel, unusual, and due to the conscious cruelty or wanton indifference of the executioner.

These petitions were filed in the Supreme Court on the day before the new date for execution, and the Chief Justice immediately called a special session of the Court to consider them. The allegations were obviously serious. It is one thing to fail to execute a man because of a simple mistake; it is quite another to subject him to this experience because of intoxication on the part of the executioner. While the torture to the condemned man may be as great regardless of why the execution failed, the culpability of the state is clear in one case and not in the other. The difficulty for the justices, however, was that in *Ex parte Hawk,* decided three years before, they had ruled that habeas corpus must first be filed in the Federal District Court rather than in the Supreme Court. Hearing Willie's case would mean overruling *Hawk.*

On that same afternoon, May 8, while de Blanc was still in Washington, the Supreme Court handed down a brief order: The petition of Willie Francis "for leave to file an original petition for writ of habeas corpus is denied for reasons set forth in *Ex parte Hawk,* 321 U.S. 114. In view of the grave nature of the new allegation set forth in this petition, the denial is expressly without prejudice to application to proper tribunals."

This rather pointed language might be roughly translated: "We are powerless to help you in view of our previous decision. But you've got a good point, and there's nothing to stop you from filing the same petition in the Federal District Court." Mr. Justice Murphy thought the petition should be granted; Mr. Justice Rutledge thought the petition should be treated as a petition for rehearing and granted and the case sent back to Louisiana for a factual hearing; and Mr. Justice Douglas took no part in the decision.

De Blanc flew back to Louisiana and immediately went to see Willie in the New Iberia jail. They had a long and serious conference. When he left the jail, de Blanc wired Wright that Willie had requested him not to initiate any further proceedings. Willie was ready to die.

The next morning, Willie Francis was taken back to St. Martinville over the same eight miles as before, past the familiar sights, around the square, and up to the front of the courthouse. The only difference was that this time the day was warmer and the hour earlier—Sheriff Resweber was taking no chances on letting Willie come through the crowd that would be gathering a little later in the day. He was put in the same cell as before. The same truck and the same heavy, portable, wooden electric chair arrived from Angola, although a new electrician accompanied it. The chair was carried to the same anteroom as before, and the wires run through the window to the truck. The generator was warmed up to its deafening pitch. Willie was shaved in the appropriate places. When the time came, shortly after noon, just as before, he was taken to the anteroom and strapped into the chair. The dozen witnesses milled about, nervous, uncomfortable, embarrassed. Willie was given the last rites and asked if he had anything to say. He didn't.

One year and six days after the first try, the switch was thrown again. It was all the same, except that this time the chair worked. Willie was gone, and all that was left was the garbled epitaph of a boy old beyond his years. "I kill Andrew Thomas and today he is lying in a grave and I am not a killer but I wonder where I am going to be lying and in what kind of grave I don't know."

### The Significance of a Case Without Precedent

On its facts, the *Willie Francis* case is an isolated event in the somewhat tortuous history of American criminal law. The faulty electrocution which Mr. Justice Reed called "without precedent" is not likely to recur. The Court's ruling, instead of taking its place as a precedent for hundreds of cases to follow, may well become something of an oddity in the Supreme Court reports, rarely cited (to date only four times by a majority of the Court) and read more as an interesting chronicle of a pathetic youngster than as a treatise on the law.

But in its larger context, the *Willie Francis* case epitomizes the role of a changing Supreme Court in our criminal jurisprudence. The problems created by fifty-one jurisdictions all enforcing their own laws are joined at the top by this Court, which is somehow expected to keep the constitutional balance clear and true and yet to respect the states in the legitimate exercise of what must, after all, be primarily a local responsibility. The Reed, Frankfurter, and Burton opinions in the *Francis* case pinpoint the entire controversy over the proper role of the Supreme Court at this juncture in our history.

A truly activist Court would have reversed or remanded the *Francis* case out of hand. A truly conservative Court would have passed it over without a qualm. It is a remarkable fact that seldom in our history have we had wholly one type of Court or the other; rather, we have had an alchemy of the two, with a single justice often swinging the balance. The trend over time, however, has been toward a more activist role by the Court in the criminal field.

Earlier opinions of the Court reflected a thinly disguised plea to the state courts to exclude tainted evidence, to allow indigent appeals, to take cognizance of police brutality, and otherwise to maintain a constant surveillance over their own processes. But many state courts continued to sanction illegal conduct, even when such conduct violated state laws and constitutions. The Supreme Court became less restrained, and its pleas turned into outright reversals.

As this activist role accelerates, however, there is an increasing tendency on the part of both lawyers and laymen to expect too much of the Court. For the Court cannot even scratch the surface of abuses in the criminal field. Too few cases come to the Court, and even fewer of these can be reviewed. The Court can only attempt to lead, to issue guidelines, and to hope that responsible officials, state and federal, will take control and follow suit.

The dilemma is exaggerated in the capital case, where each justice cannot help but know, because he is all too human, that a vote for restraint is necessarily a vote for death. Those who have watched the Court at work know the burden that each justice carries in a death case. It is the one case in which he feels the full impact of both his responsibility and his fallibility. It is the case he takes to meals and to bed; it is the case that lingers on in his mind long after it has been decided. It finally drops away only because another death case, equally troublesome, takes its place. Thus, it is in the capital case that restraint meets its most severe test, and it is in this type of case that the opening wedge is often made that leads in time to new rules for all types of criminal prosecutions. In the *Francis* case, the balance in 1947 swung by a single vote in favor of allowing the state to have its way; today, the balance could as easily swing in the opposite direction, as surely it would if the element of state culpability that was introduced late in the case were a matter of record from the outset.

The basic dilemma of the Supreme Court remains. The more forcefully it takes the lead in the criminal field, the more responsibility will tend to shift away from where it belongs—with local officials—and the more people will come to feel that all is well so long as the Supreme Court sits. As powerful as the Court is, such a feeling is nothing short of a delusion. The one hope is that an awakened citizenry, made aware by the Court of the civilized standards that should govern all criminal proceedings, will refuse to sanction further abuses.

### Table of Cases, in Order of Citation in the Text

*Louisiana* ex rel. *Francis* v. *Resweber,* 329 U.S. 459 (1947), *affirming* 31 So. 2d 697 (La. 1947); petition for rehearing denied, 330 U.S. 853 (1947); petition for writ of certiorari and petition for leave to file original petition for writ of habeas corpus denied, 331 U.S. 786 (1947).
*Ex Parte Hawk,* 321 U.S. 114 (1944).
*Palko* v. *Connecticut,* 302 U.S. 319 (1937).
*Holden* v. *Hardy,* 169 U.S. 366 (1898).
*Hebert* v. *Louisiana,* 272 U.S. 312 (1926).
*In re Kemmler,* 136 U.S. 463 (1890).

### Sources

I was fortunate in being able to obtain, in addition to the petitions and briefs on file in the Supreme Court Library, the complete file of the *Willie Francis* case kept by Judge Wright, who from 1946 to 1947 was one of Francis' attorneys. This file contained the transcript of the Board of Pardons hearings in New Orleans, letters, telegrams, notes, newspaper clippings, and other relevant papers. I also spoke by telephone to a number of participants in Francis' trial, attempted electrocution, appeals, and "second" electrocution. My general comments in regard to the Supreme Court were based on my own experience as a law clerk at the Court. I also drew from two sources—Mr. Justice Black's James Madison Lecture, "The Bill of Rights," given at New York University School of Law (February 17, 1960) and Mr. Justice Jackson's posthumous book, "The Supreme Court in the American System of Government" (Cambridge: Harvard University Press, 1955).

# 4

## SEPARATION OF CHURCH AND STATE

# *The Released Time Case*

## Frank J. Sorauf

In the summer of 1949 two members of the Supreme Court died—Justice Murphy and Justice Rutledge. They had been closely aligned with Justices Black and Douglas in what was generally called the liberal wing of the Court. These four justices had tended to vote as a bloc, particularly in civil liberties cases. This group had the four votes required to grant certiorari petitions and needed only one additional vote to control the Court's decisions. However, they were often unable to get that additional vote.

The remaining five members of the Court fell into two groups. The Chief Justice commonly joined with Justices Reed and Burton in the Court's center, while Justices Frankfurter and Jackson tended on some issues toward a community of views on the right of the Court.

The sudden disappearance of half the Court's liberal wing was bound to disturb the existing balance of forces. Truman replaced them with Tom C. Clark and Sherman Minton. Clark, a Texan, had been an official of the Department of Justice since 1937 and became Truman's Attorney General in 1945. In that connection he had an active hand in the Smith Act prosecution of top American Communists and the preparation of the Attorney General's list of subversive organizations. Minton, like Burton, had been a Senate colleague of President Truman. After one term in the Senate, where he was known as a pronounced New Dealer, he had served as administrative assistant for President Roosevelt, who in 1941 named him to a Federal Court of Appeals. These two new appointees tended to join the Vinson-Reed-Burton group to make it the dominant force on the Court.

The Vinson Court had its principal impact in the civil

liberties field. Without the votes of Murphy and Rutledge, the Court took a far more restrictive position in its view of freedom of speech, press, and association. A new Bill of Rights problem, interpretation of the religious establishment provision in the First Amendment, proved particularly difficult in various cases between 1947 and 1952, and led to some interesting new divisions of opinion on the Court.

$A$T PUBLIC SCHOOL 78, the teacher in charge of administering the released time program, Miss Wallace, would send a student monitor to every classroom. This monitor would open the classroom door and announce in a loud voice, "Church time, church time."

Similar dismissals, perhaps less dramatically announced, took place once a week in all New York City schools in the late 1940's. On the appointed days approximately one-quarter of the public school students in grades three through eight left their schools for an hour to receive religious instruction in whatever facilities the churches and synagogues could provide.

Released time religious-education programs had been prevalent in most states and in New York for many years before the constitutionality of the New York City program was challenged in 1948 in *Zorach* v. *Clauson*. Shortly after World War I communities throughout New York State had begun to experiment with released time education, and New York City began its program in 1940. After a period of rapid growth, released time enrollment reached a plateau in the late 1940's. A limiting factor was the unwillingness of many Jewish groups to support the program. Significantly, of the 110,137 New York students participating in 1950, close to 80 per cent were attending Roman Catholic classes.

The *Zorach* case was begun as a direct result of the Supreme Court decision a few months earlier in *Illinois* ex rel. *McCollum* v. *Board of Education,* which had invalidated the released time program of Champaign, Illinois. The Champaign program, like the one in New York, permitted students to leave their regular classes for one hour each week for religious instruction. Students whose parents had not requested the religious instruction continued their studies in the school building until the usual dismissal hour. Champaign, however, differed from New York City in that it provided public school rooms for the religious classes, a largesse the Supreme Court emphasized heavily in holding, eight to one, that the program had breached the wall of separation between church and state. Furthermore, the Champaign religious classes were taught by teachers approved and supervised by public school authorities, and the program was administered by the public school classroom teachers.

After the disposition of the Champaign case the question arose whether the same program with classes held on private property would also fall under the Court's ruling. In June, 1948, Tessim Zorach and Mrs. Esta Gluck sought an order in the Kings County Division of the New York Supreme Court to direct Andrew Clauson and other members of the City Board of Education and Francis T. Spaulding, State Commissioner of Education, to stop the city's released time program. They charged that the public school machinery and personnel had been used to aid sectarian education and that the released time program exerted a cumulative pressure on children and parents in favor of religious education. They charged, furthermore, that the program produced divisive effects among the children and favored formal, organized religious bodies over less institutionalized religions. With this action *Zorach* v. *Clauson* was begun.

### Twenty Years Before Zorach

Shortly after World War I school boards throughout New York State began instituting released time programs. Lacking statutory authorization by the state legislature, local boards set up programs at their own discretion which, understandably, differed considerably in detail. Legal attacks began in 1925 with a taxpayer's suit challenging the Mount Vernon program. Holding it invalid, the State Supreme Court in *Stein* v. *Brown* emphasized the use of the public school print shops to print excuses for the program. On the broader issue of the program's legality, the court noted that the legislature had not authorized such programs, nor included them in its lists of approved subjects for public school instruction, and rested its decision on the "well-established policy of the State that religious instruction shall not be given in the public schools or under their auspices." The case was never carried to the Court of Appeals.

Less than two years later the released time program of another New York community, White Plains, was subject to attack by Joseph Lewis, an avowed atheist and aggressive president of the Freethinkers Society of America. This time the suit did reach the Court of Appeals, which in *Lewis* v. *Graves* upheld the program without referring to the recent Mount Vernon case. After noting that Lewis was neither resident nor taxpayer of White Plains, Judge Cuthbert Pound asserted that the state permitted the excusing of students for music and dancing lessons. He saw no reason why the privilege should not logically be extended to religious lessons. He concluded by observing:

> Jealous sectaries may view with alarm the introduction in the schools of religious teaching which to the unobservant eye is but faintly tinted with

denominationalism. Eternal vigilance is the price of constitutional rights. But it is impossible to say, as a matter of law, that the slightest infringement of constitutional right or abuse of statutory requirement has been shown in this case.

The entire court, including its great Chief Judge, Benjamin Cardozo, concurred.

The case also marked the formal entry into the released time fray of Charles H. Tuttle, counsel for the Greater New York Federation of Churches, as *amicus curiae* urging the dismissal of Lewis' petition. Arthur Garfield Hays, a stalwart of the American Civil Liberties Union, filed a separate brief on behalf of Lewis in the lower court.

To bring uniformity to the variety of released time programs over the state and to buttress their legality, the New York legislature in 1940 amended the education law to include this clause: "Absence for religious observance and education shall be permitted under rules that the commissioner shall establish." Combining religious observance with education was a shrewd tactic: those potentially hostile to absence for religious classes— Jewish groups especially—were won over by recognition of their holy days. In signing the bill Governor Herbert Lehman made what became an often quoted defense of it.

> A few people have given voice to fears that the bill violates principles of our Government. These fears in my opinion are groundless. The bill does not introduce anything new into our public school system nor does it violate the principles of our public educational system.

Almost immediately the state Commissioner of Education formulated the regulations the law contemplated:

> 1. Absence of a pupil from school during school hours for religious observance and education to be had outside the school building and grounds will be excused upon the request in writing signed by the parent or guardian of the pupil.
> 2. The courses in religious observance and education must be maintained and operated by or under the control of a duly constituted religious body or by duly constituted religious authorities.
> 3. Pupils must be registered for the courses and a copy of the registration filed with the local public school authorities.
> 4. Reports of attendance of pupils upon such courses shall be filed with the principal or teacher at the end of each week.
> 5. Such absence shall be for not more than one hour each week at the close of a session at a time to be fixed by the local school authorities.
> 6. In the event that more than one school for religious observance and education is maintained in any district, the hours for absence for each

particular public school in such district shall be the same for all such religious schools.

In drafting the regulations the Commissioner apparently thought almost exclusively of released time programs. Two of the three times "observance" is mentioned it refers to religious schools and courses.

Later in 1940, the New York City Board of Education set up a program under its own rules and regulations. The rules, in complete accord with the Commissioner's regulations, provided that:

> 1. A program for religious instruction may be initiated by any religious organization, in cooperation with the parents of pupils concerned. There will be no announcement of any kind in the public schools relative to the program.
>
> 2. When a religious organization is prepared to initiate a program for religious instruction, the said organization will notify parents to enroll their children with the religious organization, and will issue to each enrolled pupil a card countersigned by the parent and addressed to the principal of the public school, requesting the release of the pupil for the purpose of religious instruction at a specific location. The said cards will be filed in the office of the public school as a record of pupils entitled to be excused, and will not be available or used for any other purpose.
>
> 3. Religious organizations, in cooperation with parents, will assume full responsibility for attendance at the religious center and will file with the school principal, weekly, a card attendance record and in cases of absence from religious instruction, a statement of the reason therefor.
>
> 4. Upon the presentation of a proper request as above prescribed, pupils of any grade will be dismissed from school for the last hour of the day's session on one day of each week to be designated by the Superintendent of Schools: A different day may be designated for each borough.
>
> 5. Pupils released for religious instruction will be dismissed from school in the usual way, and the school authorities have no responsibility beyond that assumed in regular dismissals.
>
> 6. There shall be no comment by any principal or teacher on the attendance or nonattendance of any pupil upon religious instruction.

Firmly established in law and regulation, the New York City released time program grew steadily through the 1940's. But early in 1948 repercussions of the Supreme Court decision in the Champaign case hit New York.

### Litigation in Search of Litigants

Immediately after the *McCollum* case decision Joseph Lewis of the 1927 White Plains case asked the State Supreme Court to direct the Commissioner of Education to end the released time programs of New York and other cities in the state. Appearing for Lewis were two of the most honored veterans in American civil liberties circles, Arthur Garfield Hays and Osmond K. Fraenkel. Hays had long been a national director of the ACLU, and Fraenkel was its general counsel. Representing the Greater New York Coordinating Committee on Released Time of Jews, Protestants, and Roman Catholics was Charles H. Tuttle, also a participant in the 1927 case. Porter Chandler and Louis Loeb appeared with him, giving the committee a counsel panel as representative as its title.

Rejecting Lewis' suit (*Lewis* v. *Spaulding*), the Supreme Court distinguished between the Champaign and New York programs. To support its contention that the two programs differed in crucial ways, the court reprinted a complete comparison of the programs submitted as an affidavit by the New York Board of Education:

| CHAMPAIGN PLAN | NEW YORK CITY PLAN |
|---|---|
| 1. No underlying enabling State statute. | 1. Education law 3210 is the enabling statute which provides that "absence from required attendance shall be permitted only for causes allowed by the general rules and practices of the public school"; and further provides that "absence for religious observance and education shall be permitted under rules that the commissioner shall establish." |
| 2. Religious training took place in the school buildings and on school property. | 2. Religious training takes place outside of the school buildings and off school property. |
| 3. The place for instruction was designated by school officials. | 3. The place for instruction is designated by the religious organization in cooperation with the parent. |
| 4. Pupils taking religious instruction were segregated by school authorities according to religious faith of pupils. | 4. No element of segregation is present. |
| 5. School officials supervised and approved the religious teacher. | 5. No supervision or approval of religious teachers or course of instruction by school officials. |
| 6. Pupils were solicited in school buildings for religious instruction. | 6. School officials do not solicit or recruit pupils for religious instruction. |

7. Registration cards distributed by school. In at least one instance, the registration cards were printed at the expense of school funds.

7. No registration cards furnished by the school or distributed by the school. No expenditure of public funds involved.

8. Non-attending pupils isolated or removed to another room.

8. Non-attending pupils stay in their regular classrooms continuing significant educational work.

9. No credit given for attendance at the religious classes.

10. No compulsion by school authorities with respect to attendance or truancy.

11. No promotion or publicizing of the released time program by school officials.

12. No public moneys are used.

Clearly, the court observed, the New York program was "free from the objectionable features" that had marked the Champaign program.

Groups long opposed to released time, such as the American Civil Liberties Union and the American Jewish Congress, were greatly concerned over Lewis' suit. The case seemed a bad one in which to test the New York program. Lewis was a militant atheist, and his litigation bore too much the unpopularity of his cause. He was neither resident of, taxpayer, nor parent or guardian of a child in the City of New York. And some thought his case had been hastily put together with too little attention to the facts of the program and the constitutional issues it raised.

The distress of these groups increased when they learned that Lewis had appealed the decision to the Court of Appeals and indicated his intention of carrying it eventually to the United States Supreme Court. They also felt it was an inopportune time for even the best-planned and best-argued case. Leo Pfeffer, the AJC expert on church-state matters, would have preferred at least a decade's wait after *McCollum* in order to consolidate gains made there; that decision had been under heavy fire from religious bodies, and group such as the AJC had done little to answer them. In conferences over the *Lewis* case the ACLU and the AJC agreed on the necessity of finding a better test of the city's released time program. Lewis agreed to drop his ill-starred case, but only if the two organizations would organize an alternative. So, born in reluctance and of necessity, the *Zorach* case was instituted.

### Two Parents Step Forward

Ideally the ACLU and AJC hoped to recruit litigants for their suit who were residents of, and property owners in, the city, who were active members of a religious body and provided religious instruction for their children, and whose children did not participate in the released time program. They hoped, furthermore, to find a Catholic, a Protestant, and a Jew to join in the challenge. Except for their inability to find a Catholic litigant, the ACLU and the AJC filled all their specifications with Tessim Zorach and Mrs. Esta Gluck.

Tessim Zorach, son of the noted American sculptor, William Zorach, had worked for a number of years in Washington as a government employee; by 1948 he was doing business in New York as a food broker. The Zorachs, members of the Holy Trinity Protestant Episcopal Church, lived with their three children in Brooklyn Heights, an area of picturesque old row and town houses. The Glucks lived in a more typical, middle-class section of Brooklyn. They were members of the AJC and of a local synagogue to which they sent their children for religious classes. Mrs. Gluck was president of the local PTA at the time the case started. As litigants, Zorach and Mrs. Gluck brought an impressive respectability to the case.

Why they became involved in the litigation is less than clear. Certainly the idea of challenging the city's released time program did not originate with either of them. "Intermediaries" from the ACLU and the AJC asked them to serve as litigants in the test case. The Zorachs' intermediary was the pastor of their church; they were assured that legal counsel would be provided and that the sponsoring organizations would absorb all costs.

The Zorachs and the Glucks entered the case for mixed and somewhat different motives. The Zorachs were attracted as a matter of principle and conviction; members of the ACLU, they had long been interested in liberal and libertarian causes. Mrs. Gluck entered more out of personal injury; her children had felt the sting of anti-Semitic taunts for nonparticipation in the program. The Zorach children suffered little or no pressure from ostracism; only a small minority of their classmates attended released time classes.

### The Parents Recede

After becoming litigants in the case, the two plaintiffs immediately dropped into the background, for their involvement in the case was primarily legal. The Zorachs had occasional visits with counsel as facts were gathered and the cases prepared, but these diminished as the case progressed. The Zorachs, in fact, had the greater share of their contacts with the ACLU and the Glucks with the AJC. Their participation was in no sense equal to that of Mrs. Vashti McCollum in her fight against the Champaign released time program; for instance, they knew little of the Lewis litigation or of the strategic considerations giving rise to "their" case.

They had been prepared for this secondary, even fleeting, role. What they had not expected as "novice" litigants was the harassment they experienced. The Glucks had by far the worse time of it: angry, sullen neighbors; insulting phone calls at all hours; COD orders placed in their names at local stores; anti-Semitic attacks by bigots; and the defection of some of their children's playmates. The Zorachs, residents of a better-educated and more cosmopolitan community, fared better. They had their share of crank phone calls, a few cold glances from neighbors and acquaintances, and a handful of business repercussions, but nothing compared to what the Glucks endured.

The real principals of the case, unlike the Zorachs and Glucks, were familiar with the business of litigating church-state issues. Leo Pfeffer, who carried the burden of AJC work in the case, had entered the *McCollum* case on an *amicus* brief and long before that had established himself with many books and articles as a leading authority on church-state relations. His *Church, State and Freedom* is one of the few indispensable works on the subject. Kenneth W. Greenawalt, a Congregationalist and member of the respected law firm of Davies, Hardy, and Schenck, served as the volunteer lawyer for the ACLU in the case. Also a specialist in church-state law, he had drafted the ACLU brief in the *McCollum* case.

Representing the other side, Charles H. Tuttle had been an *amicus curiae* in the first *Lewis* case and an intervener in the second one; he had also appeared as an *amicus* in *McCollum*. Senior member of the prestigious law firm of Breed, Abbott, and Morgan, he was counsel to both the National Council of Churches and the Protestant Council of New York. Additionally, he served as chairman and attorney of the twelve-man Greater New York Coordinating Committee on Released Time of Jews, Protestants, and Roman Catholics, which organized and ran the religious classes in the New York released time program.

### Beginnings and Pleadings

*Zorach* v. *Clauson* began slowly at first, a pace probably welcomed by its reluctant sponsors. The suit was filed in June, 1948, and prior to its initial hearing, the State Commissioner of Education unsuccessfully sought a dismissal of the petition as it applied to him. His request was denied in February, 1949, and that denial was twice affirmed on appeal. About that time the Greater New York Coordinating Committee sought to intervene as it had in Joseph Lewis' case less than two years before. It argued that it was "specifically and beneficially interested in upholding" the New York City program; its petition was granted over the objections of the plaintiffs. Also during 1949 and early 1950 the respondents in the case and the Coordinating Committee were serving their answers to the charges of Zorach and Gluck. They contained nothing beyond brief denials, except for the answer of the New York School Board. Attached to it were affidavits submitted by William Jansen, the New York Superintendent of Schools, by his assistant, and by principals of the schools the Zorach and Gluck children attended.

Jansen pointed to the differences between the New York and Champaign programs, submitting the same side-by-side comparison he had earlier prepared for the Lewis challenge.

The Jansen affidavit, with its broad assertions of fact, later assumed an enormous importance in the case, for it was the closest thing to a set of facts with which the appellate courts could work. It dealt entirely with the official plans and regulations for the program and stressed the minimal contribution the schools made:

> The planning necessary to accommodate pupils on released time is no greater than or different from that required when large numbers of pupils are absent in the schools of the City of New York for the purpose of observing religious holidays or by reason of inclement weather or serious illness in any particular community.

In short, Jansen outlined the program by drawing exclusively on the published rules and regulations of the State Commissioner of Education and the New York School Board.

Additional details were provided in the other three affidavits. C. Frederick Pertsch, Associate Superintendent of Schools, noted that the pupils not attending released time classes were given "significant education (*sic*) work with emphasis on individual and remedial instruction." The principal of P.S. 130, the school attended by the Gluck children, described the release of excused students: At 1:55 on Wednesday afternoons "the teachers advise the children that those who have been excused may leave. No further comment is made." The acting principal of the school the Zorach boys attended added: "Release of children for religious instruction on Wednesday afternoon is taken as a matter of course by the other children who remain." He had not, he added, received any complaint or criticism of the program from any parents or students.

### McCollum As a Precedent

Even as the preliminary jockeying in the *Zorach* case was taking place, it became clear that the main constitutional issue would center around whether or not the *McCollum* decision had invalidated all or only some released time programs, and if it had affected only some, whether the New York program was significantly different from Champaign's. In fact, the possibility of these issues touching the New York plan had occurred to interested parties in New York at the very time of the argument before the Supreme Court in *McCollum*. The ACLU had filed a brief as *amicus curiae* urging the invalidation of the Champaign program, while the Protestant Council of the City of New York appeared merely as a friend of the court "with special reference to the New York Statute and Judicial Decisions sanctioning 'Released Time.' "

Kenneth Greenawalt in his *McCollum* brief for the ACLU turned, after urging the unconstitutionality of the Champaign program, to issues relevant to the New York program. Referring to Bible-reading in the schools and released time classes on private property, he said:

> Each of those situations raises important constitutional questions which need careful consideration when presented. Because not here presented they are not briefed by us but merely mentioned. We think, however, that they are also unconstitutional on the same general grounds here discussed.

The *McCollum* brief of Charles H. Tuttle for the Protestant Council emphasized the differences between the Champaign and New York programs. By alerting the Court to these differences, Tuttle hoped to avoid any language in *McCollum* which could be taken as a blanket invalidation of all released time programs. The brief of the Synagogue Council of America, while urging invalidation of the Champaign program, contained no special reference to the New York experience. It did, however, mark Leo Pfeffer's formal entry into the litigation over released time.

The transcript of the oral argument in the *McCollum* case indicated that the Court itself had the New York released time plan in mind. At one point Justice Jackson asked Walter Dodd, counsel for Mrs. McCollum, "If your position is sustained, how would that affect the Released Time Plan in New York?" Dodd replied, "I don't think it would be affected by an adverse decision relative to this situation." A little later Justice Frankfurter returned to the point, "You said the New York system could survive although this system should fall. What are the decisive elements that differentiate the two?" Dodd answered that in Champaign, "they are to take their religious lessons in groups in the schools where there will be, somewhat of necessity unless the world has changed as to religion, some development of friction and trouble as between religious groups." Dodd had also distinguished between the two programs earlier in his reply brief to the Court. "The New York released time plan is directly opposed to the plan at issue in the present case," he wrote.

From the various opinions in the *McCollum* case counsel in the emerging *Zorach* case sought an answer to one question: had the Court in *McCollum* created a precedent which invalidated released time programs intrinsically? Justice Black, speaking for the majority of the Court, had clearly objected to using schoolrooms for religious classes, but his objections were more fundamental:

> Here not only are the State's tax-supported public school buildings used for the dissemination of religious doctrines. The State also affords sectarian

groups an invaluable aid in that it helps to provide pupils for their religious classes through the use of the State's compulsory public school machinery. This is not separation of Church and State.

The suggestion was clear that any system of religious education during class hours of the state's public schools would fail. A majority of the Court—Justices Black, Murphy, Douglas, Rutledge, and Burton, and Chief Justice Vinson—supported the Black opinion.

As much solace as the Black opinion brought opponents of released time, proponents of the New York plan found equal comfort in the concurrence of Justice Frankfurter. "Of course," he asserted, " 'released time' as a generalized conception, undefined by differentiating particularities, is not an issue for Constitutional adjudication. Local programs differ from each other in many and crucial respects."

Both groups of contestants in the infant *Zorach* litigation, therefore, claimed support in the *McCollum* case. Five justices had signed Black's opinion; Frankfurter's position was endorsed by three fellow concurrers—Jackson, Burton, and Rutledge—and, by implication, the dissenting Reed. Thanks to the generous embrace of both opinions by Burton and Rutledge, the Court appeared to have produced two conflicting majorities.

### To the New York Courts

In June, 1950, Judge Anthony J. DiGiovanna was chosen to preside over the case. Of all the judges of the Second District of the Supreme Court who might have been assigned to the case, he was not one that counsel for the ACLU and the AJC would have preferred. Not only was he a Roman Catholic and a fourth-degree Knight of Columbus, but also his political ties to the Democratic Party and through it to New York officialdom (which included the school board) were well known. He had been a city councilman from 1937 to 1947, the years in which the released time program had been instituted in the city; in 1946 he ran unsuccessfully for state attorney general. At the time of his appointment to the Court of Special Sessions in 1948 the New York *Times* observed that "his appointment was regarded as another step by the Democratic organization of Kings County in recognition of his service to the party in 1946 when he sacrificed certain election to the City Court bench in order to run for Attorney General on the Democratic ticket." In November, 1948, he won overwhelming election to the Supreme Court.

#### DiGiovanna Dashes a Hope

At this juncture counsel for Zorach and Mrs. Gluck hoped to explore the actual operation of the New York City released time program at a trial of issues of fact. The Jansen affidavit with its comparison of the Champaign and New York programs had raised what seemed to be triable issues. If Jansen's statement of facts were to pre-empt the attention of the courts, their case would be seriously compromised. Judge DiGiovanna, however, denied their request for a trial and held the released time program constitutional. He reviewed the city's plan, repeating the assertions of the school board and quoting verbatim Jansen's comparison of the New York and Champaign programs. Noting that it had not been the intention of the Supreme Court to strike down all released time programs in *McCollum,* DiGiovanna concluded that the New York program had none of the objectionable features of the Illinois plan. And since the second Lewis case had been decided after *McCollum,* he considered its precedent binding.

The dicta in Judge DiGiovanna's opinion confirmed the worst fears of the groups opposing released time. Despite the care and precaution of ACLU and AJC strategists their case was interpreted as an attack on organized religion. By way of admonishing the plaintiffs, DiGiovanna quoted approvingly a California court:

> Throughout her entire argument, appellant misconceives the American principle of religious freedom. What she contends for is freedom *from* religion rather than freedom *of* religion.

Furthermore, concern over the Cold War and international communism intruded.

> The denial of released time classes would be tantamount to a denial of a basic right guaranteed by the letter and the spirit of our American concept of government. It would be a step in the direction of and be consonant with totalitarian and communistic philosophies existing in jurisdictions wherein atheism and the suppression of all religions are preferred to the freedom of the individual to seek religious instruction and worship. Such would be the result or conclusion if the relief sought herein by the petitioners was to be granted.

The year of 1950, marked by the Korean War and the Berlin crisis, was clearly not a propitious one for an attempt to buttress the wall of separation.

After Judge DiGiovanna refused their petition for reargument, the plaintiffs appealed to the Supreme Court's Appellate Division for the Second Judicial District. Released time forces were jubilant at having won the first round of litigation; not only had they won the constitutional argument but they had staved off as well a lengthy and probably compromising excursion into the day-to-day administration of the program. The only facts before the courts were "theirs": the formal regulations of the State Commissioner and the New York school board, plus the affidavits of Superintendent Jansen and his lieutenants, which were submitted in the pleading.

*A Second Defeat . . .*

The Appellate Division in early 1951 upheld the DiGiovanna ruling by a three-to-two margin. Appearing as *amici curiae* for the appellants were the American Jewish Committee, American Jewish Congress, Anti-Defamation League of B'nai B'rith, Public Education Association, Committee on Academic Freedom of the American Civil Liberties Union, New York City Civil Liberties Committee, and New York Board of Rabbis. The opinion of the three-man majority, anonymously authored, concluded briefly and simply that the New York program could be distinguished from the one invalidated in *McCollum.*

The dissent of Judge Adel recognized the differences between the New York and Champaign plans; the New York program, he thought, was nonetheless void:

> in that it is integrated with the State's compulsory education system which assists the program of religious instruction carried on by separate religious sects; in that it releases pupils, who are compelled to attend public schools for secular education, from part of their legal duty upon condition that they attend religious classes; and in that the State's compulsory public school machinery is used to afford aid and assistance to sectarian groups by helping provide pupils for religious classes.

Here, succinctly stated, was the case to be made from Justice Black's majority opinion in *McCollum:* rooted in the very nature of released time programs, regardless of their differences in detail, were bonds between public education and religion that made all released time programs unconstitutional.

*And a Third*

On July 11, 1951, the New York Court of Appeals by a six-to-one vote upheld the lower court decisions. Again, the majority of the court relied on the distinctions between the New York and Champaign plans. Judge Froessel paraphrased the Jansen comparison and underscored the fact that in the New York program neither money nor school property was used directly or indirectly to aid religious bodies.

Pointing to the approved instances of the cooperation between government and religion—bus rides and textbooks, for instance—the majority argued that the Constitution did not demand "that every friendly gesture between church and State shall be discountenanced." Indeed, the court feared it would turn this "reasonable line of demarcation between friends" into an " 'iron curtain' as between foes" if it were to strike down the New York program. It noted, finally, that courts cannot ignore the rights of parents to educate their children or deny their rights of "free exercise" of religion in the name of separating church and state.

Two of the six-man majority did not join the Froessel opinion. Judge Loughran announced simply that he voted to affirm the lower court's opinion on the authority of Lewis' first case, *Lewis* v. *Graves*. Judge Desmond's concurrence went beyond the majority opinion to argue for two new constitutional doctrines. Free exercise of religion

> is absolute and not subject to any governmental interference whatever. Absolute, I insist, is the right to practice one's religion without hindrance, and that necessarily comprehends the right to teach that religion, or have it taught, to one's children.

Second, he urged a recasting of the interpretation of the no-establishment clause to prohibit only the establishing and favoring of one religion over others, or the compelling of religious affiliation or observance.

Judge Fuld alone dissented. Drawing on the Court's words, in *Everson* v. *Board of Education,* that the First Amendment prohibits any form of aid to religion, even when it is given to all religions, he outlined those forms of aid to religion involved in the New York program. Aid need not be only financial, he observed;

> what is vital and operative is not where the religious teaching is given, but that it secures its pupils through the instrumentality of the state and through the machinery and momentum of the public school system.

He disagreed, finally, that parental rights would be infringed should the court invalidate the program. No one questioned their right to send their children to whatever religious schools they chose.

In little more than a year the Zorach-Gluck forces had exhausted their legal remedies in New York. Since this litigation involved and interested important groups and religious bodies, it may be worth noting that of the thirteen New York State judges who heard the case in the three state courts, five were Catholics who voted in favor of released time; two were Jews who voted against released time; and six were Protestants, of whom five voted for released time and one opposed it.

### The Case That Never Was

Throughout its progress through the New York courts the ACLU-AJC case had been gravely compromised by the inability to win a trial of the facts of the actual operation of released time in the New York schools. The defendants had vigorously opposed one, and Judge DiGiovanna twice upheld their objections. The request for a trial on the facts, the opinion of DiGiovanna stated, was based on "a generalized allegation of maladministration in particular instances, of which no particulars are cited." In any case, he added:

> The practice or practices which may grow up in the matter of administrative details do not affect the constitutionality of the statute involved, for the statute must stand or fall by itself on this question. . . . Neither does compliance with the statute render it constitutional if it is unconstitutional, nor does administrative error render it unconstitutional if it is constitutional.

Whether the program was being conducted according to regulation was not the issue, he held. Ample opportunity existed for redress of maladministration; the remedy was administrative action against the offender. The Court of Appeals agreed; only when the administration of a statute shows "an element of intentional or purposeful discrimination" can the statute itself be struck down, wrote Judge Froessel. Hence the indicated remedy would be disciplinary proceedings against teachers or principals.

### The Phantom Facts

In none of the New York courts, then, was the issue of the facts cleanly and clearly joined. There seems to have been a monumental misunderstanding of what the plaintiffs hoped to show by a trial of the facts. Beyond the evidence of maladministration they were charging that even a faultless application of the regulations would result in clearly unconstitutional results, that the bare bones of the regulations failed to give an accurate picture of the constitutionality of the program. Their charges read:

> Administration of the system *necessarily* entails use of the public school machinery and time of public school principals, teachers, and administrative staff. . . . Operation of the released time program has resulted and *inevitably* results in the exercise of pressure and coercion upon parents and children to secure attendance . . . [and] has resulted and *inevitably* will result in divisiveness because of difference in religious beliefs and disbeliefs. [Emphasis added.]

To justify a trial on the facts, counsel for Zorach and Mrs. Gluck had collected a series of affidavits from parents, former students, and former teachers and administrators. Since a trial was never held on the facts the affidavits alleged, their authors were never cross-examined on them. They had, however, been willing to appear at a trial and defend them. The picture they painted was one considerably less impeccable than the formal regulations would have suggested.

Some of the affidavits charged flagrant misapplication of the rules of either the Commissioner or the Board of Education. Wendy, the daughter of the Glucks, stated:

> When I was in the second and third grades at P.S. 130, Brooklyn, my teacher was Miss Jeffries who was also in charge of the released time program at the school. Miss Jeffries distributed blank consent cards to the children in her class and asked the children publicly for a show of hands of those who were going to participate in the released time program. . . . Miss Jeffries scolded those students who had participated in the released time program the term before but who did not raise their hands to show that they were continuing.

A parent, Charles Stewart, claimed to have seen nuns and priests coming into the public school to meet children and escort them to the centers for Catholic instruction. His daughter Anne recalled being harassed along with other nonparticipants by another zealous teacher; their fate was to struggle with difficult long-division problems while their classmates were at religious classes. A former assistant principal deposed that in her school a student's participation or nonparticipation in the program was noted on his permanent records. A photostatic copy of one of those record cards accompanied her affidavit.

### A "Protestant Martyr"

At the same time those affidavits raised the additional issue of the inevitably objectionable results and consequences of even a precise and careful administration of the regulations. One parent, touching on the divisiveness of the program, swore:

> The released time program made my children much more aware of the fact that they were different and not members of a dominant religious group in the community. Soon after the released time program at P.S. 163, Brooklyn, my children asked me why they could not become Catholics and go to released time for religious instruction with their classmates. They were insistent in their demands and emotionally upset when I explained to them that they could not participate with the Catholic children in their released time religious instruction.

Another parent reported that his daughter felt that "she is a Protestant martyr from two to three o'clock on every Thursday when her classmates depart for religious instruction."

Other teachers and students swore that the normal school activities were inevitably disturbed. "It was extremely difficult," said one former teacher, "to teach anything which would not penalize those children who remained or which, on the other hand, would not make the released students feel that they were missing something valuable." Leona Abrams, who as a teacher had been responsible for administering a released time program, underscored the burdens which fell on the school system:

I found that my duties in connection with the released time program were very burdensome and entailed constant interruption of my teaching program, to the detriment of my own class. . . . When religious education programs were occasionally cancelled by the church centers, I had to prepare notes for the various teachers of children who attended those centers. . . . I was obliged to take time out from my own teaching in order to question those children concerning their continued absences from the religious center after they were released from the public school. . . .

The depositions clearly suggested that even the most scrupulous attention to the letter of the program would still have involved the public school system in a substantial exertion of time and resources to keep the released time classes going.

All this, to repeat, was only "what might have been." Although the argument and briefs suggested them, these data were not before any court in its decision of *Zorach* v. *Clauson*. The "case" involving the actual operation of released time in the New York schools was never decided. The resulting paucity of real, tangible facts forced the Supreme Court ultimately to decide a great constitutional issue in the "abstract," despite its own often stated hesitation to do so.

### Contestants and the Constitutional Climate

Since the counsel for Zorach and Gluck decided to bring their case to the United States Supreme Court by appeal on a substantive Federal question, rather than on certiorari, final adjudication was speeded. Furthermore, they asserted, the New York decisions had created confusion about the future of released time and the meaning of the *McCollum* precedent which only a ruling by the Supreme Court could settle. The Court granted appeal and set argument for early 1952.

Substantially the same groups that had directed the challenge and defense of the program in the New York courts participated in the final appeal to the Supreme Court. Pfeffer for the AJC and Greenawalt for the ACLU continued in dual control of the attack on the released time program, with Greenawalt presenting oral argument before the Court. Active on the same side, in a different but equally important way, were the three groups which eventually bore all the costs of litigation: the American Jewish Committee, the American Jewish Congress, and the Anti-Defamation League of B'nai B'rith. The defense remained in the hands of Tuttle and counsel for the Board of Education. New York State and the Commissioner of Education played a strictly secondary role. Furthermore, Tuttle did not confer with state representatives appearing as *amici curiae,* nor did he attempt to coordinate their briefs. The case for the defense was argued by Tuttle for the Greater New York Coordinating Committee; by Michael A. Castaldi, Assistant Corporation Counsel for New York City; and by Wendell P. Brown, Solicitor General for the state.

### A Time of "Renaissance"

As the parties to *Zorach* polished their briefs and presentations for the Supreme Court, they cannot have failed to consider the intellectual climate in which they were arguing and in which the Court was deciding. For one thing, sharp criticism of the *McCollum* decision had continued. The Jesuit weekly, *America,* had complained:

> Judicial action has been substituted for the political process. The secularization of the public schools, already too much advanced through the political process, is now declared to be a constitutional necessity. . . . The decision in the . . . case is a source of regret and alarm. The regret . . . extends to the much wider issue of the vagueness of the Supreme Court's language: the absence of limitation and definition as to what, in its interpretation of the Constitution, may at any time be declared illicit.

William J. Butler in *Catholic World* said of the justices that their "prevailing prepossession is manifestly nothing other than a general distaste for religion." On the practical level a number of communities showed their distaste for the opinion by continuing religious classes in the public schools in outright defiance of the Court's ruling. In other jurisdictions confusion prevailed. In some cities released time plans similar to New York's were declared unconstitutional. Within the Federal government the Interior Department approved a New York style program for Guam, but the Office of Indian Affairs advised an end to all released time programs.

This criticism of *McCollum* could partly be traced to another current of the times—the postwar "religious renaissance." Church membership had increased; Congress had altered the pledge of allegiance to the flag to proclaim the United States "one nation, under God"; and nationally known preachers reached millions via radio, television, books, magazines, and newspapers. The heightened interest in religion doubtless reflected a response to a variety of perils—from international communism and the Cold War to juvenile delinquency and a moral softness in American life, from John Dewey and philosophical relativism to smutty and sadistic comic books. Whatever the spur, it seemed to many Americans that a reintroduction of moral and spiritual values into American life was essential for the preservation of American traditions. The daily newspapers reminded the Supreme Court justices of these ideas and events. On the very day they heard argument on *Zorach* v. *Clauson* the Rev. Billy Graham appeared at a Washington rally and in a speech entitled "The Greatest Cocktail Party in History" compared the D.C. social whirl to Belshazzar's epic debauchery. And the week the decision was handed down the New York *Times* list of

The Released Time Case

best-selling nonfiction included *A Man Called Peter, The Greatest Book Ever Written,* and *The Power of Faith.*

### Secularism Pro and Con

In the briefs submitted to the Supreme Court it was apparent that the underlying issues of the Cold War and the battle of organized religion against secularism lay only slightly below the surface of the argument. The brief of Kenneth Greenawalt, with Leo Pfeffer "of counsel," attempted to dispel any suspicion as to the purpose of their suit. Greenawalt claimed their opposition was in no way motivated by hostility to organized religion, or even to religious education. The parties to the case were both religious people providing for the religious training of their children. "The real issues herein," he concluded, "should not be muddled by unfair references to totalitarianism, communism or atheism."

In the main body of their brief Greenawalt and Pfeffer developed a lengthy and documented argument of the constitutional issues that proceeded along these lines:

> 1. The Supreme Court had in *McCollum* invalidated *all* released time programs using the machinery of compulsory public education.
> 2. The degree of aid to religion involved in the New York plan was sufficient to invalidate it under the concept of absolute separation laid down in the *Everson* and *McCollum* cases.
> 3. No rights of parents were at stake in the case since the crucial aspect of released time is not the release, but the nonrelease of students whose parents did not request religious classes.
> 4. The lower courts erred in not permitting the appellants to prove in a trial that the New York plan, despite its formal differences from the Champaign plan, operated in clearly unconstitutional ways.

The brief of Denis M. Hurley, Corporation Counsel for the City of New York, on behalf of the Board of Education, joined the argument almost point for point. He reduced the chief issue to a preliminary rhetorical question:

> Is this minimal degree of cooperation between school and parent, the only purpose of which is to foster and encourage the well-rounded education of the child, to be condemned under the "establishment of religion" clause of the First Amendment merely because, as an incident thereto, religion generally or some sect in particular may also be involved?

His rebuttal of the contentions of the appellants touched these issues:

> 1. The New York City program differed from the specific kind of released time program the Court invalidated in *McCollum.*
> 2. Separation of church and state was not an absolute concept, and to make it one would interfere with other First Amendment rights such as

those of parents to secure a religious education for their children.

3. The main purpose of the New York program was educational and not religious; educational goals such as the providing of a new moral training predominated.

4. The case presented no triable issues of fact; since no one charged that the rules were being "consciously and purposefully manipulated and abused," the proper remedies were administrative.

The brief of Charles Tuttle and Porter Chandler for the intervening Greater New York Coordinating Committee differed markedly from the constitutionally earnest briefs of the other parties. Its testy and forceful tone was early established in its claim to speak for the hundreds of thousands of parents "who strongly resent the attempts of these two petitioners to use the courts to force upon all parents—and upon the State of New York—the petitioners' own ideas as to how other people's children, enrolled in the public schools, must be exclusively educated."

Millions of parents in the country believe, wrote Tuttle and Chandler, that "the momentum of secularism is a basic cause of the world's ills, and that it undermines the very cornerstone of our freedom as expressed in these constitutional Preambles and in the Declaration of Independence."

> If the onrushing currents of secularism throughout the world *must* exclude the religious convictions of parents from any recognition at all amid public education, then the Constitution itself can become the instrument of regimentation and of sweeping religion and the Church into a backwater of life.
>
> Such is the appalling lesson of all systems of Brown, Black and Red Shirts throughout the last twenty years—not to go back further in the history of tyranny.

The real danger confronting the American nation was secularism, "which threatens to choke the sources of spiritual power," rather than the might of the Soviet Union, they added.

In its legal arguments the Tuttle-Chandler brief dwelt heavily on the "natural right" of parents to supervise the education of their children regardless, apparently, of state education laws. Since the parent and not the state had the right and duty of educating children, the teacher, whether in a public or private school, was chiefly the agent or delegate of the parent. Therefore, "the public school is not—except in the mind of the appellants—the vassal of an all-powerful state. . . ." Otherwise their argument, while lengthy and thorough, repeated that of the other defendants. Denying that the case raised triable issues of fact, it ended with the warning that if the appeal could invalidate the New York program, "the intention of the Founding Fathers now operates in reverse, and the Bill of Rights has become an engine of tyranny."

The brief of Nathaniel L. Goldstein, New York State Attorney General, attempted chiefly to distinguish between the Champaign and New York programs. It dealt solely with the validity of the Commissioner's rules set down under the 1940 amendment to the state's education code. The National Council of Churches sought also to file a brief as an *amicus curiae,* but were refused permission. The Zorach-Gluck forces may have reasoned that to admit the Council's brief would put them in the uncomfortable position of opposing organized religion. In any event the National Council of Churches was represented indirectly in the case through its General Counsel, Charles Tuttle.

Eight states (California, Indiana, Kentucky, Maine, Massachusetts, Oregon, Pennsylvania, and West Virginia) filed *amicus* briefs supporting the New York program.

### The Last Decision

During the oral argument on the case, January 31 and February 1, 1952, observers received some preliminary hints of the developing line-up on the Court. Accounts of brief colloquies between lawyers and justices in the New York *Times* indicated Justice Frankfurter's early preoccupation with dismissed time possibilities:

> Mr. Tuttle insisted that no court could forbid schools to excuse children for "religious observances."
> "That's a very different story from this system," commented Justice Frankfurter. "Why aren't you satisfied to have every child dismissed at 2 o'clock each Wednesday and Friday?"
> "It isn't a question of my satisfaction," Mr. Tuttle replied. "The question is whether the Legislature is bound to say that 'dismissed time' is the only Constitutional alternative."

The *Times* also reported another snippet of dialogue:

> [Mr. Tuttle speaking:] "They [the parents of children] fear that under conditions of today the momentum of secularism is pushing religion and the church into the backwaters of life."
> "So they need the public schools to help them accomplish their religious purposes?" Justice Frankfurter asked.
> "They don't need the school system, they just need their children for a few minutes," cut in Justice Sherman Minton.

Three months elapsed between the completion of argument and the Court's decision. On April 28, 1952, only four years and one month after *Mc-*

*Collum,* the Supreme Court decision upheld the New York program by a six to three vote.

---

### ZORACH v. CLAUSON
#### 343 U.S. 306, 72 S. Ct. 679, 96 L. Ed. 954 (1952)

MR. JUSTICE DOUGLAS delivered the opinion of the Court.

New York City has a program which permits its public schools to release students during the school day so that they may leave the school buildings and school grounds and go to religious centers for religious instruction or devotional exercises. A student is released on written request of his parents. Those not released stay in the classrooms. The churches make weekly reports to the schools, sending a list of children who have been released from public school but who have not reported for religious instruction.

This "released time" program involves neither religious instruction in public school classrooms nor the expenditure of public funds. All costs, including the application blanks, are paid by the religious organizations. The case is therefore unlike *McCollum* v. *Board of Education,* 333 U.S. 203, which involved a "released time" program from Illinois. In that case the classrooms were turned over to religious instructors. We accordingly held that the program violated the First Amendment which (by reason of the Fourteenth Amendment) prohibits the states from establishing religion or prohibiting its free exercise.

Appellants, who are taxpayers and residents of New York City and whose children attend its public schools, challenge the present law, contending it is in essence not different from the one involved in the *McCollum* case. Their argument, stated elaborately in various ways, reduces itself to this: the

weight and influence of the school is put behind a program for religious instruction; public school teachers police it, keeping tab on students who are released; the classroom activities come to a halt while the students who are released for religious instruction are on leave; the school is a crutch on which the churches are leaning for support in their religious training; without the cooperation of the schools this "released time" program, like the one in the *McCollum* case, would be futile and ineffective. The New York Court of Appeals sustained the law against this claim of unconstitutionality. . . .

The briefs and arguments are replete with data bearing on the merits of this type of "released time" program. Views pro and con are expressed, based on practical experience with these programs and with their implications. We do not stop to summarize these materials nor to burden the opinion with an analysis of them. For they involve considerations not germane to the narrow constitutional issue presented. They largely concern the wisdom of the system, its efficiency from an educational point of view, and the political considerations which have motivated its adoption or rejection in some communities. Those matters are of no concern here, since our problem reduces itself to whether New York by this system has either prohibited the "free exercise" of religion or has made a law "respecting an establishment of religion" within the meaning of the First Amendment.

It takes obtuse reasoning to inject any issue of the "free exercise" of religion into the present case. No one is forced to go to the religious classroom and no religious exercise or instruction is brought to the classrooms of the public schools. A student need not take religious instruction. He is left to his own desires as to the manner or time of his religious devotions, if any.

There is a suggestion that the system involves the use of coercion to get public school students into religious classrooms. There is no evidence in the record before us that supports that conclusion. The present record indeed tells us that the school authorities are neutral in this regard and do no more than release students whose parents so request. If in fact coercion were used, if it were established that any one or more teachers were using their office to persuade or force students to take the religious instruction, a wholly different case would be presented. Hence we put aside that claim of coercion both as respects the "free exercise" of religion and "an establishment of religion" within the meaning of the First Amendment.

Moreover, apart from that claim of coercion, we do not see how New York by this type of "released time" program has made a law respecting an establishment of religion within the meaning of the First Amendment. There is much talk of the separation of Church and State in the history of the Bill of Rights and in the decisions clustering around the First Amendment. . . . There cannot be the slightest doubt that the First Amendment reflects the philosophy that Church and State should be separated. And so far as interference with the "free exercise" of religion and an "establishment" of religion are concerned, the separation must be complete and unequivocal. The First Amendment within the scope of its coverage permits no exception; the prohibition is absolute. The First Amendment, however, does not say that in every and all respects there shall be a separation of Church and State. Rather, it studiously defines the manner, the specific ways, in which there shall be no concert or union or dependency one on the other. That is the common sense of the matter. Otherwise the state and religion would be aliens to each other— hostile, suspicious, and even unfriendly. Churches could not be required to pay even property taxes. Municipalities would not be permitted to render police or fire protection to religious groups. Policemen who helped parishioners into their places of worship would violate the Constitution. Prayers in our legislative halls; the appeals to the Almighty in the messages of the Chief Executive; the proclamations making Thanksgiving Day a holiday; "so help me God" in our courtroom oaths—these and all other references to the Almighty that run through our laws, our public rituals, our ceremonies would be flouting the First Amendment. A fastidious atheist or agnostic could even object to the supplication with which the Court opens each session: "God save the United States and this Honorable Court."

We would have to press the concept of separation of Church and State to these extremes to condemn the present law on constitutional grounds. The nullification of this law would have wide and profound effects. A Catholic student applies to his teacher for permission to leave the school during hours on a Holy Day of Obligation to attend a mass. A Jewish student asks his teacher for permission to be excused for Yom Kippur. A Protestant wants the afternoon off for a family baptismal ceremony. In each case the teacher requires parental consent in writing. In each case the teacher, in order to make sure the student is not a truant, goes further and requires a report from the priest, the rabbi, or the minister. The teacher in other words cooperates in a religious program to the extent of making it possible for her students to participate in it. Whether she does it occasionally for a few students, regularly for one, or pursuant to a systematized program designed to further the religious needs of all the students does not alter the character of the act.

We are a religious people whose institutions presuppose a Supreme Being. We guarantee the freedom to worship as one chooses. We make room for as wide a variety of beliefs and creeds as the spiritual needs of man deem necessary. We sponsor an attitude on the part of government that shows no partiality to any one group and that lets each flourish according to the zeal of its adherents and the appeal of its dogma. When the state encourages religious instruction or cooperates with religious authorities by adjusting the schedule of public events to sectarian needs, it follows the best of our traditions. For it then respects the religious nature of our people and accommodates the public service to their spiritual needs. To hold that it may not would be to find in the Constitution a requirement that the government show a callous indifference to religious groups. That would be preferring those who believe in no religion over those who do believe. Government may not finance religious groups nor undertake religious instruction nor blend secular and sectarian education nor use secular institutions to force one or some religion on any person. But we find no constitutional requirement which makes it necessary for government to be hostile to religion and to throw its weight against efforts to widen the effective scope of religious influence. The government must be neutral when it comes to competition between sects. It may not thrust any sect on any person. It may not make a religious observance compulsory. It may not coerce anyone to attend church, to observe a religious holiday, or to take religious instruction. But it can close its doors or suspend its operations as to those who want to repair to their religious sanctuary for worship or instruction. No more than that is undertaken here. . . .

In the *McCollum* case the classrooms were used for religious instruction and the force of the public school was used to promote that instruction. Here, as we have said, the public schools do no more than accommodate their schedules to a program of outside religious instruction. We follow the *McCollum* case. But we cannot expand it to cover the present released time program unless separation of Church and State means that public institutions can make no adjustments of their schedules to accommodate the religious needs of the people. We cannot read into the Bill of Rights such a philosophy of hostility to religion.

*Affirmed.*

MR. JUSTICE BLACK, dissenting.

*Illinois* ex rel. *McCollum* v. *Board of Education,* 333 U.S. 203, held invalid as an "establishment of religion" an Illinois system under which school children, compelled by law to go to public schools, were freed from some hours of required schoolwork on condition that they attend special religious classes held in the school buildings. Although the classes were taught by sectarian teachers neither employed nor paid by the state, the state did use its power to further the program by releasing some of the children from regular class work, insisting that those released attend the religious classes, and requiring that those who remained behind do some kind of academic work while the others received their religious training. . . .

I see no significant difference between the invalid Illinois system and that of New York here sustained. Except for the use of the school buildings in Illinois, there is no difference between the systems which I consider even worthy of mention. In the New York program, as in that of Illinois, the school authorities release some of the children on the condition that they attend the religious classes, get reports on whether they attend, and hold the other children in the school building until the religious hour is over. . . . *McCollum* . . . held that Illinois could not constitutionally manipulate the compelled classroom hours of its compulsory school machinery so as to channel children into sectarian classes. Yet that is exactly what the Court holds New York can do.

I am aware that our *McCollum* decision on separation of Church and State has been subjected to a most searching examination throughout the country. Probably few opinions from this Court in recent years have attracted more attention or stirred wider debate. Our insistence on "a wall between Church and State which must be kept high and impregnable" has seemed to some a correct exposition of the philosophy and a true interpretation of the language of the First Amendment to which we should strictly adhere. With equal conviction and sincerity, others have thought the *McCollum* decision fundamentally wrong and have pledged continuous warfare against it. The opinions in the court below and the briefs here reflect these diverse viewpoints. In dissenting today, I mean to do more than give routine approval to our *McCollum* decision. I mean also to reaffirm my faith in the fundamental philosophy expressed in *McCollum* and *Everson* v. *Board of Education*, 330 U.S. 1. That reaffirmance can be brief because of the exhaustive opinions in those recent cases.

Difficulty of decision in the hypothetical situations mentioned by the Court, but not now before us, should not confuse the issues in this case. Here the sole question is whether New York can use its compulsory education laws to help religious sects get attendants presumably too unenthusiastic to go unless moved to do so by the pressure of this state machinery.

That this is the plan, purpose, design and consequence of the New York program cannot be denied. The state thus makes religious sects beneficiaries of its power to compel children to attend secular schools. Any use of such coercive power by the state to help or hinder some religious sects or to prefer all religious sects over non-believers or vice versa is just what I think the First Amendment forbids. In considering whether a state has entered this forbidden field the question is not whether it has entered too far but whether it has entered at all. New York is manipulating its compulsory education laws to help religious sects get pupils. This is not separation but combination of Church and State.

The Court's validation of the New York system rests in part on its statement that Americans are "a religious people whose institutions presuppose a Supreme Being." This was at least as true when the First Amendment was adopted; and it was just as true when eight Justices of this Court invalidated the released time system in *McCollum* on the premise that a state can no more "aid all religions" than it can aid one. It was precisely because eighteenth-century Americans were a religious people divided into many fighting sects that we were given the constitutional mandate to keep Church and State completely separate. Colonial history had already shown that here as elsewhere zealous sectarians entrusted with governmental power to further their causes would sometimes torture, maim and kill those they branded "heretics," "atheists" or "agnostics." The First Amendment was therefore to insure that no one powerful sect or combination of sects could use political or governmental power to punish dissenters whom they could not convert to their faith. Now as then, it is only by wholly isolating the state from the religious sphere and compelling it to be completely neutral that the freedom of each and every denomination and of all nonbelievers can be maintained. It is this neutrality the Court abandons today when it treats New York's coercive system as a program which *merely* "encourages religious instruction or cooperates with religious authorities." The abandonment is all the more dangerous to liberty because of the Court's legal exaltation of the orthodox and its derogation of unbelievers.

Under our system of religious freedom, people have gone to their religious sanctuaries not because they feared the law but because they loved their God. The choice of all has been as free as the choice of those who answered the call to worship moved only by the music of the old Sunday morning church bells. The spiritual mind of man has thus been free to believe, disbelieve, or doubt, withou repression, great or small, by the heavy hand of government. Statutes authorizing such repression have been stricken. Before today, our judicial opinions have refrained from drawing invidious distinctions between those who believe in no religion and those who do believe. The First Amendment has lost much if the religious follower and the atheist are no longer to be judicially regarded as entitled to equal justice under law.

State help to religion injects political and party prejudices into a holy field. It too often substitutes force for prayer, hate for love, and persecution for persuasion. Government should not be allowed, under cover of the soft euphemism of "co-operation," to steal into the sacred area of religious choice.

MR. JUSTICE FRANKFURTER, dissenting. . . .

MR. JUSTICE JACKSON, dissenting.

This released time program is founded upon a use of the State's power of coercion, which, for me, determines its unconstitutionality.

Stripped to its essentials, the plan has two stages: first, that the State compel each student to yield a large part of his time for public secular education; and, second, that some of it be "released" to him on condition that he devote it to sectarian religious purposes.

No one suggests that the Constitution would permit the State directly to require this "released" time to be spent "under the control of a duly constituted religious body." This program accomplishes that forbidden result by indirection. If public education were taking so much of the pupils' time as to injure the public or the students' welfare by encroaching upon their religious opportunity, simply shortening everyone's school day would facilitate voluntary and optional attendance at Church classes. But that suggestion is rejected upon the ground that if they are made free many students will not go to the Church. Hence, they must be deprived of freedom for this period, with Church attendance put to them as one of the two permissible ways of using it.

The greater effectiveness of this system over voluntary attendance after school hours is due to the truant officer who, if the youngster fails to go to the Church school, dogs him back to the public schoolroom. Here schooling is more or less suspended during the "released time" so the nonreligious attendants will not forge ahead of the churchgoing absentees. But it serves as a temporary jail for a pupil who will not go to Church. It takes more subtlety of mind than I possess to deny that this is governmental constraint in support of religion. It is as unconstitutional, in my view, when exerted by indirection as when exercised forthrightly.

As one whose children, as a matter of free choice, have been sent to privately supported Church schools, I may challenge the Court's suggestion that opposition to this plan can only be antireligious, atheistic, or agnostic. My evangelistic brethren confuse an objection to compulsion with an objection to religion. It is possible to hold a faith with enough confidence to believe that what should be rendered to God does not need to be decided and collected by Caesar.

The day that this country ceases to be free for irreligion it will cease to be free for religion—except for the sect that can win political power. The same epithetical jurisprudence used by the Court today to beat down those who oppose pressuring children into some religion can devise as good epithets tomorrow against those who ob ject to pressuring them into a favored religion. And, after all, if we concede to the State power and wisdom to single out "duly constituted religious" bodies as exclusive alternatives for compulsory secular instruction, it would be logical to also uphold the power and wisdom to choose the true faith among those "duly constituted." We start down a rough road when we begin to mix compulsory public education with compulsory godliness.

A number of Justices just short of a majority of the majority that promulgates today's passionate dialectics joined in answering them in *Illinois* ex rel. *McCollum* v. *Board of Education,* 333 U.S. 203. The distinction attempted between that case and this is trivial, almost to the point of cynicism, magnifying its nonessential details and disparaging compulsion which was the underlying reason for invalidity. A reading of the Court's opinion in that case along with its opinion in this case will show such difference of overtones and undertones as to make clear that the *McCollum* case has passed like a storm in a teacup. The wall which the Court was professing to erect between Church and State has become even more warped and twisted than I expected. Today's judgment will be more interesting to students of psychology and of the judicial processes than to students of constitutional law.

---

### Impact and Aftermath

While the *Zorach* decision was gratefully received in New York released time circles, it produced no dramatic impact there. The program continued as it had in the past without any great increases in student participation. Groups opposing the program, however, thought they noticed a tighter administration of the program by public school officials. Administrative action probably ended many classroom comments, some discriminatory administration of the program, and instances of zealous promotion of the program within the schools. In this manner the losers in the litigation may have produced a measure of change and reform in a program they could not overturn. For this reason or for others, however, they did not seek administrative remedies for misapplication of the regulations governing the New York program.

The impact of *Zorach* on released time throughout the country also fell somewhat short of expectations. It produced no rash of state legislation. No new legislation on released time was enacted in the states after the decision, although bills to authorize such programs were defeated in several states in the 1950's (New Hampshire, Michigan, and Arizona, for instance). Interpretive action by state attorneys general or commissioners of education, difficult to document, probably opened the way in other states. A national total of between 2,000,000 and 2,500,000 children were attending released time classes in 1953, and five years later leaders of the movement estimated the enrollment figure at close to 3,000,000. In view of the growing student population one might call the increase a modest one.

Contrary to Justice Frankfurter's resigned expectations, no flood of released time litigation followed *Zorach*. By 1962 no cases on the subject had reached the Federal courts. In the only state appellate court case squarely on the subject the Washington Supreme Court invalidated the program of School District 81 of Spokane on the grounds that permitting the recruitment of students and the distribution of permission cards in school buildings constituted a direct aid to religious bodies. Despite the absence of litigation, however, little evidence exists to think that the constitutional form of released time offered in *Zorach* has stopped the defiance of the *McCollum* ruling. As recently as 1958 most released time programs run by the Virginia Council of Churches were apparently using schoolrooms, as were many communities in other states. *Religious Education* in 1956 disclosed that a casual poll of released time programs indicated that 32 per cent still held classes in school buildings, although some paid token rentals of from five to one hundred dollars a year.

In the general debate over church-state relationships the *Zorach* decision became a weapon in the hands of individuals and groups proposing greater church-state cooperation. Since the decision marked a departure from the absolutist position of the *Everson* and *McCollum* cases, such a response was both reasonable and inevitable. But in some quarters *Zorach* was perceived somewhat recklessly; one friend of released time noted the Court had "reversed" the *McCollum* precedent, and another thought it had "cut the heart out of the McCollum decision" and "greatly modified, if not virtually overruled" it.

Regardless of interpretation, *Zorach* was mentioned in debates over church and state. When the New York Board of Regents in 1955 proposed the introduction of spiritual values into the public school curricula of the state, it cited the case to buttress its arguments. Other scholars felt it would permit nondenominational teaching "about" religion in the schools. Similar uses of the *Zorach* rule occurred in the courts. A Massachusetts court in reaffirming the legality of Bible-reading in the public schools drew attention to the Court's approval of similar religious training in *Zorach*. A New York court in 1957 dismissed a suit, brought by the ubiquitous Joseph Lewis, to forbid the public schools to use the pledge of allegiance to the flag with the phrase "under God." In so ruling, the court cited the "doctrine of accommodation" between church and state set down in *Zorach*.

### Zorach in Retrospect

In retrospect it seems entirely appropriate that the controversies surrounding *Zorach* v. *Clauson* should have arisen when and where they did. As a locale, New York offered a heterogeneous religious community in which the three major American religious traditions had a degree of community support virtually unique in the country. Beyond its mixture of religious loyalties New York also welcomed nonbelief and nonconforming belief. To accommodate this range of outlook within a single program of religious education verged on the impossible. Furthermore, in New York, unlike many homogeneous religious communities, dissenting minorities possessed the numbers, organization, and community standing to challenge the religious program. Two of the major organizations promoting a complete separation of church and state—the American Civil Liberties Union and the American Jewish Congress—had their headquarters there.

Times were also ripe for continued debate over church-state problems in the late 1940's and early 1950's. The criticism of the *McCollum* decision had been so sharp that it could scarcely have escaped the Court's notice. Justice Black, in fact, noted in his *Zorach* dissent:

> I am aware that our *McCollum* decision on separation of Church and State has been subjected to a most searching examination throughout the country. Probably few opinions from this Court in recent years have attracted more attention or stirred wider debate.

Indeed, *Zorach* was only one of a series of cases in the 1950's in which the Court was obliged to step into the raging and sensitive public debate over the place of religion and religious values in public life. The very day the Court opened oral argument in *Zorach* it also heard argument in the challenge of the New Jersey Bible-reading statute (*Doremus* v. *Board of Education*). Other controversies on birth-control legislation and Sunday closing laws were to come, and other tangential issues plaguing the Court, notably those of movie and book censorship, had religious overtones.

The public character of cases such as *Zorach* also affords the occasion par excellence for group litigation. When a controversy represents primarily the conflicting interests of major public groups, rather than the personal grievances of individuals, the invitation to group litigation is obvious. All the greater is the spur to group intervention when the groups see their interests about to be adjudicated in inept litigation they have had no opportunity to control or shape. Only groups such as the ACLU, the AJC, and the Greater New York Coordinating Committee can provide the expertise, the long-run persistence, the full-time attention, the far-seeing strategies, and the sheer financial resources needed to contest constitutional issues of this sort. The pesky, but essentially ineffective, suits of Joseph

Lewis indicate that much. Issues such as those of church and state rarely reach a final resolution in a single case. They are larger and more enduring than the individuals in whose names they are contested.

### Table of Cases, in Order of Citation in the Text

*Zorach* v. *Clauson*, 343 U.S. 306 (1952).
*Illinois* ex rel. *McCollum* v. *Board of Education*, 333 U.S. 203 (1948).
*Stein* v. *Brown*, 125 Misc. (N.Y.) 692 (1925).
*Lewis* v. *Graves*, 245 N.Y. 195 (1927).
*Lewis* v. *Spaulding*, 193 Misc. (N.Y.) 66 (1948).
*Zorach* v. *Clauson*, 198 Misc. (N.Y.) 631 (1950).
*Zorach* v. *Clauson*, 278 App. Div. (N.Y.) 573 (1951).
*Zorach* v. *Clauson*, 303 N.Y. 161 (1951).
*Everson* v. *Board of Education*, 330 U.S. 1 (1947).
*Doremus* v. *Board of Education*, 342 U.S. 429 (1952).

### Sources

The main sources for these materials on *Zorach* v. *Clauson* have been the briefs and records of the case on appeal before the United States Supreme Court. Relevant rules and regulations may also be found there. In addition I have relied on personal interviews with counsel and participants in the case, as well as with representatives of the organizations involved. The statements and depositions of facts never admitted in the case appear in Leo Pfeffer's *Church, State and Freedom* (Boston: Beacon, 1953). The New York *Times* and its index proved invaluable for background information, biographical information on the principals, general data on the released time program, and portions of the oral argument. Most of the sources used for the impact of *McCollum* are referred to in Gordon Patric's "The Impact of a Court Decision: Aftermath of the McCollum Case," 6 *Journal of Public Law* 455 (Fall, 1957). I have dealt at much greater length with the impact of *Zorach* in "*Zorach* v. *Clauson:* The Impact of a Supreme Court Decision," 53 *American Political Science Review* 777 (September, 1959).

# 5

## FREEDOM OF ASSOCIATION

# The NAACP in Alabama

## George R. Osborne

CHIEF JUSTICE VINSON died in September, 1953, and
President Eisenhower named Earl Warren to succeed him.
During Warren's first term, on May 17, 1954, in the most
portentous judicial decision thus far in the twentieth century,
the Supreme Court ruled that racial segregation in the public
schools was unconstitutional. Recognizing that this decision
would require nothing less than a social revolution to make
it effective in some sections of the nation, the Court then
waited a year before announcing that it proposed to turn enforcement back to the Federal District Courts, which were to
require school boards to develop integration plans "with all
deliberate speed."

Actually, the bringing of local pressure on segregated
schooling was left in most instances to interested local groups,
of which by far the most active was the National Association
for the Advancement of Colored People. The efforts of this
organization to try to secure compliance with the Supreme
Court mandate very quickly aroused the ire of segrega-
tionist forces, and a variety of legislative, economic, and
social pressures were used to put the local NAACP units
out of business. After its 1955 order the Supreme Court had
generally refrained from intervening in the controversies
that rapidly developed at the lower court levels, but by 1958
the efforts of Alabama to force the NAACP to suspend operations in that state required the Court to act, with the results
indicated in this account.

The 1958 Court that decided the NAACP case was somewhat changed in personnel from the 1954 Court that handed
down the original segregation decision, but it was still unanimous in this field. Justice Jackson had died in 1954, and

in his place President Eisenhower had appointed John M. Harlan, grandson of an earlier Supreme Court Justice with the same name. Harlan was a New York lawyer whom Eisenhower had previously appointed to the Federal Court of Appeals. Justice Minton retired in 1956, and was replaced by William J. Brennan, Jr., a member of the New Jersey Supreme Court. Justice Reed's retirement followed in 1957, and the new appointee was Charles E. Whittaker, a little-known member of the Federal Court of Appeals from Missouri.

# BIRMINGHAM—a sprawling industrial city of blast

furnaces and steel mills—lies in the hill country of north central Alabama. Known as the "Pittsburgh of the South," it is a town with a short but lusty history. It did not exist at the time of the Civil War yet it is now the nation's thirty-sixth largest city. The haze and smoke thrown up from the hearths and forges of the mills serve as a pungent reminder to many of the city's 340,000 residents of their dependence upon the pre-eminent steel industry.

One of Birmingham's citizens on the morning of June 1, 1956, was Mrs. Ruby Hurley, a tall and articulate woman who had spent the previous day at an out-of-state conference in her capacity as Southeastern Regional Secretary of the National Association for the Advancement of Colored People. Mrs. Hurley had come home late and was still asleep shortly after 9:00 A.M. that morning when the ring of her telephone awakened her. An Associated Press reporter was on the line. He told Mrs. Hurley of a story that was just coming over the teletype that concerned a legal action by the Attorney General of Alabama against the NAACP. He wanted to know what Mrs. Hurley knew about the action. Nothing, she told him. It was news to her, too.

### A Lawsuit Is Born

As she put down the telephone, Mrs. Hurley heard her doorbell ring. Standing there as she opened the door was a county deputy sheriff, a reporter, and a photographer. "I have some papers for you," the deputy said dryly. He handed Mrs. Hurley documents that turned out to be a summons and complaint and an injunction order. She took the papers and quickly pushed the door closed. Wide awake by now and greatly confused by all the excitement, Mrs. Hurley sat down to read what had been handed to her. She discovered that the Association had been forbidden to conduct further activities in Alabama and that the state's Attorney General had brought an action to oust it permanently from Alabama. Thus began the action styled *The State of Alabama,* ex rel. *John Patterson* v. *The National Association for the Advancement of Colored People.*

### Equality Before the Law

Founded in 1909 by a group of sixty Americans to improve the status of Negroes in American life, the NAACP has become a subject of much dispute. To its friends and supporters, it is one of the best and most effective organizations in the United States; to its opponents it is meddlesomeness personified. The controversy surrounding the Association stems directly from the role it has sought to play, *i.e.,*

> voluntarily to promote equality of rights and eradicate caste or race prejudice among citizens of the United States; to advance the interest of colored citizens; to secure for them impartial suffrage; and to increase their opportunities for securing justice in the courts, education for their children, employment according to their ability, and complete equality before the law.

Today, with over 380,000 members in 50 states and the District of Columbia, the Association is the largest civil rights organization in the United States. Members are organized into some 1,500 local branches as well as youth councils and college chapters, which in turn form 30 state conferences and several regional councils. Headquarters are in New York. The Association also maintains a Washington bureau (primarily for legislative work and contact with governmental agencies) and three regional offices—in Atlanta, Dallas, and San Francisco.

Although its opponents frequently portray the Association as having financial resources only slightly less commanding than those of Fort Knox, the organization currently operates on a budget of about $800,000 a year. Most of the money comes from annual membership dues, ranging from $2 to $25, as well as from life-membership fees and occasional fund-raising drives. The Association rarely receives large gifts from individuals or organizations and receives nothing from tax-exempt foundations or funds.

A 48-member Board of Directors (elected at an annual convention) and an employed staff headed by an Executive Secretary are responsible for running the Association. At the state and local levels, the staff is aided by volunteer officers in carrying out its policies.

### A Program of Action

Over the years, particularly since World War II, the Association has been active in the fields of housing, voting, public education, employment, transportation, and recreation. Its efforts to secure equality for Negroes, particularly since the U.S. Supreme Court's landmark 1954 decision in *Brown* v. *Board of Education* (holding segregated public schools unconstitutional), have become recurrent themes in the political and social drama. In addition to its work in obtaining favorable Federal and state legislation, executive orders, and administrative decisions, the Association seeks to break down segregation and discrimination at the community level. Like most interest groups, it would prefer to attain its objectives by discussion and agreement with local political and business groups, but this is frequently a fruitless tactic. The Association has, therefore, increasingly resorted to the judicial process. Its willingness to work through the courts—with the implicit expense and delay—has caused some other Negro groups, particularly those involved with "sit-ins" and other direct-action protests, to refer critically to the Association as being unduly "legalistic"—a backhanded compliment to its methods of operation.

The Association's work, both in and out of the courts, has been conducted on a national scale, but its efforts have been mainly concentrated in the southern states, where most American Negroes live and where the slavery heritage is strongest. Here the deep patterns of segregation have caused great resistance to change.

### "Heart of Dixie"

While "the south" has reacted in several very different manners to the Supreme Court desegregation rulings, the State of Alabama responded from the start with total intransigence. Shortly after the 1954 school desegregation decision, the Governor announced, "Anybody with any sense knows that Negro children and white children are not going to school together in Alabama . . . for a long, long time." Almost a decade later this prophecy still was true. Alabama, along with Mississippi and South Carolina, had not a single desegregated public school. The state's laws and customs requiring segregation from the cradle to the grave have remained almost intact. Only in the areas of interstate transportation and public recreation has some desegregation been enforced by Federal court orders.

The atmosphere of uncompromising resistance has been aided by a political structure that has fostered legislative inertia, as well as fear and uncertainty in whites and blacks alike. Extensive industrial and population growth has made Alabama the leading heavy-industry state in the south, but the state has lagged behind the nation-wide rate of population growth. The magnitude of racial discrimination, particularly in employment opportunities, has caused many Negroes to leave Alabama, and the Negro population has declined from 45 per cent of total state population in 1900 to 29 per cent today.

Despite major population changes, the legislature has successfully avoided any equitable apportionment of the state since 1901, when the present constitution was adopted and the population was centered in the small rural counties. (A temporary reapportionment formula was ordered into effect by a Federal court in July 1962—the first time that a Federal court actually reapportioned a state legislature since the Supreme Court ruled in March of that year that the Federal courts had such jurisdiction.) The political make-up is further aggravated by the extensive disenfranchisement of Negroes. Only about 70,000 of the state's 980,000 Negroes are registered to vote. Apathy, barriers such as the devious use of the literacy test, and the fear of physical harm and economic pressure have thus far combined to prevent any sizable number of Negroes from obtaining the ballot. As a result the rural Black Belt counties with the smallest white vote are the seats of political power. The Tennessee Valley Authority areas in north Alabama and the Mobile and Birmingham metropolitan areas are almost as poorly represented as are the Negro centers.

### The NAACP Arrives

The NAACP came to Alabama in 1918. Its first two branches were in Montgomery and Selma. By 1956 a total of fifty-eight branches had been chartered throughout the state, and the Association listed a membership of 14,566 persons. (Each branch is an unincorporated association electing its own officers and governing body and is a member of the State Conference of Branches, which coordinates state-wide functions of the Association.) In order to develop and execute its policies in the seven southeastern states more effectively, the Association decided at the 1951 annual convention to start a Southeast Regional Office in Birmingham. It opened in April, 1951, with Mrs. Hurley designated Regional Secretary. Her role was to "disseminate information to branches and the public in general concerning the enforcement of constitutional rights of Negroes and to give guidance and assistance to branches in devising means to secure community compliance with the mandate of the Federal Constitution." In nearby offices in the same building the Association also maintained its Birmingham branch. In this office W. C. Patton, formerly president of the State Conference of Branches, was employed as a field secretary "to operate within the State of Alabama to interest persons in taking an active part in the effort to secure constitutional rights of Negroes." Except for these two persons and a secretary in the Regional Office, all others connected with the organization in Alabama, whether officers or members, were unpaid volunteers.

In the years since 1918 the Association played an increasingly large role in Alabama, partly through community efforts but primarily in the courts. The Association has aided the state's Negroes both with funds and legal counsel in actions involving due process in criminal prosecutions, such as the two Scottsboro cases, *Powell* v. *Alabama* and *Norris* v. *Alabama*. (These cases involved nine Negroes charged with rape. The U.S. Supreme Court decisions established a number of legal principles regarding the right of counsel in a state court and the systematic exclusion of Negroes from a trial jury.) The Association had also brought actions attempting to secure greater voting rights for Negroes. One suit had been initiated to block the construction of segregated multiple-dwelling units built in part with Federal loan funds.

After 1954 the Association helped plaintiffs in different parts of Alabama file petitions to desegregate the public schools. It also furnished counsel to Negro student Autherine Lucy when she sought admission to the University of Alabama.

Perhaps the one episode above all others that aroused enmity was the Association's role in the successful boycott against segregated seating in the buses of Capital Motor Lines in Montgomery. The year-long boycott demonstrated what a unified and purposeful Negro community was prepared to do to achieve equality.

Indeed, the course of events at the end of 1955 gave every indication that the efforts of Alabama Negroes to attain equal rights would increase both in quantity and intensity. Throughout the state, Negroes were seeking new methods to challenge the traditional order of state-imposed segregation.

### An Outstanding Young Man

One of the state officials who was carefully watching these events was Attorney General John M. Patterson. Grandson of two Confederate soldiers, he had served in the U.S. Army in World War II and in the Korean War. He had received his undergraduate and law degrees from the University of Alabama. An aggressive and handsome young man with intense eyes, he had been an obscure practicing attorney as recently as June, 1954. But in that month his father, Albert L. Patterson, won the Democratic nomination for state Attorney General—mainly on the strength of his promise to clean the gangsters and racketeers out of his home town, Phenix City, Alabama. When the elder Patterson was murdered in an ambush only a few days after his victory in the primary, the slaying brought Phenix City under martial law. The public outcry of revulsion projected son John into state politics. Taking over his father's fight, he played a leading role in the clean-up of the city and also received his father's nomination. Easily elected in one-party Alabama, he continued his fight against crime as the Attorney General. In 1956 Phenix City won the honor of "America's Model City," while John Patterson, at thirty-five, was named one of the ten outstanding young men in America by the U.S. Junior Chamber of Commerce. Patterson was only at the beginning of a successful political career, and the racial issue had not yet involved him directly. By early 1956, however, no politician in Alabama could afford to overlook the increasing activity of the state's Negro citizens —particularly the role of the NAACP. One of Patterson's Assistant Attorneys General had mentioned that the Association seemed vulnerable to legal attack on one major ground, and Patterson began looking into the matter. His first step was to write to the Association in New York.

*"No Adequate Relief at Law"*

On Manhattan's West Fortieth Street, across from the New York Public Library and Bryant Park, in a row of grey, almost indistinct office buildings, stands the Freedom House. The fourth and fifth floors of this building house the national headquarters of the NAACP. On February 1, 1956, the morning mail brought a letter from Attorney General Patterson requesting the Association to send his office "a copy of your certificate of incorporation and by-laws, for our information and files."

The letter was received by Roy Wilkins, fifty-four-year-old Executive Secretary of the Association. A graduate of the University of Minnesota and former editor of the Kansas City *Call,* Wilkins had gone to work for the Association in 1931 and held a wide variety of positions before his appointment as the organization's chief executive. A thin, soft-spoken man, his friendly and often humorous manner covers a firm determination to win full civil rights for Negro Americans.

Wilkins' reply to Patterson, a letter dated February 7, 1956, enclosed a copy of the Association's Certificate of Incorporation and its constitution. Nothing further was heard on this matter until May 14, 1956, when Patterson again corresponded with the Association. "I would appreciate it very much," he wrote to Wilkins, "if you would furnish me with the addresses and locations of the NAACP chapters and officers in Alabama and the names of any officers or employees of said association that reside in Alabama. I need this information to complete my files." In light of the public statements by numerous Alabama officials of their intention to uphold a segregated way of life and the announced opposition to any implementation of the school desegregation decision, the state's expression of interest in the local officers and employees of the Association was not received as a friendly gesture. The association never answered this last letter.

It cannot be said at precisely what point in 1956 Wilkins and the organization's other officers became concerned about their corporate legal status in Alabama, but the letters from Montgomery left little doubt as to what was in Patterson's mind. Like most states, Alabama requires every corporation organized under the laws of another state to file with the secretary of state a certified copy of its articles of incorporation and a designation of an authorized agent and a place of business within the state "before engaging in or transacting any business." As a New York nonprofit membership corporation, the Association had assumed that it was not engaging in or transacting any "business" in the state, within the meaning of the statute. Even if this provision *were* applicable to it, the Association was later to argue, the Association is specifically exempt from such requirement since the law states it does not apply "to corporations engaging in or transacting business of interstate commerce only within the state." The Association's position was that it did no purely "intrastate" business in Alabama; all its activities were "interstate" in character. Consequently, the Association had never filed these documents. The fact that the state's enforcement authorities had not proceeded against the Association for the thirty-eight years it had operated in Alabama might indicate that the state did not construe the registration statute as being applicable to the Association; or it might suggest lax enforcement.

By the end of May, 1956, strictly applicable or not, the Association began preparing the registration papers required by the statute. However, toward the end of May the Attorney General took action by filing an equity suit in the state Circuit Court in Montgomery County. This step sought to enjoin the Association from conducting any further business or activities within the state, to dissolve all existing branches, and, upon final hearing, to oust it from the state for not having qualified as a foreign corporation before doing business in the state. The state's complaint set forth the facts of the Association's organization and membership in Alabama, referred to the solicitation and collection of dues and contributions, related the activities of the Association in connection with the efforts of Autherine Lucy to enroll at the State University and with the Montgomery bus boycott, recited the failure to comply with the Alabama foreign corporation registration provisions, and concluded that the Association was, in the language of the law, "thereby causing irreparable injury to the property and civil rights of the citizens of Alabama for which criminal prosecution and civil action at law afford no adequate relief."

When the complaint was filed, the Circuit Court, at the Attorney General's request, issued a temporary restraining order and injunction. This order restrained the Association, its employees, and its members from conducting any further business of any kind within the state, from maintaining any offices, and from soliciting members or contributions and collecting dues or contributions. Although Patterson did not request it, the court added a paragraph restraining the Association from filing "any application, paper, or document for the purpose of qualifying to do business" within the state.

Although these papers had been filed and the injunction procured during May, they were all dated June 1, 1956. Since they had been issued by the court in Montgomery without notice or opportunity for a hearing, the Association first had knowledge of the state's action when the papers were served on Mrs. Hurley in her Birmingham apartment. That same day papers were also served on W. C. Patton in the Birmingham branch office; on Rev. J. D. Hunter, president of the Selma branch; and on Robert L. Matthews, president of the Montgomery branch. Copies were also mailed to the national headquarters in New York.

### The Protagonists Meet

After reading the documents Mrs. Hurley telephoned her secretary and W. C. Patton and told them to close the two Birmingham offices. She then placed an urgent phone call to Roy Wilkins in New York, explaining the developments to him. Concerned that her mere presence would be construed as doing business in violation of the injunction order, Mrs. Hurley never returned to her office and left Alabama a few days later. Wilkins immediately called the Association's General Counsel, Robert L. Carter.

### Counsel for the Defendant

Carter was the man who would carry the major responsibility for the defense. He was educated at Lincoln University, with law degrees from Howard and Columbia. He had joined the Association's legal staff after World War II and was assistant to Thurgood Marshall when Marshall was chief counsel of the Association's Legal Defense and Educational Fund. Carter had played an important role in many Supreme Court cases dealing with segregation and had only recently been appointed General Counsel in charge of the Association's own legal office. The Legal Defense Fund was set up in 1939. Later it was made a separate corporation. By 1962 it was operating on an annual budget of about $750,000 with a permanent staff of eight attorneys (and many others throughout the country who cooperate regularly with it). It handles civil rights litigation that seeks to establish racial equality before the law on a broad national scale. On the other hand, the Association's legal staff, under Carter, works on litigation more intimately related to the organization and its membership. As an organization operated for "educational purposes," contributions to the Legal Defense Fund are tax deductible, but none of its activities may be devoted to "carrying on propaganda, or otherwise attempting to influence legislation." In contrast, the Association regularly engages in legislative and political activities. Its donors, therefore, do not enjoy this tax advantage.

Working with Carter in preparing the Association's case were two local attorneys in Alabama, Fred Gray of Montgomery and Arthur Shores of Birmingham. An ordained minister and a 1954 graduate of Western Reserve Law School, Fred Gray was just cutting his legal teeth on the bus boycott when the action began. He had assisted Carter in bringing the suit in *Browder* v. *Gayle* to abolish segregation on the Alabama public conveyances and defended dozens of Negroes arrested for participating in the boycott. (After suitable encouragement from state officials, one of his clients announced that Gray was not authorized to represent her, but, as the state was preparing to disbar Gray for barratry, he produced a written authorization that he had had the foresight to have the woman sign when he first agreed to represent her.) Gray's location enabled him to play a key role in handling the motions and appearances in the state and Federal courts of Montgomery. Shores, the oldest of the three, had been practicing in Birmingham for over twenty-five years and had gained broad experience in working with the Association's staff on a wide range of litigation. All three were to work on the briefs and other papers in the case. Carter was to present most of the argument in court.

### Hearing in the Circuit Court

The Association's first response was to file, on July 2, 1956, a demurrer to the complaint (which states, in effect, that even if everything the state said is true, there is still no legal basis for such an action) and also to file a motion to dissolve the restraining order. This motion urged, first, that the organization was not subject by virtue of its activities to the qualification requirements of the statute, and, second, that what the state sought to accomplish by the action would violate the Association's rights to freedom of speech and assembly under the Federal Constitution. The court set July 17, 1956, as the date for hearing on this motion.

Three days later the state moved the court to require the Association to produce a vast quantity of books, documents, and papers on the grounds that an examination of these was essential to its preparation for trial. The materials sought included copies of all charters of branches in the state; names, addresses, and dues of members, contributors, officers, and employees of the Association and its branches; all files, letters, and other correspondence within the preceding twelve months pertaining to or between the Association and any person, corporation, and association in the state; plus all deeds, bills of sale, canceled checks, bank statements, payrolls, and contracts. In short, a record of everybody and everything connected with the Association in Alabama during the previous year. The court set hearing on this motion for July 9, 1956, which was prior to the date for the hearing on the Association's motion to dissolve the injunction.

The morning of July 9, 1956, was the first opportunity for a full court hearing on any part of the state's action. All parties were present in the Montgomery Circuit Court for the scheduled hearing on the motion to produce. The old Montgomery County Courthouse had recently been torn down, and while a new one was under construction, hearings were held in the Knights of Pythias building. As if to emphasize the importance he attached to the action, John Patterson personally handled the presentation of the state's argument on the motion. Working with him, and present in the court that day, were two of his Assistant Attorneys General, MacDonald Gallion and Edmon L. Rinehart—both of whom would play leading roles as the case later developed.

Presiding over the court on July 9, 1956, was the Honorable Walter B. Jones, Senior Circuit Judge and Presiding Judge of the 15th Judicial Circuit of Alabama. He had issued the original temporary restraining order and injunction and was to occupy the bench on every occasion that any aspect of the case was to be heard in that court. Sixty-seven-year-old Judge Jones, a huge man—over six feet, four inches tall—bald except for a grey fringe above the ears, is a member of one of the most distinguished families in

Alabama. His father was the bearer of General Lee's flag of truce to General Grant at that historic scene at Appomattox Courthouse in 1865 and, later, was twice governor of Alabama and a U.S. District Judge. Judge Jones is a life-long resident of Montgomery. His entire life has been steeped in the history and traditions of the south. He was first elected to the Circuit Court in 1920 and has served continuously ever since. He founded the Jones Law School in 1928 and has been its president since that time. He is president of the Alabama Bible Society; president of the local law library, the public library, and the Museum of Fine Arts; president of the County Board of Jury Supervisors; past president of the Alabama Circuit Judges Association and the Alabama State Bar; a member of the National Society of Arts and Letters; senior warden of a Montgomery Episcopal church; and a member of innumerable historical societies, social clubs, and service organizations. He was presiding judge in the Phenix City crime and vice clean-up trials, and received one electoral vote for President of the United States in 1956. A prolific writer, he is the author of fifteen books. He founded the *Alabama Lawyer* in 1940 (official organ of the State Bar) and is the editor of its twenty-two volumes.

Judge Jones is also one of the south's best-known segregationists and has, since 1924, written a weekly column in the *Montgomery Advertiser* entitled "Off The Bench." One of his more famous columns in this series is "I Speak for the White Race," in which he extols the glories and accomplishments of the white race in over a dozen fields, including literature, painting, science, philosophy, and medicine. After comparing these accomplishments with the absence of achievement by the Negro race, he concludes, "We shall never submit to the demands of the integrationists. The white race shall remain forever white." On another occasion, in a speech before the Baptist Laymen of Alabama, Judge Jones declared that segregation did not conflict with the teachings of Christ, decried the "Communist-Dominated NAACP," attacked the Fund for the Republic for its $50,000 gift to the Legal Defense Fund, deplored the Supreme Court's inattention to legal precedent, and cited the Bible, "natural law," and "moral law" as "proof for segregation."

It can safely be said that the presence of Judge Jones on the bench in July, 1956, created no optimism in the minds of the Association's lawyers.

As the hearing opened, Arthur Shores rose and presented Robert Carter to the court as "associate counsel of New York City." The argument then began as Attorney General Patterson, in support of the state's motion to produce, contended that the Association could be compelled to produce the requested papers and documents because they were within the latter's exclusive knowledge and were needed for evidence in a public cause. Carter replied that the motion to produce was premature and that his demurrer to the complaint should be ruled on first. The basis of the whole action should be considered, he argued, before the court determined the necessity of producing a mass of documents that might conceivably never be used if a court should determine that the underlying action was invalid. Judge Jones ruled that Carter's point was "not well taken." Carter then argued that the motion to produce was in furtherance of a penalty or forfeiture against the Association—the ouster for failure to register—and should be dismissed on that ground. This argument was found equally unacceptable, and Judge Jones ordered the production of substantially all the documents requested by the state. In his decree issued two days after the hearing, the Judge supported this broad order by recalling "the inherent power of a Court of Equity to compel the production of books and documents when it is shown that such production is indispensable to the doing of justice as auxiliary to any proper relief." The decree required production by July 24, 1956, and the hearing on the Association's motion to dissolve the injunction was postponed until July 25, 1956—once again, *after* the court could be certain whether or not the Association would comply with the production order.

The alternatives now available to Carter and the Association were legally quite simple. They could produce the documents required by the decree, including the names and addresses of Alabama members, officers, and employees, or they could disregard all or part of the decree and run the risk of being held in contempt of court. With considerable effort they could gather and produce the books, papers, and documents ordered by the court. But they were unwilling to furnish the material called for in two paragraphs of the order:

2. All lists, documents, books and papers showing the names, addresses and dues paid by all present members in the State of Alabama. . . .

11. All lists, books and papers showing the names and addresses of all officers, agents, servants and employees in the State of Alabama. . . .

The Association feared that the production of this information, frequently referred to in the case as the "membership lists," would inevitably lead to serious economic pressure, loss of employment, harassment, and threatened or actual violence for its members.

### Climate of Alabama

The atmosphere of hostility to anyone who favored desegregation was encouraged by the state's highest officials, who, in turn, set the pattern for local political figures, civic leaders, and parents. The governor, legislators, and even judges issued public declarations that the Supreme Court's decisions must be resisted and segregation strengthened. "Abolition of segregation will never be feasible in Alabama," declared one state senator, and "Desegregation would not be possible within 100 years," said another. The legislature was called on to pass "every law to insure that segregation will remain in our schools." It responded with a resolution of "nullification" of certain Supreme Court decisions, pupil-placement laws, legislation to dissolve the entire state educational system, and a vast number of other laws and resolutions. Proposals were made to dissolve the county governments and to substitute a convention system for the state legislature in order to ensure the exclusion of Negroes from the state's political apparatus.

Organizations devoted to the maintenance of segregation developed outside the formal political structure—but often with close contacts to the political leaders. The Citizens Councils had experienced a huge growth by mid-1956, and rallies were being held throughout the state. Other groups were also formed, such as the Southerners in Alabama, and the American States' Rights Association in Birmingham. Many persons were not content with making speeches and distributing literature, and the Ku Klux Klan and other direct-action groups began to flourish. Burning crosses and other types of threats became a frequent occurrence. Bands of extra-legal night-riders and volunteer horse patrols were formed to intimidate those who sought to implement desegregation.

The NAACP was a frequent target of invective and special legislation. State Senator Englehardt told a Citizens Council rally in Macon County: "The National Association for the Agitation of Colored People forgets there are more ways than one to kill a snake. We will have segregation in the public schools of Macon County or there will be no schools." Circuit Court Judge Brady told a similar gathering in Dallas County: "The NAACP is a willing and ready tool in the hands of Communist Front organizations." What the south needs, he said, "is an organization as a slingshot to hit between the eyes of that giant monster NAACP."

Two local county laws authorized the Boards of Education to discharge school teachers belonging to organizations advocating racial integration. Another local law required any organization soliciting membership in the county to pay a $100 licensing fee, plus $5 for every member who enrolls. The act's sponsor told the legislature, "Without such a proposal it would be very easy for the NAACP to slip into Wilcox County and teach the Negroes undesirable ideas."

Threatened and actual loss of employment and other forms of economic reprisal resulted for persons who advocated compliance with the law. In Selma, Alabama, twenty-nine members of the Association signed a petition requesting the Board of Education to consider desegregating the public schools of the city in accordance with the Supreme Court decision. Within a few days the chairman of the local Citizens Council announced that sixteen of the petitioners had been discharged from their jobs. "We intend to make it difficult, if not impossible," he said, "for any Negro who advocates desegregation to find or hold a job, get credit, or renew a mortgage. We'll force the troublemakers out."

Acts of violence were directed against the more persistent or courageous Negroes. One Birmingham Negro minister who sought to test the segregation laws was beaten, his church bombed twice, and his home destroyed. Students who participated in desegregation demonstrations were attacked and beaten and their families threatened. The terror of the Klan and other groups was directed not only against Negroes but also against whites who looked favorably upon desegregation.

The police did not always try to curb lawlessness and maintain order. Occasionally, they refused to respond to calls for assistance or even actively participated in the violence. It goes without saying that the most outspoken opponents of segregation were the frequent targets of arrest.

### A Plan of Action Develops

With this background Carter's choice of alternatives on the order to produce became quite clear. Refusal to furnish the membership lists would probably subject the Association to a contempt order, and the resulting ban from carrying on any activities in the state would paralyze the organization during a presumably lengthy appeal. To produce the lists would subject the 14,566 members to uncertain but probably unfavorable consequences; in the long run it would harm the organization greatly, since many of the members would resign, and few persons would join in the future. In a twentieth-century Hobson's choice, refusal prevailed over production.

From this premise, a strategy was developed based on the filing of only three documents before the deadline. The first of these was the answer to the complaint, which set forth the major defenses: the Association was exempt from the registration statute; production would violate Article I, Section 8 of the Federal Constitution as an unreasonable burden on interstate commerce; and production would violate the Association's due process and equal protection rights under the Fourteenth Amendment, which incorporate the Association's First Amendment rights of freedom of speech and assembly. Carter was careful to frame these answers in terms of the broadest possible Federal Constitutional rights in case an appeal to the Supreme Court should be necessary. His answer also attacked what the Association considered to be the real purpose behind the state's sudden concern with the registration of out-of-state corporations:

> It is clear from the complaint that to complainant [the State] the injury it conceives respondent [the Association] has committed is not its failure to register, but its activities to secure an end to segregation and discrimination against Negroes in compliance with the Constitution and laws of the United States. In short, complainant seeks to prohibit citizens in Alabama from pursuing the rights to which they are entitled in concert with the National Association for the Advancement of Colored People.

To support this charge, Fred Gray had laboriously reviewed the available records and had discovered no prior instance where Alabama had taken action against a foreign corporation. He searched the Alabama Appellate Court decisions and failed to uncover even one instance where the state had moved to enjoin the operation of a foreign corporation because of its failure to comply with the registration statute, or barred it from complying with this law after alleged violation. (Although other foreign corporations in the civil rights or civil liberties fields had performed activities in Alabama without registering under the domestication statutes and without state interference, the NAACP lawyers were unwilling to name them, for this would not directly help their case and it might cause the state to retaliate against these other organizations.)

As a second part of this strategy, Carter filed an executed set of forms required by the registration statute, and offered to qualify if the prohibition against attempting to register were stricken from the temporary restraining order. Finally, the Association filed a motion to set aside the order to produce records, for which hearing was also set for July 25, 1956. Carter had little hope that Judge Jones would grant such a motion, but he wanted to be sure he had availed himself of every procedural move in the lower court. Recognizing the combination of forces working against him, he did not wish to be told by an Alabama Appellate Court that he had waived his right of appeal by failure to assert his motions in the Circuit Court.

### Another Round in the Trial Court

When the same cast met once again in the Circuit Court, on July 25, 1956, the only change in role was that the Association was now in violation of the order to produce records. The motion to set aside that order was heard first; in support of the motion Carter and Shores argued that the Association had now filed a full and complete answer, that the information called for by the state was already known to the Attorney General, and that the books and papers were now not material or necessary to a trial and determination of the issue raised in the suit.

In presenting testimony to support his motion, Carter called Attorney General Patterson as his witness. Reading each paragraph of the production order, he asked Patterson to explain the need for the documents it requested. On each paragraph the Attorney General's answer was basically the same: "You say that you are not doing any intrastate business; you are claiming that all your business is interstate; we say that your records are needed to show that you are doing intrastate business in Alabama." At one point the following exchange occurred:

> MR. CARTER: What purpose would the names and addresses of our members indicate to you—the names, mere names and addresses . . . ? How would our membership rolls show whether or not the Association is engaged in interstate or intrastate business?
>
> ATT. GEN. PATTERSON: I think the lists of members in the State of

Alabama will indicate that your corporation has been in the State of Alabama soliciting members and dues, and doing things in furtherance of your corporate purpose, which, as you know, is doing business in the State of Alabama.

MR. CARTER: How would a list of our members and their names and addresses prove that to you, Mr. Attorney General?

ATT. GEN. PATTERSON: Well a list of members is certainly an indication that you have gone out and have been soliciting members, wouldn't you think so?

MR. CARTER: I still want to find out specifically what the purposes of our membership list would be?

ATT. GEN. PATTERSON: I just told you what they were.

MR. CARTER: Now, as a matter of fact, Mr. Attorney General, isn't the real reason you want a list of the members . . . [so that] you may seek to embarrass these persons?

MR. GALLION: We object to that.

THE COURT: Sustain the objection, and tell him not to answer it. It is irrelevant, incompetent, immaterial, and illegal.

When Carter sought to show that revealing the names of the people soliciting membership for the Association would subject them to prosecution under the state laws, Assistant Attorney General Rinehart's objection that self-incrimination was irrelevant was sustained.

Carter then asked Patterson why, in his correspondence from February to May, 1956, he did not tell the Association that in his opinion they were illegally operating in Alabama, and the Attorney General replied that he presumed the NAACP had competent attorneys who knew the laws of the states where the organization operated.

When asked why the Association's offer to register and submit the necessary forms would not constitute sufficient compliance with the law, Patterson answered that ouster from the state was necessary to "punish" the NAACP for violating the law since 1918.

At another point, the dialogue took an unexpected turn:

MR. CARTER [reading from the order]: "All papers, books, letters, copies of letters, documents, agreements, correspondence, and other memoranda pertaining to or between the NAACP and the Montgomery Improvement Association." What is the purpose of that?

ATT. GEN. PATTERSON: The purpose of that is to show that the Montgomery Improvement Association is the same organization as the NAACP Branch Chapter.

MR. CARTER: Well, I think if you can show that, you would need all those things.

The outburst of laughter from the spectators brought a stern lecture from Judge Jones on the requisites of order, decorum, and dignity, and he threatened those who felt it necessary to laugh with a stay in the county jail.

Since Carter had from time to time referred to the effect of this lawsuit on the Association's civil rights, it was perhaps fitting that, in reply to Carter's final question, the Attorney General should give his conception of the civil rights involved in the action. Carter asked him to explain the "irreparable injury" to the people of Alabama of which the action complained. Patterson responded that the purpose of requiring a foreign corporation to register and designate an agent for service of legal process was to give the citizens of Alabama someone on whom they could serve their complaint should they have a cause of action in Alabama against that foreign corporation. "It is a very important civil right," Patterson concluded, for the failure to register "jeopardizes the public interest."

Each side then presented brief oral argument in summary and, after listening patiently, Judge Jones denied the motion to set aside the production order, stating that the grounds urged were "not well taken," since the documents and papers ordered were material to the trial of the case. At this point Judge Jones offered Carter additional time to produce the documents in question. Carter replied that additional time was unnecessary since he would not produce the documents called for, and he agreed that the Association was then guilty of "prima-facie contempt."

### Punishment for Contempt

The court then ruled the Association in contempt. Judge Jones put off all consideration of a hearing on the Association's earlier motion to dissolve the temporary restraining order, thus continuing his refusal to hear argument on the injunction or the underlying action.

The only matter now remaining before the Circuit Court was the question of punishment for contempt. Under the state's law, punishment for "criminal contempt" is limited to a $50 or $100 fine, but there is no limit on the amount of fine permissible for a "civil contempt." Criminal contempt, as the law dictionaries note, is "punitive in nature" and brought to "vindicate the dignity of the court and to punish for disobedience to its orders," while the civil variety is "remedial and coercive in nature" and brought to "compel obedience to orders and decrees." This rather slippery distinction provides substantial latitude for judicial discretion. In light of the variation in penal sums, it came as no surprise when Judge Jones announced that a civil contempt had been perpetrated in his court. But he then proceeded to define the penalty as "a punishment to vindicate the dignity and authority of the court"—the very definition of a criminal contempt.

When he got around to the monetary part of his decree, however, the judge's words were far clearer. For the contempt: a $10,000 fine, and if the Association should fully comply with the order to produce within the next five days, then it could move to have the fine reduced or set aside.

However, if it should fail to comply within such time, then the fine would be increased to $100,000.

The size of the fine was a distinct shock to the Association, for this was a lot of money to pay out of its annual budget. Refusing to accept a lower court decision in the hope that an undesirable holding can be overturned on appeal always involves a large element of risk. Since Carter felt he would receive little assistance in the Alabama Supreme Court, his only alternative would be the United States Supreme Court, assuming the case presented a sufficient Federal Constitutional issue for that Court even to consider the matter. Consequently, in an effort to stress the issue on which he thought he had the best chance of successful appellate review, Carter changed his strategy. The Association collected as much as possible of the materials called for in all paragraphs of the production order, except those dealing with the membership lists. Exact compliance with the extensive demands of the order was probably impossible, but the organization attempted to gather all that was realistically feasible.

### A Third Visit to Court

Five days later, on July 30, 1956, the deadline was at hand, and the adversaries in *Alabama* v. *NAACP* again appeared before the Circuit Court. Carter first moved to modify or vacate the contempt order, and then to stay the execution of the order pending appellate review. Both motions were denied. At this point Carter offered to file all the required documents, except the membership lists, and argued that this was substantial compliance with the production order. This was not accepted by the Court as full compliance with the order, so on the following day, July 31, 1956, Judge Jones decreed the Association to be in further contempt and increased the fine to $100,000.

The only recourse for Carter now was an appeal. Recognizing that it would appeal whatever final decree he issued, Judge Jones made certain that such appeal would be on the least favorable grounds for the Association. The state had procured the original temporary restraining order and injunction merely by requesting its issuance from Judge Jones, and the Association, as we have seen, had no opportunity to challenge this order before its issuance. This is the usual procedure with such orders, but owing to their one-sided nature they are normally reserved for extreme conditions where actions of the restrained party are causing present and irremediable harm to the other party—such as cutting down his trees. With such orders, however, the next legal step is for both parties to appear in court as soon as possible—usually within the next few days, but sometimes within hours. At this time the judge will hear both parties and decide whether a permanent injunction should be granted. By insulating the temporary restraining order and injunction from all legal attack during the hearings on the order to produce the membership lists, Judge Jones avoided a decree granting a permanent injunction. Without such a decree Carter could not appeal the restraining order, because appellate courts will not undertake to review a legal question that the lower court has not had an opportunity to pass on, even if the lower court, for that very reason, is doing everything in its power to keep from deciding the question. Thus the sole basis of appeal left open to Carter was the validity of the contempt order—and this had the unfavorable connotation of having been brought about by the Association's own deliberate refusal to comply with the order to produce.

Under Alabama law, a party in contempt of court is denied the right to proceed further with a trial of the basic action until it has purged itself of contempt (by performing the act for refusal of which it was originally held in contempt). As long as the contempt decree prevailed, therefore, the Association would never have an opportunity in the Alabama courts to challenge the restraining order or to litigate the underlying action. If for any reason the Supreme Court should be unable or unwilling to review the contempt decree, the Association was obviously in bad shape; it would either have to produce the lists or remain permanently barred from Alabama under the "temporary" restraining order.

### Views from the Higher Courts

Late in the afternoon of July 30, 1956, before Judge Jones had handed down his final contempt decree, Carter had rushed from the Circuit Court across Montgomery's broad Dexter Avenue to the Alabama Supreme Court. There he filed a motion to stay the execution of judgment and all further proceedings in the Circuit Court while an appeal was filed, and requested an immediate hearing by the State Supreme Court. The motion was supported by a three-page petition and forty-seven pages of exhibits. As the court was not in session, the clerk took the papers to the justices who were working in their chambers. Word was sent out by the chief justice that a hearing could not be granted on such a petition, for the state must also be notified and given an opportunity to present its views. Therefore, the Association was told that the following day was the proper time to bring the motion on for hearing.

#### Chief Judicial Officer

As the justices were departing for the day, Carter and the Association's lawyers spoke briefly with Chief Justice J. Edwin Livingston. An austere, imposing man, the state's highest judicial officer was a person unlikely to be sympathetic to the Association's position. In a speech before a group of students and businessmen he had once said, "I'm for segregation in every phase of life, and I don't care who knows it. . . . I would close every school from the highest to the lowest before I would go to school with colored people." The Association's lawyers pointed out to Chief Justice Livingston that Judge Jones' decree would become final the following day and, therefore, "the very purpose for which we are seeking relief is defeated if you give one-day notice." But the chief justice refused to stay the order without the other side being heard. The days of *ex parte* rulings in this case, it seems, were now over.

The following day, the contempt order now final, and the fine increased to $100,000, the Alabama Supreme Court heard argument on the motion to stay. The court denied Carter's motion, but it did so on grounds it was later to regret: "It is the established rule of this Court that the proper method of reviewing a judgment for civil contempt of the kind here involved is by a petition for common law writ of certiorari." Since Carter had not petitioned for certiorari, but had instead made a motion to stay execution of judgment, the court was telling him he had chosen the wrong procedural remedy.

A lengthy appeal process was now in view, and the Association took steps to comply with the temporary restraining order and injunction. The branches and members were notified that the Association was prohibited from engaging in any activities in the state. The Regional Office in Birmingham was moved to Atlanta, Georgia. Officers and employees of the Association stayed out of the state, except for the defense and appeal of this case, which meant that Carter and his staff were unable to participate in other litigation involving Negro rights in the state. Since the Association owned no real estate or buildings in Alabama and had only about $400 worth of office furnishings, there was little fear of an immediate levy by the state in an attempt to collect some of the fine. Under the circumstances, however, it is doubtful whether the state was really interested in execution of the judgment as long as the Association was prohibited from engaging in any activities.

*Two Petitions—No Review*

Following the instructions of the Alabama Supreme Court, Carter filed the petition for a writ of certiorari on August 8, 1956. This paper asks the appeal court to review the lower court's determination, and, unlike most appeals, granting review is discretionary with the appellate court. The petition argued that the Association had been denied its First and Fourteenth Amendment rights, and that the court below had regulated interstate activity in violation of Article I, Section 8, of the Constitution. The Supreme Court of Alabama denied the petition on August 13, 1956, with an order merely stating that "The averments of the petition for writ of certiorari in this cause are insufficient to warrant the issuance of the writ."

The petition was then revised by the Association's attorneys to add more detail and further citation of authority. On August 20, 1956, it was filed again in the Alabama Supreme Court. This time the court's response was not nearly so prompt, for its decision was not made known until December 6, 1956. Once again the State Supreme Court denied the petition, but its opinion was more explanatory this time. The certiorari remedy, the court explained, is available to review a contempt judgment, but such review is limited to very narrow questions of law—only those that affect the validity of the order of contempt:

> It is only where the court lacked jurisdiction of the proceeding, or where on the face of it the order disobeyed was void, or where the procedural requirements with respect to citation for contempt and the like were not observed, or where the fact of contempt is not sustained, that the order of judgment will be quashed.

In the court's view none of these legal deficiencies existed and therefore the contempt order was valid. Any other grievances that the Association felt it had suffered, including violations of basic Constitutional rights, could not be raised on certiorari. (It is worthy of note that even under this narrow scope of review, the Alabama Supreme Court agreed it had the authority to examine the question of whether "on the face of it the order disobeyed was void," but apparently decided that such examination did not include consideration of the Association's basic argument that the order to produce the membership lists was void as a violation of the First and Fourteenth Amendments.)

If Carter wished to have full appellate review, the court said, then he should have filed a petition for mandamus to review the order to produce records. He had chosen the wrong procedural remedy, and the correct course, the court explained, was no longer available. The opportunity to file mandamus existed only so long as the order to produce was in force, and this had been superceded since July 25, 1956, by the contempt order.

The Alabama Supreme Court had accomplished two things. By restricting the available review to narrow legal questions, and emphasizing the absence of any other means of appellate review within the state, the court's opinion upheld the contempt order and left the Association without legal recourse in the state courts. More important, however, its restriction of the review on certiorari merely to questions of state procedure had excluded from its treatment of the case all Federal Constitutional issues, and the U.S. Supreme Court has long refused to review a decision that is concerned only with state procedural matters.

Expressing the Association's growing feeling of despair, Carter summed up the Alabama Supreme Court's handling of the case with the comment,

> First they tell us a motion for stay of execution is improper, and we should have brought certiorari; then we are told the certiorari petition is insufficient; and finally they tell us that certiorari has been the wrong

remedy all along—we should have brought mandamus. I was beginning to feel like we were marching the soldiers up the hill, only to march them down again.

### To the Court of Last Resort

Soon after the Alabama Supreme Court issued its decree, the Association's attorneys began preparing their papers for appeal to the U.S. Supreme Court. On May 20, 1957, they filed a petition for certiorari with the clerk of the court.

Since the issuance of the writ is discretionary, Carter's task was to convince the High Court that valid reasons existed for allowance of the writ. He had two basic arguments. First, the judgment of the Alabama Supreme Court, while seemingly based on state procedural grounds, was nevertheless reviewable since the state had unfairly and improperly construed the scope of review available on certiorari in the Alabama courts. In presenting this argument Carter reviewed the previous Alabama cases that had extended certiorari review of contempt to include a determination of whether the petitioner had been exercising a lawful right in refusing to obey a court order. The leading Alabama case on certiorari to review a contempt finding is *Ex parte Dickens.* Here the State Supreme Court had said:

> Originally, on certiorari, only the question of jurisdiction was inquired into, but this limit has been removed, and now the court examines the law questions involved in the case which may affect its merits. . . . We think that certiorari is a better remedy than mandamus, because the office of a "mandamus" is to require the lower court or judge to act, and not to correct error or reverse judicial action . . . whereas, in a proceeding by certiorari, errors of law in the judicial action of the lower court may be inquired into and corrected.

Also, in the 1949 case of *Ex parte Morris,* the Alabama court had dealt with a case where the petitioner had been held in contempt for refusing to produce records of the Ku Klux Klan and had, on a petition for certiorari, passed upon the issues of denial of First Amendment rights in compelling production of membership lists, as well as on questions of privilege and self-incrimination. Carter's most telling point perhaps was that in its earlier denial of his motion for a stay of execution, the Alabama Supreme Court had refused it on the grounds that the proper method of review was by certiorari and, later, in his first petition for certiorari had denied it as "insufficient," not as the improper remedy.

Carter's second argument was that the action of the court below was an unconstitutional encroachment by the state upon the First Amendment rights of the Association and its members. His argument was that within the hostile circumstances existing in Alabama, production of the membership lists would be a serious interference with freedom of speech, freedom of assembly, freedom of association, and the right to seek to enforce the U.S. Supreme Court's own decision against state-enforced racial segregation.

One of the major obstacles to this argument was the 1927 U.S. Supreme Court case of *Bryant* v. *Zimmerman*. Here the High Court had sustained the power of the State of New York to require the Ku Klux Klan to produce a number of its records, including its membership lists. Carter's way around *Bryant* was to argue that a "secret oath-bound" organization such as the Klan "dedicated to unconstitutional purposes" and engaging in "illegal activities," may be required to give up its membership lists. But the Association, he emphasized, as the chief organization combating governmentally enforced racial discrimination using peaceful and legitimate means, is entitled to protection against such "proscription."

In the state's brief opposing the petition, Patterson argued that the judgment below properly disposed of the case on procedural grounds and left no Federal question to be reviewed by the U.S. Supreme Court. He asserted that in some instances Alabama's court had reviewed in full a contempt citation, but that was only because, within the special facts of those cases, there had been no opportunity to test the lower court's order by mandamus. On the Constitutional point, the state argued there was no abridgment of rights by production of the membership lists since they were necessary to the trial of the ouster action. The circumstances within the state, which the Association documented in its papers, were categorized as "various hearsay, opinions, and speculation" of which the Court could not take judicial notice. On this basis the Association rights were not infringed, particularly since the *Bryant* case had already upheld the state's power to compel disclosure.

Carter won this first round. The Supreme Court, on May 27, 1957, granted the petition. Now the parties set to work preparing the more detailed briefs in support of their petitions. Carter's brief expanded and developed the points set out in the certiorari petition and analyzed the constitutional law cases as they applied to his argument. Patterson, Gallion, and Rinehart did not substantially enlarge on the presentation developed in their earlier opposition briefs, apparently content with their initial statement of the law.

### Friends of the Court
The case had by now attracted wide attention and a great many other interest groups throughout the country became quite concerned about the outcome. Since the Supreme Court rules permit the filing of briefs and/or argument by interested parties, fourteen organized groups, most of them concerned primarily with religious and civil rights matters, combined as *amici curiae*—friends of the court—to file one such brief. Acting without prior consultation with either the State of Alabama or the NAACP, these fourteen groups were the American Jewish Congress, American Baptist Convention, Commission on Christian Social Progress, American Civil

Liberties Union, American Friends Service Committee, American Jewish Committee, American Veterans Committee, Anti-Defamation League of B'nai B'rith, Board of Home Missions of the Congregational and Christian Churches, Council for Christian Social Action of the United Church of Christ, Japanese-American Citizens League, Jewish Labor Committee, National Community Relations Advisory Council, United Synagogue of America, and Workers Defense League.

The brief of these *amici* developed the arguments that the Association's right to exist as an organization is a "liberty" within the meaning of the Fourteenth Amendment, and that the right to freedom of association necessarily includes the right to preserve, as against unreasonable demands by the state, the anonymity of those who associate. The Court rules require the consent of both parties to the filing of such a brief, or, if consent cannot be obtained, the *amici* may move the Court to accept the brief. Counsel for the Association naturally consented, but counsel for the state, not unnaturally, refused such consent, saying the brief contained "emotional and highly colored statements of opinion" and had "little relevant new material to offer." The *amici* then requested the Court on October 7, 1957, to accept the brief, urging that "since the measures taken against the NAACP here could be taken against any organization, the right of each of these organizations to exist, as well as that of the NAACP, is at stake." Three weeks later on October 28, 1957, the Court issued an order stating: "The motion for leave to file brief of American Jewish Congress *et al.,* as *amici curiae,* is denied."

As usual, the Court did not issue any reasons for this denial. Generally *amici* briefs are refused when the Court feels that they do not contribute very much by way of legal argument or citation of new authority. Here, the portion of the brief concerning the right of anonymity was the only major legal point not developed by the Association in its own brief. Regarding this as a valuable argument, the Association filed a supplementary brief (called a "reply brief"). The first three paragraphs of this document replied to a point raised in the state's brief, and the remaining ten pages were an almost verbatim copy of the anonymity argument that the *amici* had developed. This enabled the fourteen *amici,* in a roundabout way, to make their contribution to the case.

### Eighteen Eyes and Ears

Oral argument in the Supreme Court was scheduled for January 15, 1958. Late that afternoon Carter opened the case for the petitioner. His first appearance before the Court had been in 1950, when he had successfully argued *McLaurin* v. *Oklahoma State Regents* (a case involving the segregated treatment of a Negro graduate student at the University of Oklahoma). Carter had taken many cases to the High Court since that time.

He first developed his contention that Alabama had deliberately violated its procedural law in limiting the scope of certiorari review. The justices asked few questions on this topic, but when he launched into his constitutional argument, the questions from the bench became more probing. The Court, particularly Justices Black and Douglas, pressed Carter on how far he wished to carry his argument of freedom of speech and assembly. He emphasized that he was not arguing for absolute freedom from compulsory disclosure, but only that the combination of harm to the members, should their names be disclosed, plus the absence of a compelling need on the part of the state for the information sought, constituted improper interference with the rights of the Association and its members.

Carter told the Court that the Association felt the only purpose of the order to produce the membership lists and the other documents was the desire of the Alabama Courts and the Alabama Attorney General to put the Association in a position where it would either comply "and lose our right of freedom of association," or be held in contempt "and lose the right to test the order." In concluding he pointed out that the Association had made no public defiance of the Circuit Court order, and had refused to produce only the lists of its members. On the whole, Carter later recalled, he felt the Court had not given him too difficult a time in his argument.

It was then Edmon Rinehart's turn to present the case for the State of Alabama. A graduate of Princeton and Harvard Law School, Rinehart had served in World Was II in the same Army division as John Patterson, and they had become close friends. When Patterson became Attorney General in 1955, he asked Rinehart to give up his practice in New York and come to Alabama as an Assistant Attorney General; Rinehart agreed. He had thereafter worked closely with Patterson during the course of the action against the Association. On January 15, 1958, his thirty-eight birthday, Rinehart rose to argue his first case in the nation's highest Court.

It was then 4:20 P.M. and, since the Supreme Court adjourns at 4:30, Rinehart had only ten minutes to begin his argument. He led off his presentation by arguing that "This Court is without jurisdiction in the case, because it rests solely on Alabama laws." This brought him directly into the certiorari-mandamus problem, and the questions immediately started flying from the bench. Before he could develop his argument on the procedural question it was time for adjournment, but when the Court convened at noon the following day, Rinehart again took up this point. Justices Harlan and Whittaker questioned him on the scope of review in the Alabama Supreme Court. Justice Black, formerly an Alabama judge, pressed this point particularly, showing a personal familiarity with the applicable Alabama cases. It was apparent from the questioning that the Court entertained considerable doubt regarding the lower court's handling of the matter. Rinehart replied as best he could, but the questioning indicated a feeling that the state court had seemed unduly anxious not to consider the Federal questions.

Chief Justice Warren then asked, "Is there a penalty in Alabama for delinquency in filing corporate registration?" and Rinehart replied that there were two statutory penalties, one of $1,000 for failure to register, and another in the same amount for failure to appoint an agent for service of process and to designate the principal place of business. The Court seemed impressed that Alabama had provided fines for just such a situation, but did not feel it proper to invoke such penalties against the Association.

The justices asked why the state thought it needed the membership lists in determining whether or not there had been a violation of the registration statute. Justices Harlan and Frankfurter pressed Rinehart for an explanation of the relevancy and necessity of these lists, and his replies tried to support the state's compelling need for this particular information. At one point Justice Frankfurter observed that the Association had apparently received "a death sentence pro tem," even though its legal position might subsequently be upheld. Rinehart's retort was that the NAACP could and should have tested the order to produce by a mandamus petition.

Justice Brennan was especially concerned about the ouster, and asked "Has this ever been done in Alabama before?" The state's attorney replied that it had not, but he pointed out that "Alabama has never before had a case where a corporation has been so long delinquent."

The questioning up to this point had taken over fifty-five minutes, and with each side allotted only one hour, the Court gave Rinehart an extra ten minutes to develop his constitutional argument. Any interference with the Association and its members, he contended, consisted of no more than exposing the members to public criticism and possible economic and social pressure by private individuals. He added that the Fourteenth Amendment rights are not protected against individual as contrasted with state action.

On balance, Rinehart had received a more pressing examination from the justices, and, though not a wholly reliable guage of how the Court is likely to decide a case, the Association could take some comfort from this sign. When he first began developing his case, Carter felt very uncertain of eventual success, but by the time he was ready for oral argument he was much more hopeful. When the two days in Washington were finished, he felt quite confident.

### "An All-Out Fight Against the NAACP"

At the conclusion of the proceedings in Washington, the parties to a case normally bide their time and await the decision. Sometimes many months will pass before the result is announced. In this case, however, the representatives of the State of Alabama were not biding *their* time; 1958 was an election year, and with the governor prohibited by law from holding office for more than one consecutive term, the state was in line for a new chief executive. Attorney General Patterson was one of a number of Democrats who wanted the office, and since the Association had engaged so much of his time during the previous two years, he did not forget his number-one legal antagonist.

He kicked off his campaign for the gubernatorial nomination with a rousing statement: "I promise you that I will continue, as I have in the Attorney General's office, to wage an all-out fight against agitators like the NAACP." During the campaign, Patterson traveled about the state telling political rallies he "ran the NAACP out of Alabama," and repeatedly emphasized the maxim of Alabama politics that the man who wins is the one who most successfully attacks the common enemy.

One of the judiciary members up for re-election in 1958 was Judge Walter B. Jones. He announced in a televised campaign statement, "I intend to deal the NAACP, and its counterpart the Montgomery Improvement Association, a death blow from which they shall never recover." Since a judge would naturally think it ethically improper to make public statements or speeches on a case that has been, and may again be, before his court, Judge Jones did not specifically refer to *Alabama* v. *NAACP*. A group called the "Friends of Walter B. Jones" did this for him. One Montgomery attorney, in a speech on behalf of Judge Jones, recalled how the Judge:

> . . . with characteristic courage and fidelity to his oath and his conscience [imposed the fine on the Association] . . . and thereby incurred the wrath and perpetual hatred of the Communist tainted organization, which was formed by renegade white men for exploitation of the Negro, and which has destroyed the domestic tranquility of our country.
> . . . in the coming attempts to integrate the schools, public swimming pools, parks and amusement areas, these issues will be tried in the courts and these matters should be entrusted to a tested and experienced man such as Judge Jones.

Other lawyers in town made similar speeches endorsing the candidacy of Judge Jones.

Assistant Attorney General MacDonald Gallion was another Alabama figure with political ambitions, and he had taken a leave from office in order to conduct a campaign for the nomination for Attorney General. An Assistant Attorney General since 1945, he had run third in the 1954 campaign for Attorney General and later participated in the Phenix City clean-up. With a pleasant, easy manner, Gallion was soon to prove he was not just a political "also-ran." He, too, bore down hard on the NAACP in his speeches.

The voices of Alabama's political candidates calling for the destruction of the Association, and the legal steps that they had taken to achieve this goal, were only one phase of what had become, by early 1958, a wholesale attack on the Association throughout the entire south. Almost every southern state had embarked on a crusade either to harass or to annihilate the organization.

Following Alabama's lead, other states applied the corporation registration and taxation laws to strike at the Association. Texas enjoined the Association from operating for failure to pay proper franchise taxes and for soliciting and inciting civil rights litigation. Louisiana dusted off its twenty-two-year-old Ku Klux Klan Act (never previously applied against any group), and temporarily enjoined the Association from further operations in the state. The revenue commissioner of Georgia set out on a tax-evasion investigation and came up with a court order requiring production of the Association's business records. The organization's reluctance to cooperate led to a $25,000 fine and imprisonment of the president of the Atlanta Chapter.

Another technique used by many states was a legislative investigation of the Association and its members, ostensibly in a search for the "Communists" who were inspiring desegregation. Florida and Virginia were especially persistent in their attempts to reveal the sinister role allegedly played by the Association in the Communist conspiracy.

Statutes were passed in Arkansas, Tennessee, Texas, and Virginia purporting to regulate lobbying, and requiring individuals or organizations soliciting contributions for racial legislation or litigation to register specific information—such as the names of all contributors—with the state.

At least five states (Georgia, Mississippi, South Carolina, Tennessee, and Virginia) directed their efforts at the Association's legal staff and passed a group of litigation statutes redefining the common-law offenses of barratry, champerty, and maintenance to apply to the efforts of the Association to encourage and aid Negroes to secure their constitutional rights by legal action.

Other efforts were made to hinder the Association by penalizing its members—particularly public school teachers. After a Louisiana court had enjoined the organization from pursuing any activities in the state, the legislature enacted statutes providing for dismissal of school employees who are members of, or contributors to, any group that is "by law or injunction prohibited from operating in the state." Mississippi required all teachers to file a list of the organizations of which they were members during the preceeding five years, and South Carolina prohibited any member of the Association from holding a state or local governmental job.

The Association tested many of these statutes in the state courts and appealed the unfavorable court orders. The state courts rarely failed to support the legislation, but in the Federal courts the Association succeeded, after much delay and expense, in overturning most of the south's anti-NAACP laws.

In no state, however, was the attack on the Association more sustained, more carefully planned, or more successful than in Alabama.

*The "Second Contempt Action" Begins*

Soon after the Alabama political campaign began, the state showed once again that it had other things in store for the Association. An unincorporated organization known as the Alabama State Coordinating Association for Registration and Voting, had been organized in the state during 1952 to conduct community clinics on voter registration. Since its creation, the ASCARV had operated solely in Alabama and, as there were no membership fees or dues, had relied for financial support on contributions at public meetings. In addition to his work as field secretary for the Association, W. C. Patton had been president of the ASCARV since its founding. After the 1956 injunction Patton had not worked for the NAACP in Alabama, but had continued in his position with the ASCARV.

On April 9, 1958, at the height of his campaign for the gubernatorial nomination, Patterson took off sufficient time to enter the Circuit Court and request Judge Jones to issue an order to show cause why the Association should not be adjudged guilty of contempt of court for failure to obey the temporary restraining order and injunction. Enumerating the activities that violated the restraining order, Patterson alleged that the Association and Patton had "gained and exercised control over" the ASCARV in order to evade the restraining order; that the activities of the ASCARV are "in fact and in reality" the activities of the Association since the voter registration group is "a mere device and subterfuge to cover and hide the operations and business activities" of the Association in Alabama; and that through the ASCARV the Association had "engaged in corresponding with individuals in Alabama, distributing circulars, soliciting memberships, holding meetings, circulating propaganda and carrying on other business activities in furtherance of its program." The state also served subpoenas on the NAACP and the ASCARV, requiring each organization to produce all books, records, and correspondence relating to the other group for the period beginning with the Association's ouster in 1956.

The Association's reaction to this second contempt action was to state not only that the allegations were false but that the action was but one more part of the state's design to prevent the Association from carrying on its activities in Alabama. General Counsel Carter, Executive Secretary Roy Wilkins, and Director of Branches Gloster Current all emphasized in subsequent discussions about this action that the Association made a genuine and substantial effort to avoid carrying on any activities in Alabama, indirectly as well as directly. The Association, in Wilkin's words, "ceased operations completely." "Since Alabama's front door is barred," Wilkins said, "we will not sneak through the back. We're just not that kind of organization." The Association could also hope that ultimately the legal roadblocks might be cleared away if it kept its hands clean and obeyed "the law"—even what it regarded as injustice masquerading as law—but if it were caught actually attempting to circumvent the restraining order, it would have greater difficulty seeking fairness and equity in the courts. This is, no doubt, one of the considerations that has prevented the Association from following the advice, occasionally received as the legal obstacles have become ever more interminable, that it should test the restraining order and injunction by deliberately violating it and appealing the citation for contempt.

The Association's reply to the show-cause order did not treat the factual allegations, but argued that the court lacked jurisdiction since the matter was then pending in the Supreme Court.

### Neither Bias Nor Prejudice

During the last week of June, 1958, after Patterson, Gallion, and Judge Jones had won their respective nominations, hearings were held on the second contempt action. Hardly had Judge Jones opened the proceedings when Carter moved to have the presiding judge disqualify himself because of prejudice and bias. Carter introduced evidence of the speeches made by, or on behalf of, Judge Jones. Then Fred Gray and Rev. Solomon Seay, head of the Montgomery Improvement Association, testified to having heard the judge state that he would deal a death blow to the NAACP. After Patterson's sharp and caustic cross-examination failed to shake the testimony of Gray and Seay, Carter asked Judge Jones to take the witness stand. Refusing to do this, he did agree to "testify from the bench under my oath as Circuit Judge."

Carter first referred to Judge Jones' speech before the Baptist Laymen of Alabama and the political speeches by others on behalf of the Judge, and asked if he believed the Association to be Communist-dominated. "That is my belief," Judge Jones answered. Patterson was on his feet immediately, obviously concerned that things might be getting a little out of hand. On the Attorney General's motion, Judge Jones ordered Carter's question and his own answer struck from the record, saying, "I don't think that has any particular material bearing right here at this time and I grant your motion."

The Association's General Counsel then attempted to elicit the Judge's beliefs and attitudes regarding other statements made in various speeches, but Judge Jones declined to answer, usually with the statement, "I don't think it has any particular relevancy to this particular issue here." Finally Carter asked Judge Jones if he had said in the campaign that he would deal the NAACP a death blow from which it would never recover. "That is sub-stantially correct," the Judge replied. He explained that during the campaign he had come to the conclusion that the NAACP was fighting his candidacy, and he was simply saying to the people that if they renominated him, it would be a "blow to any organization that attempts to further its own interests by having judges elected who might be subservient to its will."

After a fifteen-minute recess, Judge Jones returned to the bench and denied the motion to disqualify himself, since the Association's contentions were "inadequate" to justify such a disqualification. Wishing to recite one or two instances of his "good will for the Negro race," Judge Jones told of his efforts to have a library built for Negroes and to secure for them the advantages of a bookmobile. He then explained:

> I do not know nor am I conscious of anything said or done by me which in law disqualifies me. . . . I stand legally indifferent between the parties and have neither bias for the State nor prejudice against the Respondent [NAACP]. In my judgment I can impartially hear and determine the issues now before the Court.

Carter then asked Judge Jones to postpone the hearings until he could appeal to the State Supreme Court on the issue of the judge's fitness to preside over the case. The judge ruled that the question of his fitness should be raised on appeal of the entire case and refused a postponement.

This completed the Association's attempts to remove Judge Jones, and the court then considered the matter of the Association's relationship with the ASCARV. Carter testified that the Association's files did not contain any books, records, or correspondence of any kind relating to the ASCARV during the past two years. The Association has "scrupulously obeyed" the injunction, he stated. Carter urged the Attorney General to offer some proof of the existence of the records he sought, instead of a "fishing expedition" and "mere allegations that some organization is our alter ego."

W. C. Patton then testified as head of the voter-registration group. The subpoena allegedly served on his organization had actually been left with a visitor in his office, he explained, and therefore the ASCARV was under no legal obligation to bring anything along to court.

Patterson was by now obviously annoyed; he requested, and received, a one-week continuance to permit proper service on Patton. Judge Jones thus scheduled the hearing on a day Carter was to be in Washington, D.C., and refused to permit another hearing date. When Carter sought to have a different date set, he and Judge Jones engaged in heated argument, cut short only when the Judge stopped all discussion with his statement, "That's an Order of the Court." Carter was furious that the Attorney General had requested a delay until a time when he could not be present, and the often acrimonious hearing ended when Carter shouted, "You have no right to choose the attorney for the Respondent in this case, Mr. Patterson."

But the "second contempt" hearings did not reach a final adjudication, in part because, more than five months after oral argument, the Supreme Court in Washington made known its decision.

### "Free Enjoyment of the Right To Associate"
When the Supreme Court convened on June 30, 1958, the last day of the term, its unanimous opinion in *NAACP* v. *Alabama* was announced by

John M. Harlan, a justice with particular skill at writing technical opinions in procedural cases.

---

## NATIONAL ASSOCIATION FOR THE ADVANCEMENT OF COLORED PEOPLE v. ALABAMA
### 357 U.S. 449 78 S. Ct. 1163, 2 L. Ed. 2d 1488 (1958)

MR. JUSTICE HARLAN delivered the opinion of the Court.

We review from the standpoint of its validity under the Federal Constitution a judgment of civil contempt entered against petitioner, the National Association for the Advancement of Colored People, in the courts of Alabama. The question presented is whether Alabama, consistently with the Due Process Clause of the Fourteenth Amendment, can compel petitioner to reveal to the State's Attorney General the names and addresses of all its Alabama members and agents, without regard to their positions or functions in the Association. . . .

### I.

We address ourselves first to respondent's contention that we lack jurisdiction because the denial of certiorari by the Supreme Court of Alabama rests on an independent non-federal ground, namely, that petitioner in applying for certiorari had pursued the wrong appellate remedy under state law. Respondent recognizes that our jurisdiction is not defeated if the nonfederal ground relied on by the state court is "without any fair or substantial support," *Ward* v. *Love County*. It thus becomes our duty to ascertain, ". . . in order that constitutional guarantees may appropriately be enforced, whether the asserted non-federal ground independently and adequately supports the judgment." *Abie State Bank* v. *Bryan*. The Alabama Supreme Court held

that it could not consider the constitutional issues underlying the contempt judgment which related to the power of the State to order production of membership lists because review by certiorari was limited to instances ". . . where the court lacked jurisdiction of the proceeding, or where on the face of it the order disobeyed was void, or where procedural requirements with respect to citation for contempt and the like were not observed, or where the fact of contempt is not sustained. . . ." The proper means for petitioner to obtain review of the judgment in light of its constitutional claims, said the court, was by way of mandamus to quash the discovery order prior to the contempt adjudication. Because of petitioner's failure to pursue this remedy, its challenge to the contempt order was restricted to the above grounds. Apparently not deeming the constitutional objections to draw into question whether "on the face of it the order disobeyed was void," the court found no infirmity in the contempt judgment under this limited scope of review. At the same time it did go on to consider petitioner's constitutional challenge to the order to produce membership lists but found it untenable since membership lists were not privileged against disclosure pursuant to reasonable state demands and since the privilege against self-incrimination was not available to corporations.

We are unable to reconcile the procedural holding of the Alabama

Supreme Court in the present case with its past unambiguous holdings as to the scope of review available upon a writ of certiorari addressed to a contempt judgment. . . .

For example, in *Ex parte Morris*, decided as late as 1949, the petitioner had been held in contempt for his refusal to obey a court order to produce names of members of the Ku Klux Klan. On writ of certiorari, constitutional grounds were urged in part for reversal of the contempt conviction. In denying the writ of certiorari, the Supreme Court concluded that petitioner had been accorded due process, and in explaining its denial the court considered and rejected various constitutional claims relating to the validity of the order. There was no intimation that the petitioner had selected an inappropriate form of appellate review to obtain consideration of all questions of law raised by a contempt judgment.

The Alabama cases do indicate, as was said in the opinion below, that an order requiring production of evidence ". . . *may* be reviewed on petition for mandamus." But we can discover nothing in the prior state cases which suggests that mandamus is the *exclusive* remedy for reviewing court orders after disobedience of them has led to contempt judgments. Nor, so far as we can find, do any of these prior decisions indicate that the validity of such orders can be drawn in question by way of certiorari only in instances where a defendant had no opportunity to apply for mandamus. Although the opinion below suggests no such distinction, the State now argues that this was in fact the situation in all of the earlier certiorari cases, because there the contempt adjudications, unlike here, had followed almost immediately the disobedience to the court orders. Even if that is indeed the rationale of the Alabama Supreme Court's present decision, such a local procedural rule

. . . cannot avail the State here, because petitioner could not fairly be deemed to have been appraised of its existence. Novelty in procedural requirements cannot be permitted to thwart review in this Court applied for by those who, in justified reliance upon prior decisions, seek vindication in state courts of their federal constitutional rights.

That there was justified reliance here is further indicated by what the Alabama Supreme Court said in disposing of petitioner's motion for a stay of the first contempt judgment in this case. . . . In denying the motion, the Supreme Court stated:

"It is the established rule of this Court that the proper method of reviewing a judgment for civil contempt of the kind here involved is by a petition for common law writ of certiorari." . . .

We hold that this Court has jurisdiction to entertain petitioner's federal claims. . . .

### III.

We thus reach petitioner's claim that the production order in the state litigation trespasses upon fundamental freedoms protected by the Due Process Clause of the Fourteenth Amendment. Petitioner argues that in view of the facts and circumstances shown in the record, the effect of compelled disclosure of the membership lists will be to abridge the rights of its rank-and-file members to engage in lawful association in support of their common beliefs. It contends that governmental action which, although not directly suppressing association, nevertheless carries this consequence, can be justified only upon some overriding valid interest of the State.

Effective advocacy of both public and private points of view, particularly controversial ones, is undeniably enhanced by group association, as this Court has more than once recognized by remarking upon the close nexus between the freedoms of speech and assembly. *De Jonge* v. *Oregon; Thomas* v. *Collins.* It is beyond debate that freedom to engage in association for the advancement of beliefs and ideas is an inseparable aspect of the "liberty" assured by the Due Process Clause of the Fourteenth Amendment, which embraces freedom of speech. See *Gitlow* v. *New York; Palko* v. *Connecticut; Cantwell* v: *Connecticut; Staub* v. *Baxley.* Of course, it is immaterial whether the beliefs sought to be advanced by association pertain to political, economic, religious or cultural matters, and state action which may have the effect of curtailing the freedom to associate is subject to the closest scrutiny.

The fact that Alabama, so far as is relevant to the validity of the contempt judgment presently under review, has taken no direct action . . . to restrict the right of petitioner's members to associate freely, does not end inquiry into the effect of the production order. See *American Communications Asso.* v. *Douds.* . . . In the domain of these indispensable liberties, whether of speech, press, or association, the decisions of this Court recognize that abridgement of such rights, even though unintended, may inevitably follow from varied forms of governmental action. Thus in Douds, the Court stressed that the legislation there challenged, which on its face sought to regulate labor unions and to secure stability in interstate commerce, would have the practical effect "of discouraging" the exercise of constitutionally protected political rights . . . and it upheld the statute only after concluding that the reasons advanced for its enactment were constitutionally sufficient to justify its possible deterrent effect upon such freedoms. Similar recognition of possible unconstitutional intimidation of the free exercise of the right to advocate underlay this Court's narrow construction of the

authority of a congressional committee investigating lobbying and of an Act regulating lobbying, although in neither case was there an effort to suppress speech. *United States* v. *Rumely; United States* v. *Harriss.* The governmental action challenged may appear to be totally unrelated to protected liberties. Statutes imposing taxes upon rather than prohibiting particular activity have been struck down when perceived to have the consequence of unduly curtailing the liberty of freedom of press assured under the Fourteenth Amendment. *Grosjean* v. *American Press Co.; Murdock* v. *Pennsylvania.*

It is hardly a novel perception that compelled disclosure of affiliation with groups engaged in advocacy may constitute as effective a restraint on freedom of association as the forms of governmental action in the cases above were thought likely to produce upon the particular constitutional rights there involved. This Court has recognized the vital relationship between freedom to associate and privacy in one's associations. When referring to the varied forms of governmental action which might interfere with freedom of assembly, it said in *American Communications Asso.* v. *Douds:* "A requirement that adherents of particular religious faiths or political parties wear identifying arm-bands, for example, is obviously of this nature." Compelled disclosure of membership in an organization engaged in advocacy of particular beliefs is of the same order. Inviolability of privacy in group association may in many circumstances be indispensable to preservation of freedom of association, particularly where a group espouses dissident beliefs. Cf. *United States* v. *Rumely* (concurring opinion).

We think that the production order, in the respects here drawn in question, must be regarded as entailing the likelihood of a substantial restraint upon the exercise by petitioner's members of their right to freedom of association. Petitioner has made an uncontroverted showing that on past occasions revelation of the identity of its rank-and-file members has exposed these members to economic reprisal, loss of employment, threat of physical coercion, and other manifestations of public hostility. Under these circumstances, we think it apparent that compelled disclosure of petitioner's Alabama membership is likely to affect adversely the ability of petitioner and its members to pursue their collective effort to foster beliefs which they admittedly have the right to advocate, in that it may induce members to withdraw from the Association and dissuade others from joining it because of fear of exposure of their beliefs shown through their associations and of the consequences of this exposure.

It is not sufficient to answer, as the State does here, that whatever repressive effect compulsory disclosure of names of petitioner's members may have upon participation by Alabama citizens in petitioner's activities follows not from *state* action but from *private* community pressures. The crucial factor is the interplay of governmental and private action, for it is only after the initial exertion of state power represented by the production order that private action takes hold.

We turn to the final question whether Alabama has demonstrated an interest in obtaining the disclosures it seeks from petitioner which is sufficient to justify the deterrent effect which we have concluded these disclosures may well have on the free exercise by petitioner's members of their constitutionally protected right of association. See *American Communications Asso.* v. *Douds; Schneider* v. *Irvington.* Such a ". . . subordinating interest of the State must be compelling." *Sweezy* v. *New Hampshire* (concurring opinion). It is not of moment that the State has here acted solely

through its judicial branch, for whether legislative or judicial, it is still the application of state power which we are asked to scrutinize.

It is important to bear in mind that petitioner asserts no right to absolute immunity from state investigation, and no right to disregard Alabama's laws. As shown by its substantial compliance with the production order, petitioner does not deny Alabama's right to obtain from it such information as the State desires concerning the purposes of the Association and its activities within the State. Petitioner has not objected to divulging the identity of its members who are employed by or hold official positions with it. It has urged the rights solely of its ordinary rank-and-file members. This is therefore not analogous to a case involving the interest of a State in protecting its citizens in their dealings with paid solicitors or agents of foreign corporations by requiring identification. See *Cantwell* v. *Connecticut; Thomas* v. *Collins.*

Whether there was "justification" in this instance turns solely on the substantiality of Alabama's interest in obtaining the membership lists. During the course of a hearing before the Alabama Circuit Court on a motion of petitioner to set aside the production order, the State Attorney General presented at length, under examination by petitioner, the State's reason for requesting the membership lists. The exclusive purpose was to determine whether petitioner was conducting intrastate business in violation of the Alabama foreign corporation registration statute, and the membership lists were expected to help resolve this question. The issues in the litigation commenced by Alabama by its bill in equity were whether the character of petitioner and its activities in Alabama had been such as to make petitioner subject to the registration statute, and whether the extent of petitioner's activities without qualifying suggested its permanent ouster from the State. Without intimating the slightest view upon the merits of these issues, we are unable to perceive that the disclosure of the names of petitioner's rank-and-file members has a substantial bearing on either of them. As matters stand in the state court, petitioner (1) has admitted its presence and conduct of activities in Alabama since 1918; (2) has offered to comply in all respects with the state qualification statute, although preserving its contention that the statute does not apply to it; and (3) has apparently complied satisfactorily with the production order, except for the membership lists, by furnishing the Attorney General with varied business records, its charter and statement of purposes, the names of all of its directors and officers, and with the total number of its Alabama members and the amount of their dues. These last items would not on this record appear subject to constitutional challenge and have been furnished, but whatever interest the State may have in obtaining names of ordinary members has not been shown to be sufficient to overcome petitioner's constitutional objections to the production order.

From what has already been said, we think it apparent that *New York ex rel. Bryant* v. *Zimmerman* cannot be relied on in support of the State's position, for that case involved markedly different considerations in terms of the interest of the State in obtaining disclosure. There, this Court upheld as applied to a member of a local chapter of the Ku Klux Klan, a New York statute requiring any unincorporated association which demanded an oath as a condition to membership to file with state officials copies of its ". . . constitution, by-laws, rules, regulations and oath of membership, together with a roster of its membership and a list of its officers for the current year. . . ." In its opin-

ion, the Court took care to emphasize the nature of the organization which New York sought to regulate. The decision was based on the particular character of the Klan's activities, involving acts of unlawful intimidation and violence, which the Court assumed was before the state legislature when it enacted the statute, and of which the Court itself took judicial notice. Furthermore, the situation before us is significantly different from that in Bryant, because the organization there had made no effort to comply with any of the requirements of New York's statute but rather had refused to furnish the State with *any* information as to its local activities.

We hold that the immunity from state scrutiny of membership lists which the Association claims on behalf of its members is here so related to the right of the members to pursue their lawful private interests privately and to associate freely with others in so doing as to come within the protection of the Fourteenth Amendment. And we conclude that Alabama has fallen short of showing a controlling justification for the deterrent effect on the free enjoyment of the right to associate which disclosure of membership lists is likely to have. Accordingly, the judgment of civil contempt and the $100,000 fine which resulted from petitioner's refusal to comply with the production order in this respect must fall.

## IV.

Petitioner joins with its attack upon the production order a challenge to the constitutionality of the State's ex parte temporary restraining order preventing it from soliciting support in Alabama, and it asserts that the Fourteenth Amendment precludes such state action. But as noted above, petitioner has never received a hearing on the merits of the ouster suit, and we do not consider these questions properly here. The Supreme Court of Alabama noted in its denial of the petition for certiorari that such petition raised solely a question pertinent to the contempt adjudication. "The ultimate aim and purpose of the litigation is to determine the right of the state to enjoin petitioners from doing business in Alabama. That question, however, is not before us in this proceeding." The proper method for raising questions in the state appellate courts pertinent to the underlying suit for an injunction appears to be by appeal, after a hearing on the merits and final judgment by the lower state court. Only from the disposition of such an appeal can review be sought here.

For the reasons stated, the judgment of the Supreme Court of Alabama must be reversed and the case remanded for proceedings not inconsistent with this opinion.

*Reversed.*

---

### Citadel of Liberty or Servant of the NAACP?

Reaction to the Supreme Court decision was predictable. John Patterson was personally unavailable for comment but the Attorney General's office announced that it would "continue the fight to keep the NAACP from operating in Alabama," and noted that the ruling did not stop the state from proceeding with a new contempt action against the Association. Officials in other southern states roundly condemned the decision, with Louisiana's Senator Allen J. Ellender calling it "another heavy blow at the basic foundation of our government—the sovereign states." Louisiana State Senator W. M. Rainch warned that the court ruling "gives the green light to the Ku Klux Klan," and William Shaw, attorney for the Louisiana Joint Legislative Committee on Segregation, condemned "the subservience of the court to the NAACP."

The *Alabama Journal* in Montgomery, expressing the editorial opinion of most of the southern newspapers, decried the decision in these words:

> The relief given the organization in rescinding the fine is incidental. The approval given secret membership in such organizations as the NAACP is another of the dangerous precedents the High Court has been establishing since 1954.
>
> Underground organizations operating in secrecy have been a menace to American institutions for a long time. Whatever it may be, the Ku Klux Klan, the Clan-na-Gael, the Mafia, Al Capone's gangsters, the slimy and slinky communist cells, the NAACP, or anything else, they are not American.

For the opposite view, the New York *Times* editorialized:

> Again the United States Supreme Court has proved itself to be a towering citadel of American liberty. Monday's decision on freedom of association is one more case to prove the point.

A determined campaign of harassment by Alabama and other Southern states against the National Association for the Advancement of Colored People has been stopped in its tracks—though not yet overcome—by the Court's unanimous ruling.

The sentiment of those within the Association are expressed in a letter of thanks Robert Carter sent to Fred Gray on July 3, 1958:

I never thought that I would know how it feels to save $100,000. I don't know about you, but I'm afraid I feel as poor as ever. When you read the opinion, if you have not already done so, it will be gratifying to see how closely the Court structures its approach along the lines developed in our brief.

### The State Rests

The Supreme Court mandate was formally sent down to the Alabama Court on August 1, 1958, but that was as far as it was ever to go. Three months later the Alabama Supreme Court had done nothing, and the Association moved that the mandate be forwarded to the Circuit Court for the "further proceedings" which the High Court had required. This motion was renewed on November 19, 1958, and again on December 19, 1958, by mailing it to the Attorney General and filing with the Alabama Supreme Court copies of the original motion.

Also in mid-December of 1958, Attorney General Patterson (now Governor-Elect) filed in the State Supreme Court a "Brief and Argument to the Mandate of the U.S. Supreme Court." Here Patterson explored the various alternatives that he thought were open to the Alabama Supreme Court—none of which included following the mandate—and concluded that the State Supreme Court should "refuse the motion to forward the mandate, and leave in force the contempt judgment."

Two more months went by and still nothing was done with the Association's motions. Then on February 12, 1959, the Alabama Supreme Court handed down an opinion denying the motion to send the case back to Judge Jones, and, instead, "again affirmed" the contempt adjudication and reinstated the $100,000 fine.

### The U.S. Supreme Court Is "Mistaken"

The Association was originally held in contempt "for its willful and deliberate refusal to produce the documents" described in the production order, but on appeal both the state and the Association had argued, and the Supreme Court had decided, the issue of disclosure of only the membership lists. Since the case developed around that question, the state had not asserted in the first appellate process that the Association had otherwise failed to produce documents required by the order. Now in its 1959 decision the Alabama Supreme Court sought to widen the issues and bring into question the adequacy of the Association's compliance with the other paragraphs of the production order.

The fact that the U.S. Supreme Court had rested its decision on the understanding that refusal to produce the membership lists was the sole reason the Association was held in contempt was cast aside by the Alabama Court as a "mistaken premise." The court asserted: "There is nothing in the record here before us upon which we could bottom a conclusion that petitioner has apparently complied satisfactorily with the production order, except for the membership list." Thus the Association was still in contempt for failure to produce the other "certain books, papers, and documents" thereby "necessitating another affirmance of the judgment." After twenty-six months of appeals the case was now exactly where it had been in December, 1956.

The Association once again had only one legal move open—back to the U.S. Supreme Court. Hopeful that the High Court might hear the case before its term ended in June, 1959, Carter filed another petition for certiorari in Washington less than three weeks after Alabama had handed down its second "affirmance." His petition asserted that the Alabama decision was not supported by the facts and that the state's continuing effort to proscribe and banish the Association as a punishment for contempt violated an inherent right of defense secured under the due process clause. Manifesting the Association's growing sense of frustration, Carter concluded:

> The history of this case makes obvious the fact that various stratagems, technicalities, distortions of fact and unvarnished delays have been applied and will continue to be applied in Alabama to frustrate petitioner's right to test the validity of its *ex parte* ouster in the courts of Alabama and to seek a review of this holding, if necessary, in an appropriate appellate court.

On March 25, 1959, the State's new attorney general, MacDonald Gallion, took the place of John Patterson, now governor. Henceforth Gallion was to play the leading role on behalf of Alabama. Long familiar with the case, he had no difficulty in assuming his new position.

### Supreme Court Revisited

After reviewing the Association's petition and the response of the state, the Supreme Court, on June 8, 1959, handed down a brief *per curiam* opinion (one that is rendered by the Court as a whole, and not by a single Justice with whom others concur), which granted the Association's petition.

The opinion pointed out that in the former proceedings before the Supreme Court, both the state and the Association raised the identical constitutional question of the right to refuse to produce the record of membership, and stated that Alabama "made not even an indication that other portions of the production order had not been complied with." The case was "briefed and argued before us by both sides" on the single issue of the membership lists, and "that was the view of the record which underlay this Court's conclusion that petitioner had 'apparently complied satisfactorily with the production order, except for the membership lists' and that was the premise on which the Court disposed of the case."

"The State plainly accepted this view of the issue presented by the record and by its arguments on it," the Court's opinion explained, "for it did not seek a rehearing or suggest a clarification or correction of our opinion in that regard." Regarding the state's assertion that it "has never agreed, and does not now agree" that the Association had complied with the order to produce with the exception of the membership lists and "in fact, specifically denies" such compliance, the opinion concluded:

> This denial comes too late. The State is bound by its previously taken position, namely, that decision of the sole question regarding the membership lists is dispositive of the whole case. . . .
> In these circumstances, the Alabama Supreme Court is foreclosed from re-examining the grounds of our disposition. "Whatever was before the Court, and is disposed of, is considered as finally settled."

The Court then "reversed" the judgment of the Alabama Supreme Court and added a final point: "We assume that the State Supreme Court, thus advised, will not fail to proceed promptly with the disposition of the matters left open under our mandate for further proceedings."

Governor Patterson issued a statement expressing his "disappointment" at the result, and commented:

> There is no room in Alabama for such an organization as the NAACP and every effort will be made to prevent them from ever returning to this state. They should stay in New York where they came from and stop kindling the fires of racial hatred in the South. . . . The NAACP is no credit to the Negro race and has set the Negroes' cause back 100 years in Alabama.

Attorney General Gallion stated that "The fine should have stuck." Noting that "the NAACP is still enjoined from doing business in Alabama," he promised that "the Attorney General's office will continue to vigorously fight this case."

### How "Temporary" Is a Restraining Order?

The Supreme Court's mandate is the formal written judgment of the Court that directs the court below, whose decision it has reviewed, to proceed in accordance therewith. After receipt of this mandate by the Alabama Supreme Court, it had been "assumed" that it would, in turn, be sent down to the Circuit Court and a trial on the merits would begin, for until the lower court actually receives this mandate it has no legal authority to proceed in the manner prescribed therein. But on receipt of the mandate the State Supreme Court first issued an order, on August 5, 1959, saying that it was "withholding action" on the mandate pending a hearing by the High Court of the state's request for a rehearing. When this was denied by the U.S. Supreme Court on October 12, 1959, the State Supreme Court had no apparent legal reason for detaining the mandate.

By the end of October the state had still done nothing with the mandate. The Association then filed a motion with that court requesting immediate remand to the Circuit Court. No response was forthcoming and similar motions were made during November. Late that month the clerk of the Alabama Supreme Court sent the following letter to Fred Gray in Montgomery:

> We have received and filed, on October 23, 1959, your motion to remand. Your subsequent motions are substantially, if not identical with the original motion, [sic] so the Court has instructed me not to file these motions but to return them to you, since they serve no purpose.
>
> The Court instructed me to inform you that this case will receive attention as soon as practicable commensurate with the rest of the important business of the Court.

"I think you can understand how we felt," Fred Gray has commented, "when we merely asked the State Supreme Court to perform the simple task of dropping the mandate in the mail, and were told, after three and one-half years of delay, to cease such efforts since they 'serve no purpose.' "

There was no way of telling when the mandate would, if ever, find its way to the top of the court's other "important business." The state's approach became completely clear, however, when Attorney General Gallion, on December 22, 1959, requested the State Supreme Court to retain the mandate since the Association "is at the present time under proceedings of contempt in the Circuit Court of Montgomery County for violating the injunction of that Court." Gallion referred to the order to show cause, which had been filed in April, 1958, in connection with the ASCARV matter, and concluded that the "NAACP is not entitled to a hearing [on the merits] at this time" since "a party in contempt or against whom a prima-facie case of contempt has been presented has no standing in court to proceed with the merits of the cause until the contempt is purged." This was the same principle of state law that had prevented a trial on the merits all during the period when the Association was in contempt for violating the production order.

Judge Jones then set February 23, 1960, as the date for another hearing on this second contempt action, but this was of little help to the Association. If the unsubstantiated allegations of the complaint in that action were held sufficient to bar a trial of the ouster action itself, then the Association feared that a series of such complaints, together with lengthy and desultory hearings and with motions and appeals back and forth between the Circuit Court and the State Supreme Court, could, perhaps for years, prevent any attack on the "temporary" restraining order.

Subsequent effects were made to have the State Supreme Court send down the mandate or issue a reason for not doing so, but these proved as unavailing as the earlier attempts. The hearings on the second contempt action were rescheduled for March, and then for April. A motion in the Circuit Court to set a date for a hearing on the real merits was denied by Judge Jones since he could not act without the mandate. Finally the Association itself, during April and May of 1960, requested further time extensions on the contempt hearings, for Carter and the others working with him had long since grown weary of shadowboxing in the Alabama state courts, and they were looking for another legal approach. In their struggle to get back in business in Alabama, it seemed highly unlikely that any assistance would be forthcoming from the state judiciary. Once again the Federal courts appeared to be the only legal recourse.

### Legal Progeny: NAACP v. Gallion

On June 23, 1960, Carter entered the U.S. Federal District Court in and for the Northern Division of the Middle District of Alabama. The Honorable Frank M. Johnson, Jr., U.S. District Judge for the Middle District of Alabama, presided. Here Carter filed a complaint in civil action No. 1622-N against MacDonald Gallion, Attorney General of Alabama, and Mrs. Bettye Frink, Secretary of State of Alabama.

On the offensive now, for the first time in four years, the Association's action, authorized by Federal civil rights statutes, was for a permanent injunction to prohibit the Attorney General from enforcing the *ex parte* temporary restraining order of June 1, 1956, and to prohibit him and other officials of the state from proceeding against the Association and its members pursuant to the restraining order in any court in the state. The second part of the action was for a permanent injunction to enjoin the Secretary of State from refusing, pursuant to the restraining order, to register the Association as an out-of-state corporation. By an order issued the following day, Judge Johnson set the case down for a hearing on July 13, 1960.

Perhaps alarmed at the Federal Court's scheduling a hearing so quickly, the state moved, on June 30, 1960, for a resetting at a later date. The motion explained that both Attorney General Gallion and Mrs. Frink had long planned to attend the National Democratic Convention, which convened in Los Angeles on July 11, 1960, since both were duly elected delegates. Judge Johnson's scheduling of the hearing for July 13, 1960, would obviously conflict with their plans. But the Federal Court promptly denied the motion.

The Attorney General's response to the Association's action was not made public, but Mrs. Frink was somewhat less reserved. "We are not going to let them do business in Alabama," she declared. "I don't believe a federal court has the right to tell us what to do." One of the Montgomery newspapers, under a headline "Frink Pledges Fight Against NAACP" quoted her as saying: "Judge Johnson is a fine Alabama citizen working for the Alabama citizens. I don't think he would tell elected officials how to run their office. I have faith in Judge Johnson that he will tell the NAACP they have been outlawed in Alabama, and should remain outlawed as long as they don't comply with Alabama law."

Judge Johnson, a lifelong Republican from Winston County, Alabama —a county that seceded from the state after the state seceded from the Union—was a successful lawyer in Walker County before his appointment as a district attorney in Birmingham. In 1955, at the age of thirty-five, he was appointed a Federal judge by President Eisenhower. As the representative of the Federal Judiciary in Montgomery, his task has not been easy. Some of his rulings have, for example, desegregated interstate transportation facilities and enjoined county voter registration boards from continuing their deliberate denial of Negro voting rights. As a result, he has earned the enmity of the segregationists, and Alabama newspapers have called for his "deportation."

### Should Comity Yield to Constitutional Right?

Carter's case essentially amounted to the argument that Alabama's use of its contempt power deprived the Association of the right to present a defense on the merits and thus violated due process of law. The continued determination of state officials to use state courts as a major implement to destroy the Association, he contended, made adequate redress in the state courts unlikely, and action in the Federal Court the only possible remedy.

The biggest obstacle to the Association's case was the rule of "comity." Even if Carter could make his case on the legal points involved, he would still have to convince Judge Johnson that he should, as a matter of discretion, exercise the Federal Court's power to enjoin the state. This principle of comity is a tradition of courtesy and deference that the Federal Courts have adopted out of regard for the independence of the state governments.

After full argument (during which Attorney General Gallion announced that the Alabama Supreme Court had just remanded the case to the Circuit Court with directions to "undertake such proceedings as may be deemed proper") Judge Johnson denied the request for an injunction. His decision, issued on August 11, 1960, stressed that this was a case "where an action is in the breast of a state court" and concluded:

> The Court must and does now assume that the public officials of the State of Alabama recognize that they are just as solemnly committed by their oaths . . . to protect the constitutional rights of all citizens, as is this Court. It would be necessary for the Court to assume otherwise in order to justify granting plaintiff the relief it seeks.

How much longer he had to look before he found a Federal Court that would cease "assuming" and start "enjoining," Carter did not know, but his search next took him to New Orleans to the U.S. Court of Appeals for the Fifth Circuit, which hears appeals from the District Courts of Alabama and five surrounding states.

### The Oppression Is Not Manifest

A busy court, whose case load has increased substantially under the pressure of litigation dealing with many aspects of segregation, the Fifth Circuit Court was unable to hear oral argument on the case until well into the spring of 1961.

The tone of the Court and the questions from the bench during oral argument in April left Carter somewhat pessimistic, and with good reason, for when the decision was announced on May 15, 1961, he had lost again. The opinion, written by Judge Warren Jones, stated that the Court could not find sufficient evidence to indicate that the State Court remedy was inadequate or, as Carter had argued, "nonexistent." Regarding the Association's argument that the public officials of Alabama, including its judiciary, are committed to a policy of maintaining racial segregation at all costs, including the defiance of Federal authority, and that the Association is itself a prime object of attack, the opinion dismissed this "climate in Alabama" and the numerous references, citations, and quotations in Carter's brief that detailed the situation, stating, "We are unable to take judicial notice of these excerpts or of the facts which they purport to relate." The opinion then explained: "[O]nly manifest oppression will justify the interference by a federal court with state administrative officers acting under color of office in a good faith effort to perform their duties."

Judge Warren Jones spoke for two of the three members of the Court of Appeals. Chief Judge Elbert P. Tuttle dissented.

> In this case, I would have not the slightest doubt that the failure of the Alabama Supreme Court to make possible further proceedings in the State's trial court by its failure to take the simple ministerial act of sending down the mandate for a period of more than eight months, and then sending it

down only after suit was filed in the United States Court, presented a classic example of a case in which the assumption that the State Court would act promptly to permit a trial of the rights of an aggrieved party has been demonstrated to be false.

Almost nine months had now passed since the Alabama Supreme Court mandate had been sent down to the Alabama Circuit Court, and Judge Walter Jones still had not set a date for hearings on the trial of the action. Carter's recourse was again to the nine men in Washington.

### Washington, D.C., Round Three

On October 23, 1961, without oral argument or extended briefs, the High Court handed down a one-paragraph order which vacated the judgment of the Court of Appeals and directed Judge Johnson's Federal District Court to proceed with a trial of the issues raised in Carter's action "unless within a reasonable time, no later than January 2, 1962," the state granted the Association a hearing upon its motion to dissolve the restraining order and upon the merits of the ouster action. As an indication of the reason for taking the unusual step of giving a state ten weeks within which to hold a trial or face the consequences of a probable Federal injunction, the Supreme Court merely cited a section of the 1921 case of *Truax* v. *Corrigan* dealing with fairness in the law:

> The [Constitution] requires that every man shall have the protection of his day in court and the benefit of the general law—a law which hears before it condemns, which proceeds not arbitrarily or capriciously but upon inquiry, and renders judgment only after trial.

The order, in effect, agreed with the opinion of Judge Tuttle in the Court of Appeals and gave the State of Alabama its last opportunity either to hold a trial or face the probability of a Federal injunction. On receipt of the mandate, Judge Johnson ordered immediate as well as monthly statements from both the state and the Association to keep him advised of the status of the case.

After a year-long struggle in the Federal courts, Carter still had not received his injunction, but time was fast running out for Alabama. The tactics of delay had succeeded for over five years, but now a new approach would have to be found.

### Hearing on the Merits

Within a month, the Circuit Court set December 27–29, 1961, as the date for a hearing on the merits and ordered a pre-trial conference for early

December. At the conference, the state changed its original complaint in the 1956 ouster action and now added all the charges of violating the restraining order that it had brought against the Association in 1958 concerning its relationship with the ASCARV. Furthermore, the Association was accused of falsely charging (in the complaint in *NAACP* v. *Gallion*) various state executives and judicial officials with "arbitrary, vindictive, and collusive proceedings" to prevent the Association from contesting its ouster in the courts, of falsely charging agents of the state "with acts which constitute a violation of the criminal conspiracy statutes," and was accused of having "encouraged, aided and abetted the unlawful breach of the peace in many cities in Alabama" and of similarly engaging in a course of conduct "seeking to deny to the citizens of Alabama the constitutional right to voluntarily segregate."

All of these activities, the complaint concluded, rendered the Association "totally unacceptable to the State of Alabama and its people," and Attorney General Gallion asked that the Association "be forever barred and enjoined from further business dealings or activity of any kind" within the state.

Without further delays, the case was permitted to come to trial as scheduled, on Wednesday, December 27, 1961, in the new, modern County Courthouse on Washington Street in Montgomery. Seated at the counsel table for the State of Alabama were Attorney General Gallion and five Assistant Attorneys General, including Gordon Madison, who was to present the case for Alabama. The Association's counsel were Carter, Gray, and Shores, together with two other attorneys from Birmingham.

Promptly at ten o'clock Judge Jones entered the large, oak-paneled courtroom and took his seat behind the bench. The Circuit Court first disposed of the preliminary motions and not unexpectedly denied Carter's request to order the desegregation of courtroom seating. (Judge Jones had expressed his attitude on this subject in the February, 1961, libel trial of the *New York Times,* with the ruling that if the Fourteenth Amendment rights of due process and equal protection were ever construed to require him to desegregate his Court, then "the Fourteenth Amendment has no standing whatever in this Court, it is a pariah and an outcast.") The State of Alabama then began presentation of its evidence to show that the Association had been doing business since 1956 in violation of the temporary injunction. The state's strategy was to try to prove that the ASCARV was in fact the "alter ego" of the NAACP. To show this, Assistant Attorney General Madison had one factor in his favor: the position of W. C. Patton. Head of the ASCARV since its founding in 1952, Patton also had served as an NAACP employee in Alabama up to June, 1956. Since the injunction, he had been employed in the NAACP office in Memphis, Tennessee, but had maintained his residence in Birmingham and continued as head of the ASCARV in Alabama. Thus, Patton was vulnerable to the charge that his Alabama activities were but a cloak for the continued operation of the NAACP—especially since both groups were engaged in voter registration work.

Consequently, in his questioning of the witnesses, Madison first brought out that in 1957 Patton had attended an NAACP-sponsored meeting of voter registration groups in Atlanta, and in 1961 had sent a telegram to the ASCARV's treasurer, who was attending a meeting of the National Negro Funeral Directors Association in Washington, D.C., authorizing him to represent "our Association" in a plea for contributions. The state presented no evidence to show that these activities did not relate to Patton's work with the ASCARV, but merely implied that this constituted doing business by the NAACP.

Madison then developed a point that he was to bring out frequently during the trial. Most, if not all, of the officers of the ASCARV were also members or officers of NAACP branches in Alabama prior to June, 1956. The ASCARV officials had been active in many civil rights groups in Alabama both before and after the injunction, but all (except Patton) had ceased to be members of the NAACP in 1956. Starting with this overlapping membership, Madison inferred that continued functioning of ex-NAACP members after 1956 in other Alabama organizations such as the ASCARV was merely a subterfuge for the continued business activities of the NAACP. Thus, such a group was an "alter ego" of the enjoined Association. If such reasoning did not actually prove the NAACP was engaging in undercover activities, the state apparently hoped that it would create the desired inference.

One of the techniques Madison used to substantiate this argument was to pass over the fact that the ASCARV had functioned continuously since its creation in 1952. Instead, he concentrated on the year 1957, when the organization was incorporated in Alabama. To make the point clear, in his questioning he continually referred to 1957 as the year ASCARV was "founded" or "organized." Therefore, the argument ran, since the NAACP was enjoined in 1956, and the ASCARV was "formed" but a few months later, then the ASCARV was the "alter ego" of the NAACP.

The state next sought to place in evidence the records of the Southern Bell Telephone Company showing the hundreds of telephone calls made by Patton from his Birmingham residence from June, 1956, to the date of trial. Many of the persons called were NAACP officials, and Madison suggested:

> . . . Since these people have nothing to do with the other corporation I referred to [the ASCARV], and since he called these people over the telephone talking to them long distance at various and sundry times, I think there is a rather strong inference that he was talking and dealing in NAACP business in Alabama. . . . I don't see how anybody could make that many phone calls unless he was.

Since there was no way of knowing what Patton actually said during the phone calls, Fred Gray strongly objected to the state's using such fragile and insubstantial evidence as a "fishing expedition." But Judge Jones ruled the evidence admissible, and Madison retorted, "It may be a fishing expedition, but it hooked a pretty good fish."

The reading of the telephone company records took over three hours, and as the court adjourned for the day, Carter—fearful that the stage was being set for further delays—suggested that the judge consider holding night sessions to complete the trial in the allotted three days. This rankled Judge Jones, and the following morning antagonism among the participants—thus far kept beneath the surface—was brought into full view when he tried to bar Carter from the court. The judge asked if the "attorneys outside the jurisdiction" had complied with the rule requiring a letter of introduction and recommendation from a member of the Board of Commissioners of the State Bar. (Carter had been introduced and accepted by the court when the case began in 1956, but the rules had since been made more stringent.) Carter produced the requisite letter. Judge Jones then remarked that even with the letter the matter is still discretionary with the judge, for there is no requirement that he must allow an attorney from another state to participate. He nevertheless granted Gray's motion to admit Carter, but did so with an admonition against any further suggestions about "how this court should be run," such as night sessions or desegregated seating, and pointed out that Carter was being admitted only "for this one case."

As the tension eased, the trial resumed, and the state presented its final two items of evidence: a form letter signed by a Birmingham dentist and his wife and sent in December, 1960, to a friend in Orville, Alabama. It explained that the senders had donated the usual Christmas card money to the NAACP in New York and requested the recipient to do the same. The second was a copy of the *NAACP News,* mailed to residents of Alabama in 1954 by the Tuskegee branch. The first was introduced, Madison explained, because it could be inferred that the form was "prepared by the NAACP," and such solicitation of funds clearly constituted doing business in violation of the injunction; the second was presented to show that the Association was engaged in intrastate business prior to 1956.

This concluded the state's case, and it was then the Association's turn to place its evidence before the court.

### *"We Like To Run Our Own Business"*

The Association's case was designed to make three points. Carter first wished to present the Association's view of the "inferences" to be drawn from the state's evidence, as well as to put forth a full denial of the allegations of illegal operation. To do this he called Roy Wilkins as his first witness. After explaining the purposes, methods of operation, and accomplishments of the NAACP since its founding, Wilkins described the organization's pre-1956

activities in Alabama, emphasizing that the Association had ceased all operations in the state in June, 1956. He then explained that the Atlanta meeting
in 1957, at which Patton had been present, was attended by representatives
of a number of southern organizations active in the campaign to increase
Negro voter registration, and that Patton's participation as head of the
ASCARV was not barred by the 1956 decree.

Under Carter's questioning, Wilkins then told the Court about the 1960
Christmas card appeal. He explained that the campaign had been conceived
and organized by the National Links, a nation-wide women's social club, to
solicit funds for the NAACP as part of its Christmas project. The appeal
was not conducted or supported in any way by the Association, he testified,
and was unconnected with the NAACP's own Christmas seal campaign.

Responding to a question as to whether or not the Association was connected with the ASCARV or the Montgomery Improvement Association,
Wilkins said, "No. In no way whatsoever. Not organically, structurally,
financially or otherwise. . . . It is our policy to work independently whenever possible. We like to run our own business."

When Madison cross-examined Wilkins, he asked him if the officials of
the ASCARV "could be former members of the NAACP." Wilkins' reply
that "they could be former Elks also" emphasized the Association's contention that it made no difference how many organizations these people belonged to as long as they were not engaging in activities on behalf of the
NAACP.

After further unproductive questioning regarding the Patton phone calls,
Madison referred to the actions brought in Alabama by the Department of
Justice under the 1960 Civil Rights Act, charging discrimination against
prospective Negro voters, and asked Wilkins:

> Q. Has the NAACP had anything to do with jogging up the Justice De-
> partment in bringing these suits down here?
> A. I think our influence with the Justice Department has probably been
> exaggerated. I don't think anybody has to jog Robert Kennedy. He's sort of
> a self-starter. . . . The Justice Department certainly didn't consult us
> about what they were going to do in Alabama. . . . We didn't help them
> at all. . . .
> Q. Well, you are well aware that they are keeping us pretty busy, aren't
> you?
> A. I would hope, Mr. Madison, that they would keep you even busier.
> Q. All right. No further questions.

Wilkins' testimony was the only light moment of the entire trial. Gordon
Madison later recalled this exchange with much humor, "I really stuck my
chin out on that one," he said.

Instead of attempting to prove the absence of intrastate activities prior to 1956, the Association sought to place the case in what it thought was the proper perspective. Its second point, therefore, was to show that Alabama had never previously brought any action against a nonprofit foreign corporation for failure to register. Fred Gray consecutively called to the stand the Attorney General, both the Clerk and the Register of the Circuit Court (a nephew of Judge Jones), and the Secretary of State, Mrs. Frink. (An attractive twenty-eight-year-old homemaker and mother and a candidate for State Auditor in the Democratic primary, Mrs. Frink had that morning announced, in a statement Fred Gray read to the Court, that she would prefer to resign her job rather than to register the NAACP to do business in the state because "to turn this bunch loose again on Alabama would be like turning loose a pack of wild dogs.") Gray had subpoenaed the four officials to bring the records of their offices showing any prior action by the state against any other nonprofit foreign corporation. But Judge Jones upheld the failure to comply with the subpoenas by ruling that he had no authority to require the "bringing of State records into Court," and then refused to permit any testimony except as restricted to a corporation having the "same line of activity, the same objectives, and the same methods" as the NAACP. Aside from creating a distinction not found in the registration statute between types of nonprofit foreign corporations, this ruling further annoyed the NAACP for, in its view, it effectively blocked any meaningful testimony. The Association's only legal recourse was to read into the Trial Record a summary of Fred Gray's research showing the absence of any prior actions by the state against a corporation such as the NAACP. (Such inadmissible material, however, has no evidentiary standing and cannot be used by a court in deciding the case.)

To develop its third point, the Association called the Chief of the State Franchise Tax Division who testified about a letter he had received in September, 1960, from the nonprofit First Manassas Corporation of Virginia. The letter asked whether under Alabama law the Virginia corporation should first register or secure a license in order to solicit funds for the Civil War Hall of Fame, a commemorative battlefield shrine. When Fred Gray attempted to elicit from the witness the state's reply, Madison objected and the courtroom spectators received a lesson on historical terminology from Judge Jones:

> I don't see where this so-called Civil War—there never was any Civil War on this continent. There was a war between the Union and the Confederacy, sometimes called the War of Rebellion and sometimes called the War Between the States, but it was only the War between the Union and the Confederacy; I just don't believe this is admissible.

Regardless of whether this ruling set forth a valid legal basis for excluding the testimony, Gray's only alternative was to read the reply into the

Record: "Our legal division has held," the witness wrote, "that your organization is exempt from qualifying in Alabama as a foreign corporation." This evidence was one of the major points the Association had sought to establish, for it substantiated the contention it had made since the case began in 1956—that under Alabama law a nonprofit foreign corporation is exempt from registration. The refusal of the court once again to permit any testimony thoroughly nettled the Association's lawyers—especially since they felt the judge had been unduly lenient in admitting some of the doubtfully relevant evidence and testimony of the state's witnesses.

After the Association completed its case on the third day, the trial ended with the closing arguments. Madison first summarized the "ample evidence" of the Association's doing business in violation of the temporary injunction. Perhaps out of realistic appraisal of the probity of most of the evidence he had presented, however, he then said, "Our case does not center . . . on whether or not they have engaged in activities since 1956." Thus discounting the sometimes none too relevant factual revelations of the trial, Alabama's case amounted to little more than it had in 1956: The Association had engaged in intrastate business without prior corporate registration, and, therefore, should be ousted from the state.

Arthur Shores then summed up the Association's position. He pointed out that none of Patton's alleged undercover activities with the ASCARV rested on factual proof. He dismissed the Birmingham phone calls by urging that as an employee of the Association in Tennessee, Patton would normally make some phone calls from his home to officials outside the state, concerning NAACP business outside of Alabama, and such calls were not prohibited by the 1956 decree. The Christmas Fund appeal of the Links was "meaningless," since the sender of the letter was not a member of the NAACP and, as a private individual, had a right to engage in civil rights activities. Urging that there was no showing of irreparable injury to the state justifying such drastic action as a permanent injunction, Shores then stated, "the NAACP has been the whipping boy of the politicians in this state for seven years." He concluded with a development of the Association's belief that the real purpose of the entire litigation was to prevent Negroes from securing their Constitutional rights.

### The Injunction Is Made Permanent

Three days of testimony produced the expected result. On the afternoon of Friday, December 29, 1961, the third day of the trial, Judge Jones handed down his final decree, which ordered the Association "permanently restrained and enjoined from conducting any further business of any description within the State of Alabama," and from "exercising any of its corporate functions" except as may be protected by the interstate commerce clause of the U.S. Constitution. Calling the evidence of illegal operation "overwhelming," the Judge, in a brief order, noted that the U.S. Supreme Court directive "prevented" him from writing a full opinion before the January 2, 1962, deadline expired, but he reserved the right "at a future date" to state in an opinion his findings of fact and rulings of law.

After five years and seven months, the Association had, at last, received a trial of the action. In the perverse logic the situation demands, Carter was at least relieved to be ousted. Now he had a final decree on the merits of the case that he could and would appeal.

Judge Jones denied, on January 12, 1962, a petition for rehearing and the case went on appeal to the Alabama Supreme Court. In the likely event that the Association is unsuccessful there, the next step will be to the U.S. Supreme Court for a fourth time. A total of 21 judges in 5 courts have already handed down 67 separate orders, decrees, and rulings, and the case, in a sense, has just begun.

### To What End?

After six long years of litigation, what has happened to the parties involved? The Association has, to be sure, been out of business in Alabama for more than six years. Its state-wide organization has been destroyed and its activities on behalf of the state's Negroes have been completely disrupted.

It has also experienced substantial direct expenses and damages. The Association's own General Counsel has handled much of the legal work, thus avoiding a major cost, but attorney's fees have been paid to the local counsel in Alabama. Carter recently estimated that the total cost to date of defending the state action and bringing the Federal suit was between $25,000 and $30,000. The major "expense" to the Association, however, has been a loss of income. For the twelve-month period before June, 1956, a total of $27,309 was received in dues and contributions from members and contributors in Alabama. This income has practically ceased, for only 29 Alabama members remain—each sending their dues directly to the national office. It is probable that during this period of over six years the state-wide membership would have increased—as it has in many states—and the total loss here may well approach $200,000. On the other side of the case, the total amount that has thus far been paid out of the Treasury of the State of Alabama is incalculable.

As far as Alabama is concerned, the case has remained at the center of state politics. Attorney General Gallion and six other candidates ran for the 1962 gubernatorial nomination in the Democratic primary. "Who was it that put the NAACP out of business in Alabama?" the Attorney General rhetorically asked the crowds as he toured the state, and replied, "It was MacDonald Gallion, that's who it was." He promised to maintain this position in a "forceful but dignified" manner. Discussing the case at a campaign rally in Birmingham, he predicted: "I have no doubt that the Alabama

Supreme Court will uphold the permanent injunction on appeal, and as for the U.S. Supreme Court, I don't know what federal constitutional issues exist in this case, but they may cook up some."

Although Gallion was not the winner in the primary, Alabama's Governor-elect, George C. Wallace, promised to be equally vigilant against the NAACP. Wallace, a forty-two-year-old former Circuit Court Judge, received national prominence in 1959 when he impounded the voter registration records of Barbour and Bullock Counties and refused to turn them over to agents of the Federal Civil Rights Commission. Calling Judge Johnson "an integrating, scalawagging carpet-bagger," Wallace campaigned by promising the Alabama voters he would fight the "Federals" and "face our enemies face to face, hip to hip and toe to toe" to maintain segregation, "even to the point of standing at the schoolhouse door in person."

The over-all racial situation in Alabama continues to be tense. Sit-ins, protest marches, and economic boycotts have occurred. The demonstrations have frequently been broken up and the leaders arrested and jailed. Bloody rioting greeted the visits of the Freedom Riders in May, 1961. Legal actions followed. They led to the effective desegregation of interstate transportation facilities in Montgomery, Birmingham, and elsewhere. Other court orders have not been effective. In Birmingham, faced with a Federal court order to integrate public recreational sites, the community centers, swimming pools, and parks were closed and posted with "No Trespassing" signs. The sites remain officially closed, but unofficially some are used on a segregated basis. Birmingham is perhaps the most fiercely resistant city remaining in the south, and the coming efforts to desegregate its schools can be expected to arouse strong opposition.

Two more recent developments have demonstrated Alabama's ingenuity in opposing those who endeavor to assist Negro civil rights efforts. The State refused to renew the notary public commissions of attorneys who have defended or initiated legal actions on behalf of Negroes seeking desegregation. In February, 1962, the Secretary of State and the Attorney General rejected the application of the Congress of Racial Equality to register to do business in Alabama as a nonprofit foreign corporation. CORE promptly brought suit seeking to require the state to register the group. This action, pending in the Federal court, created a curious legal position: in 1956, the state ousted the NAACP for its failure to comply with the foreign corporation statutes before doing business; then, six years later, the state prohibited CORE from complying with the identical statutes when it sought to register prior to doing business.

During the Association's six-year absence, other Negro groups throughout the state have pushed forward in their drive for equal rights. The ASCARV has been the major state-wide unit in the voter registration field, but other groups, such as the Montgomery Improvement Association, the Non-Partisan Voters League in Mobile, the Midway Improvement Association in Bullock County, and the Tuskegee Civic Association in Macon County, have played a large role.

In many ways, the whole cluster of issues involved in *Alabama* v. *NAACP* is symbolized by the motto of the State of Alabama. It is carved on a granite supporting wall of the steps leading up to the State Capitol in Montgomery—a white, ante-bellum structure that is perhaps the most handsome statehouse in the nation. *Audemus jura nostra defendere,* the motto declares; "We dare defend our rights." Just what rights and whose rights the State of Alabama has been defending since 1954 is the deeper question of the case. The final resolution of that issue will not be made in Montgomery or even in Washington but in the notion of constitutional rights adopted by the final tribunal: the national consensus on what is equality and justice for Americans. That consensus, for better or worse, will ultimately make itself felt throughout the entire fabric of American public law.

### Table of Cases, in Order of Citation in the Text

*Brown* v. *Board of Education,* 347 U.S. 483 (1954).
*Powell* v. *Alabama,* 287 U.S. 45 (1932).
*Norris* v. *Alabama,* 294 U.S. 587 (1935).
*Lucy* v. *Adams,* 350 U.S. 1 (1955).
*Browder* v. *Gayle,* 352 U.S. 903 (1956).
*Alabama* v. *NAACP,* 265 Ala. 356 (1956).
*Alabama* v. *NAACP,* 265 Ala. 699 (1956).
*Alabama* v. *NAACP,* 265 Ala. 349 (1956).
*Ex parte Dickens,* 162 Ala. 272 (1909).
*Ex parte Morris,* 252 Ala. 551 (1949).
*Bryant* v. *Zimmerman,* 278 U.S. 63 (1927).
*McLaurin* v. *Oklahoma St. Regents,* 339 U.S. 637 (1950).
*NAACP* v. *Alabama,* 357 U.S. 449 (1958).
*Alabama* v. *NAACP,* 268 Ala. 531 (1959).
*NAACP* v. *Alabama,* 360 U.S. 240 (1959).
*NAACP* v. *Gallion,* 190 F. Supp. 583 (M.D. Ala. 1960).
*NAACP* v. *Gallion,* 290 F. 2d 337 (5th Cir. 1961).
*NAACP* v. *Gallion,* 368 U.S. 19 (1961).
*Truax* v. *Corrigan,* 257 U.S. 312 (1921).

### Sources

The major sources have been the transcripts of the proceedings in the Montgomery County Circuit Court in 1956, 1958, and 1961, and the petitions and briefs filed in the United States Supreme Court (No. 91, October 1961 Term; No. 753, October 1958 Term; and No. 303, October 1961 Term). Copies are on file in the Columbia University Law Library as well as in other law schools.

Information on the NAACP and on developments in Alabama generally was obtained from an examination of the newspaper clipping files from 1954 to 1962 of the Montgomery *Advertiser,* the Montgomery *Alabama Journal,* the Birmingham *News,* and the Birmingham *Post-Herald.* An examination of the *Southern School News* from 1954 to 1962 yielded much factual data.

The following persons have kindly given their time for interviews and discussions and have assisted me with recollections and materials: Robert L. Carter, Gloster Current, Attorney General MacDonald Gallion, Dr. Charles G. Gomillion, Fred D. Gray, Mrs. Ruby Hurley, Assistant Attorney General Gordon Madison, William P. Mitchell, Assistant Attorney General Edmon L. Rinehart, Arthur D. Shores, and Roy Wilkins. I am also grateful to Judge Frank M. Johnson, Jr., and Judge Walter B. Jones, for their helpful interviews. Since this case is still under the jurisdiction of Judge Johnson's Federal District Court, and since the case may again return to Judge Jones' Circuit Court, no part of the discussions with these judges concerned any factual, legal, or judicial aspect of *Alabama* v. *NAACP* or *NAACP* v. *Gallion.*

Quotations from the oral argument before the United States Supreme Court were secured in part from the above newspapers, but are based primarily on the recollections of Robert L. Carter and Edmon L. Rinehart.

The more useful printed sources, for general background as well as analysis of the legal issues posed by this case, have been: Robert B. McKay, "The Repression of Civil Rights as an Aftermath of the School Segregation Cases," 4 *Howard Law Journal* 9 (1958); Walter F. Murphy, "The South Counterattacks: The Anti-NAACP Laws," 12 *Western Political Quarterly* 371 (June, 1959); Jack W. Peltason, "Fifty-Eight Lonely Men" (New York: Harcourt, Brace & World, Inc., 1961); Joseph B. Robinson, "Protection of Associations from Compulsory Disclosure of Membership," 58 *Columbia Law Review* 614 (1958); James Rorty, "The Embattled NAACP," *Antioch Review* (Fall, 1959), p. 379; and Stanley Rowland, "The Legal War on the NAACP," 184 *The Nation* (February 9, 1957), p. 115.

Two "Notes," "Anonymity: An Emerging Fundamental Right," 36 *Indiana Law Journal* 306 (1961), and "Group Action: Civil Rights and Freedom of Association," 54 *Northwestern Law Review* 390 (1959), were also helpful.

For the racial climate of Birmingham, Alabama, as well as the author's experience in that city, see Osborne, "Boycott in Birmingham," 194 *The Nation* (May 5, 1962), p. 397.

# 6

## GOVERNMENT LOYALTY-SECURITY PROGRAMS

# *Subversion and the Cold War*

## Leonard G. Miller

AFTER the racial segregation issue, probably the most controversial area for the Court in the 1950's was that of national security. Concern about communism at all governmental levels led to a variety of legislative programs aimed at uncovering, countering, or punishing subversion. The Smith Act was used to prosecute communists for advocating the violent overthrow of the government. The Taft-Hartley Act required officers of labor unions to sign a non-Communist oath. Congressional committees, particularly the House Committee on Un-American Activities and Senator McCarthy's group, carried on full-time inquiries into alleged subversive activities. Federal, state, and local employees were required to take oaths that they did not believe in the overthrow of the government by force and violence, or belong to organizations having such goals. Active programs to check on the loyalty of public employees were instituted.

The Vinson Court had generally upheld the constitutionality of these programs or refused to pass upon them at all. The Taft-Hartley non-Communist oath was sustained in 1950. The Smith Act was declared constitutional in 1951. Several state oath requirements for public officials were upheld. Claims that congressional committees were abusing the constitutional rights of persons haled before them were rejected.

On the Warren Court, however, a renewed concern arose about the constitutional aspects of national security programs, owing in considerable part to the active interest of the Chief Justice and Justice Brennan. They joined Justices Black and Douglas to reconstitute a four-judge liberal bloc such as had existed prior to the deaths of Murphy and Rutledge. Between 1955 and 1958 the Warren Court moderated the excesses of a number of security programs in very substantial fashion. Central figures on the Court, notably Frankfurter and Harlan, swung to a more critical view of loyalty-security practices during this time. Perhaps the most famous decisions were *Watkins* v. *United States* (1957), which indicated an intention to restrict the investigatory practices of congressional communist-hunting committees, and *Yates* v. *United States* (1957), which imposed some substantial limitation on further use of the Smith Act in convicting communists. The present case is one of a series in which the Court effected some limitations on the operation of the loyalty-security program for Federal employees.

The only change in the Court was occasioned by the retirement of Justice Burton in 1958. President Eisenhower's fifth appointee to the Court was Potter Stewart, a 43-year-old Republican and member of the Federal Court of Appeals from Ohio.

WHEN William Vincent Vitarelli walked with his attorney into the hearing room of the Senate Subcommittee on Constitutional Rights on November 23, 1955, he had been out of a regular job for more than a year. In September, 1954, he had been fired as a "security risk" from his government position as an educational administrator in the South Pacific. Since that time, he had been able to find odd jobs, but nothing worthy of a man with a doctorate in education and substantial professional experience. Yet the hearings conducted by the subcommittee symbolized the beginning of a sober second look at loyalty-security practices as they had evolved in the United States in the postwar period. Thus, as he spelled out his story, Vitarelli still clung to the hope that his name might be cleared.

The *Vitarelli* case began in the Executive Branch, attracted significant attention in the Legislative Branch, and culminated in the Judicial Branch of the government. In many ways it represented the continuing constitutional debate that had polarized around two views of government security. One view held that the government had to protect itself against employees who were actual or potential security risks, and that these determinations could be made without affording the employee the kind of hearing he would be entitled to in a court. The other position recognized that the government normally may discharge employees with no particular procedures being required, but contended that security-risk dismissals, which can destroy a man's reputation and ruin his livelihood, could constitutionally be made only after due process of law. The proper balance between the government's right to self-protection and the employee's right not to suffer because of arbitrary or unjustified action was in serious dispute.

Off and on since 1952, Vitarelli had been fighting for his professional life within the Executive Branch and, more recently, within the court system. His case was soon to go back to court, and eventually to the Supreme Court itself, where he won reinstatement, and then back into court again for a money judgment.

### Loyalty Programs Old and New

As far back as the Civil War, the United States Government had had a fairly rigorous Federal loyalty system. The genesis of the modern program, however, was in Section 9-A of the Hatch Act of 1939, which forbade Federal employment to members of a party or organization "which advocates the overthrow of our constitutional form of government. . . ." Two years later, in 1941, this proscription was extended to include personal advocacy. During World War II the military departments had the power of "immediate removal" of civilian employees when "warranted by the demands of national security." But by the end of the war, the machinery of these programs had largely run down.

Increasing hostility between the United States and the Soviet Union in the postwar period revived concern over internal security, which was intensified by the discovery of Soviet espionage coupled with reports of widespread Communist infiltration in American government and institutions. The military and the Department of State hastily improvised security programs, but these programs were unduly harsh on governmental employees and of doubtful effectiveness.

The quest for a more systematic program resulted in the issuance of Executive Order (E.O.) 9835 by President Truman on March 21, 1947. That Order established the Employee Loyalty Program—"the first thorough, all-inclusive screening of Federal employees," as one observer described it. At the apex of this new loyalty apparatus was the Loyalty Review Board, empowered to hear appeals from employees who thought they had been unfairly discharged. Congress took steps to supplement this program in August, 1950, with the passage of Public Law 733. This Act authorized the heads of eleven Federal agencies that had especially close links with the national security to suspend summarily any employee if it were "necessary or advisable in the interest of national security. . . ." It also guaranteed to workers who held permanent civil service appointments a statement of charges, a hearing, and administrative review before dismissal. Thus, while the Loyalty Review Board was concerned with loyalty, Public Law 733 dealt with the broader concept of security.

This dual system remained in effect until May, 1953, when the new President, Eisenhower, signed E.O. 10450 in an attempt to establish one general security program. At that time the Truman order was revoked, and the provisions of Public Law 733 were extended to all executive agencies. Furthermore, agency heads were required to list all those positions in which an employee could have "a material adverse effect on the national security" and to set up programs within each department in the spirit of the new Executive Order. Interdepartmental avenues of appeal, such as the Loyalty Review Board, were thus abolished.

The new program, whatever the President's intentions, made it far easier for agencies to rid themselves of undesirable or troublesome employees. There was virtually no higher administrative review of the operation of the various departmental programs, nor any machinery to check possible abuses. The White House did not fill the void created by the abolition of the old Loyalty Review Board. An additional feature of E.O. 10450 was that it placed a greater burden on the employee to clear himself of charges than had been imposed even during the Korean War under the Truman program. As a last measure, the Order expanded the list of grounds for dismissal to include the excessive use of intoxicants, drug addiction, sexual perversion, mental illness or instability, or susceptibility to blackmail.

A year and a half later, the Civil Service Commission announced that in the May 28, 1953–June 30, 1954 period, 6,926 Federal employees had been dismissed as "security risks" or resigned because adverse information was in their personnel files. Less than a quarter of the cases involved subversive associations or disloyal activities—still, of course, a substantial figure. The most common transgressions included chronic alcoholism, sexual perversion, and mental instability. Yet all the fired workers were classified as "security risks." Some saw cause for unrestrained joy at these figures. Republican National Chairman Leonard Hall, for instance, said:

> The elimination of 6,926 subversives and security risks from the federal government demonstrates the difference between the Eisenhower and the Truman administrations. This administration is cleaning up instead of covering up. It represents the best argument for a Republican-controlled House and Senate next month.

What the Eisenhower Administration had accomplished was the erasure of the legalistic distinction between "loyalty risks" and "security risks." Only the latter classification remained, although few Americans recognized the distinction. So far as the public was concerned, a dismissal on security grounds was almost conclusive proof that an employee was disloyal. A disloyal American, obviously, is not one that any employer is eager to hire.

### The Government Hires an Educator

William Vitarelli graduated from Newark Teachers College in 1933. He thereafter held several teaching posts, including an appointment as Professor of Industrial Arts at West Georgia State College, where he directed a Rosenwald Fund project on improving rural teaching and school facilities. Subsequently, he held several teaching appointments at Columbia University, including one as research associate for a program in Bucks County, Pennsylvania, similar to the Rosenwald project.

In 1949 Vitarelli received his Ph. D. from Teachers College of Columbia University. A year later he applied to the United States Department of the Interior for an overseas teaching job and was hired. He left for the West Caroline Islands in the South Pacific in November, 1950, and was joined by his wife and four children a few months later.

Vitarelli was assigned to the Palau district of the Trust Territory of the Pacific Islands, which was held by the United States under a U.N. trusteeship and administered by the Department of the Navy. He was responsible for organizing a school system, supervising school construction, and formulating adequate curricula. Vitarelli received preliminary clearance from the Navy and, when the territory was placed under the jurisdiction of the Interior Department a few months later, a full-scale security investigation. Thereafter he received "good" or "outstanding" ratings on performance at six-month intervals.

### A "Routine" Set of Interrogatories

In October, 1952, while on leave in the United States, Vitarelli received from the Interior Department Loyalty Board a "routine" set of "interrogatories" requiring written answers under oath. Although the questions were expressly declared not to constitute charges, they specifically demanded:

> Do you have any information concerning, or explanation of, a report that you have been associated with F——, a member of many Communist Front organizations? Do you have any information concerning, or explanation of, a report that you have been associated with W——, a member of and leader in the Communist Party? Do you have any information concerning, or explanation of, a report that you have received the USSR Information Bulletin by mail?

Vitarelli submitted a sworn five-page reply a few days later, unequivocally asserting that he "never knew" either F—— or W—— to be in any way connected with the Communist Party or with Communist-front activities. He then listed, to the best of his recollection, the full extent of his associations with these two men. He remembered meeting them in connection with his professional activities around 1943 or 1944, while teaching industrial arts at West Georgia State College. His association with F——, he stated, had been casual and short-lived, although he might subsequently have written F—— a letter. He conceded that he had attended a political rally with W—— and entertained him at his home, yet he insisted that "My interest in Mr. W—— had always been solely from the point of view of a scholar and teacher who was interested in building good relationships between the school and the community."

In answer to the third interrogatory, he stated that he had subscribed to the USSR Information Bulletin for use in a course he had taught at Columbia University Teachers College in the late 1940's or early 1950's, devoted in part to an examination of competing political ideologies. But he added that he had also subscribed to the bulletins issued by several non-Communist nations in order "to have on hand information about various countries of all political orientations."

### Interior Suspends an Educator

Vitarelli's reply was dated October 13, 1952. Not until February, 1954, did he learn from his immediate superior that he and four other Island employees were under consideration as security risks. On March 13 the Guam *Daily News* carried a story to this effect, quoting the High Commissioner of the Trust Territory as the source of information. While Vitarelli was not identified by name, the Commissioner gave as an example of a security risk a known conscientious objector, and said that "an advocate of pacifism is out of place in so sensitive and strategic an area." It was well known in the Territory that Vitarelli was a Quaker and had declared himself a pacifist during World War II.

Vitarelli had still not been officially informed of any action; three days after the newspaper story appeared, the Commissioner arrived at Palau and told Vitarelli he was suspended, giving pacifism as a reason. Then on March 30 Secretary of the Interior Douglas McKay wrote a letter suspending Vitarelli, which was received in Palau on April 8. The letter listed the following charges, "which are as specific as security interests permit":

> That during the years 1941 to 1945, inclusive, but not limited thereto, you were either a member of, affiliated with, or in sympathetic association with the Communist Party, and members of the Communist Party, including but not limited to the following particulars as to such affiliation and sympathetic association. . . .

Four points were contained in the bill of particulars. First was Vitarelli's "sympathetic association with persons who were members of, affiliated with, or in sympathetic association with the Communist Party," namely,

F——, W——, and R——. Second, "in the year 1945 while you were a resident of New York City you registered a preference for the American Labor Party. . . [which] has been cited as being under the domination and control of the Communist Party or members thereof by a Special Committee on Un-American Activities of the House of Representatives." Third, there was the admitted subscription to the USSR Information Bulletin. Fourth, it was alleged that Vitarelli's sworn statements of October 13, 1952, that F—— was only a casual acquaintance, and that F—— and W—— were not known to him as being in sympathetic association with the Communist Party were untrue. Based on these allegations, the Secretary's letter reached this conclusion:

> Your behavior, activities and associations tend to show that you are not reliable or trustworthy, and the facts above alleged furnish reason to believe that you have deliberately misrepresented, falsified, or omitted material facts in connection with your said behavior, activities, and associations, and these facts also furnish reason to believe that you may be subjected to coercion, influence, or pressure which may cause you to act contrary to the best interests of national security.

Finally, the letter indicated the steps that Vitarelli could take if he wished to contest the suspension.

> You are hereby advised of your right and opportunity to submit any [sworn] statements, answer, or affidavits to the Secretary of the Interior within 30 days after receipt of this notice to show why you should be reinstated or restored to duty. . . . You may also request a hearing before a board duly constituted for that purpose. I will review and consider such statements, answer, and affidavits, if any are submitted by you, and the recommendation of the hearing board if a hearing is requested, and within 30 days thereafter you will be notified of my decision to either terminate your employment if I shall determine that such termination is necessary and advisable in the interests of the national security of the United States, or to reinstate you to your former employment. . . .

### Answering the Charges

This notice placed Vitarelli in a dilemma. To contest the suspension, he would have to return to Washington within thirty days. However, he lacked funds for plane travel, and the High Commissioner's office had ruled that he could not travel at government expense unless he first resigned. Vitarelli appealed to the American Friends Service Committee, and owing largely to its intercession, the Department granted him the travel allowance. Since it covered only himself, his wife and four children remained on the Islands.

On returning to his home in Erwinna, Bucks County, Pennsylvania, Vitarelli retained a prominent Philadelphia law firm to advise him in preparing a written answer to the charges. The case was assigned to Allen S. Olmsted, II, whose experience covered forty years of general practice, though this was his first loyalty-security case.

On June 4 Vitarelli submitted to Secretary McKay a ten-page answer. At the outset he said emphatically, "I have never been a member of, affiliated with, or in sympathetic association with the Communist Party . . . [and] have never knowingly been intimately or sympathetically associated with members of the Communist Party . . . [or] with individuals who were known to be Communist sympathizers." He also emphatically denied the allegation that in his 1952 statement he had "deliberately . . . falsified or omitted material facts."

Vitarelli conceded that he had registered for the American Labor Party in New York City in 1945, but said he had no idea at the time that it was under the "domination and control" of the Communist Party as now charged. This party had been founded with the support of many labor unions in 1936. In 1944 President Roosevelt received almost 500,000 votes on the Labor Party ticket in New York, and by 1947 party registrants numbered 228,668.

To refute the charge that "your behavior, activities, and associations tend to show that you are not reliable or trustworthy," Vitarelli called attention to the forty-four affidavits which he appended to his answer. Twenty of the forty-four represented the opinions of American families residing in the Pacific district where Vitarelli worked. These persons not only swore unconditionally as to his loyalty and freedom from communistic leanings and practices, but were emphatically affirmative as to the superior quality of the work he had performed in fostering and administering an educational program for the natives. Several of the other affidavits were from Columbia University professors, stating that Vitarelli's duties as an assistant in a course taught there included the obtaining of copies of the Communist *Daily Worker* and *New Masses* to show the various methods of propaganda.

In conclusion Vitarelli demanded reinstatement to his position. However, if the answer and affidavits were deemed insufficient to warrant this, he requested a hearing at the earliest possible time.

### The Security Board Hears the Evidence

On June 11 Secretary McKay rejected the demand for reinstatement, but granted the request for a hearing, which was held at the Interior Department in Washington on June 22 and July 1, 1954. The Hearing Board was composed of three officials from other agencies—Commerce, Justice, and Agriculture—none of whom had previously met Vitarelli.

In accordance with the usual procedures in security matters, there were substantial departures from the standards that prevail in judicial hearings. Vitarelli was represented by counsel (Olmsted), but he was not confronted with any witnesses against him and, therefore, could not cross-examine his accusers or answer or rebut their allegations. Nor was he given the text of any derogatory statements that might have been made against him. Moreover, he did not have the right to subpoena witnesses in his own behalf.

Vitarelli was on the stand during the entire session of June 22. The solicitor of the Department of the Interior, J. Raoul Armstrong, prosecuted the Department's case, and all the Board members joined in the cross-examination. Armstrong conceded that Vitarelli's loyalty was not an issue, the only question being whether he was a security risk.

The main charge against Vitarelli was that in his answer to the 1952 interrogatories he had not been completely frank or candid in disclosing his receipt of the USSR Information Bulletin or his relationship with F——and W——. Vitarelli responded that he had never intentionally concealed any pertinent information. As to the Bulletin, he reaffirmed his earlier statements, although he could not recall whether he had subscribed to it, requested it, or whether someone had sent it to him.

The cross-examination of Vitarelli was not restricted to such reasonably relevant matters. He was questioned rather extensively concerning his social, economic, and political philosophy, as well as his political conduct. He was asked whether he thought the Eisenhower security program was a Republican plot to get rid of Democrats; what views he entertained while in Georgia as to racial segregation; whether he thought Jews were discriminated against through educational quotas and restrictive employment practices; whether he knew of various organizations that were not listed in the letter of charges, including the National Council for Soviet-American Friendship, Southern Conference for Human Welfare, Joint Anti-Fascist Refugee Committee, Negro Youth Congress, Abraham Lincoln Brigade, and Consumers' Union; whether he had been "active" in the Progressive Party of 1948; about "Black Mountain Transcendentalism" (a puzzler to everyone subsequently connected with this case, including the Supreme Court); and whether he had voted for Henry Wallace for Vice President in 1940. Vitarelli was even asked whether he had "kidded," "chided," or "ridiculed" a fellow teacher back in Georgia "as being of the bourgeoisie because she had purchased a house." Here are samples of the interchanges:

> QUESTION: The file indicates that you referred to and spoke about a people's movement.
> ANSWER: My interest in a people's movement is a philosophical, vague thing. It had no connection with organization that I remember.
> Q.: If philosophical, let us hear it.
> A.: In the context of the Constitution and the rights of the people to have free speech, meaning all people including Negroes and Jews.

Q.: Do I interpret your statement that maybe Negroes and Jews are denied some of their constitutional rights at present?

A.: Yes.

Q.: File indicates that you were quite hepped up over the one-world idea.

A.: I am still interested in the idea of world cooperation among all people in order that we may have peace, but I am cynical now about its possibilities.

Q.: At one time or two you were a strong advocate of the U.N. Are you still?

A.: I am still.

The second day of the hearing, July 1, was devoted exclusively to the testimony of four witnesses Vitarelli presented in his own behalf, including the commander of his local American Legion post, a justice of the peace, and the noted author James Michener. The cross-examination of the witnesses presented by Vitarelli, like that of Vitarelli himself, wandered far afield, as these excerpts make clear:

The Doctor [Vitarelli] indicated that he was acquainted with and talked to Norman Thomas on occasions. Did you know about that? . . . How about Dr. Vitarelli? Is he scholarly? . . . A good administrator? . . . Did you consider Dr. Vitarelli as a religious man? . . . Was he an extremist on equality of races? . . .

This whole process of attempting to rebut the undisclosed material in the confidential file was most frustrating, as Olmsted caustically noted in the nineteen-page brief he filed on July 22. Thus he particularly urged that the Board clear Vitarelli of any imputation of disloyalty. He observed that under the Eisenhower Executive Order, one "can be a security risk, even though found to be loyal." But "the public does not understand this, and takes inference of treasonable tendencies (or at least disgraceful ones, such as sex deviation) from a finding of security risk." He demanded that the Board at least "specifically find the unquestioned fact that Vitarelli is 'of complete and unswerving loyalty to the United States.' Anything else would blast the future of a very talented teacher, needlessly, and without basis in fact."

### Vitarelli Dismissed

Secretary McKay's "Findings and Final Determination" in the Vitarelli case were dated on September 2, and forwarded to Vitarelli by the Director of the Office of Trust Territories on September 3. The Secretary recited that on August 26 the Hearing Board had recommended "that the employment of William Vincent Vitarelli is not clearly consistent with the interests of national security," and that its recommendation had been accompanied by the required memorandum of reasons. After having "carefully reviewed" the case, he went on, he found it

> advisable and necessary that the employment of William Vincent Vitarelli should be terminated in the interest of national security for the reasons specifically set forth in the letter of March 30, 1954.
>
> IT IS, THEREFORE, DETERMINED AND ORDERED that the employment of William Vincent Vitarelli, an employee of this Department of the Interior, be, and the same is hereby, terminated in the interest of national security at the close of business on September 10, 1954.

### Unsuccessful Administrative Appeals

Olmsted protested that he never got the Hearing Board's "decision." Armstrong replied that the Department had never given a copy of the Board's "so-called decision" to a suspended employee since it was "only a recommendation," which the Secretary need not have consulted in determining whether to dismiss him. Olmsted objected to the characterization of the Board's action as "a mere recommendation by a subordinate clerk," pointing out that Executive Order 10450 referred to a "decision" of the Hearing Board and provided that this decision "will be reviewed and considered" by the Secretary.

Olmsted then requested a conference in Washington to find out "what may be done to assure the possibility of future employment and to protect him against unjust inference." The Department agreed to discuss the matter and on September 24 Olmsted conferred with Armstrong and two high-ranking security officers of the Department. Armstrong conceded that the Department had no complaint as to Vitarelli's service in the Pacific area and that it had based its decision to terminate his employment entirely on his activities prior to entering government service, especially in Georgia and at Columbia.

Armstrong also revealed that the Department had largely relied on a confidential FBI report containing information damaging to Vitarelli. He contended that the report had been made by a person who was a confidential agent and that, consequently, the Department could not divulge its contents, except to indicate that it did not concern Vitarelli's activities in the Pacific. Moreover, Armstrong maintained that the agent's statement seemed to be fortified by Vitarelli's own testimony. He explained that several times during the hearing Vitarelli was given an opportunity to enlighten the Board on the matter touched on by the agent, and though his answers indicated his awareness of what was being hinted at, he deliberately chose to withhold pertinent information on that point. Olmsted confronted Vitarelli with these charges, but Vitarelli vigorously insisted that he had been completely candid.

No further significant developments in the case occurred until late in the summer of 1955. Although his family had returned to the States in November, 1954, Vitarelli was unable to obtain permanent employment commensurate with his professional capabilities. Friends at Teachers College advised him not to seek an educational position. "They said it would be better to wait until I got cleared; on a number of occasions I was advised not to try to get into education because it would be like butting my head against a stone wall until I got cleared." However, he did make several applications and received one answer, "but all of a sudden everything was dropped and I did not hear from them again." The best educational job offered him was at a salary of $2,400 at a private school in Massachusetts. Thus he was compelled to accept various odd jobs, such as designing swimming pool brochures and doing part-time construction work. His earnings were meager, and he was practically destitute. Yet the likelihood of a material improvement in his condition was faint as long as the security dismissal remained on his official personnel record.

## The Case Reopened

A remarkable coincidence gave new life to his case. In September, 1955, at an airport in Lucknow, India, Olmsted, who was concluding a trip around the world, struck up a conversation with Nat Logan-Smith, who identified himself as an Interior Department personnel officer stationed in the Pacific Trust Territory. In response to Olmsted's expressed interest in Vitarelli's case, but unaware that he was serving as the latter's attorney, Logan-Smith freely divulged what he knew of the matter.

According to Logan-Smith, Vitarelli's dismissal had in no way been predicated upon his associations prior to entering government service, but had been based entirely upon his conduct and activities in the Pacific, which clearly indicated that he lacked "common sense." This information directly contradicted the Department's announced position that it had no complaint as to Vitarelli's performance as a public servant but objected only to certain conduct and associations prior to his employment by the government.

## Further Unsuccessful Administrative Appeals

Startling as Logan-Smith's revelations were, Olmsted was uncertain as to his next course of action. For, as he cautioned Vitarelli:

> From your point of view a practical question is how it would affect you and your future activities to bring out that you were really fired for reasons which might be classified as inefficiency. A kindly disposed person would merely say that you were a square peg in a round hole and that you were too independent and full of good ideas to fit into the government bureaucracy. An unkindly disposed person would say, however, that you were just no damn good.

Yet, after weighing the alternatives, Olmsted decided to bring Logan-Smith's statements to light. He informed Armstrong that important new evidence had been discovered, though he did not divulge its nature, and requested a rehearing at which it might be placed officially upon the record. Armstrong assured him that the Department wanted to be fair and granted his request. Accordingly, on November 14, Logan-Smith appeared before Undersecretary of the Interior Clarence Davis and was quizzed by both Olmsted and Armstrong. His testimony virtually confirmed the earlier story.

On November 18 Olmsted wrote to the Undersecretary reiterating his "first and primary" demand that Vitarelli be reinstated in the light of Logan-Smith's testimony for it indicated that the matter giving rise to the dismissal "should be classified as suitability rather than as security risk." Olmsted reassured Davis that "Vitarelli is prepared to relieve the Department of all embarrassment in the matter by resigning after he is reinstated."

The Department failed to respond. Meanwhile, Olmsted and Vitarelli accepted invitations to appear before the Senate Subcommittee on Constitutional Rights, which was making a comprehensive review of government security procedures, and on November 23 they testified concerning the development of the case to date. Subcommittee Chairman Hennings was sufficiently impressed by their testimony to request Secretary McKay to provide further pertinent information. The Secretary refrained from making any extensive comments since, he said, "the entire record is again being . . . carefully reviewed" to determine whether the petition Olmsted had filed should be granted.

### Preparing for Court Action

The Interior Department took no action. It did not even indicate when the pending review of the whole record might be completed. Vitarelli and Olmsted concluded that the time had come to go to the courts. Because Olmsted was not a member of the District of Columbia bar, where the suit would have to be filed, he secured a Washington attorney, Clifford J. Hynning, to serve as Vitarelli's counsel.

Hynning immediately conferred with various people in an effort to secure Vitarelli's reinstatement. He discussed the case with Harry Cain of the Subversive Activities Control Board and with Dr. Benjamin Ginzburg, Staff Director of the Subcommittee on Constitutional Rights. In late February, 1956, Hynning had an informal talk with the chairman and another member of Vitarelli's Security Hearing Board and reported, "They are plainly disturbed about the case, which is indicated by the speed with which I could arrange the meeting. But they did not know what to do. . . . They were bothered by the great amount of irrelevancies in the record and tried to blame Vitarelli for introducing them." Finally, on April 9, Hynning filed a memorandum with Davis re-emphasizing that what Vitarelli wanted "was clearance of his name, not a job with the Department of the Interior." But on May 11, Davis, who was now Acting Secretary of the Interior in place of the recently resigned McKay, officially denied the petition for reinstatement or an entirely new hearing. The only recourse left was a suit for reinstatement in the Federal District Court.

Vitarelli's chances for success in the courts were difficult to evaluate. Two Supreme Court decisions that dealt with the Truman Loyalty Program had failed to resolve any constitutional questions. In *Bailey* v. *Richardson* (1951), the Court had divided four to four (Justice Clark not participating), thus affirming a lower Federal Court decision that because government employment was a privilege, not a right, the procedures used to dismiss a Federal employee need not conform to the standards of procedural due process. The decision in *Peters* v. *Hobby* (1955), although conceding that dismissal on loyalty grounds fastened a "badge of infamy" on the fired worker, confined itself to the narrow ground that E.O. 9835 did not authorize the Loyalty Review Board (abolished under the Eisenhower security program) to reverse agency decisions favorable to the employee.

On June 11, 1956, however, the Supreme Court handed down its decision in *Cole* v. *Young,* the first case to reach the Court under the Eisenhower program. Here the Court ruled that the power to remove Federal workers under the Act of August 26, 1950, invoked by the Department of the Interior in removing Vitarelli, was limited to "sensitive" positions, that is, those in which there was some special relationship to the national security. Because Vitarelli's position had never been designated "sensitive" and therefore under the Interior Department's own regulations had to be considered "nonsensitive," the decision gave hope that his reinstatement might still be secured without a court test. On June 12 Hynning made a written demand on the new Secretary of the Interior, Fred Seaton, to order Vitarelli's immediate restoration to duty on the ground that the *Cole* decision had rendered his dismissal a "nullity." But Secretary Seaton failed to comply, pending a determination by the Justice Department as to the effect of the *Cole* decision on security removals in general.

When no action was immediately forthcoming, preparations were made to bring suit in the District Court. Olmsted succeeded in obtaining a grant of $2,000 from the Rights of Conscience Committee of the American Friends Service Committee, of which he was a member, to defray the expenses involved. He and Hynning journeyed to Vitarelli's home in Bucks County to map their strategy. The principal question to be resolved was whether the complaint should be limited to the contention that, in the light of the *Cole* decision, Vitarelli's dismissal had technically been a nullity, or whether to strive to obtain his complete vindication. Because reinstatement on a "technicality" was undesirable, they decided to pursue the latter alternative.

### Vitarelli's Complaint and the Government's Answer

On July 10 the complaint was filed by Hynning, with Olmsted remaining of counsel. It asked for a declaratory judgment that Vitarelli's removal be set aside as illegal and void, and for a mandatory injunction directing that he be reinstated with back pay. The complaint alleged that the procedures employed by the Department in dismissing Vitarelli violated his rights under the departmental security regulation issued under the Act of August 26, 1950, and E.O. 10450, and also the broader constitutional guarantees of the due process clause of the Fifth Amendment.

These specific constitutional objections were entered against the dismissal:

(1) The statement of charges was insufficiently specific.

(2) The hearing was not fair or impartial since the board "wandered far afield, without any discernible standards of relevancy and materiality from the matters set forth in the letter of charges."

(3) There was no evidence to support the board's findings.

(4) Vitarelli was never furnished with a copy of the findings and conclusions reached by the board.

(5) His dismissal as a security risk "branded him with 'a badge of infamy' . . . arbitrarily and capriciously, without basis in fact, without a fair hearing or procedure," because of which his "reputation as a professional educator has been destroyed and it has become virtually impossible for him to obtain employment in his field of training."

In a detailed answer to the complaint, the government denied that any of the procedures followed in Vitarelli's suspension were unlawful or unconstitutional. It claimed that the letter of charges was as "specific as security regulations permit" and that the Security Board hearing was impartial. And, despite Armstrong's earlier concession on the record, it even denied that Vitarelli's loyalty was unquestioned.

## Courtroom Tactics

The next move was a surprising one. On October 10 the government, without previous warning, submitted to the court two sworn affidavits from the Department of the Interior and the Civil Service Commission attesting that those agencies had voluntarily expunged from their records all adverse findings made with respect to Vitarelli under E.O. 10450. Attached to these affidavits was a photostatic copy of the standard civil service form entitled Notification of Personnel Action, which had just been entered in Vitarelli's employment file, reciting that it was "a revision of and replaces the original," issued in 1954. The revised notification of termination of employment deleted the crucial statement contained in the original that the action was "taken in accordance with the provisions of Executive Order 10450." Like the original, however, it was dated September 21, 1954, and nothing on its face indicated that it was not issued on that date, or that it was issued in October, 1956.

This shift in government strategy, it was later learned, had been taken by the Justice Department as a result of its study on the effect of the *Cole* decision on the status of other dismissed Federal employees. The government conceded that in the light of *Cole* the removal of Vitarelli from a nonsensitive position was unauthorized by either the Act of 1950 or E.O. 10450 and, therefore, reliance on this ground for removal had to be eliminated from the record. This did not mean that the government was ready to concede that Vitarelli's removal was unjustified; it merely meant it recognized the need to find a new reason to justify the removal. Nor was this hard to do, since Vitarelli's own counsel had repeatedly asked the government why it had not, if it wanted to be rid of Vitarelli, removed him from his unprotected Schedule A position by simple executive action.

This was precisely the stand the government now took. Along with the notice of revision in Vitarelli's file, the administration submitted a motion to dismiss his suit or, alternatively, for summary judgment denying his claim on the ground that the Secretary's removal action was not subject to review.

### *The District Court Trial—The Dismissal Sustained*

On October 16 the case was heard before District Judge James W. Morris. Neither party introduced testimony, limiting the proceedings to presentation of oral argument. To Hynning the issue was clear-cut. "Can the Government fire the man for the wrong reasons and the wrong procedures and blacken his name and the name of his family and then say we aren't responsible, because we could have fired him in a perfectly lawful manner which wouldn't have blackened his name? I think that question answers itself."

Donald M. McGuineas, who represented the government, formulated the issue quite differently. Vitarelli was an employee at will of the Secretary of the Interior, having an indefinite, not a fixed term, appointment. Further, Vitarelli lacked protection under the Veterans' Preference Act and the civil service laws. "Therefore . . . the Secretary, in the exercise of the executive authority to hire and fire employees, was free to dismiss the plaintiff at any time, on any grounds or for no ground, with procedure or without procedure, as he might see fit."

At the conclusion of the argument, Judge Morris ruled in favor of the government. He said, "I really don't see how this Court has the right to say that he [Vitarelli] shall be reinstated when the Secretary had the right to terminate his service, even if he terminated [it] for a wrong reason." An employee at will, he continued, although removed by a wrong procedure for the wrong reason, is still without a remedy as far as reinstatement is concerned, because if a court should restore him, he could be fired again that very same day.

Judge Morris then invited each side to submit language for a court order that would carry this ruling into effect and that would exonerate Vitarelli as far as possible from the "security risk" stigma. The order, issued on October 29, stated:

This cause having been heard on cross motions of plaintiff and defendants for summary judgment; and it appearing that the removal of plaintiff as a "security risk" under the Act of August 26, 1950 . . . has been conceded by the defendants not to have been authorized under that act; that the defendants have taken all practical steps, short of reinstating plaintiff or giving him back pay, to remove the stigma, if any, which may have resulted from his removal by expunging from the records of the Department of the Interior and the Civil Service Commission all adverse statements with respect to plaintiff as a "security risk" under Executive Order 10450; that the position to which plaintiff seeks reinstatement was and is a "Schedule A" position, which is excepted from the competitive civil service and from which plaintiff could be summarily removed with or without cause under the general authority of the executive branch to appoint and remove employees excepted from the competitive civil service; and that this Court cannot order the reinstatement of plaintiff whose tenure, as a "Schedule A" employee, is only at the will of the employing Government.

### The Decision To Appeal

Vitarelli was dissatisfied with the phraseology of the order and wanted to appeal the decision. As he wrote Hynning:

> I believe that the only way I can re-establish myself in the educational field is to win a reinstatement with all the rights and standing I had before I was so unjustly wrenched from my work. . . . The most important fact to remember . . . is that I have been branded and that . . . expunging has not removed the brand [since it automatically followed from the rationale of the *Cole* decision].

Hynning too considered the District Court order inadequate and wanted to make an appeal. Olmsted, on the other hand, at first thought that nothing significant stood to be gained from an appeal since the District Court order was "framed in such words as to indicate [Vitarelli's] freedom from taint as a security risk." He was finally persuaded, however, "as a citizen outraged by the conduct of the Department of the Interior," that an appeal should be made. The Rights of Conscience Committee agreed to permit the unexpended balance of its earlier allocation to defray the actual filing costs of the appeal.

Hynning, after giving notice of his intention to appeal, successfully negotiated with the government for an extension of the period for filing the appeal. He wished to await a Supreme Court decision in the pending case of *Service* v. *Dulles*. On June 17, the Court (Justice Clark not participating) unanimously ordered the reinstatement of Service, a State Department foreign service officer, on the grounds that the Secretary of State had manifestly failed to observe the regulations that he himself had prescribed and had bound himself to follow in security cases.

This decision was pertinent to Vitarelli's claim, for in his letter of suspension Secretary McKay purported to be acting under Departmental Order 2738, which he had issued in November, 1953, extending certain procedural rights to "all" employees suspended "in the interest of national security." In Hynning's opinion Vitarelli had been denied several of these protections and, therefore, according to the *Service* case, was entitled to reinstatement.

## The Opposing Arguments in the Court of Appeals

Hynning's brief presented a threefold argument. First, as in the District Court, the "prime issue" was the constitutional right of an educator to pursue his profession without being arbitrarily defamed by the government. Second, even if the dismissal did not violate fundamental constitutional guarantees, the rule of the *Service* case was sufficient to compel his reinstatement. For Secretary McKay had by departmental order guaranteed certain procedures applicable to "all" security removals, which Vitarelli had not enjoyed. Third, though the Secretary clearly lacked the legal authority to dismiss Vitarelli under the Act of August 26, 1950, and E.O. 10450, the fact that he *purported* to do so was of decisive significance and prevented the government from subsequently seeking to justify his action under the executive's plenary removal power.

In its reply the government contended that the judgment of the District Court should be affirmed because Vitarelli's dismissal violated none of his legal rights. As to the constitutional issue, the government again argued that whatever stigma might have been fastened on him by dismissing him as a security risk had been completely removed by the voluntary recision of all references to the adverse security findings from his personnel records. Regarding Vitarelli's statutory rights, the government had two answers: first, he had none; second, even if the departmental security regulations were deemed applicable to Vitarelli's discharge, they had been complied with fully.

## Another Unfavorable Decision—The District Court Upheld

On February 13, 1958, the three-judge Court of Appeals, with one judge dissenting, affirmed the decision of the District Court in *Vitarelli* v. *Seaton*. The court admitted that a government employee lacking statutory job protection was "entitled to be free from dismissal on unconstitutional or flagrantly arbitrary grounds," but found that Vitarelli's treatment by the Secretary "was in no way arbitrary or lacking in due process." He was given written charges and an opportunity to answer them, together with a hearing.

The court also pointed out that one of the grounds of dismissal announced by Secretary McKay, untrustworthiness and deliberate misrepresentation, furnished a "clear basis" for the dismissal; since this finding appeared "rational and proper," the courts could not "review the evidence or examine the merits thereof." The fact that this charge "was intimately related" to the expunged security charges was deemed immaterial. In other words the charge of untrustworthiness, though purportedly made in a security hearing, nonetheless survived a voluntary expunging of the adverse security charges. At any rate that revision "is equivalent to the maximum relief a court might have been justified in granting under all the circumstances of the case." Thus Vitarelli was "legally discharged, even though the proceedings were improperly labeled as being brought under the authority of the Act of 1950 and Executive Order No. 10450."

One judge dissented on the ground that the charge of untrustworthiness could not be read "as in any case independent" of the expunged security charges. He found, under the ruling in *Cole,* "the basis for the original termination disappears, and with it the validity of that termination." He concluded that the second notice of dismissal, filed in the District Court on October 10, 1956, but which purported to dismiss Vitarelli as of the date of the original termination, "could not relate back as attempted, and at most could be effective only as of the time it was taken. . . ."

### Appeal to the Supreme Court

Before applying for a writ of certiorari to the Supreme Court, it was necessary to raise funds for filing fees and printing costs. A favorable recommendation by the District of Columbia Bar Association enabled Hynning to secure an award of $2,500 from the Robert Marshall Civil Liberties Trust, while Olmsted obtained a further grant of $500 from the Friends' Rights of Conscience Committee.

On May 5, 1958, upon a motion submitted by Hynning two days earlier, Chief Justice Warren issued an order, extending for an additional thirty days, until June 13, the time in which to file the petition for certiorari. This meant that Vitarelli's petition would not be lost in the morass of such applications accumulated at the end of the term. Hynning prepared a draft of the petition and submitted it to Olmsted, who suggested several revisions. He proposed that greater stress be placed upon the graphic fact that "the 1956 letter of discharge was a phony reprehensibly lacking in frankness." He further urged elimination from the petition of the elaborately developed arguments and extensive quoting from cases, which in his judgment were more appropriate in a brief than in a petition for certiorari. Hynning was willing to incorporate the former suggestion, but rejected the latter because of "the importance of drafting a petition for certiorari so fully that, if the Court were so minded, it might lead to a reversal *per curiam* without a submission on the merits."

A detailed petition was submitted to the Supreme Court on June 12. The issue was "whether respondent Secretary can defame and stigmatize petitioner as a threat to the security of his country through following the formalities of an adjudicatory proceeding without observing the most elementary requirements of a fair hearing." The government filed a motion in opposition to granting the writ, reiterating its contention (accepted by the two lower courts) that Vitarelli was entitled to no further judicial relief since he was unprotected by any statute or regulation, and since the adverse security findings had been voluntarily expunged from government records. The Supreme Court granted certiorari on October 27.

In December, while Hynning was drafting his brief, Olmsted was appointed to the Court of Common Pleas of Delaware County, Pennsylvania. He then officially withdrew from active participation in the case. One of his partners, Harry E. Sprogell, replaced Olmsted as "of counsel" to Hynning. Vitarelli's brief for the most part simply reiterated the contentions raised and developed before the Court of Appeals. The constitutional right against being stigmatized with a "badge of infamy" was again the "prime issue."

### A Government Offer of Settlement Spurned

Before filing its reply the government tried to settle the case out of court. On February 5, Samuel Slade, a Justice Department attorney, informally told Hynning that his Department was willing to settle by reimbursing Vitarelli's back pay, although only up to 1956, but was encountering strong resistance from Interior, which feared the precedent such action would set for other cases. Hynning tentatively rejected the "offer," since he believed that Vitarelli desired, in addition to back pay, reinstatement and reassignment to the Pacific. However, Hynning did transmit the government's suggestion to Vitarelli, Olmsted, and Sprogel. Vitarelli pronounced it absolutely unacceptable. "Any settlement for back pay . . . without *reinstatement* . . . is out of the question," he stated. He regarded reinstatement as

> crucial in order to re-establish my credentials and to convince future employers that the "clearance" was substantial *in fact* as well as theory. As for my returning to the Islands, I feel that again—the very fact that I would resume employment where I had left off and that my credentials would show (*technically*) that I had been employed from *1950 to 1959* by the Department of the Interior would not make prospective employers wonder about the big gap during my "suspension" until I had a chance to explain and show the documentation.

Hynning likewise strongly opposed the compromise. Vitarelli should "insist on reinstatement with all the rights that follow therefrom," he declared.

> We are now so close to a final decision and an authoritative one at that, that I feel that we should proceed. In my opinion Vit runs little or no risk of losing in the Supreme Court. . . . To now rush into a last minute settlement would be disastrous in terms of the long fight that he has made in this case.

On February 14 Hynning received a phone call from Slade. With the consent of the Interior Department, Justice made a specific offer to give Vitarelli five months back pay, from his suspension in April, 1954, to the termination of his employment on September 10, 1954. In addition, the offer included re-employment for Vitarelli "somewhere in the Pacific" instead of reinstating him, with the stipulation that this was without prejudice to his rights to bring suit in the Court of Claims for additional back pay. Slade gave his assurance that this was an authentic offer of re-employment, and that thereafter Vitarelli would not be harassed or confronted with any of the charges.

Hynning immediately conveyed the substance of the conversation to Vitarelli for his consideration. Three days later, after delineating the alternatives, Hynning recommended to Vitarelli that the offer be rejected and the case proceed on its merits. But Vitarelli (and his wife) had already decided to reject the offer after studying Hynning's letter of February 14, and thus Hynning's recommendation only confirmed their decision. As Vitarelli said, "five months of back pay falls far short of an equitable adjustment [and] 're-employing you as a teacher somewhere in the Pacific' is far too vague and uncertain. . . ."

### Oral Argument in the Supreme Court

The government made no further offer of settlement and, accordingly, filed its brief in the Supreme Court. The brief was a restatement of the arguments presented in the Court of Appeals. Oral argument was heard before the Supreme Court on April 1 and 2, 1959. At the outset Justice Harlan, who subsequently wrote the opinion of the Court, inquired why the transcript of the hearing before the Security Hearing Board was not in the printed official record before the Court. Hynning explained that since the case went up on a motion for summary judgment, the substance of the proceedings before the Board was merely summarized in the complaint and admitted by the government for purposes of that motion. Consequently, there was no occasion to introduce the transcript officially into the record before the Court. Chief Justice Warren then inquired whether the government objected to making a copy available to the Court; the attorney for the government, John G. Laughlin, Jr., had no objection. Needless to say, Hynning wanted it to be introduced, for he considered the transcript more damaging to the government than the complaint. This assertion was later borne out by the fact that footnotes to the opinion of the Court contained many more detailed references to anti-Semitism than appeared in the original complaint. The Court had apparently read the transcript meticulously.

An interesting piece of repartee occurred near the conclusion of the oral argument on April 1. The Chief Justice requested Laughlin to explain the reference in the transcript to "Black Mountain Transcendentalism." Justice Frankfurter quipped that it would be impossible to decide the case until the

Court learned more about it. In response to a question from Justice Douglas Hynning said that he did not have the foggiest idea what it was. The next day Laughlin sheepishly volunteered that "Transcendentalism" was a type of philosophy prevalent in New England during the nineteenth century, while "Black Mountain" referred to some mountains in India. The Court was apparently satisfied. On June 1 its decision appeared.

---

## *VITARELLI* v. *SEATON*
### 359 U.S. 535, 79 S. Ct. 968, 3 L. Ed. 2d 1012 (1959)

MR. JUSTICE HARLAN delivered the opinion of the Court.

[The opinion begins with a summary of the facts in the case, which have already been recounted.]

The Secretary's letter of March 30, 1954, and notice of dismissal of September 2, 1954, both relied upon Exec. Order No. 10450, . . . the Act of August 26, 1950, . . . and Department of the Interior Order No. 2738, all relating to discharges of government employees on security or loyalty grounds, as the authority for petitioner's dismissal. In *Cole* v. *Young,* . . . this Court held that the statute referred to did not apply to government employees in positions not designated as "sensitive." Respondent takes the position that since petitioner's position in government service has at no time been designated as sensitive the effect of *Cole,* which was decided after the 1954 dismissal of petitioner, was to render also inapplicable to petitioner Department of the Interior Order No. 2738, under which the proceedings relating to petitioner's dismissal were had. It is urged that in this state of affairs petitioner, who concededly was at no time within the protection of the Civil Service Act, Veterans' Preference Act, or any other statute relating to employment rights of government employees, and who, as a

"Schedule A" employee, could have been summarily discharged by the Secretary at any time without the giving of a reason, under no circumstances could be entitled to more than that which he has already received—namely, an "expunging" from the record of his 1954 discharge of any reference to the authority or reasons therefor.

Respondent misconceives the effect of our decision in *Cole.* It is true that the Act of August 26, 1950, and the Executive Order did not alter the power of the Secretary to discharge summarily an employee in petitioner's status, without the giving of any reason. Nor did the Department's own regulations preclude such a course. Since, however, the Secretary gratuitously decided to give a reason, and that reason was national security, he was obligated to conform to the procedural standards he had formulated in Order No. 2738 for the dismissal of employees on security grounds. *Service* v. *Dulles.* . . . That Order on its face applies to *all* security discharges in the Department of the Interior, including such discharges of Schedule A employees. *Cole* v. *Young* established that the Act of August 26, 1950, did not permit the discharge of non-sensitive employees pursuant to procedures authorized by that Act if those procedures were more summary than those to which the employee would have been entitled by virtue of any pre-existing statute or regulation. That decision cannot, however, justify noncompliance by the Secretary with regulations promulgated by him in the departmental Order, which as to petitioner afford greater procedural protections in the case of a dismissal stated to be for security reasons than in the case of dismissal without any statement of reasons. Having chosen to proceed against petitioner on security grounds, the Secretary here, as in *Service,* was bound by the regulations which he himself had promulgated for dealing with such cases, even though without such regulations he could have discharged petitioner summarily.

Petitioner makes various contentions as to the constitutional invalidity of the procedures provided by Order No. 2738. He further urges that even assuming the validity of the governing procedures, his dismissal cannot stand because the notice of suspension and hearing given him did not comply with the Order. We find it unnecessary to reach the constitutional issues, for we think that petitioner's second position is well taken and must be sustained.

Preliminarily, it should be said that departures from departmental regulations in matters of this kind involve more than mere consideration of procedural irregularities. For in proceedings of this nature, in which the ordinary rules of evidence do not apply, in which matters involving the disclosure of confidential information are withheld, and where it must be recognized that counsel is under practical constraints in the making of objections and in the tactical handling of his case which would not obtain in a cause being tried in a court of law before trained judges, scrupulous observance of departmental procedural safeguards is clearly of particular importance. In this instance an examination of the record, and of the transcript of the hearing before the

departmental security board, discloses that petitioner's procedural rights under the applicable regulations were violated in at least three material respects in the proceedings which terminated in the final notice of his dismissal.

*First,* § 15(a) of Order No. 2738 requires that the statement of charges served upon an employee at the time of his suspension on security grounds "shall be as specific and detailed as security considerations, including the need for protection of confidential sources of information, permit . . . and shall be subject to amendment within 30 days of issuance." Although the statement of charges furnished petitioner appears on its face to be reasonably specific, the transcript of hearing establishes that the statement, which was never amended, cannot conceivably be said in fact to be as specific and detailed as "security considerations . . . permit." For petitioner was questioned by the security officer and by the hearing board in great detail concerning his association with and knowledge of various persons and organizations nowhere mentioned in the statement of charges, and at length concerning his activities in Bucks County, Pennsylvania, and elsewhere after 1945, activities as to which the charges are also completely silent. These questions were presumably asked because they were deemed relevant to the inquiry before the board, and the very fact that they were asked and thus spread on the record is conclusive indication that "security considerations" could not have justified the omission of any statement concerning them in the charges furnished petitioner.

*Second,* §§ 21(a) and (e) require that hearings before security hearing boards shall be "orderly" and that "reasonable restrictions shall be imposed as to relevancy, competency, and materiality of matters considered." . . . [T]hese indispensable indicia of a meaningful hearing were not observed. It is not an overcharacterization to say that as the hearing proceeded it developed into a wide-ranging inquisition into this man's educational, social, and political beliefs, encompassing even a question as to whether he was "a religious man."

*Third,* § 21(c)(4) gives the employee the right "to cross-examine any witness offered in support of the charges." It is apparent from an overall reading of the regulations that it was not contemplated that this provision should require the Department to call witnesses to testify in support of any or all of the charges, because it was expected that charges might rest on information gathered from or by "confidential informants." We think, however, that § 21(c)(4) did contemplate the calling by the Department of any informant not properly classifiable as "confidential," if information furnished by that informant was to be used by the board in assessing an employee's status. The transcript shows that this provision was violated on at least one occasion at petitioner's hearing, for the security officer identified by name a person who had given information apparently considered detrimental to petitioner, thus negating any possible inference that that person was considered a "confidential informant" whose identity it was necessary to keep secret, and questioned petitioner at some length concerning the information supplied from this source without calling the informant and affording petitioner the right to cross-examine.

Because the proceedings attendant upon petitioner's dismissal from government service on grounds of national security fell substantially short of the requirements of the applicable departmental regulations, we hold that such dismissal was illegal and of no effect.

Respondent urges that even if the dismissal of September 10, 1954, was invalid, petitioner is not entitled to reinstatement by reason of the fact that he was at all events validly dismissed in October, 1956, when a copy of the second "Notification of Personnel Action," omitting all reference to any statute, order, or regulation relating to security discharges, was delivered to him. Granting that the Secretary could at any time after September 10, 1954, have validly dismissed petitioner without any statement of reasons, and independently of the proceedings taken against him under Order No. 2738, we cannot view the delivery of the new notification to petitioner as an exercise of that summary dismissal power. Rather, the fact that it was dated "9–21–54," contained a termination of employment date of "9–10–54," was designated as "a revision" of the 1954 notification, and was evidently filed in the District Court before its delivery to petitioner indicates that its sole purpose was an attempt to moot petitioner's suit in the District Court by an "expunging" of the grounds for the dismissal which brought Order No. 2738 into play. In these circumstances, we would not be justified in now treating the 1956 action, plainly intended by the Secretary as a grant of relief to petitioner in connection with the form of the 1954 discharge, as an exercise of the Secretary's summary removal power as of the date of its delivery to petitioner.

It follows from what we have said that petitioner is entitled to the reinstatement which he seeks, subject, of course, to any lawful exercise of the Secretary's authority hereafter to dismiss him from employment in the Department of the Interior.

*Reversed.*

MR. JUSTICE FRANKFURTER, whom MR. JUSTICE CLARK, MR. JUSTICE WHITTAKER and MR. JUSTICE STEWART join, concurring in part and dissenting in part.

An executive agency must be rigorously held to the standards by which it professes its action to be judged. See *Securities & Exchange Comm'n* v. *Chenery Corp.* . . . Accordingly, if dismissal from employment is based on a defined procedure, even though generous beyond the requirements that bind such agency, that procedure must be scrupulously observed. See *Service* v. *Dulles*. . . . This judicially evolved rule of administrative law is now firmly established and, if I may add, rightly so. He that takes the procedural sword shall perish with that sword. Therefore, I unreservedly join in the Court's main conclusion, that the attempted dismissal of Vitarelli in September 1954 was abortive and of no validity because the procedure under Department of the Interior Order No. 2738 was invoked but not observed.

But when an executive agency draws on the freedom that the law vests in it, the judiciary cannot deny or curtail such freedom. The Secretary of the Interior concededly had untrammelled right to dismiss Vitarelli out of hand, since he had no protected employment rights. He could do so as freely as a private employer who is not bound by procedural restrictions of a collective bargaining contract. The Secretary was under no law-imposed or self-imposed restriction in discharging an employee in Vitarelli's position without statement of reasons and without a hearing. And so the question is, did the Secretary take action, after the abortive discharge in 1954, dismissing Vitarelli?

In October, 1956, there was served upon Vitarelli a copy of a new notice of dismissal which had been inserted in the Department's personnel records in place of the first notice. Another copy was filed with the District Court in this proceeding. This second notice contained no mention of grounds of discharge. If, instead of sending this second notice to Vitarelli the Secretary had telephoned Vitarelli to convey the contents of the second notice he would have said: "I note that you are contesting the validity of the dismissal. I want to make this very clear to you. If I did not succeed in dismissing you before, I now dismiss you, and I dismiss you retroactively, effective September 1954."

The Court disallows this significance to the second notice of discharge because it finds controlling meaning in the suggestion of the Government that the expunging from the record of any adverse comment, and the second notice of discharge, signified a reassertion of the effectiveness of the first attempt at dismissal. And so, the Court concludes, no intention of severance from service in 1956 could legally be found since the Secretary expressed no doubt that the first dismissal had been effective. But this document of 1956 was not a mere piece of paper in a dialectic. The paper was a record of a process, a manifestation of purpose and action. The intendment of the second notice, to be sure, was to discharge Vitarelli retroactively, resting this attempted dismissal on valid authority—the summary power to dismiss without reason. Though the second notice could not pre-date the summary discharge because the Secretary rested his 1954 discharge on an unsustainable ground, and Vitarelli could not be deprived of rights accrued during two years of unlawful discharge, the prior wrongful action did not deprive the Secretary of the power in him to fire Vitarelli prospectively. And if the intent of the Secretary be manifested in fact by what he did, however that intent be expressed—here, the intent to be rid of Vitarelli—the Court should not frustrate the Secretary's rightful exercise of this power as of October 1956. The fact that he wished to accomplish more does not mean he accomplished nothing.

To construe the second notice to mean administratively nothing is to attribute to the Secretary the purpose of a mere diarist, the corrector of entries in the Department's archives. This wholly disregards the actualities in the conduct of a Department concerned with terminating the services of an undesired employee as completely and by whatever means that may legally be accomplished. If an employer summons before him an employee over whom he has unfettered power of dismissal and says to him: "You are no longer employed here because I fired you last week," can one reasonably escape the conclusion that though the employer was in error and had not effectively carried out his purpose to fire the employee last week, the employer's statement clearly manifests a present belief that the employee is dismissed and an intention that he be foreverafter dismissed? Certainly the employee would have no doubt his employment was now at an end. Of course if some special formal document were required to bring about a severance of a relationship, cf. *Felter v. Southern Pacific Co.,* . . . because of non-compliance with the formality the severance would not come into being. But no such formality was requisite to Vitarelli's dismissal.

This is the common sense of it: In 1956 the Secretary said to Vitarelli: "This document tells you without any ifs, ands, or buts, you have been fired right along and of course that means you are not presently employed by this Department." Since he had not been fired successfully in 1954, the Court concludes he must still be employed. I cannot join in an unreal interpretation which attributes to governmental action the empty meaning of confetti throwing.

---

### Restoration and Back Pay

On the day the decision was announced, Vitarelli was teaching manual arts at a high school in Langhorne, Pennsylvania. The decision of the Court appeared to provide the "complete vindication" which he had sought for five years. Indeed, to the extent that the decision was meant to secure his reinstatement and restoration to duty in the Pacific, the Department of the Interior sought to comply forthwith, even though a final order would not be entered by the District Court until November. On June 15 the High Commissioner of the Trust Islands offered Vitarelli the post, stationed on Guam, of Assistant to the Education Director for the Islands. This position bore the same civil service grade as his former post. Vitarelli enthusiastically accepted. The Department ordered him reinstated as of June 26, then placed him on one month's annual leave to enable him to put his personal affairs in order. On August 4 he departed for his new assignment.

The settlement of his claim for back pay was not so easily reached, however. At the time of his unlawful suspension he was employed at a basic salary of $6,140 per year, plus 25 per cent territorial post differential (TPD), authorized by the Civil Service Commission. Hynning argued that Vitarelli should now receive approximately $42,000 gross, covering the basic pay and TPD accumulated since the date of his suspension, the payments, by the day, for the entire period of his absence from his official post in the Pacific, the general statutory salary increases granted by Congress in 1955 and 1958 and the periodic pay raises that had occurred since his suspension, and the annual leave which would have accrued had he not been unlawfully removed. From this total Vitarelli's "interim net earnings" should be deducted, which in turn should be computed as the earnings he had received from his private employment since his suspension (approximately $22,000) minus the legal fees incurred in vindicating his right to his professional position.

The Departments of Justice and Interior, on the other hand, believed that he was entitled to receive only his basic pay for the five-year period, plus the TPD for the seven-month period from April 10 to November 11, 1954, during which his family actually remained overseas awaiting his orders to return to the mainland, less his "interim net earnings," from which no deduction might be made for legal expenses. By this calculation, the sum due would be approximately $11,000.

Even this amount could not be immediately obtained. On June 15 the General Accounting Office (GAO) announced that, on the basis of previous decisions of the Comptroller General, it would not authorize or approve the disbursement of *any* back pay to Vitarelli since his lack of civil service tenure or veteran's status prevented his qualifying under any appropriation statute or organic law.

### The Case in the Court of Claims

Thus it became necessary to institute suit in the Court of Claims. Petition was filed by Hynning on June 30. Soon thereafter the Comptroller General informed the Department of Justice that the GAO had changed its views and was willing to approve the "noncontroversial" claim that the Departments of Justice and Interior had agreed should be paid. Settlement was eventually reached in mid-January, 1960, in the amount of $10,917.42.

This still left to be resolved by the Court of Claims Vitarelli's suit for the additional sums he was claiming for legal fees, annual leave, pay increases, daily payments, and TPD—a total of approximately $31,000. On June 8 a decision was rendered that amounted to a clear-cut victory for neither party. The Court held that Vitarelli should recover the monetary equivalent of the annual leave that would have accrued during the period of his removal, the payments, by the day, from the date of his suspension until the hearings before the Security Board were completed, and the 25 per cent post differential for the entire period since November, 1954; but that he should not receive the periodic increases or legislative raises that had occurred during his separation, nor should he be permitted to exclude his legal fees from "interim net earnings." On December 30, 1960, final judgment was entered in the amount of $10,630, and payment of the judgment was effected in January, 1961. Adding the earlier settlement of the uncontested claim, Vitarelli's total recovery was $21,517.42.

### Aftermath and Appraisal

The day following the decision, the New York *Times* reporter covering the Supreme Court, Anthony Lewis, predicted that *Vitarelli* v. *Seaton* would have "reverberations for all security programs." Many of the agency regulations, he wrote, require standards of fairness similar to those of Interior Departmental Order 2738, "but in fact many security hearings are said to have the same faults as in this case." On June 4 the *Times* editorially commended the decision and observed that "it is a healthy thing for government to be bound by its own regulations, especially in security cases, where judicial standards may be lacking."

In avoiding the larger constitutional issues which this case presented, the Court was following the line of its earlier decisions, such as *Cole* and *Service,* which also reversed particular applications of the security regulations without finding constitutional faults in the entire system. There seems little doubt that the Court was deliberately following a cautious policy in dealing with the security issue. On the one hand was the Court's clear distaste for the unjudicial procedures which had characterized the employee-security operations. On the other hand the Court had just come through a period of violent criticism for its national security decisions of 1957 and 1958. Moreover, the Federal courts have traditionally been reluctant to interfere with Executive Branch employee dismissals. By reversing administrative security actions, but on relatively narrow grounds, the Court may have felt that it was making the most effective use of its power of judicial review.

Four weeks after *Vitarelli* the Court decided a security case arising in private industry, *Greene* v. *McElroy*. Here the Court came closer to taking a stand on the constitutional issues, but again avoided actually basing the decision on such grounds. An engineer in a private firm had been denied the security clearance necessary to work on classified government contracts, and since his firm had no unclassified projects he had to be dismissed. As in other security proceedings, he was not informed of the source of the charges against him or permitted to confront his accusers. The Court, with only one dissent, ruled that a hearing of this type "failed to comport with our traditional ideas of fair procedure," but went on to find that neither Congress nor the President had authorized security procedures which dispensed with the confrontation safeguard. The *Vitarelli* case was cited incidentally by Justice Harlan in a concurring opinion as supporting the wisdom of abstaining from constitutional decisions wherever possible.

The cautious tactics which the Court followed in *Vitarelli* and the other security decisions between 1955 and 1959 may have been justified, but they failed to provide any constitutional rules and left each case to be decided on the basis of its particular facts. In a June, 1961, decision, *Cafeteria and Restaurant Workers Union* v. *McElroy,* the Court, by a five-to-four vote, for the first time found that the facts of a case justified the dismissal on security grounds. Here a woman employee of a cafeteria operated under contract on the premises of the Naval Gun Factory in Washington was denied access to the installation by the post commander on security grounds, without a hearing or statement of reasons for the action.

The Court majority supported this security decision, relying on the time-honored right of a military commander to exclude civilians from the area of his command. The Court was even able to use the *Vitarelli* case to buttress its conclusion, for it had been recognized there that the Secretary of the Interior could have summarily discharged Vitarelli, who was unprotected by civil service laws, at any time without giving a reason.

The "reverberations" of the *Vitarelli* case have been limited to establishing the principle that in security matters a government agency must scrupulously follow its declared procedures. Viewed in this light *Vitarelli* may properly be considered a reaffirmation and extension of *Service,* and it takes its place as an important part of the legal cornerstone of procedural fairness governing dismissal of Federal employees.

Those who regarded the procedures of the Federal security program as odious and dangerous to individual rights had hoped for much more from the Court, but the enunciation of the "Service-Vitarelli" rule and its acceptance by almost the entire Court cannot fail to act as a measure of judicial restraint on the recurrence of another McCarthy era. Moreover, the cumulative impact of the government's reversals in *Cole, Service, Vitarelli,* and *Greene* undoubtedly diminished the scope and curbed several excesses of the security program.

The Cinderella ending of the *Vitarelli* case was atypical of security dismissals generally. This detailed account of the traumatic effects of a security dismissal on one individual dramatizes a tortured period in American history. To be branded a "security risk" for alleged sympathetic association with those who were alleged to be in sympathetic association with communism is guilt by association twice removed. While Vitarelli's political beliefs were undoubtedly to the left of center, this long proceeding left no support for the inference that he was disloyal. This is a tragic tale of a disrupted career, personal heartbreak, administrative ineptitude or worse, and time and money wasted in a proceeding that should never have been started.

Litigants in constitutional law cases, even important ones, tend to recede into obscurity after the Supreme Court has rendered its decision. Yet the lingering effects of a security-risk dismissal, although judicially reversed, never completely disappear. Vitarelli learned to his dismay how enduring those effects may be. His career went well after his return to the South Pacific, and in 1962 he obtained a substantial promotion to the position of Community Development officer for the entire Trust Territory. But one of his neighbors on Guam persisted in referring to him as a Communist, and was finally dissuaded from this practice only by Vitarelli's threat to bring suit against him. The "badge of infamy" had not been removed by the Supreme Court's decision.

## Table of Cases, in Order of Citation in Text

*Watkins* v. *United States,* 354 U.S. 178 (1957).
*Yates* v. *United States,* 354 U.S. 298 (1957).
*Bailey* v. *Richardson,* 341 U.S. 918 (1951).
*Peters* v. *Hobby,* 349 U.S. 331 (1955).
*Cole* v. *Young,* 351 U.S. 536 (1956).
*Service* v. *Dulles,* 354 U.S. 363 (1957).
*Vitarelli* v. *Seaton,* 253 F. 2d 338 (1958).
*Vitarelli* v. *Seaton,* 359 U.S. 535 (1959).
*Vitarelli* v. *United States,* 279 F. 2d 878 (1960).
*Greene* v. *McElroy,* 360 U.S. 474 (1959).
*Cafeteria and Restaurant Workers Union* v. *McElroy,* 367 U.S. 886 (1961).

## Sources

The primary sources consulted for this treatment of the *Vitarelli* case included the transcript of proceedings of both the 1954 hearing before the Security Hearing Board and the 1955 rehearing before Undersecretary of the Interior Davis, and the petitions and briefs filed before the Federal District Court for the District of Columbia, the Court of Appeals for the District of Columbia, the United States Supreme Court, and the Court of Claims. Copies of the Supreme Court materials are deposited in the libraries of the leading law schools throughout the country. I also used a transcript of the arguments and proceedings before the District Court, which is available in the library of the court in Washington. Clifford Hynning and Allen Olmsted, Vitarelli's two attorneys, gave me unrestricted access to their files, which contained pertinent correspondence, memoranda, and newspaper clippings, and granted me interviews which illuminated aspects of the case which could not be ascertained from the files. The testimonies of Vitarelli and Olmsted before the Senate Subcommittee on Constitutional Rights appear in *Hearings Pursuant to S. Res. 94, Security and Constitutional Rights (84th Congress, 2d Session),* 1955, pp. 653–72. A paper on the *Vitarelli* case written by Lawrence Apple for Professor Westin's course at Columbia University was also drawn upon.

The secondary literature on the loyalty-security program is extensive. The most valuable works are: Ralph Brown, *Loyalty and Security: Employment Tests in the United States* (New Haven: Yale University Press, 1958); Eleanor Bontecou, *The Federal Loyalty-Security Program* (Ithaca: Cornell University Press, 1953); and *Report of the Special Committee on the Federal Loyalty-Security Program of the Association of the Bar of the City of New York* (New York: Dodd, Mead, 1956).

# 7

## PROBLEMS OF FEDERALISM

# The Offshore Oil Cases

## Lucius J. Barker

IN SPITE of the emphasis on Federal regulation of industrial relations and on civil liberties in this book, it is important to remember that one of the major roles of the Supreme Court is to act as umpire for the Federal system. The Court must adjudicate disputes between the national and the state governments, and it is this kind of problem that has resulted in some of the Supreme Court's greatest decisions.

Under Chief Justice Marshall, in the historic case of *McCulloch* v. *Maryland* (1819), the Court protected the Bank of the United States from destructive state taxation, and inaugurated an entire theory of intergovernmental tax immunity. Beginning with *Gibbons* v. *Ogden* (1824), the Court has dealt with countless versions of the conflict between federal and state governments over the regulation of commerce. Advocates of states' rights have periodically appealed to the Tenth Amendment to preserve state spheres of action from Federal dominance, and on some occasions they have been successful in persuading the Supreme Court of the validity of their position. In general, however, the Court has been one of the important nationalizing influences in American public life.

The Federal-state issue treated in this series of cases—the right to exploit subsurface minerals under the seaward boundaries of the United States—generated a public controversy that lasted for more than two decades. Congress was consistently of the opinion that offshore oil rights belonged to the states. The Supreme Court consistently took the view that the Federal government had paramount rights in that area. Under President Truman the executive office safeguarded the national position, but with Eisenhower the powerful forces of the Presidency went over to the state position, and against a united executive-legislative phalanx the Supreme Court had to yield.

W HEN Governor Stevenson invaded the Lone-Star State on October 17, 1952, two days after General Eisenhower had campaigned to cheering Texas audiences, rumors were widespread that he would encounter violence. "I have been warned," the Illinois Governor said at Fort Worth, "that there is political intimidation and coercion in Texas these days and that I, a candidate for President of the United States of the Democratic Party, might be exposed to disorder created by organized hoodlums." Stevenson went on to discount these rumors, however, by saying he did not believe that such opposition "will start or ever live in the fiercely free heart of Texas." In Fort Worth the Illinois Governor received a cool reception. In Dallas the crowds were more enthusiastic. Speaking in Dallas before a state fair crowd of about twenty thousand, the Democratic nominee held firm to his position on the submerged lands. Governor Stevenson said:

> I have been astonished at the false propaganda which has been spread about the effect of Supreme Court decisions. The Republicans—and I am ashamed to say, a few erstwhile Democrats—have charged that the Government is trying to steal your inland rivers, your filled lands and even your ranches.
>
> They have told you falsely that the school children of Texas are being robbed of $2,500 apiece. They have even made the ridiculous claims that Washington is trying to kidnap the oysters of Chesapeake Bay and grab the buildings along the shores of the Great Lakes.
>
> There is not one crumb of truth in any of these charges which the General talked about so blithely during the well-deserved birthday reception you had for him.

As Stevenson spoke, Ike fans paraded about with placards reading: "Adlai—What about Hiss?" "Adlai—What about the Tidelands?" and "Adlai means Trumanism—with a Harvard accent."

The Dallas incident typified one of the most intriguing, fascinating, and bitterly fought political-legal controversies in the past half-century. Seldom has there been a more vivid and dramatic portrayal of the scope and complexity of the American governmental process. This drama was replete with shadowy characters, shady deals, behind-the-scenes manipulators, the undue influence and temptation of big money—all of which foster the charge that politics is dirty. In a more positive vein, however, the controversy also illuminated the many procedures by which public policies are formulated: the interdependence of legislators, administrators, and judges in policy formation, and the influence of the "people" on the policy-making process.

### The Great Debate Unfolds

The controversy, popularly but erroneously called the tidelands oil controversy ("offshore oil" would have been a more apt term), was between those who felt that the submerged lands and resources belonged to the states and those who felt that such lands and resources belonged to the national government. Chiefly, it was a battle over the oil under the marginal sea. Monetary stakes were enormous, estimates running high into the billions of dollars. But more than money was involved. Some saw the controversy as a struggle for the preservation of states' rights as opposed to an ever increasing and dangerous trend toward centralized government. Others viewed it as a fight to protect the national interest against encroachments from selfish, narrow interests parading under the banner of states' rights. Some thought the outcome would determine whether a vital natural resource (oil) would be properly conserved or wastefully exploited. In any event the stakes were high and the issue was charged with emotion.

Participation in the controversy was far-reaching. Teacher associations, chambers of commerce, fisherman associations, oil companies, library groups, grocer associations, public officials, bar associations, political parties, government agencies—all played roles in this political-legal drama. These participants generally divided into two broad interest groups, one favoring state control of the offshore oil lands and the other favoring national control. Before turning to the case itself, it is helpful to sketch the major contending forces and their basic arguments in this conflict.

#### The States' Righters

Those favoring state control of the offshore lands were far more numerous than those who favored national control, with the impetus for state control coming from officials of California, Louisiana, and Texas—the three states that stood to gain billions from offshore oil. The state-control group sought, as its central tactic, to secure Congressional enactment of quitclaim legislation, by which the Federal government would grant whatever rights it had to the states. Leadership and co-ordination of this drive for Congressional action was in the hands of the National Association of Attorneys General. Price Daniel, then Attorney General and later Governor of Texas, helped lead the Attorneys General into the state-control camp.

An impressive array of organizations favored state ownership—American Bar Association, American Association of Port Authorities, Conference of

Governors, Council of State Governments, Interstate Oil Compact Commission, National Association of State Lands Officials, United States Conference of Mayors, National Institute of Municipal Law Officers, National Association of Secretaries of State, National Reclamation Association, Southern States Industrial Council, United States Wholesale Grocers Association, and Independent Petroleum Association of America. Several of these, such as the Association of State Land-Officials, expressed their position through special resolutions they passed. Other organizations took the additional step of having representatives at Congressional hearings.

In one way or another each of these organizations felt it would be affected by the outcome of the controversy. The American Title Association, for example, felt that the decision of the Court in the *California* case favoring national control of the offshore oil lands had jeopardized titles of lands granted by the states under their navigable waters, and that these titles had been acquired in good faith. "As a political question," an Association spokesman said, "it is no concern to us who owns or who administers any particular area of land. The whole interest of our Association is in the sound establishment, the stability, and the accurate determination of real property."

In addition to the host of state and local officials who supported their cause, state-control forces had strong representation in the national government. A Congressional majority overwhelmingly favored state control and maintained this position throughout the controversy. Before 1952, however, there was very little support for state control in the judicial and executive branches.

Those members of the oil industry who were active in the controversy also favored state control. Oil interests were inconspicuous at Congressional hearings before 1949 since state-control leaders had decided that too much participation by oil companies would adversely affect the public. After 1949, however, oil interests were well represented at Congressional hearings.

### The National Controllers: A Small but Determined Crew

From the beginning of the controversy through 1952 national government officials and agencies formed the core of the national-control group. President Truman, through his use of the veto, demonstrated his strong support of national control. Moreover, Harold Ickes, Tom Clark, and Philip Perlman, leading figures within the Executive Branch, supported national control. Representatives of the Interior, Justice, and Defense Departments frequently appeared before Congressional Committees in opposition to quitclaim legislation and in support of national control of the tidelands. Before 1953 the Supreme Court majority supported the national-control position in three separate instances.

Additionally, national-control forces maintained quite an active representation, although a minority one, in Congress. Numerous techniques were used by this small but very active group to delay legislation. Senators

Douglas, Lehman, Anderson, O'Mahoney, Donnell, Hill, Morse, Humphrey, and Kefauver, and Representatives Celler and Sabath were especially active in support of national control; almost all of these men were Democrats.

Those who had applied for Federal leases on the basis of the Leasing Act of 1920 naturally favored national control. These applicants were constantly represented at Congressional hearings by a small number of lawyers; one of the most active was former Senator Burton K. Wheeler. Wheeler's position, and generally the position of those seeking Federal leases, was that since the Supreme Court had decided that California did not own the submerged lands, they (the submerged lands) became part of the public lands and were therefore subject to provisions of the Mineral Leasing Act of 1920. Of course Federal applicants had been saying all along that the Act of 1920 gave the Secretary of Interior sufficient authority to lease those lands.

During 1949–1952 there was a marked increase in the number of organizations supporting national control. One factor that caused this increase was the introduction of the Hill Amendment, the so-called oil-for-education amendment, which would have provided that moneys accruing to the Federal government from the offshore oil lands be used by all the states for educational purposes. Organizations supporting the Hill Amendment, several of which had already come out for national control, included the National Grange, National Farmers Union, American Federation of Teachers, American Federation of Labor, Congress of Industrial Organizations, Americans for Democratic Action, and the American Library Association.

### Seeds of Conflict: U.S. v. California

In 1921 the California legislature authorized the issuance of leases to private enterprises in state lands containing oil deposits. State lands were defined to include "school sections, tidelands and parts of navigable lakes and rivers." At that time no one seriously questioned California's ownership of the offshore oil deposits and few realized their size and significance. Although there were some lawyers who questioned California's right to grant these leases, official spokesmen of the national government took the position that the submerged lands belonged to the states. As late as 1933 Secretary of Interior Harold Ickes wrote a letter to an applicant for a Federal lease in which he reiterated this position.

Although the position of Secretary Ickes and other officials of the national government was definite, others believed that these lands belonged to the national government rather than to the states. By 1937, with the growing importance of offshore oil, so many applicants insisted that the land belonged to the United States that Secretary Ickes began to have some doubts about his own position. President Roosevelt also began to question state ownership of these lands. From 1937 on, bills were periodically introduced in Congress authorizing the Attorney General to take action to eject state lessees. After 1937, action on all applications for Federal leases, of which there were about 200, was suspended pending judicial settlement of the matter. This change in Interior Department policy was strongly attacked by state-control advocates. Consequently, 1937 marks the real beginning of the controversy. Ickes himself was one of the first to admit that his action represented a complete reversal of what had been the policy of the Interior Department.

> This, I hastily concede, was a change from the earlier action of myself and of the Department. I did not, when I assumed office a good many years ago, take an oath that I would always be right nor even that I would never change my mind. I did take an oath to do my duty and I viewed my duty in this matter as plain, once I realized that the ownership of the submerged lands had not in fact been settled by the courts. Show me a man who takes stubborn pride in the fact that his mind, once made up, is unchangeable, and I will show you a man who is not fit to be a public servant.

### National Control Choice: A Judicial Determination

Ickes' abrupt change in policy on applications for Federal leases gave added incentive to those who felt that the national government rather than the states should control the "tidelands." National government officials were the most active among national-control advocates. They chose to take the battle into the courts. On May 29, 1945, Attorney General Biddle filed the government's suit against Pacific Western Oil Corporation, a lessee of California. In a news release issued the same day Biddle said:

> The suit is designed to settle a problem which has been the subject of genuine controversy and which has overhung titles in the marginal sea. The suit does not involve tidelands or lands under inland waters, though the status of these will no doubt be clarified to some extent by the decision.

The question of who influenced the Attorney General to instigate the suit aroused much dispute and remains somewhat unclear. Senator Downey of California, for one, felt that the suit was urged by Secretary Ickes and was obviously filed as a deliberate attempt to block legislation to cede all Federal titles to the states. While Secretary Ickes was the prime mover behind a judicial determination of the matter, he actually objected to Biddle's strategy in filing the suit in District Court. Said Ickes, "I objected that it would probably be 15 or 16 years before it could reach the Supreme Court, and that under the Constitution he could file an original suit in the Supreme Court. That I urged him to do. It had not been done when he [President Roosevelt] died."

Ickes was determined to take the issue directly to the Supreme Court. He discussed the idea of an original suit with President Truman on one or two occasions, and Truman agreed to it. His discussions with Attorney General Clark, a Texan, proved less fruitful since Clark saw no reason for dismissing the suit in the District Court and starting it anew in the Supreme Court. Generally speaking, Clark's position was that he did not want to reverse his predecessor. Apparently, however, Ickes persuaded Clark to bring the suit in the Supreme Court, but became impatient over Clark's delay in filing the papers. Ickes once again went to President Truman, who finally ordered Clark to file an original suit against California, dismissing the Pacific Western suit. The original suit was filed October 19, 1945.

### State Advocates Respond: "Congress Should Decide"

While proponents of national control were concentrating on the judicial front, state-ownership proponents concentrated on Congress. State officials of California took the lead in this rapidly growing state-control group. California Attorney General Robert Kenny, a left-of-center Democrat, was the key man among this group of officials.

In preparing for this battle to save California's offshore oil lands, in February, 1945, Kenny employed William W. Clary, a member of a prominent Los Angeles law firm, as Special Assistant Attorney General of California. Clary's job was to help Kenny prepare legislation, briefs, legal memoranda, and to explain legal aspects of the tidelands issue whenever it was necessary to do so. California advanced Clary $500 as a retainer fee and left the balance unfixed. Part of this balance was actually paid by interests other than the state, including those oil companies that were operating under leases from California.

State-control proponents introduced a host of bills in Congress to declare good title in the states to the submerged lands. (Significantly, many of these bills were introduced before the Pacific Western suit in October, 1945.) The history of H.J. Res. 225, introduced on June 28, 1945, by Representative Hatton Summers (D., Texas), reveals the techniques and strategy that state-control forces used in drafting and piloting the legislation through Congress. It also shows how strongly adherents of state control pursued a legislative rather than judicial settlement, no doubt because of the impact a Congressional quitclaim act might have upon the courts.

The quitclaim bills of 1945 were drafted by several cooperating lawyers —California Attorney General Kenny; Judge Myers, a senior law partner in the Clary law firm; and William Clary. Copies of the proposed legislation were sent to the attorneys general of Texas and New York, and to both the attorney general and governor of Louisiana. It was also discussed with Lee Shelley, attorney for the American Association of Port Authorities. Kenny submitted the proposed legislation to California oil firms and "other tidelands lessees" who studied and approved the draft legislation and "may have even suggested minor changes." Representative Herbert of Louisiana introduced the bill, after receiving a copy for that purpose from Governor

Davis of Louisiana. Sixteen similar bills were introduced at the same time.

Clary and Kenny were also active in stimulating interest among the various state attorneys general in quitclaim legislation during 1945. In April, 1945, Clary, at Kenny's direction, sent a letter to all state attorneys general enlisting their support and signature for a brief prepared by Kenny and himself. This letter not only contained the brief, but a copy of the proposed legislation. The brief, signed by forty-six of the forty-eight attorneys general, was filed at the joint Senate-House hearings in June, 1945. (The Pacific Western suit was filed May 29, 1945. The two attorneys general who did not sign the brief were those of Washington and Arizona.) The document analyzed numerous court decisions and interpreted these decisions as showing that the states rather than the Federal government owned the lands (and hence the oil) in question.

Calling his brief a "landmark in legislative history," Kenny commented:

> Never before have the attorneys general of forty-six states joined in full cooperation and agreement on an important proposition of law and upon the necessity for a particular piece of Congressional legislation. It should be borne in mind that the attorney general is the highest legal officer of the state, and this combined expression of these people's lawyers, of legal opinion, is, I believe, entitled to great respect.

The government's filing of the Pacific Western suit (May 29, 1945) cast a shadow over the propriety of enacting quitclaim legislation while the suit was pending. But state-control advocates were determined to erase this uncertainty. Perhaps one of the most lucid statements in this respect was made by the American Association of Port Authorities:

> Any argument that Congress should refrain from acting until the courts have passed upon this matter is obviously fallacious. The highest court in the land has already passed upon the question, and it has done so more than once. If those desiring to expropriate submerged lands are unwilling to abide by the past decisions of the Supreme Court, there is no reason to believe that they will abide by its decision in this newly initiated case. Only congressional action can put an end to the matter. The initiation of the present suit [Pacific Western], accompanied as it has been by announcement casting doubt upon the title to submerged and reclaimed lands throughout the country, is a strong argument for the adoption of the pending bills.

The House Judiciary Committee, in recommending passage of H.J. Res. 225, said there was "no justification for subjecting the states and their successors who have long had the ownership and possession of their tide and submerged lands to the expense and vexation of litigation." In addition, quitclaim advocates such as Representative Allen of Louisiana said that the Court by a "long line of decisions" had already decided the matter. Allen said:

> This question is before us because an effort is being made upon the part of some to upset this long line of decisions. The Supreme Court of the United States in the last few years has upset so many long-standing decisions that I think it is right and proper that Congress should now step in and once and for all settle this question. . . . Moreover, it is a question of policy to be established by Congress more than it is a legal question to be determined by the courts.

Accordingly, the House was in no mood to wait for a judicial determination. With only a scattering of opposition votes, the House passed H.J. Res. 225 on September 20, 1945, by a vote of 108 to 11.

### Wait for the Court?—H.J. Res. 225 in the Senate

Action in the Senate on H.J. Res. 225 did not come until early 1946. By this time, the propriety of enacting quitclaim legislation while litigation was pending had been heightened by the government's dismissal of the Pacific Western suit and the filing of original proceedings against California in the Supreme Court on October 19, 1945.

The impact of the original suit was soon apparent. In the Senate hearings conducted February 5–7, 1946, Secretary Ickes sharply criticized the attempt to enact legislation while litigation was pending. He also lashed at the techniques and strategy being used to push this legislation through Congress. "I do not suppose," he said, "that anyone will deny that the purpose of H.J. Res. 225 is to have Congress rather than the Supreme Court settle this issue." Furthermore, Ickes thought it was

> certainly a novel way to litigate a law suit and the attorney general of California must indeed be peripatetic in attempting to argue his law case simultaneously in the Supreme Court and in the Congress. . . . I am not here to argue the law with California or the oil companies, indeed, I could not do so with propriety while the case is pending in the Supreme Court and under the control of the Attorney General.

Secretary Ickes insisted that the contest was not over "an invasion of states' rights," or an "overruling of settled law," but was a contest for oil. He pointed to the presence of the oil company lessees of California with the forty-six states' attorneys general and the American Association of Port Authorities in supporting the quitclaim legislation, and particularly criticized the manner in which the forty-six attorneys general were solicited to sign the brief supporting the legislation. Said Mr. Ickes:

> I have no doubt that most of the state attorneys general are thoroughly learned men, but when I was a practicing lawyer I signed briefs only when I had thoroughly studied the problem and never in response to telegraphic solicitation. I might add, although it has only an indirect bearing on the

issue, that there is much to be said for the old-fashioned practice of law, when counsel relied upon his authorities and not upon the number of signatures that he was able to collect. I should think that Congress, as well as the courts, would be suspicious of a legal argument conducted along the lines of a bathing-beauty contest.

But state-control leaders were not to be outdone; they countered with a most distinguished witness, Professor Manley O. Hudson of Harvard Law School. A former member of the World Court and a noted international jurist, Hudson said he saw no impropriety in Congress taking action while a case was pending in the Supreme Court. He said that the issue was one of general policy, and that Congress may "very properly pronounce itself at any time upon such a question of policy. . . . You will not be pronouncing upon the issues which may be raised in a particular case that is pending," he said, "though your declaration of policy be based upon what you deem to be the legal situation existing or upon the changes which you consider proper in the existing situation."

In its report to the Senate, the Judiciary Committee urged passage of H.J. Res. 225 saying that "Congress should not permit itself to be embarrassed in its consideration of legislation by the subsequent institution of judicial proceedings by another branch of the Federal Government." The Committee said, without naming cases, that in twenty-six cases in which the Supreme Court took original jurisdiction, the Court needed an average of over 9 years to decide those cases. "It is not unreasonable to assume," the Committee stated, "that the Supreme Court will decide this, one of the most complicated of all of original jurisdiction, within its average period of 9 years."

Debate in the Senate mainly concerned the question of whether Congress should pass legislation on a matter pending before the Court. Senator Barkley, for one, contended that the "obvious purpose of the joint resolution is to nullify the original proceeding now pending in the United States Supreme Court between the United States and the State of California." Noting that the litigation had progressed to the point where final arguments were about to be given, Barkley said that "on the eve of the argument and a decision, there is no justification, and it is hardly in the public interest, for Congress to resolve the issue of law adversely to the Federal Government, which this proposed resolution seeks to do." He felt that the issue was a legal one to be decided by the Court.

But proponents of the legislation fought back. They explained that the suit in the Supreme Court was filed subsequent not only to the introduction of quitclaim legislation, but subsequent to its passage by the House on September 20, 1945. (The original suit was filed October 19, 1945, but the Pacific Western suit was filed May 29, 1945.) Accordingly, argued California's Senator Knowland, "the suit in the Court is an attempt to take away from the Congress of the United States jurisdiction to determine policy. "If we admit the doctrine," he continued, "that the mere filing of a case in the courts when there is legislation pending in the Congress . . . is sufficient to take jurisdiction from Congress, there is not a piece of legislation that has ever been proposed in the Congress . . . that could not be blocked by such a theory."

Despite the arguments and a last-ditch attempt by Senator Morse to attach an anti-poll-tax amendment to H.J. Res. 225, the Senate passed the resolution 44 to 34, with 18 not voting.

### Truman Blocks Congress

While Congress saw the virtues of quitclaim, President Truman did not. He erased whatever hopes quitclaim proponents had of getting Congress to act before the Court could decide the case by vetoing H.J. Res. 225. In his veto message the President stated that if the Court decided that the United States had no title to or interest in the submerged lands, no quitclaim legislation was necessary. However, he said that the issue presented a legal question of great importance which (according to the advice given him by his Attorney General, Clark) had not been previously determined by the Court. Hence he concluded that "Congress is not an appropriate forum to determine the legal issue now before the Court," and "that the jurisdiction of the Supreme Court should not be interfered with while it is arriving at its decision."

On August 2, 1946, a House attempt to override the President's veto failed. The storm center of the controversy was thereby shifted from the legislative halls to the judicial arena, where both sides were in the midst of preparations to defend their causes before the Supreme Court.

## Enters the Court: United States v. California (1947)

### Preliminaries to Court Decision

In its complaint in *United States* v. *California* the government asked the Court to declare that the United States was and is the owner or possessor of paramount rights in the lands, minerals, and other things of value lying under the Pacific Ocean, seaward of the ordinary low-water mark on the coast of California, extending three nautical miles, and bounded on the north and south by the State of California. The government contended that the issue involved is the "three-mile belt on the *open sea,*" and that the Court had "never held that title to the bed of the ocean within the three-mile belt is in the individual states."

California answered the United States' complaint with one of the most elaborate briefs ever filed before the Court. A 14-page table of contents outlined three volumes of 822 pages. According to Interior Secretary Ickes, it weighed three pounds, nine ounces. The United States asked the Court to strike the entire brief because the answer "is prolix and so replete with arguments, evidentiary matter and conclusion, both of law and fact, that it is virtually impossible to segregate and identify the well-pleaded facts for the purpose of determining the issues intended to be rendered."

While admitting that her brief was long, and contained much evidentiary matter and some conclusions of law and fact, California felt that the "ends of justice in a controversy between sovereigns could best be attained by presenting the claims of the State in their full strength." Eventually, California filed a new 508-page brief to which the 822-page "Answer" was added as an appendix. A 258-page brief was filed by the United States to confront California's new brief.

The O'Melveny and Myers firm was paid $150,000 for its work in 1947 on the *California* case. For the three-year period (1945–47) Clary and the O'Melveny and Myers firm were paid $328,000 of which $58,200 was paid by California and $270,000 by other clients, mainly oil companies having state leases.

California and the United States were not the sole combatants in this legal battle, however. Ten *amicus curiae* briefs were submitted. Only one, that of an applicant for a Federal lease, supported Federal control; the others favored state control. The brief supporting state control expressed grave concern over the probable ramifications of the pending litigation. The American Association of Port Authorities, representing state and municipal port authorities, contended that the government's suit "directly challenges and beclouds" the titles of states and their grantees to lands upon which they have erected port improvements in excess of $860,000,000. The National Institute of Municipal Law Officers discussed the suit's implications respecting rights of municipalities to use harbors and bays in exercise of municipal functions and powers.

A brief of the State of New York declared that while it would not be bound by adjudication in this specific case, it, as one of the thirteen original states, was "deeply disturbed" by some of the claims and issues raised by the United States in the pending litigation.

### The California Decision[1]

On June 23, 1947, the long-awaited decision was given. The Supreme Court held that California was not the owner of the three-mile strip, and that the Federal Government had "paramount rights in and power over" the three-mile coastal area of California. Justice Black delivered the opinion of the Court and was joined by five of his colleagues—Justices Vinson,

---

[1] In view of the complex and lengthy decision, this case relies on the author's condensation rather than on edited excerpts from the decision itself—Ed.

Douglas, Murphy, Rutledge, and Burton. Justices Frankfurter and Reed dissented, and Justice Jackson did not participate.

Justice Black first disposed of two technical arguments raised by California. One was that the pleadings presented no "case or controversy," under Art. III, Sec. 2 of the Constitution, but only difference of opinion between state and national officials. However, said Justice Black, it was not only a difference as to who owned or had paramount rights in and power over the lands in question, but also who had the superior right to take, or authorize the taking of, vast quantities of oil and gas from these lands. Justice Black wrote that

> Such concrete conflicts as these, constitute a controversy in the classic legal sense, and are the very kind of differences which can only be settled by agreement, arbitration, force, or judicial action. . . . The justiciability of this controversy rests therefore on conflicting claims of alleged invasions of interests in property and on conflicting claims of governmental powers to authorize its use.

As to the state's contention that it is impossible to identify the subject matter of the suit as to render a proper decree, Justice Black noted that the Court had previously disposed of difficulties concerning submerged lands boundaries and, therefore, he saw no reason why the Court in subsequent hearings might not determine with greater definiteness particular segments of the boundary.

A second contention of California was that the case should be dismissed on the ground that the Attorney General had not been granted the power to file or maintain the suit. Though it did not deny that the Attorney General had been given broad authority by Congress to initiate and conduct litigation on behalf of the government, California did say that such broad authority had been restricted since Congressional actions over a long period of time had manifested a clear policy of state rather than Federal ownership of the submerged lands. Justice Black stated that an Act passed by Congress and signed by the President could certainly limit the authority of the attorney general, but nothing like that had been passed here. The justice took special notice that in 1946 Congress passed H.J. Res. 225, quitclaiming the three-mile belt to the respective states, but he also noted that the resolution was vetoed by the President and the veto was subsequently sustained. "Plainly," said Justice Black, "the resolution does not represent an exercise of constitutional power of Congress to dispose of public property under Art. IV, Sec. 3, Clause 2."

Having disposed of these jurisdictional issues, the case could now be considered on its merits. Justice Black held that the United States government "rather than the state has paramount rights in and power over that belt, an incident to which is full dominion over the resources of the soil under that area including oil." Black continued:

> The crucial question on the merits is not merely who owns the bare legal title to the lands under the marginal sea. The United States here asserts rights in two capacities transcending those of a mere property owner. In one capacity it asserts the right and responsibility to exercise whatever power and dominion are necessary to protect this country against dangers to the security and tranquility of its people incident to the fact that the United States is located immediately adjacent to the ocean. The government also appears in the capacity as a member of the family of nations. It asserts that proper exercise of these constitutional responsibilities requires that it have the powers unencumbered by state commitments, always to determine what agreement will be made concerning the controls and use of the marginal sea and land under it.

The Court also rejected the contention raised by California that the conduct of certain governmental agencies had implied the state's legal title to these lands. Justice Black emphasized that "even assuming that the governmental agencies have been negligent in failing to recognize or assert the claims of the Government at an earlier date, the great interest of the Government in this ocean area is not to be forfeited as a result." In this same connection, the Court disposed of the contention that vast improvements have been made by public and private agencies near or along the shores and that if state ownership was not "maintained," such improvements could result in great losses to investors. A "great national question is not dependent upon what expenses may have been incurred upon mistaken assumptions," the Court responded. California's argument that the original colonies acquired all rights previously possessed by the Crown including the three-mile belt adjacent to the sea, and that since she was admitted on an "equal footing" with the other original states she too acquired such lands, was also rejected by the Court. Said Justice Black:

> [Acquisition of the three-mile belt] has been and is a function of national external sovereignty. . . . That the political agencies of this Nation both claim and exercise broad dominion and control over our three-mile marginal belt is now a settled fact. And this assertion of national dominion over the three-mile belt is binding upon this Court.

One part of the Court's opinion did give some hope to the state-control people. The Court noted that Congress' power, in relation to its constitutional authority "to dispose of and make all needful rules and regulations respecting the territory and other property belonging to the United States," is without limitation. "Thus," said Justice Black, "neither the Courts nor the executive agencies could proceed contrary to an Act of Congress in this congressional area of national policy."

### "Paramount Rights Not Involved"—Two Dissent

Justices Frankfurter and Reed dissented. Frankfurter chided the majority for deciding the case on the basis of "paramount rights." "Rights of ownership are here asserted," said Frankfurter, "and rights of ownership are something else." He failed to see how the United States acquired any proprietorship in these lands. Even if ownership was not in California, Frankfurter reasoned that on a "fair analysis of all the evidence," it would seem that the lands were unclaimed, and as such, this is a "political question not for this Court." Indeed, said Frankfurter, "the disposition of the area, the rights to be created in it, the rights heretofore claimed in it through usage that might be respected though it fall short of prescription, all raise appropriate questions of policy, questions of accommodation, for the determination of which Congress and not this Court is the appropriate agency." Frankfurter concluded by saying that "considerations of judicial self-restraint would seem to me far more compelling where there are obviously at stake claims that involve so many far-reaching, complicated, historic interests, the proper adjustments of which are not readily resolved by the materials and methods to which this Court is confined."

Justice Reed likewise thought the question of ownership and nothing else was involved. To him that ownership turned on whether the thirteen original states prior to the formation of the union owned the marginal lands. If so, then California, admitted on an "equal footing," had the same rights. And in Reed's opinion the majority's citations of authorities supported, rather than refuted, ownership of the marginal lands in the thirteen states, and hence California likewise had such ownership. State ownership of these lands would not in any way interfere with "the needs or rights of the United States in war or peace" since "the power of the United States is plenary over these undersea lands precisely as it is over every river, farm, mine, and factory of the nation."

### The Court Decision: Reaction and Aftermath

Editorial opinion, as expected, produced a mixed reception to the *California* decision. The St. Louis *Post-Dispatch,* a leader in the fight for national control, hailed the decision as a "victory for the principle of judicial, not legislative, decisions of lawsuits." The Washington *Post,* which also favored the decision, cautioned that Congress still had the power to "give this asset away," but to do so "would be a most reckless profligacy."

On the other hand editorial reactions in the three states directly concerned were unanimous in condemning the decision. Both the New Orleans *Times Picayune* and the San Francisco *Chronicle* expressed hope that Congress would settle the issue, although the *Times Picayune* plaintively asserted that the veto barrier posed by President Truman still existed. The Dallas *Morning News* took a somewhat aloof attitude toward the decision since the "United States' claim is not expected to affect Texas because of the unusual situation" by which that state became part of the union. However, the paper said that "Congress could simplify the whole matter by legislation conceding" the tidelands to the states.

### California Asks Rehearing: The "Overlooked Principles"

Soon after the June 23 decision, California asked for a rehearing and reconsideration of the majority opinion and decision. The petition, about forty pages long (and one of the more succinct statements filed by California in the entire controversy) tramped over what by now was well-traveled ground. It contained rather bold insinuations that the justices had not done their homework, and this "caused the Court to overlook at least six established principles of law." Most of these "overlooked" principles were old arguments tailored to fit a new situation—the majority opinion.

The National Association of Attorneys General, the steering committee of the state-control group, also filed a brief in support of California's petition for rehearing. However, all these efforts came to naught since, on October 13, 1947, the Court denied California a rehearing.

### Problems! Problems!

On July 26, 1947, the United States and California entered into what was to be the first of a series of interim agreements based on the Court's decision. These stipulations provided for state administration of operations in the offshore lands pending enactment of pertinent legislation by Congress for Federal management, administration, and control of the lands. Moneys from these lands were to be held in escrow pending final determination of boundaries. These stipulations, usually for one-year periods, continued up to 1953.

In addition to continuing operations, there remained the problem of putting the *California* decision into effect. On September 13, 1947, the United States filed its suggestions for a decree with the Court. The proposed decree asked the Court to declare that the United States was "possessed of paramount rights of proprietorship in and full dominion over the lands, minerals, and other things underlying the Pacific Ocean lying seaward of the ordinary low-water mark. . . ."

On October 27, 1947, the Court issued its decree which followed substantially the language suggested by the United States with one exception: the Court struck out the words "of proprietorship" and used the same wording as in its decision; i.e., "the United States . . . is possessed of paramount rights in and full dominion and power over. . . ." But delineating what were national and what were state boundaries remained the most thorny problem accruing from the *California* decision. While this issue was being litigated between 1947 and 1951, the central conflict shifted back to the Congressional front.

### The Political Arena: Reaction and Inaction

#### Decision Spurs Congress

Following the *California* case, Congress was deluged with bills attempting to "clear up" this controversy. Although some supported the decision of the Court, an overwhelming majority of the bills were aimed at overcoming that decision. Two of these deserve special consideration: S. 1988, because of the extensive hearings conducted on it and H.R. 5992, because of its overwhelming passage by the House.

Senator Edward H. Moore of Oklahoma introduced S. 1988 on January 6, 1948, "a bill to confirm and establish the titles of the states to lands and resources in and beneath navigable waters within state boundaries and to provide for the use and control of said lands and resources." Price Daniel, Attorney General of Texas, and Fred Howser, Attorney General of California (who succeeded Kenny in 1948), were primarily responsible for drafting the bill.

Hearings on S. 1988 and similar bills were held during February and March. By far the most extensive hearings held on the submerged lands question, the proceedings provided an excellent forum to air the controversy in wake of the *California* decision. The state-control people made the most of it, presenting a well-organized contingent of witnesses, including a host of state officials, representatives of organizations such as the National Association of Attorneys General, and a few oil men. On the other hand officials of the national government, applicants for Federal leases, and one or two organizations such as the National Grange constituted the group in favor of national ownership.

The high point of the hearings centered on the testimony of U.S. Attorney General Tom Clark. Clark, speaking for the Executive Branch, viewed the Court's ruling as holding that the Federal government has "paramount rights in and dominion over" the three-mile belt, which to Clark meant that the "Federal Government has the right to minerals in such belt. . . ." The House passed its quitclaim bill (H.R. 5992) and sent it on to the Senate, but Congress adjourned before the Senate could act.

#### The Election Interlude: Issue Kept Alive

Though the tidelands died in Congress, the issue remained alive during the 1948 Presidential-Congressional elections. Both state- and national-control advocates realized the importance of the election to their respective causes. This was particularly true of state-control adherents who still had vivid memories of President Truman's veto of the 1946 quitclaim legislation. But the tidelands did not become a central issue in 1948, nor was it important in the outcome of the election. However, during the campaign, charges were made that oil interests were behind the Dixiecratic movement hoping to split the Democrats so that the Republicans, who supported state control, could capture the Presidency. But, even if true, these and any other efforts proved valueless since President Truman was re-elected. Hence the political situation remained virtually unchanged with Congress favoring state control and the President favoring national control. Consequently, action in the judicial arena took on added importance.

### The "Submerged" Court: Problems Old and New

*Separating Mine from Thine*

Two separate proceedings began in the Supreme Court in 1948. In the first, a direct sequel to the *California* ruling, the United States filed a motion asking for specific action to define national-state boundaries in certain rich oil areas off the California coast. On June 21 the Supreme Court appointed a Special Master to determine what portions of the boundary necessitated "precise determination and adjudication" and to make recommendations as to Court procedure in fixing boundary lines.

On June 27, 1949, the Master issued a report listing seven areas off the California coast as appropriate for precise boundary determination. On the same day, the Court ordered the Master to "proceed with all convenient speed" in framing the issues and defining the evidence to be submitted in dealing with these seven areas. On May 22, 1951, a second Master's Report was filed, leading the Court to give the case to a Special Master who was directed to conduct hearings and submit recommendations for an order applying the proper principles of law to the seven coastal segments in dispute.

The answers to these questions—involving such complex issues as the status of channels between the mainland and offshore islands, the status of bays or harbors, and the setting of low-water marks—were submitted to the Court in the Master's Report on October 14, 1952. This was not to be acted on, as we shall see, because of ensuing developments in Congress.

*What About Louisiana and Texas?*

The second legal action growing out of the *California* decision was a suit filed by Attorney General Clark on December 21, 1948, against Louisiana and Texas. This suit asked the Court to enjoin both states, and all persons claiming under them, from continuing to trespass upon the submerged lands in violations of rights of the United States.

The action of the Attorney General was not unexpected. At hearings on quitclaim legislation earlier that year (March, 1948), Attorney General Clark had indicated that the cases against Texas and Louisiana were "in preparation," and that he intended to file suit against every state which he thought was affected by the *California* decision. Texas officials, while not surprised, reacted angrily. Governor Jester told reporters, "You can't print what I think," and Attorney General Price Daniel commented, "Wait until I get my blood pressure down."

The United States, insofar as the litigation was concerned, was in a fairly good position. For one thing the Court in the *California* case had said that the issue in that case had not been decided in any previous cases—a definite blow to the state-control people. Hence it appeared that the *California* case would be controlling in the two pending cases. Moreover, the government contended that the California decision was applicable to the area outside of the three-mile limit so that the acts of state legislatures which sought to extend state boundaries beyond the three-mile limit could not take precedence over the *California* decision.

As to the alleged "special position" of Texas, the government admitted that Texas had and did claim all the "vacant and unappropriated lands" lying within its borders at the time of annexation and did so in accordance with annexation agreements; but these lands, the government argued, did not include those under the marginal sea. Thus the national interests, responsibilities, and concerns basic to the "paramount rights" of the United States in the *California* case, were equally applicable to both Louisiana and Texas.

The greatest task facing those who worked on the Louisiana brief was to try to distinguish their case from the *California* case. Louisiana contended that Congress had never asserted ownership of, or authority over, the submerged lands of the Gulf; that the United States did not have fee-simple title to lands and minerals underlying waters off the Gulf; and that the paramount rights of the United States did not extend to proprietary interests in minerals and other things within the territorial limits of the states.

Texas put forth two main arguments. She argued first that her case was entirely different from, and could not be controlled by, the *California* case. Such a special reason, according to the Texas argument, had been fully developed by Charles Cheney Hyde of Columbia, Professor Emeritus of International Law, in a memorandum attached to the Texas brief. Texas' second contention was that the government pleadings raised "mixed issues" of law and fact, and that the state should be allowed to present evidence in support thereof. The discussion of this argument, which included a detailed analysis of the many agreements and arrangements entered into by Texas both as a republic and as a state, and its applicability to the instant case, occupied some 200 pages of Texas' 240-page brief.

*"Treat Them like California"*

On June 5, 1950, about two months after the oral arguments had been given, the Court issued its decisions in both the *Louisiana* and *Texas* cases, favoring the national government; seven justices participated. Justice Jackson (a former U.S. attorney general) and Justice Tom Clark (appointed to the Court in 1949) did not take part. For a six-man majority, with Justice Frankfurter in sole dissent, Douglas wrote regarding the *Louisiana* case:

> We think *United States* v. *California* controls this case. . . . The marginal sea is a national, not a state concern. National interests, national responsibilities, national concerns are involved. The problems of commerce, national defense, relations with other powers, war and peace focus there. National rights must therefore be paramount in that area. That is the rationale in the *United States* v. *California*. There is one difference . . . between Louisiana's claim and California's. The latter claimed rights in the three-mile belt. . . . Louisiana claims rights 24 miles seaward of the three-mile belt. . . . The ocean seaward of the marginal belt is perhaps even more directly related to the national defense, the conduct of foreign affairs, and world commerce than is the marginal sea. Certainly, it is not less so. So far as the issues presented here are concerned, Louisiana's enlargement of her boundary emphasizes the strength of the claim of the United States to this part of the ocean and the resources of the soil under that area, including oil.

The question that posed a significant difference between the *Texas* case and the *Louisiana* and *California* cases was whether Texas' ownership (dominion) of her coastal area as a fully sovereign nation prior to her becoming a state gave her a claim to that area. Justice Douglas, again speaking for the Court, denied this contention, saying that even if Texas had both dominion and imperium (governmental powers of regulation and control) in and over the marginal belt when she existed as an independent Republic, any claim that she may have had to the marginal sea was relinquished to the United States when Texas ceased to be an independent nation and was admitted to the Union on an "equal footing" with the existing states. Accordingly, the "equal footing" clause negates any implied, special limitation of any of the paramount powers of the United States in favor of a state.

But some of Justice Douglas' colleagues, who had agreed with him in the *Louisiana* case, took sharp issue with his opinion regarding the applicability of the *California* case to Texas. Justice Reed, in a dissenting opinion joined in by Justice Minton, noted that the majority opinion conceded that prior to the Resolution of Annexation, the United States recognized Texas' ownership of three leagues (about ten and one-half miles) of offshore territory. Assailing the "equal footing" argument used to overcome this fact, Justice Reed said:

> "Equal footing" has heretofore brought to a state ownership of river beds, but never before has that phrase been interpreted to take away from a newly admitted state property that it had theretofore owned. . . . The

necessity for the United States to defend the land and to handle international affairs is not enough to transfer property rights in the marginal sea from Texas to the United States. Federal sovereignty is paramount within national boundaries, but Federal ownership depends on taking possession, as the *California* case holds; on consent, as in the case of places for Federal use; or on purchase, as in the case of Alaska. . . . The needs of defense and foreign affairs alone cannot transfer ownership of an ocean bed from a state to the Federal Government any more than they could transfer iron ore under uplands from state to Federal ownership. National responsibility is no greater in respect to the marginal sea than it is toward every other particle of American territory.

Justice Frankfurter wrote a brief opinion which he made applicable to both the *Louisiana* and *Texas* cases. He said that "time has not made the reasoning of *United States* v. *California* more persuasive, but the issue there decided is no longer open for me." Justice Frankfurter continued:

It is relevant, however, to note that in rejecting California's claim of ownership in the offshore oil the Court carefully abstained from recognizing such claim of ownership by the United States. This was emphasized when the Court struck out the proprietary claim of the United States from the terms of the decree proposed by the United States in the *California* case.

I must leave it to those who deem the reasoning of that decision right to define its scope and apply it, particularly to the historically very different situation of Texas. . . . As is made clear in the opinion of Mr. Justice Reed, the submerged lands now in controversy were part of the domain of Texas when she was on her own. The Court now decides that when Texas entered the Union she lost what she had and the United States acquired it. How that shift came to pass remains for me a puzzle.

Texas' case was decided by a four-to-three vote. The majority consisted of Chief Justice Vinson and Justices Black, Douglas, and Burton; Justices Reed, Minton, and Frankfurter dissented.

Six months after the *Louisiana* and *Texas* decisions, the Court issued decrees giving the United States "paramount rights in and full dominion and power over the lands, minerals and other things underlying the Gulf of Mexico extending seaward twenty-seven marine miles in Louisiana, and extending 'outside of inland waters' in Texas." Both states were to account for all moneys accruing from these lands since June 5, 1950. Since the government had wanted the states to account for all moneys received since the 1947 *California* decision, these decrees were something of a mixed victory for the Federal government.

Because Congress had not passed legislation providing for the administration of the tidelands, it became apparent that if the Interior Department were to administer the "paramount rights" of the United States in these lands, the Department would have to seek authority from Executive Order 9633. This order, issued by President Truman in 1945, placed the natural resources of the submerged lands under the "jurisdiction and control of the Secretary of the Interior for administrative purposes pending enactment of legislation." (Under E.O. 10426, issued January 16, 1953, President Truman transferred control of these lands to the Secretary of the Navy.) Secretary Chapman thought that E.O. 9633 gave him sufficient authority to administer the lands. Accordingly, he issued notices allowing operations to continue under state leases for specified periods, usually thirty- or sixty-day periods. Operators were to pay to the national treasury all rentals, royalties, and other fees which would have otherwise been due to the states under state leases since December 11, 1950. On June 26, 1952, the Interior Department specified that operations would continue for an indefinite period, subject to amendment or revocation on thirty days' notice.

### Was the Court "Right"?

Reacting to the Court's ruling in the *Louisiana* and *Texas* cases, an overwhelming majority of those who expressed opinions stated that the Court had made fundamental errors in arriving at its decisions, particularly in the *Texas* case. In the opinion of Professor John Hanna of the Columbia University Law School:

> There have been few judicial decisions that have been contrary to the expressed views of more well-informed lawyers. . . . Four men in the strategic position of members of the Supreme Court thus decided against Texas what may have been the greatest land suit in history. Disregarding lawyers directly or indirectly concerned with litigation relating to submerged lands, this quartet of justices in its opinion stands almost alone among the able lawyers who have studied this controversy.

Probably the most vigorous criticism of the Court's decisions came in the form of a "Symposium on the Texas Tidelands Case," published in the 1951 Winter issue of the *Baylor Law Review* of the Baylor University of Texas. The entire issue was devoted to the Symposium. Different aspects of the Texas case were analyzed by such recognized authorities as Dean Roscoe Pound, James William Moore, Charles Cheney Hyde, Ireland Graves, John Hanna, and Price Daniel. Most of these men had been of counsel for the State of Texas, and some were especially sharp. Professor Moore, for example, entitled his article, "Expropriation of the Texas Tidelands by Judicial Fiat."

The Court's decisions also produced reverberations in the annual meeting of the National Association of Attorneys General, the organization which had led the fight for state control. Attorney General-elect Si Garrett of

Alabama, in supporting a minority resolution that the Association's efforts
now be directed toward fostering national control, said:

> The Supreme Court of the United States has told this association not once,
> but over and over again, that the belief that we have or that the Associa-
> tion has, that these properties belong to the State is wrong and that they
> belong to the United States of America.
>
> We have either spent, or misspent, most of the time and most of the
> efforts and most of the energies and most of the effectiveness of this As-
> sociation in that mistaken belief and now we are asked to say, "To hell
> with what the Supreme Court of the United States has said."

On the other hand, Attorney General Daniel of South Carolina severely
criticized the Court for overruling what he said had been for a hundred
years an established doctrine of the Court. Daniel commented:

> I think that those Court decisions covering a hundred years ought to mean
> something. When we come up here and seek to change them all, just be-
> cause the present Court has said "We are going to overrule everything the
> former courts have said," it is rather humiliating. . . . We have never be-
> fore had so great an amount of brains on the Supreme Court bench as it
> now has, and it is going to show you that it believes in its ability by over-
> ruling all those former decisions and announcing a new doctrine and de-
> claring a new covenant by which it will let their tidelands be taken away
> from the states and taken up into Washington and of the disposition of it
> up there, nobody will know.

National and state officials from Texas were tartly outspoken in their
criticism of the Court decisions. Representative Gossett commented that
"the Supreme Court has given the nation another long shove down the road
to national socialism." Attorney General Price Daniel said, "As far as I'm
concerned, the fight has just begun." In Baton Rouge, Louisiana, Attorney
General Bolivar Kemp commented that Louisiana's hope "has always been
in Congress." The most vehement verbal blast to come from a state official,
however, came after the Court had denied, on October 16, 1950, a Texas
petition for rehearing. Bascom Giles, State Land Commissioner of Texas,
said that he'd "go to jail" before turning over to the government the more
than $8,000,000 in rents and royalties claimed through its ownership of off-
shore lands.

Newspaper reaction in the three states primarily concerned was also
quite critical of the Court's decisions. "Like Hitler after Munich," said the
Dallas *Morning News,* "the Federal Government can change its mind after
making an agreement." The New Orleans *Times Picayune* referred to the
Court decision as a "legalistic grab of the tidelands. . . ."

On the other hand the St. Louis *Post Dispatch* reasserted its often repeated position that "these areas are public domain." The Washington *Post* also favored the decisions. The New York *Times* thought that the decisions clarified, but did not settle the "tidelands" issue; given the Court's ruling, the *Times* thought that the production and conservation of offshore oil by private interests could be carried on "more appropriately and more effectively" under Federal rather than state control.

### The States "Appeal" to Congress

Just as they had done after the *California* decision, state-control advocates took the battle to Congress. On July 30, 1951, they succeeded in getting legislation (H.R. 4484) through the House, but only after fierce and pointed debate. For example, Representative Halleck (R., Indiana) declared:

> Once again we face a familiar issue: encroachment by big government. Once again that encroachment is cloaked in the all too familiar guise of beneficent paternalism. Once again the Congress is called upon as a bulwark to resist the schemes of the planners who would chip away, piece by piece, the foundation of American freedom established by customs and the Constitution.

On the other side of the ledger Congressman Bailey (D., West Virginia) pleaded with his colleagues not to pass quitclaim, saying that "today's proposals by the oil lobby" made President Roosevelt's court-packing plan look "tame indeed." "Though my voice may ring through these sacred Halls as the voice of one crying in the wilderness," said Bailey, "I make bold to denounce this rape of the judiciary."

Though successful in the House, quitclaim proponents had a harder time in the Senate. On January 14, 1952, Senator Tom Connally (D., Texas) moved to dismiss the anti-quitclaim Interior and Insular Affairs Committee from further jurisdiction over H.R. 4484, the quitclaim measure passed in 1951. This strategy stirred the Committee to action, but instead of reporting out the House bill, the committee voted to submit a bill introduced by Senators O'Mahoney and Anderson (S.J. Res. 20) calling for interim operation of submerged lands under Federal control pending enactment of permanent legislation by Congress. It was understood, however, "that some members of the Committee voted 'yes' just to get the bill to the floor so it could be revised more in line with the straight quitclaim bill previously passed by the House." Once on the floor quitclaim proponents successfully amended S.H. Res. 20 to conform to H.R. 4484, the House quitclaim measure. However, the Senate bill differed from the House version in one fundamental respect, it did not relate at all to the continental shelf. After a House-Senate conference the House agreed to accept the Senate version, and the quitclaim measure was passed and sent to the President.

Again the quitclaim victory in Congress was short-lived. On May 29 President Truman cast another veto. In his explanatory message the President indicated that Federal ownership of these lands had been affirmed and reaffirmed by the Supreme Court, and that he would not turn over to certain states as a "free gift" that which belonged to all the people. Though sharply critical of the President's veto, state-control forces in the Senate did not attempt to override it. Undoubtedly, they had decided to take the issue to the electorate in the 1952 Presidential election.

### Oil at the Polls: The 1952 Presidential Election

#### Conventioneering

President Truman's veto of S.J. Res. 20 more than anything else pointed up the importance of this Presidential election to the state-control forces. And, unlike the 1948 election, the tidelands issue was a major one in this campaign and election.

Long before the conventions the most prominent candidates in both parties had made known their positions on the offshore oil issue. The three leading candidates for the Republican nomination—Senator Robert Taft of Ohio, Governor Earl Warren of California, and General Dwight Eisenhower—had all voiced support of state ownership. On the other hand Senator Richard Russell of Georgia was the only Democratic hopeful to support state ownership. Senator Estes Kefauver, winner of many Presidential primaries, prided himself on denouncing state control while at the same time overwhelmingly carrying California in its Presidential primary. Governor Adlai Stevenson and Governor Averell Harriman also favored national control.

The unanimity for state control among the Republican candidates made it apparent that both the platform and the party's candidate would support that position. This idea became even more tenable to Republican strategists who foresaw the oil issue as a possible chance to crack the traditionally Democratic solid south, especially since Democratic leaders were in the national-control camp.

Hence, the Republican convention meeting in Chicago wasted little time in adopting a party platform which included a plank favorable to state control. And with the nomination of General Eisenhower state-control forces beamed with confidence. As early as 1948, long before the General entered the active political arena, state-control forces had sought and received his support for their cause.

On the other hand it was generally known that the top echelon of the Democratic party, with President Truman heading the list, favored national control. Democratic leaders also knew that the Republican platform was highly appealing to their southern brethren, both in respect to the oil issue as well as to civil rights. A plank calling for outright national control would have been considered an affront by many southerners—not only those from Texas and Louisiana, but those also from other states which had by this time come to view the offshore oil issue as one of "states' rights" versus "centralized government." Still, state-control forces probably felt they had little to gain by pushing a tidelands plank since its force would greatly depend on the attitude of the nominee. Whatever the explanation, the Democrats decided not to include a plank on the oil issue. However, the subsequent nomination of Governor Stevenson left little doubt as to how this void in the platform would be interpreted.

### An "Oily" Campaign

After the party conventions, it was quite apparent that the tidelands was destined to become a major campaign issue. For one thing, it represented a clear choice between the two Presidential candidates, and this difference was sharpened during the campaign. For example, in both Texas and Louisiana Governor Stevenson stated his unequivocal opposition to state control. Said the Governor in a Louisiana speech:

> I am not surprised . . . that Louisiana has been greatly disappointed in the decision of the Supreme Court, holding that the right to the oil beneath the coastal submerged lands is vested in all the people of the United States and not just those of Louisiana. The people and Governor of Illinois would be similarly disappointed had they lost a similar lawsuit.
>
> But I am not running for Governor and if I am elected on November 4, I will be representing all of the people and not just some.
>
> . . . If the submerged lands, by virtue of the ruling of the United States Supreme Court, are a national and not a state asset, the question presented is one of wise policy in the disposition of that asset.
>
> I do not think it is wise policy for the Congress to institute a practice of giving away such national assets to individual states. . . .

General Eisenhower strongly endorsed state control, with some difference in tone and clarity, however, between Eisenhower's position before his nomination, and his position during the campaign. On June 15, 1952, before his nomination, Eisenhower admitted that he was not familiar with the tidelands controversy at the time he first endorsed the state-control position.

> I was in Texas a number of years ago and they showed me some documents. These documents consisted of two resolutions, one passed by the Republic of Texas in 1838 and the other a resolution of our Congress taking Texas into the Federal Government, the Federal Union.
>
> The first document, which recited certain conditions under which Texas had won its independence from Mexico, stated that along with the ground soil they took the seaward side of their nation to include three leagues, and

I was under the impression the agreement recognized those three leagues and roughly 10 miles. So I always thought those 10 miles of shore belonged to Texas.

Now when I said that, I didn't know there was a great struggle going on, and I found out later that there had been a Supreme Court decision on it, and I am one of those who obeys the Supreme Court.

Now I might have my own ideas as to what those documents meant, but I believe in obeying the Supreme Court, so I kept still from there on, because I know too little about it, but I still think that I read the thing correctly.

When Candidate Eisenhower spoke on the issue in Texas during that campaign, his position was strong and clear.

The Supreme Court has declared in very recent years that there are certain paramount Federal rights in these areas. But the Court expressly recognized the right of Congress to deal with the matters of ownership and title.

Twice by substantial majorities, both Houses of Congress have voted to recognize the traditional concept of state ownership of these submerged areas. Twice these acts of Congress have been vetoed by the President.

I would approve such Acts of Congress.

My opponent has announced that he agrees with the President's veto of these laws. . . .

The intense campaigning on the oil issue, coupled with the election of General Eisenhower, was a distinct victory for the state-control forces. Eisenhower's tremendous victory not only split the traditionally Democratic solid south—the Republicans carried Texas, Tennessee, Virginia, and Florida—but also captured Congress for the Republicans. What was important was that for the first time since the controversy began, the state-control forces had a friend in the White House.

### The Submerged Lands Act: Promise and Compromise

#### Teamwork At Last

Before the Eisenhower administration took office, President Truman made a last-minute effort to preserve the submerged lands for the national government. On January 16, 1953, he issued an executive order, setting aside the submerged lands as a naval reserve, and transferred the administration of these lands from the Secretary of the Interior to the Secretary of the Navy. While irritated by the move, state-control leaders were too jubilant to be deterred by a lame-duck President. They would look to the White House come January 20. Accordingly, state-control advocates wasted little time introducing the long-awaited legislation, and the battle in Congress was begun anew.

Many tidelands bills were introduced during the first session of the Republican-controlled 83rd Congress, a few supporting national control but an overwhelming majority providing for state control. The two major state-control bills were S.J. Res. 13 and H.R. 4198. Hearings on these and similar bills were conducted during February and March, 1953, by the Senate Committee on Interior and Insular Affairs and the House Judiciary Committee.

Undoubtedly the high point of the hearings before both committees was the testimony of Federal officials who, for the first time since the controversy began in 1937, favored state control.

Attorney General Herbert Brownell adopted a state-control position with some reservations, in the form of six recommendations. The first of these caused great concern in state-control quarters. It read:

> For the purpose of minimizing constitutional questions, I consider it of primary importance that any statute combine a program (a) authorizing the States to administer and develop the natural resources from the submerged lands within a line marking their historic boundaries with (b) specific authorization to the executive branch of the Federal Government to develop the lands outside of that line, with the income therefrom going to the entire Nation. The statutes also should reserve to the United States its powers to regulate navigation, conduct the national defense, and conduct international relations in the so-called State areas.
>
> My recommendation would mean, in legal terms, that instead of granting to the States a blanket quitclaim title to the submerged lands within their historic boundaries, the Federal Government would grant to the States only such authority as required for the States to administer and develop the natural resources. I do not thereby intend to cast any doubt upon the constitutionality of a so-called quitclaim statute, but merely to draw to your attention a method of minimizing if not eliminating altogether the constitutional point raised by witnesses before this committee.

Some state-control advocates, such as Senator Daniel of Texas and Senator Long of Louisiana, were not at all pleased with Brownell's testimony. Long criticized Brownell's stand for "exclusive federal control" of the continental shelf as less favorable than that taken by the Truman administration. Brownell replied that his Department had approached the question from a purely "non-political viewpoint and felt that to give the Federal Government exclusive control in the continental shelf was in the interest of the United States Government as a whole."

Neither were advocates of state control satisfied with the testimony of Jack B. Tate, Deputy Legal Adviser to the State Department. Tate presented the views of the Department with respect to the international aspects of the submerged lands problem. He pointed out that "the State Department was not concerned with the issue of Federal versus State ownership or control," but only with the possible effect pending legislation might have upon the conduct of foreign affairs.

Such testimony on the part of Federal officials caused state-control advocates to wonder whether the President had changed his position. However, Eisenhower reassured them that he was adhering to his campaign promise. Senator Daniel, after a luncheon with the President, declared that "President Eisenhower still is for vesting full ownership of offshore lands, within the historic boundaries in the states." Daniel said unequivocally that the President did not share Brownell's views. The Senator said, "I can say that there has been no change whatever in the position in favor of state ownership which the President first took in 1948."

President Eisenhower, in a news conference on March 5, 1953, reaffirmed his position that the states should have clear title to the submerged lands within their historic boundaries. This statement helped to clear doubts raised by Federal officials, especially Brownell. When asked by a reporter whether Brownell's view that the states should get "developmental rights but not title" agreed with his concept, the President replied, "Well . . . the Attorney General has to delve into the legal questions involved, but every state has within its historic boundaries certain public lands that belong to the state. Now that is the way he [Brownell] looked upon this."

On March 24 the House Judiciary Committee approved H.R. 4198. It was evident from the outset that opponents of quitclaim had no chance of bottling up the legislation in the House, although they did put up a game fight. Finally, on April 1, the quitclaim measure passed by a 285-to-108 vote and was placed on the Senate Calendar the same day.

### Filibustering Oil Unproductive: Action in the Senate

Other than for explanations of the legislation by sponsors Senators Cordon and Holland, national-control Senators did most of the talking during the Senate debate, with Douglas leading a group of critics composed of Hill, Fulbright, Lehman, Morse, Humphrey, Anderson, and Kefauver. Douglas was so active in the debate that as early as April 9 Senator Long insinuated that the Illinois Senator was filibustering. Douglas retorted that he did not believe in filibusters, but did believe in a "thorough discussion" of such an important piece of legislation. He said, "I feel strong and vigorous and I am ready to continue"—and continue he did. In fact quitclaim opponents began resorting to all types of maneuvers to delay what was, according to all odds, an inevitable defeat. On April 10 Senator Anderson offered his own Federal-control bill, S. 107, as a substitute to the quitclaim bill, S.J. Res. 13. Immediately after this action Senator Hill submitted his "oil-for-education" amendment, providing that oil revenues accruing to the Federal government should be used to benefit the educational system of the entire nation.

On April 14 Senator Taft urged the Senators to cut short their remarks or face the possibility of late adjournment. He said that from the time the debate started on April 14, 300,000 words had been spoken on the subject. "Therefore," the Ohio Senator said, "I do believe that from this moment on, it will not be possible for any Senator to utter one word which has not been uttered already."

### Debate Continued Nevertheless

On April 23 Senator Morse erased all doubts that a filibuster was really in progress. Morse took the floor at 11:40 A.M. on April 23 and spoke for twenty-two hours and twenty-six minutes, his speech ending at 10:05 A.M., April 24. The speech began innocently enough with the Senator giving his "weekly report" to the country on behalf of the Independent party, of which he was the only member. But before finishing, Morse had covered a variety of subjects, ranging from sliced bologna to tidelands oil.

On April 27 state-control advocates began the drive to bring the legislation to a vote. Senator Taft, the majority leader, succeeded, 56 to 33, in tabling the Anderson substitute (national-control bill), which included the Hill "oil-for-education" amendment.

Then, after the unanimous-consent agreement entered into on April 28, providing for a vote on all amendments, and S.J. Res. 13 on May 5, the pace in the Senate quickened. State-control forces time and again defeated amendments designed to weaken quitclaim legislation. Finally on May 5 the Senate passed S.J. Res. 13 by an overwhelming 56-to-35 majority. Immediately thereafter, and in accordance with the unanimous-consent agreement, the House quitclaim bill was amended to strike out everything after the enacting clause and insert instead the text of S.J. Res. 13. With this done the Senate passed H.R. 4198.

One major difference between the House and Senate bills should be carefully noted. The House bill provided for the administration and control of the continental shelf by the Federal government. The Senate bill, by specific wording, did not undertake to deal with this area. Under ordinary circumstances a conference would have been held between the two Houses to resolve their differences. This time none was held. Instead, on May 13, the House, by a 278-to-116 vote, agreed to accept the Senate version, thus avoiding another full-scale Senate debate. On May 14 the bill was sent to the President.

### Keeping a Promise

On May 22, 1953—five months after his inauguration—President Eisenhower made good his compaign promise by signing the quitclaim bill. The ceremony took place in the presence of more than forty Senators and Representatives, both Democrats and Republicans, all of whom had been staunch supporters of the measure. In signing the legislation the President said:

> I am pleased to sign this measure into law recognizing the ancient rights of the states in the submerged lands within their historic boundaries. As I have said many times, I deplore and I will always resist Federal encroachment upon rights and affairs of the states. Recognizing the states' claim to these lands is in keeping with the basic principles of honesty and fair play.

Almost immediately after the President had signed the bill, Republican National Committee Chairman Leonard Hall hailed it as a states' rights victory—"the first sharp turn from the drift toward the superstate in America." He said the action of the President "re-establishes the Jeffersonian principles of states' rights and bolsters the basic conception of our Founding Fathers that government should be so subdivided that the power never could rest in the hands of a few."

### A Pyrrhic Victory?

Concurrent with the Submerged Lands Act, Congress also enacted the Outer Continental Shelf Lands Act, providing for Federal control of lands and resources beyond state boundaries and extending to the edge of the continental shelf. While this legislation clearly posed potential limitations on the operation of the Submerged Lands Act, state-control leaders had little choice but to accept it. The Administration and Republican Congressional leaders, both key elements in the state-control coalition, strongly supported the continental shelf legislation and insisted on its passage in conjunction with the Submerged Lands Act. Such legislation was needed to help counteract the charge made by some Democrats that in passing the Submerged Lands Act the Republican party was beginning a big "giveaway" program. Moreover Attorney General Brownell thought the legislation would "minimize constitutional questions" which might be raised concerning the Submerged Lands Act. In any event many state-control leaders felt constrained to go along with Federal control of the continental shelf.

### "Constitutionalizing" State Control

Shortly after passage of the Submerged Lands Act, Alabama and Rhode Island sought to initiate original suits in the U.S. Supreme Court against Texas, Louisiana, California, Florida, and the national government (the suit named certain Federal officials) by challenging the constitutionality of that Act. Alabama and Rhode Island argued that Congress did not have the authority to dispose of its paramount rights in these lands since paramount rights is not synonymous with "property" as used in the Constitution (Art. IV, Sec. 3). Paramount rights in *United States* v. *California* and the other submerged lands cases was considered an aspect of national sovereignty which could not be given away by the Federal government without endangering its responsibility to conduct foreign affairs. Furthermore, Alabama and Rhode Island contended that even if Congress had sought refuge under the property clause, the Submerged Lands Acts would be unconstitutional since Congress acts as trustee for all the people, and its disposition of property must be in keeping with its trusteeship. They argued that for Congress to act otherwise would preclude equal footing for all states, and equal footing, they contended, demanded equality of treatment by Congress.

### Court Defers to Congress

In a brief *per curiam* opinion, a Court majority of six justices denied the motions of Alabama and Rhode Island to file bills of complaint. (Eight justices participated in the decision with the new Chief Justice Earl Warren of California not taking part.) The Court cited as the controlling factor in the case the unlimited power of Congress to dispose of property belonging to the United States. Congress not only exercises legislative power over the public domain, said the Court, but also powers of proprietorship. While the Court left unanswered many of the issues raised by the complainants, Justice Reed in a concurring opinion replied to the specific challenges of Alabama and Rhode Island.

### Are Oceans "Territory"?—Black and Douglas Dissent

In a tersely worded dissenting opinion Justice Black said that in view of the "equal footing" principle he doubted the power of Congress to give to a few states ocean resources which are the common property of all. He also questioned Congress' authority to treat the oceans as "territory" within the meaning of the Constitution. If so treated and if Congress could give away three miles of ocean, he reasoned, what would keep it from later ceding 150 miles or more? "And I have trouble also," said Justice Black, "in thinking Congress could sell or give away the Atlantic or Pacific Ocean." Hence he felt that the issues were "too grave and too doubtful" to be summarily dismissed without a more careful examination than the Court afforded. Justice Douglas also wrote a dissent opposing dismissal without full consideration by the Court.

The Court's ruling drew the expected reaction from state-control and national-control spokesmen. Senator Thomas Kuchel (R., California), who had criticized the Court's earlier decisions, extolled the 1954 ruling, observing that it wrote the finish "to an ill-starred bureaucratic theory of paramount [federal] rights which was both an affront to California's sovereignty and an assault . . . upon traditional American constitutional government."

The Dallas *Morning News* said that "Texas is glad that the only course open to Congress under a wrongful Court ruling is sustained by a right one."

From the other camp, Senator Wayne Morse (D., Oregon) predicted that opponents of the decision would "take it to the voters." The St. Louis *Post-Dispatch,* long a champion of the national-control position, called the 1954 Court decision "an astonishing repudiation of [its] decision in 1947, twice reaffirmed in 1950."

But the Court had spoken, and the constitutionality of the Submerged Lands Act had been upheld. However, as we shall soon see, California was the only state (of those primarily involved) whose oil was thus secured. Most of her known oil reserves are within the three-mile zone, and California's narrow continental shelf makes further underseas operations and exploration difficult and impractical. In contrast the gently sloping continental shelf off the Gulf Coast makes underwater operations possible out to a distance of 70 to 140 miles, before reaching a depth of 600 feet and dropping sharply. Much of the known and potential oil deposits of the Gulf states, particularly Louisiana and Texas, is beyond the three-mile zone.

### The "Third" House: Judicial Legislators

#### Coalition in Conflict

State and Federal officials who had joined to pass the Submerged Lands Act and to defend its constitutionality now found themselves feuding over the meaning of that very Act. In 1955 the Justice Department interpreted the Act to give the states rights within their "historic boundaries," and this meant rights within three miles and no more. While the Act implied that states on the Gulf Coast that could prove their "historic boundaries" extended beyond three miles would have rights in such boundaries, the Justice Department held such an implication improper. Based on this construction of the Act, and under the authority of the Outer Continental Shelf Lands Act (passed in conjunction with the Submerged Lands Act), the Justice Department claimed that all lands beyond three miles were under exclusive Federal jurisdiction and control.

Following this Justice Department position, the Interior Department attempted to issue leases for lands beyond three miles off the Louisiana coast. Louisiana contended that these lands were within its "historic boundaries." (Louisiana claimed boundaries extending twenty-seven miles seaward). When Louisiana refused to stop operations beyond three miles, the United States in 1956 brought suit against Louisiana in the Supreme Court.

On May 27, 1957, Texas filed an *amicus curiae* brief urging the Court to restrict its decision to Louisiana only. Texas deemed such an intervention necessary since Louisiana used Texas' three-league claim to support its own claim to three leagues. (Texas might have sought to be an official intervener in the case, since if the government won the Louisiana litigation it could use that as a precedent in future litigation against Texas.) The only issue before the Court, Texas argued, was the extent of Louisiana's boundary at the time she entered the Union or as approved by Congress prior to the passage of the Submerged Lands Act, and nothing else.

However, on June 24, 1957, the Court decided that the issues in the *Louisiana* case were so closely related to the possible interests of Texas and other Gulf states, "that the just, orderly and effective determination of such issues requires that they be adjudicated in a proceeding in which all interested parties are before the Court." Accordingly, Alabama, Florida, Mississippi, and Texas were made parties to the original Louisiana suit.

Three more years of litigation followed, but the issues and statutory situation facing the Court in the original *Louisiana* case remained unchanged. This was particularly true of the government's position relative to the extent of Texas' boundaries, although the views of the President and the Justice Department appeared to conflict on this point. The President had repeatedly stated that Texas was entitled to a ten-and-one-half-mile boundary, while the Justice Department had maintained that no state's boundaries could exceed national boundaries, which were three miles.

On October 23, 1957, William Rogers was appointed Attorney General, replacing Herbert Brownell, who had resigned to re-enter law practice in New York. State-control leaders were pleased over Brownell's resignation, for several saw him as the key figure in what they considered to be an all-out Justice Department drive to Federalize everything, and to pursue Federally enforced integration in southern public schools. Rogers' attitude on the tidelands was much friendlier to the states, at least to Texas. As Attorney General, Rogers immediately stated that he fully agreed with the President's views concerning Texas, and that the position of the Justice Department would no longer be in conflict with those views. Despite this assurance, when the government presented its oral arguments before the Court in 1959, its position remained unchanged. With Solicitor General Rankin presenting the oral arguments, the government contended, as it had since 1955, that state boundaries, including those of Texas, could not exceed the national boundaries of three miles.

In one sense these events could be interpreted as proving the accuracy of the Presidential statement that while he endorsed Texas' three-league claim, this was his personal view, and it was up to others to delve into "legal questions." On the other hand if one focuses on the conflict between the President and the Justice Department, it is clear that the President was either unwilling or unable to change the position of the Solicitor General's office when the case was argued before the Court.

*Three Miles or Ten Miles?—The Court Decides*

The Supreme Court decision was rendered on May 31, 1960. Mr. Justice Harlan delivered the principal opinion of the Court and in doing so disposed of the Texas, Louisiana, Mississippi, and Alabama cases. The justices wrote six opinions, totaling 139 pages. Chief Justice Warren, former Governor of California, and Justice Clark, former U.S. Attorney General, took no part in the decision of the cases.

To Harlan the main issue in all the cases was the geographical extent to which the Submerged Lands Act of 1953—"this ill-drawn statute," he called it—ceded to the states Federal rights as proclaimed by the Court in the earlier *California, Louisiana,* and *Texas* cases.

In the first part of his opinion Harlan discussed the issues on which all the states disagreed with the Federal government, after showing that the statute itself was unclear as to how a boundary was to be defined. Justice Harlan resorted to legislative history. "Repeated expressions of the Act's sponsors," said Harlan, "make it absolutely clear that no boundary in excess of three miles was fixed for any state, but that a state would have to establish the existence of such a boundary in judicial proceedings." Although Congressmen made statements that the Act would give Texas and Florida three leagues, these were only "individual expressions," and the Court had to make "an independent judicial inquiry and adjudication on the subject, as contemplated by Congress."

In view of the "purely domestic purposes of the Act" Harlan said the Court could see no irreconcilable conflict between the traditional three-mile executive policy and the fact that under the Submerged Lands Act the seaward boundaries for some states may be more than three miles. Harlan thus concluded that Congress intended to grant states, subject to a three-league limitation, lands they would have owned had existing court decisions on the marginal sea been applied.

Having attempted to clarify the Act by its legislative history, Harlan then applied the Act to the individual states. Although Congress had not approved a three-league provision of an 1836 Texas Boundary Act when it brought Texas into the Union in 1845, Harlan found that such a provision was included in the Treaty of Guadalupe-Hildago (1848), which fixed the boundary between the United States and Mexico. This to him indicated the desire of the United States to follow the 1836 Texas statute. And since under the Submerged Lands Act Congress "intended, in substance, to define a state's present boundaries by reference to events surrounding its admission," Harlan concluded that Texas was entitled to a three-league boundary, and the Court so held.

Justice Douglas sharply disagreed with the *Texas* ruling, denying that the 1848 Guadalupe Treaty intended to give effect to Texas' three-league claim under the 1836 Boundary Act. The purpose of the three-league provision in the Guadalupe Treaty was merely to mark the zone wherein our law-enforcement agencies could maintain effective patrols regarding customs and smuggling. However, if the standard of proof were thus relaxed for the benefit of Texas, Douglas felt the same should be done for all the states, since their claims "are as clear as those of Texas."

This is just what Justice Harlan, speaking for the Court, denied. The claims of Louisiana, Mississippi, and Alabama, he held, were nowhere "as clear as those of Texas." He found no historical evidence to substantiate the claims of these states to boundaries of more than three miles.

Justice Black concurred in the *Texas* case, but dissented in the *Louisiana, Mississippi,* and *Alabama* cases. He thought that a fair construction of the Submerged Lands Act would entitle not only Texas but the other states as well to a three-league boundary. In a brief over-all concurring opinion Justice Frankfurter said that Congress did not vest the Court "with determination of a claim based on 'equity' in the layman's loose sense of the term for it could not. . . . Congress," he continued, "may indulge in largess based on consideration of policy, [but] Congress cannot ask this Court to exercise benevolence on its behalf."

Florida's right to a three-league boundary was decided on a single point—that the Constitution which the state adopted when it was readmitted to the Union in 1868 described the state's boundary as extending three leagues. To Justice Black, who spoke for the Court, Congressional approval of Florida's Constitution (which included the three-league provision) was sufficient to substantiate that state's claim under the Submerged Lands Act.

This time, Justice Harlan, who had spoken for the Court in the *Texas, Louisiana, Mississippi,* and *Alabama* cases, dissented. He thought that "different considerations" prevailed in a state being readmitted to "representation in Congress" than one being "originally admitted" into the Union. In the situation that prevailed in 1868 Congress "was engaged in 're-establishing the broken relations of the State(s) with the Union. . . .'"

### Jubilation, Disappointment, Relief

Once again, the Court's decision drew praise and criticism depending on who got title and oil. Officials of Texas and Florida hailed the decision as "wonderful"—a victory for "states' rights." Florida's Attorney General Ervin said he was especially pleased because he "thought the Federal Government was intent on nationalizing everything. It is heartening to see a ruling in favor of the states." But officials from Louisiana, Mississippi, and Alabama did not share the jubilation of their sister states—they had lost. Louisiana was by far the biggest loser. As a result of the decision, that state would have to surrender more than $308,000,000 which had been escrowed pending determination of the dispute. As Louisiana Attorney General Gremillion put it, "We was robbed. This is awfully hard to swallow."

Perhaps the most striking and ambivalent reaction came from the St.

Louis *Post-Dispatch,* the newspaper which had long championed national control. The paper favored the Court decision since it brought some "small measure of order" to an otherwise chaotic situation. But, the *Post-Dispatch* continued, "the best thing to do with the Submerged Lands Act is to tow it well out to sea and sink it in about 40 fathoms."

### The Losers "Appeal" to Congress

The 1960 decision has not ended the controversy. On December 12, 1960, the Court issued its decree. For the decree to be effectively implemented, however, an exact determination of boundaries must be made, which first depends on determining the baseline from which the three-mile limit is to be measured. This could prove especially difficult in some cases, for example, Louisiana, and will pose many engineering and cartographic problems. Furthermore, those dissatisfied with the Court decision (after being denied a rehearing) have once again "appealed" to Congress. Bills have been introduced in the 87th Congress that would extend the boundaries of Louisiana, Mississippi, and Alabama to three leagues, the same as those approved by the Court for Texas and Florida. Since the stakes are high, and the interests large, the tidelands, like many deeply embedded constitutional-political issues, will pose thorny problems for years to come.

### Offshore Oil in Perspective

In many ways the offshore oil controversy illuminates the dynamics of the American political system; especially does it affirm the interrelation of Court, Congress, and President as participants in the policy-making process. In the earlier *California* (1947), *Louisiana* (1950), and *Texas* (1950) cases the Court was asked to determine whether the national or state governments owned the submerged lands. Since the Court found no guidelines to follow, it had wide discretion to fashion a national policy for the submerged lands. Hence, when the Court decided that the states did not own these lands, but that the national government had "paramount rights in and power" over them, the Court was acting more as a formulator of policy than as a reviewer or interpreter of established policy. In any case, state-control advocates refused to accept the decisions of the Court as final and intensified their fight for a legislative determination of the matter. In 1953 they succeeded in passing the Submerged Lands Act, which gave to the states what the Court had concluded belonged to the nation. The passage of this law illustrated how the state-control group was able to overcome the adverse Court decisions.

In 1954, however, national-control forces challenged the constitutionality of the Submerged Lands Act. Unlike the earlier cases in 1947 and 1950, the

# Louisiana Weighs Cost to State
# Of Decision on Offshore Oil

Alexander in the Philadelphia *Bulletin*

**"Two on a see-saw."**

Court was now asked to adjudge the constitutionality of a specific Congressional policy, the Submerged Lands Act. Here the court exercised its power of judicial review and upheld the validity of the law. Nevertheless, this 1954 decision, unlike the earlier ones, supported state rather than national control and marked the first time in the controversy that the activity of the Court could be so interpreted. But by 1954 there had been: (1) a Presidential election in which the "tideland" was a major issue—an election in which the Court had been criticized for its decisions in the dispute; (2) the election of the Presidential candidate who disagreed with the Court's decisions; (3) a law, the Submerged Lands Act, passed by Congress and supported by the newly elected President; and (4) changes in Court personnel. These factors might help explain the change in the Court's position. Apparently, the 1954 Court majority was not concerned with squaring the Submerged Lands Act with the basic rationale of the earlier cases but, rather, showed great deference to the judgment of Congress and the President as to the disposal of the submerged lands. As Justice Douglas aptly observed in dissent: changes in time and Court personnel had brought with them changes in the Court's position.

The issue was once again before the Court in 1960. This time the Court was asked to interpret the Submerged Lands Act. Since this "ill-drawn statute," as Justice Harlan termed it, was so unclear, and since the Court chose to clarify it, the Court had to do more "legislating" than would have been necessary had the statute been more definitive and clear. But given the compelling and conflicting pressures at work in the legislative process, especially when big stakes are at issue, Congress sometimes finds it expedient to frame statutes that "pass the buck" (the thorny problems) to the judges.

In general, control of the Presidency seems to have been the turning point in the controversy. Through 1952 Congress supported state control while the Court, by its decisions, supported national control. Neither would change its position. As long as the national-control group had the Court and the President on its side, the much larger state-control group was unable to accomplish its goal. But once the President changed sides as a result of the 1952 election, the state-control group was able to overcome the national-control interest, which included the decisions of the Court.

The characteristic role of members of Congress and of the President in interest representation is also illuminated by the controversy. The more diffused interest (national control) was represented by the President (Truman), the more intense (state control) by the Congressional majority. The relationship of Congressional organization and procedure to this result is apparent. But a Presidential election may change the position of the President's relation to various groups. In a Presidential election it is important to get the support of mobile-intense groups. A mobile-intense group, like the state-control group, may have leverage over a Presidential candidate that it may lose after his election. Certainly Eisenhower's position after his election, though still friendly to state control, seemed much more general and unclear than it had during the campaign.

The importance of organization and intensity in determining the outcome of a conflict is demonstrated by the activity of the state-control group. To many state-oriented organizations, such as the National Association of Attorneys General, the issue was one of preserving "states rights" against an ever growing national bureaucracy. To the oil industry, the stakes were potentially very high, profit being the apparent purpose of their economic activity. To California, Louisiana, and Texas, the principal beneficiaries of increased state revenues from leases, the amounts in question were much larger than they would have been for the much more numerous potential beneficiaries of national income from oil leases. This then provided the hard core of the state-control group. The objectives of this group were clear and definite, its leadership readily discernible. On the other hand, the size, distribution, and leadership of those who supported national control were more unclear. Official spokesmen of the national government, supported national control through 1952, but apart from them, the membership of this group was less discernible. Those who supported national control were more general in their objectives than those who supported state control. Moreover organizations supporting national control, such as the National Grange, were not intensively involved in the oil issue. The issue was not central or vital to the life of these organizations as, say, a farm or labor issue would be. The "Hill strategy" (oil-for-education) of trying to bring into this diffused national-control group the well-defined group supporting public education was very clever—it was also a confession of weakness. But it did not turn the tide of battle.

### Table of Cases, in Order of Citation in the Text

*United States* v. *California*, 332 U.S. 19 (1947).
*United States* v. *Louisiana*, 339 U.S. 699 (1950).
*United States* v. *Texas*, 339 U.S. 707 (1950).
*Alabama* v. *Texas* et al., 347 U.S. 272 (1954).
*United States* v. *Louisiana* et al., 363 U.S. 1 (1960).

### Sources

Principal sources used in this treatment of the tidelands cases include: (1) Copies of Supreme Court records and briefs that are in the University of Wisconsin Law Library, Madison; (2) Hearings before the House and Senate Judiciary Committees and the Senate Interior and Insular Affairs Committee, published between 1938 and 1953. The most informative and extensive of these were the *Joint Hearings before Committees on the Judiciary on S. 1988 and*

*Similar Bills* (80th Congress, 1st Session); and (3) the *Congressional Record*, as referred to in text, for floor debates and other materials.

The New York *Times* provided the main newspaper source, supplemented by the Dallas *Morning News,* Washington *Post,* St. Louis *Post-Dispatch,* and the New Orleans *Times-Picayune.*

Published materials relating to the tidelands are plentiful. Some of the more useful include: Ernest Bartley, *The Tidelands Oil Controversy: A Legal and Historical Analysis* (Austin: University of Texas Press, 1953); William K. Metcalfe, "Tidelands Controversy: A Study in Development of a Political-Legal Problem," *Syracuse Law Review,* 4: 39–89 (Fall, 1952); and "Congress Again Considers Far-Reaching Tidelands Oil Controversy," *Congressional Digest,* 27: 229–56 (October, 1948). Brief references to the issue are found in *The Secret Diary of Harold Ickes* (New York: Simon and Schuster, 1953); and *Memoirs* by Harry S. Truman, Vol. 2 (Garden City, L. I.: Doubleday, 1956). A recent publication, Robert Engler's *The Politics of Oil* (New York: Macmillan, 1961), discusses the tidelands as a "fragment of a much larger picture" in an attempt to describe "the political behavior of the petroleum industry and its impact upon political processes throughout the United States."

For a detailed study of the tidelands see the author's doctoral thesis, *The Offshore Oil Controversy: A Study in Public Policy Making (1954);* a copy is available in the University of Illinois Library, Urbana. The study contains an extensive bibliography on the tidelands issue, pp. 237–42. For the author's other views on the issue in published form see "The Offshore Oil Controversy since 1953," *Wisconsin Law Review,* 107–27 (January, 1958); and "The Supreme Court As Policy Maker: The Tidelands Oil Controversy," *Journal of Politics,* 24: 350–66 (May, 1962).

# 8

RELIGION AND COMMERCE

# *The Sunday Closing Cases*

## Sister Candida Lund

ON JUNE 25, 1962, the Supreme Court ruled that a twenty-two-word "nondenominational" prayer prescribed by the New York Board of Regents for daily recital in the schools of that state, though not made compulsory for students, was unconstitutional because it amounted to an establishment of religion contrary to the First and Fourteenth Amendments. This decision provoked an uproar of protest and threatened retaliatory action that in bitterness and widespread character was probably unique in the current century. Even in the case of the segregation decision, the attacks were no more savage, and they tended to be limited to one section of the country, whereas in the school prayer case the reaction was nation-wide. It seemed that only a comparatively few public figures—a group which included President Kennedy—had seriously undertaken to examine the constitutional problems involved or to appraise the potential consequences of the Court's coming to the opposite conclusion and approving religious worship services as a part of the public school program.

The Supreme Court, unlike most of its critics, had been giving the most serious thought to the meaning of the First Amendment ban on establishment of religion for more than a decade. In 1947 the Court by a five-to-four vote had upheld public payment of bus fare for students attending parochial schools. How the Court came to approve the release of public school students so that they could attend church-sponsored education off the school premises but during school hours has been recounted earlier in this volume.

In the following case, the Supreme Court was asked to consider whether laws requiring businesses to close on Sundays have a religious purpose which renders them unconstitutional and whether they infringe the liberties of religious groups which observe a day other than Sunday as their Sabbath. However, the religious issues were complicated and to some extent overshadowed by the fact that two of the cases were economic controversies growing out of rivalry between older downtown commercial retailers in large cities and the newer outlying discount houses with huge parking lots whose evening and Sunday operations have seriously damaged the business of the central city merchants. The bona fide religious problems involved were somewhat obscured by this commercial element in the controversy.

CHRISTMAS shoppers crowding into the "Two Guys from Harrison" discount house outside Allentown, Pennsylvania, on December 8, 1957, had been attracted by the promise of bargains. These shoppers, in fact, were flocking to a store founded on a new strategy in American retailing. It was a low-overhead, high-volume store built far from the main business center. It was surrounded by a giant parking lot and stocked with an enormous variety of merchandise sold at a low markup. This particular store had made another departure from tradition. It stayed open on Sundays.

December 8 was a Sunday. As the aisles of the store filled with customers, no one paid particular attention to a small group of men that filed into the building. These men were interested not in bargains but in enforcing a law. They were the District Attorney of Lehigh County, his first assistant, and his police officers. They began to arrest members of the Two Guys' staff for violation of the state Sunday closing laws.

A few years earlier a somewhat similar action had taken place in Springfield, Massachusetts. There, a modern kosher market, closed on Saturday for reasons of faith, had been selling its goods on Sunday to provide for the religious dietary needs of its customers.

These two cases represented a welter of conflicts, economic, social, recreational, and religious. People wanted to shop on Sunday; the receipts of the stores proved that. Saturday Sabbatarians, furthermore, felt that they had a constitutional right to choose their own day of rest. But at the same time, tradition had long held that the Lord's Day was Sunday and a day of rest. The resolution of the conflicts finally fell to the United States Supreme Court, where both cases were ultimately heard.

### Sunday Closing: An American Tradition

Laws requiring that business and other worldly activities cease on Sunday date back to early colonial history. Introduced in a spirit of intense and intolerant religious fervor, they were once vigorously enforced against "Sabbath violators." Their observance, however, steadily declined in the nineteenth and twentieth centuries. By 1880 a speaker at the third annual meeting of the American Bar Association declared:

> The laws for the observance of Sunday, though on the statute books of all of our states, have fallen into such disuse that they seldom come to the attention even of our profession, except when used as a shorthand way of getting rid of some nuisance on Sunday which is not otherwise prohibited; or when pleaded by some corporation as a defense to some action for neglect of duty.

After World War II, however, the development of Sunday merchandising practices reawakened interest in the Sunday closing problem. Of the forty-four states having a comprehensive restriction of Sunday activity, forty-one in the decade of the 1950's enacted amendments to their Sunday laws, providing either new exemptions or new prohibitions. It was this wave of activity on the Sunday closing front that produced the Supreme Court decisions of 1961.

The legitimacy of state Sunday closing laws had been before the Supreme Court in earlier periods. Prior to 1901 the Court had upheld the Sunday laws of two states in *Hennington* v. *Georgia* (1896) and *Petit* v. *Minnesota* (1900). Another case, *Soon Hing* v. *Crowley* (1885), contained dicta to the same effect. These earlier cases, however, had not involved challenges on religious grounds, since it was not until 1925 that the Supreme Court ruled the First Amendment to be a restraint on the states.

By the fall of 1960 the Court had four Sunday closing cases on its docket; all had come to the Court on appeal. The Massachusetts case was *Gallagher* v. *Crown Kosher Super Market;* it was the only one in which the state law had been declared unconstitutional. Two cases had been decided in favor of Pennsylvania's laws, *Two Guys from Harrison-Allentown* v. *McGinley* and *Braunfeld* v. *Brown.* In the fourth case the Maryland law had been upheld by the state's Supreme Court in *McGowan* v. *Maryland.* Two of the cases, *Crown Kosher* and *Braunfeld,* involved complaints against Sunday closing laws by Orthodox Jewish merchants. The other two, *Two Guys* and *McGowan,* arose out of discount house operations on Sunday. One case from each pair is selected for discussion here.

### The Crown Market Case

The Crown Kosher Super Market opened in Springfield, Massachusetts, in 1953. In accordance with the religious convictions of its stockholders and customers, the store followed a policy of closing at sundown on Friday and not reopening until Sunday, when it remained open for the entire day. Operating in this manner, the market soon claimed a weekday volume that averaged around $15,000 in gross sales and a Sunday volume of some $5,000. The owners estimated their Sunday clientele at an average of 500 persons.

From its August opening to the following May the store had no difficulty with law-enforcing agencies, although it was violating the infrequently enforced Sunday closing law. In May, the Chief of Police, Raymond P. Gallagher, unexpectedly ordered the arrest of Harold Chernock, part owner and manager of Crown Market, for violating the Sunday law of Massachusetts, a statute whose progenitor was enacted in 1692. Parts of the General Laws involved read:

> Whoever on the Lord's day keeps open his shop, warehouse, or workhouse, or does any manner of labor, business or work, except works of necessity and charity, shall be punished by a fine of not more than fifty dollars.

Another section spelled out the exceptions to the law.

That his name might long be remembered as part of an historical court case held no charm for Chief Gallagher. In turn taciturn and aggressive he gave the impression that he wished he had never heard of Sunday closing or Saturday Sabbatarians. He refused to give Springfield reporters the names of those whose complaint had caused Harold Chernock's arrest. The answer, however, could be found in the small kosher butchers scattered around town. For instance, an old-time kosher butcher shop on a corner of Dwight Street stands in marked contrast to the newer, glossier Crown Kosher Super Market on Sumner Avenue. Its owners are Milton Chernick (cousin of Harold Chernock although the family name is spelled differently) and his partner, Sydney Brown. Milton Chernick and some of the other kosher butchers went to see Chief Gallagher about enforcing the Sunday law against Harold Chernock. These men wished to work a five-day week but were disturbed by the competitive advantage that Crown Market had through its policy of staying open on Sunday—although this was not the supermarket's only advantage.

The kosher butchers of Springfield were joined in a quasi-formal trade association, with Harold Chernock as president. According to his cousin Milton, Harold Chernock "defected" in the following way: Sam Smith, a wealthy wholesaler and retailer in Hartford, wished to open a store in Springfield, but wanted to go into business there with someone who already had a kosher sign. The Springfield butchers were wary of anyone who increased competition. They were suspicious of Harold Chernock and asked him if he intended to go into partnership with Smith; Chernock denied such a plan. In the words of his cousin, "He really double-crossed us—and as president." Once his fellow butchers were certain that Chernock had become

Sam Smith's partner, they "threw him out" and elected a new president of their association.

The new Crown Kosher Super Market, operating on a six-day week and calling itself a "one-stop store," did provide hard-to-meet competition. Milton Chernick claimed that he lost approximately 40 per cent of his business to his cousin. If so, he apparently still fared better than several other butchers whose stories he told: "Kaplan was knocked out of business. Sugarman was knocked out of business."

The butchers took a number of steps. They solicited the help of the minister whose church was across the street from the Crown Kosher Super Market, but he was unable to aid them. Some of the butchers went to Boston to see if the Hebrew butchers' union there could help induce Harold Chernock to conform to their pattern. There they were told that they would have to join the union. The Springfield butchers were going to do this, but after further consideration decided that joining would be too expensive. The Boston organization, nevertheless, sent one of its lawyers to Springfield to look into the situation. After his investigation, the lawyer told the kosher butchers he could do nothing for them—"too much politics."

City officials, their eyes on future elections, did not wish to offend the opponents of Sunday closing any more than they wished to offend its adherents. Sometimes, however, they had difficulty in knowing where a man stood. For example, one of them made the mistake of saying to one of Chernock's competitors, "We're trying to do all we can to help Harold Chernock."

With this background the litigation provoked by Chernock's arrest began in the state courts, where it was known as *Commonwealth* v. *Chernock*. Chernock, a short, balding man, maintained throughout, "I think I am doing the right thing," and "My Rabbi is standing behind me." His interest in the case naturally enough did not include the legal subtleties. To him it was a matter of the Torah and also a bread-and-butter issue. In May, 1954, the Springfield District Court fined the defendant fifteen dollars for each complaint with which he was charged. Appeal was then taken to the Superior Court of Hampden County, which also found him guilty. Chernock then appealed to the Supreme Judicial Court of Massachusetts during its September sitting, and that court affirmed his conviction. No effort was made to obtain review of this judgment in the Supreme Court of the United States.

### In the Federal Court

Instead, Sam Smith, Chernock's Connecticut partner, petitioned in the Federal District Court for an injunction against enforcement of the Sunday closing law. The complaint was brought on behalf of the Crown Market, three Orthodox Jewish customers, and the chief rabbi of Springfield. The defendant was Raymond P. Gallagher, Springfield chief of police. The Hartford firm of Ribicoff and Kotkin acted for Smith. The firm in turn sought the help of Herbert B. Ehrmann, a Boston lawyer, who had early in his career gained recognition for serving as counsel with William Thompson to Sacco and Vanzetti. Before the *Crown* case was over he was elected president of the American Jewish Committee.

Because the constitutionality of a state statute was questioned and injunctive relief requested, a three-judge court for the District of Massachusetts was convened to hear the case. Counsel for petitioners argued that the statute amounted to an establishment of religion by setting Sunday apart as a religious Sabbath. The Commonwealth was thereby using its criminal machinery to enforce the holy day of a particular faith. Counsel also argued that the statute constituted a deprivation of religious freedom for the petitioners. The corporate petitioner, because of the religion of its officers, directors, and stockholders, was unable to open between sundown on Friday and sundown on Saturday. If the state would not permit the store to operate on Sunday, it would lose approximately one-third of its business. Customers, moreover, were denied an opportunity to provide for their prescribed religious dietary needs. The rabbi was hindered both in his function of supervising the food to be eaten by his congregation and in his effort to have his congregation preserve due observance of the Jewish Sabbath and dietary laws.

The other side prepared its case less carefully. Counsel for the chief of police made little more than routine contributions. They filed a standard motion to dismiss the complaint on May 28, 1958, assented to an amendment of the complaint on July 11, 1958, submitted defendant's answer on July 25, 1958, and filed a six-page brief. Counsel for Chief Gallagher were several Springfield attorneys and Joseph H. Elcock, Jr., Assistant Attorney General of the Commonwealth. Elcock had expected Springfield counsel to conduct the case, but at the hearing they deferred to him. He had to step in virtually unprepared.

From the beginning, George Fingold, the Attorney General, was as reluctant to defend the Federal suit as were the Springfield solicitors. The issue was politically too explosive. At the time the suit was brought, Fingold was running for governor on the Republican ticket. Consequently, he decided not to defend the suit. On August 31, 1958, before the gubernatorial election took place, Fingold died suddenly. Edward McCormack, favorite nephew of Speaker of the House John McCormack, was appointed in his place. He felt no inclination to defend the suit either. Such defense could easily offend the many Jewish contributors to the Democratic party and, if it could be avoided, so much the better for the party and for the state Attorney General who hankered for a seat in the United States Senate. McCormack, however, was caught in a crossfire. The most persistent volleys came from Federal District Judge William McCarthy, imperious and irascible. McCarthy had unsuccessfully needled Fingold to defend the suit, and his denunciation of him for not doing so, pre-mortem and post-mortem, was bitter and extreme. He continued his goading with the new Attorney General, McCormack. The weekly Catholic paper of the Boston archdiocese, the *Pilot,* also spoke out for Sunday closing.

A few days before the suit was to be argued, the Attorney General's office decided to defend it. No investigation of the facts was made at that late date, and the worth of such an investigation was questionable anyway. Elcock was rushed in to make a motion to dismiss, which he did, on the grounds that there was no equitable jurisdiction, and that the corporation was estopped by the judgment in the previous state litigation, the *Chernock* case. He did make an opening statement at the hearing on November 13, 1958, and cross-examined the petitioners' only witness, Harold Chernock, but the state offered no evidence of its own.

The Attorney General's brief in the District Court was merely three typed pages. It cited four cases to establish lack of standing and two cases on the merits, but did not include *People* v. *Friedman* (1950), a New York case which had important bearing on the current one. The *amicus* brief filed on the side of the Commonwealth made only the most casual reference to the *Friedman* case, thus failing to emphasize a helpful precedent.

At issue in the *Friedman* case was New York Sunday legislation similar to that of Massachusetts. The statute had originated in the seventeenth century and at that time was a reflection of the religious leanings of the people. By 1950 it had come to be known as "Penal Law, Article 192—Sabbath." It contained a general prohibition of Sunday labor, except for works of necessity and charity, various specific prohibitions of Sunday trades, and numerous specific exceptions to the prohibitions. The two defendants, Sam Praska and Sam Friedman, had been charged with, and convicted of, selling uncooked meat to the public in violation of the statute.

The *Friedman* case had presented a more attractive set of facts than did *Crown.* Whereas the latter was identified with the trappings of a big supermarket, Friedman and Praska were kosher butchers in a poor neighborhood where refrigeration could pose a problem for their customers who wished to provide for their dietary needs in accordance with their religion. After their conviction they appealed to the New York Court of Appeals, which affirmed the conviction. Then the defendants sought review in the United States Supreme Court. Their appeal presented the following questions: whether the New York Sabbath law was an establishment of religion, whether it unconstitutionally denied freedom of religion because it failed to exempt persons recognizing a day other than Sunday as a holy day of rest, whether it denied equal protection and due process because of its alleged arbitrary and discriminatory inclusion and exclusion of goods and services, and, lastly, whether the law was discriminatorily applied against the defendants and persons similarly situated. The Supreme Court dismissed the appeal with a statement that it presented no substantial Federal question. It had been held that such a dismissal, unlike a denial of certiorari, is regarded as a disposition on the merits of the case and as an authoritative precedent.

### Amici Curiae: Friends of the Court

In the early stages of the *Crown* case the Attorney General decided not to permit the filing of any *amicus* brief. Thus petitions to file from the Southern New England Conference of Seventh Day Adventists, the International Religious Liberty Association, the Lord's Day League of New England, the Boston Archdiocesan Council of Catholic Men, and the Massachusetts State Labor Council were denied. Later, however, permission was granted to the Seventh Day Adventists and the International Religious Liberty Association for the filing of a joint brief, and to the Lord's Day League and the Archdiocesan Council of Catholic Men for a joint brief.

The Seventh Day Adventists, numbering in 1959 more than 330,000 adult members in America, is the largest Christian group observing the Saturday Sabbath. From the time of the denomination's founding in 1844, its members have found Sunday closing laws a hardship. The Southern New England Conference is the Adventist organization covering Massachusetts, Connecticut, and Rhode Island. Created and controlled by the Seventh Day Adventists, the International Religious Liberty Association is a corporation whose avowed purposes are to disseminate the principles of religious liberty throughout the world and to safeguard the right of all to worship as each shall choose. Attorneys for this pair of *amici curiae* were Leo Pfeffer and Howard Whiteside. Pfeffer, head of the American Jewish Congress' Commission on Law and Social Action, had earned a national reputation for dogged and devoted fighting for separation of church and state. He was counsel in the earlier important Sunday case, *People* v. *Friedman,* and has written extensively on the subject of Sunday legislation.

The Lord's Day League of New England, founded in 1895, labels itself "a Christian civic organization." Its general secretary was a Protestant minister, the Rev. Vaughn Shedd, a gentle, unsophisticated man with a Dickensian touch. The Boston Archdiocesan Council of Catholic Men is an affiliate of the National Council of Catholic Men. The usual way for the Catholic Church in Boston to present its views on legislation to the legislature or any of the courts is through this Archdiocesan Council. The League and the Council are not affiliated with each other and have, in fact, diverse purposes, so that it is unusual to see the organizations in tandem. In their brief, nevertheless, they declared their mutual aim of preventing the further secularization and commercialization of the Lord's Day.

### The Court's Ruling—and Dissent

On May 18, 1959, the court handed down its opinion. In a two-to-one decision the court found for the plaintiffs on all possible grounds and granted them an injunction against enforcement of the statute. The dissenter was Judge William McCarthy.

Chief Judge Calvert Magruder, with Judge Peter Woodbury in agreement, spoke for the court. An Episcopalian, Magruder had been on the bench since 1939 and was soon to retire. He had resigned as vice-dean of the Harvard Law School in order to accept the appointment from President Roosevelt. In ruling for the plaintiffs on all scores the court did not explicitly declare that the statute was an establishment of religion, but this was implicit in the opinion. It did firmly hold that the Sunday closing law was an unconstitutional denial of freedom to practice the Jewish religion and also ruled that the statute constituted a denial of due process and of equal protection.

A few weeks after the majority opinion was filed, Judge McCarthy filed his dissent, which was not without spleen. He stated that he was in complete disagreement with his colleagues as to what constituted the facts in the case. In his view there was a marked disparity between the Agreed Statement of Facts in *Commonwealth* v. *Chernock* and the basic facts accepted by the court in the *Crown Market* case. This could not be: same market, same man, therefore same facts, he syllogized. To him there was no violation of freedom of religion or of equal protection, the two issues he considered basic to the case.

### The Case of the Two Guys

Similar to *Crown* in the economic motivation prompting it but lacking that market's predication of religious freedom, *Two Guys from Harrison-Allentown* v. *McGinley* was to come to a different conclusion in the three-judge District Court that heard it. The history of Two Guys had something of a robber-baron flavor. The warring "barons" were the owners of Hess's Department Store and of Two Guys from Harrison-Allentown, Inc., a discount house. Hess's is the outgrowth of a dry-goods store, founded in Allentown, Pennsylvania, in the 1890's. Today it is the average man's Neiman-Marcus, its aggressive advertising making it known throughout the northeastern United States. For the 1960 fiscal year Hess's had gross sales in excess of $30,000,000—a dollar volume of about $300 per year for each person in Allentown. Max Hess, son of one of the founders, is president; named one of "America's Twelve Master Salesmen" in a nation-wide poll by *Forbes* magazine, Hess is the bellwether of Allentown's merchants.

The Two Guys in Allentown is one of a large chain of discount houses that the Hubschman brothers, Herbert and Sidney, parlayed from a New Jersey diner. In 1933 they operated the diner across from the main gate of the Harrison plant of the Radio Corporation of America. They were able to get appliances at reduced cost, which they sold to their customers as a sideline. Because they were doing a bigger business in appliances than in hamburgers and hot dogs, they decided to go into the discount business. Stock in the chain is traded on the New York Stock Exchange under the corporate name, Vornado, Inc. George Hubschman, a nephew, managed the Allentown store.

The store, located on the Seventh Street Pike in Whitehall Township, Lehigh County, a short ride from the city of Allentown, employed some 300 persons. It opened on October 22, 1957, with an announced policy of a seven-day week, its Sunday hours being from noon until 10 P.M. Before making the final decision to open in the area, the Hubschmans had investigated to see if the Pennsylvania Sunday closing laws were enforced there. Learning that the laws had not been enforced for six years, they went ahead with their plans. This Two Guys, like all others in the chain, sells nationally advertised merchandise at low markup. It is able to do this because it has a low rental, it is adjacent to a population center, it has a large (4,000-car-capacity) parking lot, centralized warehousing and buying, computer inventory control, volume purchasing, low advertising, spare décor, and an almost total absence of sales service.

Perhaps the first indication that Hess and the other Hamilton Street merchants were going to oppose their new competitor was given by a stockholder's suit against Two Guys. Irving W. Coleman, a stockholder in the corporation and a man considered close to Max Hess, brought a lawsuit in the Lehigh County Court a few weeks after the store opened. Coleman claimed that by maintaining Sunday hours the store was breaking the Pennsylvania Sunday Blue Law of 1794. The violation, he claimed, placed the charter of the corporation in jeopardy, thus endangering his investment. The County Court refused to grant the preliminary injunction which he requested, and the case was left pending. It was generally believed that Coleman had purchased the stock for Hess with the intention of bringing a stockholder's suit.

Max Hess made the next move. On Tuesday, December 3, 1957, he ran an ad in the Allentown papers which announced that Hess's would be open Sundays from 1:00 to 5:30 P.M. until Christmas for the added shopping convenience of its customers. Several other Allentown merchants joined in this new policy. Subsequent happenings made it apparent that Hess took this step to give District Attorney Paul McGinley an opportunity to act.

### The District Attorney Enforces a Law

Previously, McGinley had taken a neutral stand on the Blue Laws which, in the light of new developments, he was to abandon. In April, 1957, the South Side Businessmen's Association of Bethlehem announced that it would ask McGinley to help enforce the Sunday Blue Laws. The *Morning Call,* an Allentown paper, carried the District Attorney's comments regarding this announcement. "First of all," McGinley said, "the businessmen are coming to the wrong place when they appeal to the district attorney's office." He explained that, as in other similar complaint cases, an information must first be signed in an alderman's office, and legal steps taken from there. His office would enter the picture if a conviction were appealed in the Court of Quarter Sessions and would then represent the Commonwealth. He added that under the Blue Laws

> you are not allowed to ride a horse or carriage on Sunday and, in its strictest interpretation, you cannot drive a car. If the law is to be enforced, then, it would have to be enforced for every type of business opened on a Sunday, including the little grocery store, gas stations, and all other businesses.

Later in the case, the discount house ran a full-page advertisement reproducing this article from the *Morning Call* and emblazoned in inch-high, bold-faced letters across the top of the page was the question *"Who* or *What* Made You Change Your Mind, Mr. District Attorney McGinley?"

That the District Attorney did change his mind cannot be doubted. Following Hess's announcement that his store would be open Sundays until Christmas, Paul McGinley ordered Lehigh County police to "crack down" on business establishments violating the state's Sunday law. He declared that if local law-enforcement agents did not comply with the order, the county detectives and state police would be directed to enforce the law.

This was the kind of militancy Max Hess wanted. After McGinley's order, Hess ran a new ad on December 6. Its heading read, "Hess Brothers Will Be Closed on Sundays," and in parentheses, "and we couldn't be happier about it." The subhead praised the District Attorney: "Our Hats Are Off to District Attorney Paul McGinley for His Dynamic Action Against Sunday Selling." In the body of the ad Hess's reasons were given in ringing words: "It was a most difficult decision for us to make several days ago, when we opened the attack by announcing that Hess Brothers would be open on Sundays. We asked for widespread violations! We asked for public indignation! We asked for action! And we got it!" He also pointed out that if Sunday selling were not stopped now, "it would rapidly become the public disgrace that confronts many cities and many counties in many parts of the United States." He recognized that "the battle is *only* begun . . . not yet won," and he closed with the statement that Hess Brothers was unalterably opposed to Sunday selling.

Enforcement of the Sunday laws took shape in a series of arrests made at the Two Guys the following Sunday, December 8, 1957, and succeeding Sundays for two years. Later, pending prosecution in the Pennsylvania courts of two test cases of employees who had been arrested, the District Attorney, by agreement, limited his arrests to ten employees of the Two Guys each Sunday. During this time a few arrests were made at other stores operating on Sunday, but counsel for the discount house termed these "merely window dressing." In all, more than 800 arrests of employees at the Two Guys were made. The Sunday law which defendants were charged with violating read in part:

> Whoever does or performs any worldly employment or business whatsoever on the Lord's day, commonly called Sunday (works of necessity and charity only excepted), or uses or practices any game, hunting, shooting, sport or diversion whatsoever on the same day not authorized by law, shall, upon conviction thereof in a summary proceeding, be sentenced to pay a fine of four dollars ($4), for the use of the Commonwealth, or, in default of the payment thereof, shall suffer six (6) days' imprisonment.

The procedure followed in these arrests was to try the parties before an alderman or a justice of the peace. The hearings were scattered all over the county, in order, counsel for the Two Guys felt, "to keep us jumping— Emmaus, Bethlehem, all over the place." Also, in their opinion this spread endeared the District Attorney to the magistrates as there is a statutory fee of $9 per case.

### In the Court of Quarter Sessions

In some instances the alderman or justice of the peace dismissed defendants for lack of identification. In the great majority of cases, however, defendants were found guilty of violating the Pennsylvania Blue Law and ordered to pay fines of $4, or serve six days in jail, plus costs.

The discount house decided to appeal the first seventy-five convictions to the Court of Quarter Sessions of Lehigh County. After that no appeals were made, but the Two Guys paid the $4 fine for each employee and the court costs which ranged from $12 to $18. Counsel for the Two Guys, George Joseph and Morris Efron, tried to get an agreement to merge the seventy-five appeals into one or, failing that, put ten into one. They could reach no accord with the District Attorney's office and regarded this unwillingness as part of the economic pressure put on the Two Guys. Eventually, however, counsel reached an understanding with the state to limit the cases to two which would control the other seventy-three. Thus the cases of *Commonwealth* v. *Milton Bauder* and *Commonwealth* v. *Helen Mills* came before the court.

In these two cases appellants petitioned to appeal their summary convictions. Their petitions raised the issue of the constitutionality of the Pennsylvania Sunday Blue Law as applied to them. Presiding Judge James F. Henninger of the Court of Quarter Sessions of Lehigh County denied the petitions. Appellants then appealed from this court to the Superior Court of Pennsylvania.

*In the Superior Court of Pennsylvania*

In the Superior Court counsel elaborated on the arguments they had used in the court below. Counsel contended that the statute was unconstitutional because it was discriminatory, vague, and established a religion. They argued that a pattern of discrimination had been created by four means: (1) statutory classification; (2) judicial exception; (3) administrative fiat; and (4) failure to enforce. The claim was made that the "District Attorney has, in fact, by administrative fiat and by discriminatory enforcement, rewritten the Sunday Blue Law so that it applies in Lehigh County solely to persons employed at the Two Guys from Harrison store." Vagueness in the law was asserted because no one "could possibly know that he would not be in violation of it if he sold a house on Sunday, operated a gasoline station, or fixed a railroad track, or if, in Lehigh County, he operated a bowling alley, florist shop, or any one of a multitude of retail establishments—but that he would be in violation of the statute in Lehigh County if he were to work for Two Guys from Harrison, Inc." Working from *Everson* and *McCollum,* counsel based their establishment argument on the assertion that the Pennsylvania Sunday Blue Law was adopted pursuant to a religious purpose and in operation attempted to influence persons to go to church and preferred certain religions over others in violation of United States Supreme Court rulings on religious establishment.

The Commonwealth opened its argument with a dictum from an earlier Pennsylvania case, *Commonwealth* v. *American Baseball Club of Philadelphia* (1927): "Christianity is part of the common law of Pennsylvania, and its people are Christian people. Sunday is a holy day among Christians." More than seventeen pages of the Commonwealth's thirty-two-page brief consisted of long quotations from earlier opinions. The Commonwealth, however, had a decided advantage in that virtually all the highest courts in Pennsylvania, as well as in her sister states, had upheld Sunday laws. Nevertheless, the argument was not put forth in its most effective form. The brief relied most heavily on *Specht* v. *Commonwealth,* which declared that the statute was essentially a civil regulation made for the government of man as a member of society. The Commonwealth denied the alleged discrimination, asserting that the way the law was administered would in itself have no bearing on the defendant's guilt or innocence, nor on the alleged unconstitutionality of the law.

The Superior Court on November 14, 1958, upheld the statute in a five-to-two decision. The majority did not file an opinion but handed down an order affirming the Court of Quarter Sessions' dismissal of appeal. The dissenting judges were Blair F. Gunther and G. Harold Watkins. Judge Gunther took note of changing customs and practices, pointing out that what once "may have been considered evil practices or acts which debauch the mind and corrupt the morals of this commonwealth are accepted today as perfectly proper. What may have been considered as nonessential worldly employment of that day may well be considered employment of necessity today." He further said that he was dissenting from the majority "for the admitted discrimination which I consider arbitrary and in violation of the equal protection clause of the Federal Constitution."

The next decision to make was whether to take the case to the State Supreme Court. Since the Superior Court decision was a divided one, it would seem logical to do so. In view of certain new developments, however, it seemed wise to go into the Federal courts with a new case.

*Popular Pressures*

The newspapers persistently pressured the District Attorney to continue his enforcement. Throughout the litigation the papers gave McGinley preferential treatment. Allentown's newspapers (all under the same ownership) hailed McGinley editorially and offered "congratulations to Max and Paul" for their Sunday closing campaign.

Whether the District Attorney had popular support was another question. McGinley's term was to expire in December, 1959. He chose not to seek re-election, but instead became a candidate on the Democratic ticket for the State Senate. He was of the opinion that his enforcement of the Blue Laws would help him. Many people, however, thought that the Sunday closing campaign had been engineered by Max Hess and considered the whole thing ridiculous. McGinley lost the election to the incumbent, John Van Sant, who received 37,088 votes to McGinley's 32,765.

It would not be correct to say that the Allentown newspapers succeeded at any time in marshaling public opinion regarding the Sunday sales controversy. McGinley spoke hyperbolically of mass meetings and marches upon city hall. A *Sunday Call-Chronicle* reporter recounted that church and citizen groups, protesting vehemently against Sunday opening, bought newspaper space, circulated petitions, and held meetings. The executive secretary of the Greater Allentown Council of Churches, Dr. Donald Timmerman, headed one citizens group that operated rather ineffectually, but received considerable publicity. The churches played a very small part. According to George Joseph, the Catholic Church played no part at all.

As the managing editor of the *Call-Chronicle* papers, commenting on public opinion in January, 1961, said, "There was no great steam up against it. No great steam up for it." He added that the number of people who bought at the Two Guys on Sunday indicated they favored Sunday opening. Very soon after McGinley began making arrests at the Two Guys, the discount house claimed to have "many thousands of petitions signed by residents of our county asking for local referendum on the question."

The candidates to succeed McGinley were George Joseph, who had originally represented Two Guys in court, and Ernest Ritter, Assistant District Attorney and brother-in-law of McGinley. Blue Law enforcement was a principal issue in their campaign. The question was raised on the few occasions when the two candidates debated face to face. Joseph said that the Blue Laws came up at the fifty-odd kaffeeklatsches that he attended while electioneering. Ritter declared that if elected, he would enforce the Blue Laws; he would not initiate prosecutions but when violators were brought into court he would take action. George Joseph said the same thing. In fact, Ritter's approach in the campaign was the opposite of what the District Attorney's office was doing, for it was initiating prosecutions. George Joseph was elected.

### New Legislation

Early in December, 1958, Paul McGinley had changed his tactical approach. He announced that because of deliberate attempts to flout the law, he would begin a program of criminal prosecutions based on conspiracy charges. As part of this new program, conspiracy charges were sworn out against twenty-three persons involved in Blue Law violations at the Two Guys discount house. Conviction on such charges involves a $500 fine and/ or up to two years in jail, and the guilty party would carry a criminal record throughout his lifetime. It was primarily this development that prompted the Two Guys to bring a bill in equity in the Federal District Court for the Eastern District of Pennsylvania to enjoin enforcement.

While this case was pending, the state legislature in August, 1959, amended the Sunday closing law to impose additional and heavier penalties on those who sold or offered to sell at retail certain enumerated merchandise on Sunday. The act read as follows:

> Whoever engages on Sunday in the business of selling, or sells or offers for sale, on such day at retail, clothing and wearing apparel, clothing accessories, furniture, housewares, home, business or office furnishings, household, business or office appliances, hardware, tools, paints, building and lumber supply materials, jewelry, silverware, watches, clocks, luggage, musical instruments and recordings, or toys, excluding novelties and souvenirs, shall, upon conviction thereof in a summary proceeding for the first offense, be sentenced to pay a fine of not exceeding one hundred dollars ($100), and for the second or any subsequent offense committed within one year after conviction for the first offense, be sentenced to pay a fine of not exceeding two hundred dollars ($200) or undergo imprisonment not exceeding thirty days in default thereof.
>
> Each separate sale or offer to sell shall constitute a separate offense. . . . P.L. No. 212, 18 Purd. Stat. 4699.10.

Although opponents of the bill persistently charged that it had a religious purpose, this was denied by every speaker who favored the bill. For instance, Senator Walker remarked in debate,

> As I read this bill, I find nothing in it which is of a religious nature. The bill is prompted by the thousands of letters that we have all received in the Senate of Pennsylvania, asking us to do something for the men and women who work in the department stores. These people are not asking to go to church; they are asking for a day of rest.

Senator Van Sant, in whose district Allentown lay, voted in favor of the law. Later he explained: "While I was not wholly in agreement with the 1959 amendment to the Sunday Law I voted favorably feeling that the majority of my people favored strengthening the Sunday Closing Law."

Of the six senators who spoke against the bill, four did so because they considered it a religious bill. One of them, Senator McGinnis, stated on the floor of the Senate that "ninety-five percent of my mail is letters favoring this bill. However, I think it is unconstitutional; it is a religious bill. . . . Every letter I get says: 'I want to go to church on Sunday.' . . ."

Once this law was passed, the bill in equity that the Two Guys had brought in the Federal District Court was amended to include an attack on the constitutionality of this act on the same grounds used in attacking the earlier statute. Thus the suit alleged that the Pennsylvania Sunday laws were unconstitutional because: (1) they were laws respecting the establishment of religion; or (2) laws which prefer or place at an advantage one religion over others; (3) they deny equal protection because discriminatory; and (4) District Attorney Paul McGinley was applying the law to appellant in a willfully discriminatory manner.

The court issued a temporary restraining order and, on September 11, 1959, after a hearing, a three-judge court granted a preliminary injunction halting enforcement of the Sunday laws against the discount house until the case could be heard on its merits.

### The Decision of the Federal District Court

In October the case came to trial, and the court upheld the Commonwealth. Circuit Judge William H. Hastie wrote the opinion, in which District Judge John W. Lord concurred, while District Judge George A. Welsh concurred in part and dissented in part.

The court concerned itself only with the 1959 amendment to the law. It admitted that the earlier Supreme Court Sunday cases, *Hennington* and *Petit,* could no longer serve as dependable precedents because of the development of constitutional concepts in the present century, and it turned to *Friedman* v. *New York* as a reliable guide. In the District Court's opinion, the United States Supreme Court had been urged in the *Friedman* case to find the same constitutional infirmities in the New York Sunday statute that the District Court was being asked to find in the Pennsylvania law. Without permitting oral argument, the Supreme Court had dismissed the case "for want of a substantial federal question."

As an inferior court, the District Court declared that it could not escape from the obligation to apply the Supreme Court's *Friedman* ruling unless the Pennsylvania law differed significantly from the New York law. To the court there was no such difference. Both statutes had a common background and originally were designed to the same end. Judge Hastie found no help in Chief Judge Magruder's treatment of this problem in *Crown*. He wrote, "That opinion disposes of this problem of controlling authority in a brief footnote which is not elaborate enough to make the court's reasoning clear to us."

To answer the equal protection argument, the District Court again used the *Friedman* case. In *Friedman* the argument of arbitrary classification seemed to have been made as strongly as the First Amendment argument. Yet the Supreme Court had not found it persuasive.

The court did not rule on the claim that District Attorney McGinley had willfully and discriminatorily enforced the Sunday law against the Two Guys. It would not make an anticipatory finding with respect to the future because McGinley's term would expire on December 31, 1959. Judge Welsh expressed the view that the legislature lacked the power to pass the 1959 act. He wrote: "The amending act actually is one to regulate business and to deal with competition among businessmen."

### Preparation for the Supreme Court

In this way two Federal courts had arrived at opposite conclusions regarding the validity of Sunday closing laws. Would the Supreme Court, confronted by two contrary opinions from inferior Federal courts, now be more willing to hear arguments concerning the Sunday closing laws? The losing parties in *Crown* and *Two Guys* hopefully appealed to the Supreme Court. On April 25, 1960, the Court noted probable jurisdiction.

Because of the earlier attitude of indifference and delay on the part of the Commonwealth of Massachusetts, the task of preparing the case to present to the Supreme Court was much heavier for it than for the other parties. This attitude was now changed, however, and the Attorney General secured the assistance of a distinguished law professor, Arthur E. Sutherland of Harvard. Professor Sutherland worked with the Assistant Attorney General, Joseph Elcock, and his staff, but Sutherland was responsible for the composition of the brief.

Almost half of the 79-page brief was devoted to procedural argument, and attention was directed chiefly at the question of standing. In Sutherland's opinion, however, the most telling argument for the Commonwealth lay in the wide judicial support that Sunday laws had always enjoyed. A long appendix listing the states, their Sunday statutes, and the holdings of the highest courts in the states buttressed this argument in the brief.

In supporting the lay character of the Sunday holiday as against its clerical character, the brief followed the lines of the Brandeis-brief theory. A consensus indicated that many people favor a single day of nonbusiness in the week. The Soviet government, hardly religious-minded, introduced in 1929 a rotation of days off, but found it necessary in 1940 to return to Sunday as a common day of rest so that workers and their families could enjoy the day together.

The arguments of the Commonwealth with respect to the merits of the case could be summed up in the following manner: first, Sunday laws, once religious, are now economic and social regulations; second, Saturday closing is not imposed by state action; third, the United States Supreme Court has previously recognized the economic and social character of such laws, as have inferior courts; fourth, the wide adoption of such laws indicates that they are not unreasonable or contrary to the equal protection and due process clauses of the Fourteenth Amendment.

Counsel for Crown Market reworked their brief, but presented substantially the same arguments they had used in the lower court. A similar policy was followed by the parties in *Two Guys*.

### Amici Curiae

When the Sunday closing cases were appealed to the Supreme Court, some old friends cautiously disappeared and new ones appeared. No *amicus* brief was filed for the Commonwealth in either *Crown* or *Two Guys*. The Boston Archdiocesan Council of Catholic Men and the Lord's Day League, the two organizations that had appeared as *amici* for the state in the *Crown* case when it was in the District Court, no doubt realized that their presence would add a religious tone. The Boston Council would not file without the cooperation of the National Council of Catholic Men in Washington, and under the circumstances such cooperation was unlikely.

However, *amici curiae* in the *Braunfeld* case did speak for the constitutionality of Sunday laws. These were the Retail Clerks International Association (AFL-CIO), the National Retail Merchants Association, and the Pennsylvania Retailers Association. This last organization had pressed vigorously for the passage of the 1959 Pennsylvania Sunday law.

For the Crown Market the following filed *amicus* briefs: the General Conference of Seventh Day Adventists; the American Civil Liberties Union jointly with the Civil Liberties Union of Massachusetts; the Synagogue Council of America jointly with the National Community Relations Advisory Council; and the American Jewish Committee jointly with the Anti-Defamation League of B'nai B'rith. The American Civil Liberties Union also appeared as *amicus* for the Two Guys.

### Oral Argument

On December 7–8 in a crowded courtroom the Supreme Court heard several hours of oral argument which Elcock, with Yankee drive, opened.

He said that if the state could insist on a weekly day of rest, it could, for convenience, pick the day already respected by many as a day of worship. Justice Stewart, noting that Massachusetts already had a law requiring one day off in seven, inquired why it was necessary to have a statute specifying Sunday a compulsory day of rest. Elcock explained that those who fell within the exemptions of the Sunday law would otherwise have no protection. If husbands and wives did not have a common day off, family problems might result. Justice Stewart observed that California did not have a Sunday law and yet seemed to have no problem. Justice Douglas questioned, "Do you think the fact that this is a kosher market rather than some other market is significant here?" "No," replied Elcock, "It makes no difference. Some of the foods sold there were not kosher foods."

Ehrmann—assured, urbane, competent—argued that the Massachusetts statute still had a religious purpose. He stressed that the act placed a heavy burden on the Orthodox owners of the market, their customers, and their rabbi. Justice Douglas asked, "Would the case be different if the market were run by an atheist?" Ehrmann answered: "Under one of our principles it would be. . . . As applied to the atheist, there would be no discrimination because he would still have to take only one day off. But the Orthodox Jew must take off two days." Justice Black asked: "Would your argument be different if nothing in the case showed the motive for the legislation? . . . Suppose the statute merely said the restrictions were imposed to create a day of rest." Ehrmann responded, "I find it difficult to express an opinion on a statute with whose history I am not familiar." He then tried to bring Justice Black back to the Massachusetts statute so as to keep the issue as narrow as possible. Later Justice Harlan returned to Black's question, saying, "On your establishment of religion point, don't you ultimately have to face up to the basic question suggested by Mr. Justice Black—whether a state has a right to prescribe a day of rest?" To this Ehrmann answered: "We will run into that if you do not find this to be a religious statute. . . . If it is a day-of-rest statute, then the Court must weigh the damage to the economic interests and interferences with religious observances against the purpose to be accomplished." Harold Chernock slept peacefully through Ehrmann's afternoon argument, only to be warned of his unseemly conduct by the Court's roving bailiff. Upon dozing a second time he was ejected for sleeping on so solemn an occasion in what has been called the Taj Mahal of Washington.

Counsel for the Two Guys discount house, Harold Kohn, took up this question of a prescribed day of rest in his argument. He told the Court that Pennsylvania had a right to declare a mandatory day of rest, but not to choose a day that conflicted with the religious sensitivities of some persons. He argued that the Pennsylvania Sunday laws were intended "to enforce respect for a religious doctrine that we think is forbidden by the Constitution."

Harry J. Rubin of the Pennsylvania Department of Justice pointed out to the Court that the discount house could not plead religious injury. "This plaintiff simply wants to remain open seven days a week," he stated.

Throughout the argument most of the questions directed at counsel came from Warren, Frankfurter, Stewart, and Black. Douglas, Harlan, and Brennan asked a few questions, Whittaker one or two, Clark none.

### The Supreme Court Decides

On May 29, 1961, the Supreme Court ruled that the statutes under consideration in the four Sunday closing cases were constitutional. Five justices—Warren, Black, Clark, Harlan, and Whittaker—voted to uphold the Sunday laws in all the cases. Justice Frankfurter joined these five in every case except *Braunfeld*, where he thought that the case should be remanded to the District Court to give the appellants a chance to prove their allegations that the 1959 Pennsylvania statute was irrational and arbitrary. Justices Brennan and Stewart voted with the majority in *McGowan* and *Two Guys*, but dissented in *Crown Kosher* and *Braunfeld*, on the issue of the free exercise of religion. Justice Douglas dissented in all four cases on both the establishment and free exercise of religion grounds. All of these separate statements made it a very long set of opinions, Justice Frankfurter's views alone running to over a hundred pages in the Reports, including appendixes and tables. While separate opinions were written by Chief Justice Warren for all four cases, his principal discussions were in the *McGowan* and *Braunfeld* opinions.

---

*McGOWAN* v. *MARYLAND*
*GALLAGHER* v. *CROWN KOSHER SUPER MARKET*
*TWO GUYS FROM HARRISON-ALLENTOWN* v. *McGINLEY*
*BRAUNFELD* v. *BROWN*
366 U.S. 420, 81 S. Ct. 1101, 6 L. Ed. 2d 393 (1961)

MR. CHIEF JUSTICE WARREN [from *McGowan* v. *Maryland*].

. . . Appellants contend that the statutes violate the guarantee of separation of church and state in that the statutes are laws respecting an establishment of religion contrary to the First Amendment, made applicable to the states by the Fourteenth Amendment. . . .

The essence of appellants' "establishment" argument is that Sunday is the Sabbath day of the predominant Christian sects; that the purpose of the enforced stoppage of labor on that day is to facilitate and encourage church attendance; that the purpose of setting Sunday as a day of universal rest is to induce people with no religion or people with marginal religious beliefs to join the predominant

Christian sects; that the purpose of the atmosphere of tranquility created by Sunday closing is to aid the conduct of church services and religious observance of the sacred day. . . . There is no dispute that the original laws which dealt with Sunday labor were motivated by religious forces. But what we must decide is whether present Sunday legislation, having undergone extensive changes from the earliest forms, still retains its religious character.

Sunday Closing Laws go far back into American history, having been brought to the colonies with a background of English legislation dating to the thirteenth century. . . . Clearly . . . the English Sunday legislation was in aid of the established church.

The American colonial Sunday restrictions arose soon after settlement. Starting in 1650, the Plymouth Colony proscribed servile work, unnecessary travelling, sports, and the sale of alcoholic beverages on the Lord's day and enacted laws concerning church attendance. The Massachusetts Bay Colony and the Connecticut and New Haven Colonies enacted similar prohibitions. . . . The religious orientation of the colonial statutes was equally apparent. . . .

But, despite the strongly religious origin of these laws, beginning before the eighteenth century, nonreligious arguments for Sunday closing began to be heard more distinctly and the statutes began to lose some of their totally religious flavor. In the middle 1700's, Blackstone wrote, "[T]he keeping one day in the seven holy, as a time of relaxation and refreshment as well as for public worship, is of admirable service to a state considered merely as a civil institution. It humanizes, by the help of conversation and society, the manners of the lower classes; which would otherwise degenerate into a sordid ferocity and savage selfishness of spirit; it enables the industrious workman to pursue his occupa-

tion in the ensuing week with health and cheerfulness." 4 Bl. Comm. 63. . . . The preamble to a 1679 Rhode Island enactment stated that the reason for the ban on Sunday employment was that "persons being evill minded, have presumed to employ in servile labor, more than necessity requireth, their servants. . . ." With the advent of the First Amendment, the colonial provisions requiring church attendance were soon repealed. . . .

More recently, further secular justifications have been advanced for making Sunday a day of rest, a day when people may recover from the labors of the week just passed and may physically and mentally prepare for the week's work to come. . . . The proponents of Sunday closing legislation are no longer exclusively representatives of religious interests. Recent New Jersey Sunday legislation was supported by labor groups and trade associations. . . . Almost every State in our country presently has some type of Sunday regulation and over forty possess a relatively comprehensive system. . . . Some of our States now enforce their Sunday legislation through Departments of Labor. . . . Thus have Sunday laws evolved from the wholly religious sanctions that originally were enacted. . . .

In order to dispose of the case before us, we must consider the standards by which the Maryland statutes are to be measured. . . . The First Amendment, in its final form, did not simply bar a congressional enactment *establishing a church;* it forbade all laws *respecting an establishment of religion.* Thus, this Court has given the Amendment a "broad interpretation . . . in the light of its history and the evils it was designed forever to suppress. . . ." *Everson* v. *Board of Education.* . . . It has found that the First and Fourteenth Amendments afford protection against religious establishment far more extensive than merely to forbid a national or state church. . . .

However, it is equally true that the "Establishment" Clause does not ban federal or state regulation of conduct whose reason or effect merely happens to coincide or harmonize with the tenets of some or all religions. In many instances, the Congress or state legislatures conclude that the general welfare of society, wholly apart from any religious considerations, demands such regulation. Thus, for temporal purposes, murder is illegal. And the fact that this agrees with the dictates of the Judaeo-Christian religions while it may disagree with others does not invalidate the regulation. So too with the questions of adultery and polygamy. . . . The same could be said of theft, fraud, etc., because those offenses were also proscribed in the Decalogue. . . .

Throughout this century and longer, both the federal and state governments have oriented their activities very largely toward improvement of the health, safety, recreation and general well-being of our citizens. Numerous laws affecting public health, safety factors in industry, laws affecting hours and conditions of labor of women and children, week-end diversion at parks and beaches, and cultural activities of various kinds, now point the way toward the good life for all. Sunday Closing Laws, like those before us, have become part and parcel of this great governmental concern wholly apart from their original purposes or connotations. The present purpose and effect of most of them is to provide a uniform day of rest for all citizens; the fact that this day is Sunday, a day of particular significance for the dominant Christian sects, does not bar the State from achieving its secular goals. To say that the States cannot prescribe Sunday as a day of rest for these purposes solely because centuries ago such laws had their genesis in religion would give a con-

stitutional interpretation of hostility to the public welfare rather than one of mere separation of church and State. . . .

But this does not answer all of appellants' contentions. We are told that the State has other means at its disposal to accomplish its secular purpose, other courses that would not even remotely or incidentally give state aid to religion. . . . It is true that if the State's interest were simply to provide for its citizens a periodic respite from work, a regulation demanding that everyone rest one day in seven, leaving the choice of the day to the individual, would suffice.

However, the State's purpose is not merely to provide a one-day-in-seven work stoppage. In addition to this, the State seeks to set one day apart from all others as a day of rest, repose, recreation and tranquility—a day which all members of the family and community have the opportunity to spend and enjoy together, a day on which there exists relative quiet and disassociation from the everyday intensity of commercial activities, a day on which people may visit friends and relatives who are not available during working days.

Obviously, a state is empowered to determine that a rest-one-day-in-seven statute would not accomplish this purpose; that it would not provide for a general cessation of activity, a special atmosphere of tranquility, a day which all members of the family or friends and relatives might spend together. Furthermore, it seems plain that the problems involved in enforcing such a provision would be exceedingly more difficult than those in enforcing a common-day-of-rest provision.

Moreover, it is common knowledge that the first day of the week has come to have special significance as a rest day in this country. People of all religions and people with no religion regard Sunday as a time for family activity, for visiting friends and relatives, for late sleeping, for passive and active entertainments, for dining out and the like. . . . Sunday is a day apart from all others. The cause is irrelevant; the fact exists. It would seem unrealistic for enforcement purposes and perhaps detrimental to the general welfare to require a state to choose a common-day-of-rest other than that which most persons would select of their own accord. For these reasons, we hold that the Maryland statutes are not laws respecting an establishment of religion. . . .

MR. CHIEF JUSTICE WARREN [from *Braunfeld* v. *Brown*].

. . . Concededly, appellants and all other persons who wish to work on Sunday will be burdened economically by the State's day of rest mandate; and appellants point out that their religion requires them to refrain from work on Saturday as well. Our inquiry then is whether, in these circumstances, the First and Fourteenth Amendments forbid application of the Sunday Closing Law to appellants.

Certain aspects of religious exercise cannot, in any way, be restricted or burdened by either federal or state legislation. Compulsion by law of the acceptance of any creed or the practice of any form of worship is strictly forbidden. The freedom to hold religious beliefs and opinions is absolute. . . .

However, the freedom to act, even when the action is in accord with one's religious convictions, is not totally free from legislative restrictions. . . . The statute at bar does not make unlawful any religious practices of appellants; the Sunday law simply regulates a secular activity and, as applied to appellants, operates so as to make the practice of their religious beliefs more expensive. Furthermore, the law's effect does not inconvenience all members of the Orthodox Jewish faith but only those who believe it necessary to work on Sunday. And even these are not faced

with as serious a choice as forsaking their religious practices or subjecting themselves to criminal prosecution. Fully recognizing that the alternatives open to appellants and others similarly situated—retaining their present occupations and incurring economic disadvantage or engaging in some other commercial activity which does not call for either Saturday or Sunday labor—may well result in some financial sacrifice in order to observe their religious beliefs, still the option is wholly different than when the legislation attempts to make a religious practice itself unlawful.

To strike down, without the most critical scrutiny, legislation which imposes only an indirect burden on the exercise of religion, i.e., legislation which does not make unlawful the religious practice itself, would radically restrict the operating latitude of the legislature. Statutes which tax income and limit the amount which may be deducted for religious contributions impose an indirect economic burden on the observance of the religion of the citizen whose religion requires him to donate a greater amount to his church; statutes which require the courts to be closed on Saturday and Sunday impose a similar indirect burden on the observance of the religion of the trial lawyer whose religion requires him to rest on a weekday. The list of legislation of this nature is nearly limitless.

Needless to say, when entering the area of religious freedom, we must be fully cognizant of the particular protection that the Constitution has accorded it. Abhorrence of religious persecution and intolerance is a basic part of our heritage. But we are a cosmopolitan nation made up of people of almost every conceivable religious preference. These denominations number almost three hundred. . . . Consequently, it cannot be expected, much less required, that legislators enact no law regulating conduct that may in some way result in an economic disadvantage to some religious sects and not to others because of the special practices of the various religions. We do not believe that such an effect is an absolute test for determining whether the legislation violates the freedom of religion protected by the First Amendment. . . .

. . . If the purpose or effect of a law is to impede the observance of one or all religions or is to discriminate invidiously between religions, that law is constitutionally invalid even though the burden may be characterized as being only indirect. But if the State regulates conduct by enacting a general law within its power, the purpose and effect of which is to advance the State's secular goals, the statute is valid despite its indirect burden on religious observance unless the State may accomplish its purpose by means which do not impose such a burden.

Appellants . . . contend that the State should cut an exception from the Sunday labor proscription for those people who, because of religious conviction, observe a day of rest other than Sunday. By such regulation, appellants contend, the economic disadvantages imposed by the present system would be removed and the State's interest in having all people rest one day would be satisfied.

A number of States provide such an exemption, and this may well be the wiser solution to the problem. But our concern is not with the wisdom of legislation but its constitutional limitation. Thus, reason and experience teach that to permit the exemption might well undermine the State's goal of providing a day that, as best possible, eliminates the atmosphere of commercial noise and activity. Although not dispositive of the issue, enforcement problems would be more difficult since there would be two or more days to police rather than one and it would be more difficult to observe whether violations were occurring.

Additional problems might also be presented by a regulation of this sort. To allow only people who rest on a day other than Sunday to keep their businesses open on that day might well provide these people with an economic advantage over their competitors who must remain closed on that day; this might cause the Sunday-observers to complain that their religions were being discriminated against. With this competitive advantage existing, there could well be the temptation for some, in order to keep their businesses open on Sunday, to assert that they have religious convictions which compel them to close their businesses on what had formerly been their least profitable day. This might make necessary a state-conducted inquiry into the sincerity of the individual's religious beliefs, a practice which a State might believe would itself run afoul of the spirit of constitutionally protected religious guarantees. Finally, in order to keep the disruption of the day at a minimum, exempted employers would probably have to hire employees who themselves qualified for the exemption because of their own religious beliefs, a practice which a State might feel to be opposed to its general policy prohibiting religious discrimination in hiring. For all of these reasons, we cannot say that the Pennsylvania statute before us is invalid, either on its face or as applied. . . .

MR. JUSTICE BRENNAN, concurring and dissenting [from *Braunfeld* v. *Brown*].

I agree with the Chief Justice that there is no merit in appellants' establishment and equal-protection claims. I dissent, however, as to the claim that Pennsylvania has prohibited the free exercise of appellants' religion. . . .

The issue in this case . . . is

whether a State may put an individual to a choice between his business and his religion. The Court today holds that it may. But I dissent, believing that such a law prohibits the free exercise of religion. . . .

Admittedly, these laws . . . do not say that appellants must work on Saturday. But their effect is that appellants may not simultaneously practice their religion and their trade, without being hampered by a substantial competitive disadvantage. Their effect is that no one may at one and the same time be an Orthodox Jew and compete effectively with his Sunday-observing fellow tradesmen. This clog upon the exercise of religion, this state-imposed burden on Orthodox Judaism, has exactly the same economic effect as a tax levied upon the sale of religious literature. . . .

What . . . is the compelling state interest which impels the Commonwealth of Pennsylvania to impede appellants' freedom of worship? What overbalancing need is so weighty in the constitutional scale that it justifies this substantial, though indirect, limitation of appellants' freedom? . . . It is the mere convenience of having everyone rest on the same day. It is to defend this interest that the Court holds that a State need not follow the alternative route of granting an exemption for those who in good faith observe a day of rest other than Sunday.

It is true, I suppose, that the granting of such an exemption would make Sundays a little noisier, and the task of police and prosecutor a little more difficult. It is also true that a majority —21—of the 34 States which have general Sunday regulations have exemptions of this kind. We are not told that those States are significantly noisier, or that their police are significantly more burdened, than Pennsylvania's. . . . The Court conjures up several difficulties with such a system which seem to me more fanciful than real. . . .

In fine, the Court, in my view, has exalted administrative convenience to a constitutional level high enough to justify making one religion economically disadvantageous. . . .

MR. JUSTICE STEWART, dissenting [from *Braunfeld* v. *Brown*].

. . . Pennsylvania has passed a law which compels an Orthodox Jew to choose between his religious faith and his economic survival. That is a cruel choice. It is a choice which I think no State can constitutionally demand. For me this is not something that can be swept under the rug and forgotten in the interest of enforced Sunday togetherness. I think the impact of this law upon these appellants grossly violates their constitutional right to the free exercise of religion.

MR. JUSTICE DOUGLAS, dissenting [in all four cases].

. . . I do not see how a State can make protesting citizens refrain from doing innocent acts on Sunday because the doing of those acts offends sentiments of their Christian neighbors.

The institutions of our society are founded on the belief that there is an authority higher than the authority of the State; that there is a moral law which the State is powerless to alter; that the individual possesses rights, conferred by the Creator, which government must respect. . . .

Those who fashioned the First Amendment decided that if and when God is to be served, His service will not be motivated by coercive measures of government. . . . The First Amendment . . . means, as I understand it, that if a religious leaven is to be worked into the affairs of our people, it is to be done by individuals and groups, not by the Government. This necessarily means, *first,* that the dogma, creed, scruples, or practices of no religious group or sect are to be preferred over those of any others;

*second,* that no one shall be interfered with by government for practicing the religion of his choice; *third,* that the state may not require anyone to practice a religion or even any religion; and *fourth,* that the state cannot compel one so to conduct himself as not to offend the religious scruples of another. The idea, as I understand it, was to limit the power of government to act in religious matters . . . not to limit the freedom of religious men to act religiously nor to restrict the freedom of atheists or agnostics.

The First Amendment commands government to have no interest in theology or ritual; it admonishes government to be interested in allowing religious freedom to flourish—whether the result is to produce Catholics, Jews, or Protestants, or to turn the people toward the path of Buddha, or to end in a predominantly Moslem nation, or to produce in the long run atheists or agnostics. On matters of this kind government must be neutral. This freedom plainly includes freedom *from* religion with the right to believe, speak, write, publish and advocate antireligious programs. . . . Certainly the "free exercise" clause does not require that everyone embrace the theology of some church or of some faith, or observe the religious practices of any majority or minority sect. . . . The "establishment" clause protects citizens also against any law which selects any religious custom, practice, or ritual, puts the force of government behind it, and fines, imprisons or otherwise penalizes a person for not observing it. The Government plainly could not join forces with one religious group and decree a universal and symbolic circumcision. Nor could it require all children to be baptized or give tax exemptions only to those whose children were baptized.

Could it require a fast from sunrise to sunset throughout the Moslem month of Ramadan? I should think not. Yet why then can it make criminal the doing of other acts, as innocent as eating, during the day that Christians revere? . . .

The issue of these cases would . . . be in better focus if we imagined that a state legislature, controlled by Orthodox Jews and Seventh-Day Adventists, passed a law making it a crime to keep a shop open on Saturdays. Would a Baptist, Catholic, Methodist, or Presbyterian be compelled to obey that law or go to jail or pay a fine? Or suppose Moslems grew in political strength here and got a law through a state legislature making it a crime to keep a shop open on Fridays? Would the rest of us have to submit under the fear of criminal sanctions? . . .

The Court picks and chooses language from various decisions to bolster its conclusion that these Sunday Laws in the modern setting are "civil regulations." No matter how much is written, no matter what is said, the parentage of these laws is the Fourth Commandment; and they serve and satisfy the religious predispositions of our Christian communities. . . .

It seems to me plain that by these laws the States compel one, under sanction of law, to refrain from work or recreation on Sunday because of the majority's religious views about that day. The State by law makes Sunday a symbol of respect or adherence. Refraining from work or recreation in deference to the majority's religious feelings about Sunday is within every person's choice. By what authority can government compel it? . . .

These laws are sustained because, it is said, the First Amendment is concerned with religious convictions or opinion, not with conduct. But it is a strange Bill of Rights that makes it possible for the dominant religious group to bring the minority to heel because the minority, in the doing of acts which intrinsically are wholesome and not antisocial, does not defer to the majority's religious beliefs. Some have religious scruples against eating pork. Those scruples, no matter how bizarre they might seem to some, are within the ambit of the First Amendment. . . . Is it possible that a majority of a state legislature having those religious scruples could make it criminal for the nonbeliever to sell pork? Some have religious scruples against slaughtering cattle. Could a state legislature, dominated by that group, make it criminal to run an abattoir?

The Court balances the need of the people for rest, recreation, late sleeping, family visiting and the like against the command of the First Amendment that no one need bow to the religious beliefs of another. There is in this realm no room for balancing. I see no place for it in the constitutional scheme. A legislature of Christians can no more make minorities conform to their weekly regime than a legislature of Moslems, or a legislature of Hindus. The religious regime of every group must be respected—unless it crosses the line of criminal conduct. But no one can be forced to come to a halt before it, or refrain from doing things that would offend it. That is my reading of the Establishment Clause and the Free Exercise Clause. . . .

The State can of course require one day of rest a week: one day when every shop or factory is closed. Quite a few States make that requirement. Then the "day of rest" becomes purely and simply a health measure. But the Sunday laws operate differently. They force minorities to obey the majority's religious feelings of what is due and proper for a Christian community; they provide a coercive spur to the "weaker brethren," to those who are indifferent to the claims of a Sabbath through apathy or scruple. . . .

There is an "establishment" of religion in the constitutional sense if any practice of any religious group has the sanction of law behind it. There is an interference with the "free exercise" of religion if what in conscience one can do or omit doing is required because of the religious scruples of the community. Hence I would declare each of those laws unconstitutional as applied to the complaining parties, whether or not they are members of a sect which observes as its Sabbath a day other than Sunday.

When these laws are applied to Orthodox Jews . . . or to Sabbatarians their vice is accentuated. If the Sunday laws are constitutional, Kosher markets are on a five-day week. Thus those laws put an economic penalty on those who observe Saturday rather than Sunday as the Sabbath. For the economic pressures on these minorities, created by the fact that our communities are predominantly Sunday-minded, there is no recourse. When, however, the State uses its coercive powers—here the criminal law—to compel minorities to observe a second Sabbath, not their own, the State undertakes to aid and "prefer one religion over another"—contrary to the command of the Constitution. . . .

### In the Wake of the Decision

Controversy concerning Sunday sales did not cease when the Supreme Court handed down its decision; on the contrary, it intensified. Once again the forum became the state legislature and the state courts. Throughout the states new Sunday closing laws were enacted or proposed, some more stringent, others more relaxed than before. Existing laws were enforced with new vigor and readied for tests in the courts. The locales of these events read like a train caller's litany.

In Brunswick, Maine, the citizens voted down (1,696 to 1,172) an article expanding the Sunday closing law so as to permit Sunday sales at general merchandise stores: elsewhere in Maine the voting showed a widespread inclination to allow business on Sunday. As Maine goes, so goes the nation; everywhere this same diversity was reflected. In Austin, the Texas legislature passed a law forbidding a store to remain open both Saturday and Sunday, but in Jackson the Mississippi house defeated a bill to permit certain Sunday sports already prohibited under the Blue Laws. In Hammond, Indiana, the police increased enforcement of the 1905 Indiana Sunday law, yet in Columbus, Ohio, the police chief frankly stated that he did not have the manpower to devote to such arrests and that, furthermore, there were too few convictions to justify the expenditure of police pay. In Springfield, the Illinois Supreme Court refused to uphold a 1961 statute banning the Sunday sale of automobiles; whereas in Jefferson City, the Missouri Supreme Court upheld the state's Sunday law.

Everywhere there was considerable feeling that the laws should be made more realistic and workable by bringing them into line with present-day needs. Obviously, it was difficult to reach consensus on what constituted present-day needs.

### In Massachusetts

In Massachusetts, Attorney General McCormack immediately plumped for strict enforcement. He cautioned police officials that it was their duty to enforce the Sunday statute as long as it remained state law. To strengthen his enforcement policy, he sought the help of state troopers. Behind McCormack's action was an awareness that rigid, impartial enforcement of the law could lead to its re-examination and even revision. "If the public doesn't like the law," he declared, "it should change it, not ask the police to turn their backs on it."

The Attorney General, therefore, was not surprised when his policy brought protests. Selectmen in different towns met with police officials to determine what could be done. Petitions for immediate legislative revision were circulated in resort areas. Different groups clamored for a special legislative session.

Despite more vigorous enforcement, businessmen found loopholes. Many gift-shop owners continued to stay open by procuring a license to sell candy or ice cream. The bakery in Pittsfield which sold sticks of gum for 23¢ each and included a 22¢ loaf of bread was not an isolated case. Nor was the Nantucket gift-shop owner who on Sunday put a sign outside his shop reading: "Blue Laws Alas! Today Only, All Prices 10 Percent Above Weekday Prices to Help Pay the $50 Blue Law Fine." Inside a second sign read, "Welcome, Customers and State Police."

To study the problems of Sunday legislation, Governor Volpe appointed a blue-ribbon committee with Arthur Sutherland as chairman. Representatives of business, labor, and religion helped to make up the twenty-one-member committee.

In November the committee presented its report to the governor. Although no member proposed either the complete abolition of Sunday laws or the retention of the laws precisely as they were, there was a clear division as to the substance of the law. The majority report continued the present law with certain clarifications. It kept the principle of a lengthy list of exceptions including an exception for bona fide non-Sunday Sabbatarians. The minority, which included Professor Sutherland, recommended that only three forms of activity be prohibited: manufacturing, construction, and sale of goods. Under these three headings there were a number of exceptions.

Twenty bills with respect to Sunday legislation were filed in the 1962 session of the General Court. Near the end of the session the House of Representatives passed a bill which included a "compromise" that had been worked out with Sabbatarian proponents: stores with not more than three workers, including the proprietor, which sold goods, wares, merchandise, and food were permitted to stay open Sundays. As a number of Saturday Sabbatarians operated stores of this nature such owners would be helped.

The Senate, in a surprise maneuver, added an amendment to permit Sabbatarians to open their businesses on Sunday. The amendment, introduced by Senator A. Frank Foster, a Jewish Democrat from Dorchester, passed by a roll-call vote of 21 to 14. Unfortunately it proved to be a fateful amendment.

The *Pilot,* the weekly paper of the Catholic Archdiocese of Boston, denounced the Senate action. In an editorial entitled "Assault on Sunday" it sternly declared:

> The Massachusetts Senate, in a shocking assault on the day of rest statute, voted this week to except sabbatarians from the requirements of the Sunday Law. In simplest terms the Senators responded to pressures that will destroy the Sunday observance in favor of those—principally Jews and Adventists—who worship on Saturday. If the legislation is given final approval, Sunday in Massachusetts will soon be a "business as usual" day for some of our citizens and a day of rest for none of our citizens. . . .
>
> It [the bill] clearly gives commercial advantage to one minority in the community while it penalizes another, and it strikes at the heart of the day of rest which Sunday has been in our society for centuries. . . . It is *bad* legislation, passed under pressure.

In addition, the *Pilot* carried the names of those Senators who had "so unwisely" supported the amendment, and expressed the hope that they would "reconsider."

Losing no time, the Senate on Monday, June 11, reversed itself, killing the Sabbatarian amendment, 31 to 8, in a manner described by some Jewish legislators as "frightening." Five Republicans and three Democrats voted for the amendment; nine Republicans and twenty-two Democrats voted against it. In addition to—and probably springing from—the criticism in the *Pilot,* Senators claimed they were beleaguered by telephone calls asking for prompt action to kill the amendment. Senator John Beades, Democrat from Boston, made the motion to reconsider the action. Having originally voted in its favor, he attempted to explain the reversal: "It has been brought to our attention that the amendment goes further than we thought." In addition to its reversal the Senate also limited the opening of small stores on Sunday to those selling only food; defined the small store as one employing two persons, including the owner, during the week; and banned all Sunday dancing.

Rabbi Joseph Shubow expressed surprise at the reaction in the Senate. He said, "I am disturbed by the statement issued by my good friends of the *Pilot* that the law was passed by the Senate because of the 'pressure' of Jews and other Sabbatarians." He added, "We must remember that minority groups, so-called, do not have the power possessed by majorities when it comes to pressure."

The bill went back to the House where debate on it became acrimonious. The Sabbatarians, however, lost the battle. Ignoring the pleas of the Sabbatarian groups, the governor, away at the annual governors' conference, requested the lieutenant-governor to sign the bill so that it could be in effect by the Fourth of July.

The Boston *Globe,* perhaps hyperbolically, hailed the act with the acclamation, "Massachusetts has become an up-to-date state today" and declared, "The term 'Blue Laws' has been wiped off the books." The act, in addition to liberalizing certain Sunday proscriptions, liberalized previously restricted holidays. This was why the Legislative and Executive Branches wished the act in effect by the Fourth of July. Hundreds of business establishments were eager to be open on such a lucrative holiday.

The statute allowed the following on Sundays and particular holidays: (1) souvenir, antique, and gift shops to remain open; (2) sale of food in stores employing no more than two persons (including the proprietor) seven days a week; (3) showing of real estate for rent or sale; (4) a homeowner to work on his own house provided he does not create a public nuisance; (5) rental and sale of sports equipment to be used on the premises; (6) sale of bait and sale or rental of fishing and boating equipment; (7) transportation of goods by water, rail, or air, and loading or unloading of such goods; (8) pet shops to open and sell; (9) art galleries to open and sell; (10) nurseries to open and sell; and (11) sale of kosher food by a natural person who is a bona fide Sabbatarian.

### In Pennsylvania

In Pennsylvania, a policy of immediate enforcement was not recommended, but rather the contrary. There, too, the Attorney General, Anne X.

Alpern, shortly to be appointed to the Pennsylvania Supreme Court, was more successful than the Attorney General of Massachusetts in keeping herself removed from the controversy. It was the city solicitor of Philadelphia, David Berger (who had argued the *Braunfeld* case before the Supreme Court), who advised that enforcement should not begin until pending legal matters were cleared up.

The management of the Two Guys discount house saw to it that legal matters were prolonged as much as possible. It used several ways to effect this. First, it submitted a routine petition for review of the Supreme Court decision, which the Court turned down. The discount house also joined in a further test of the constitutionality of the law, petitioning the State Supreme Court to permit it to appear as *amicus* in a case to which Bargain City discount house was a party. This latter discount house had brought the matter of Sunday closing once again to the Pennsylvania courts, arguing that although the United States Supreme Court had declared the law not to be a violation of the Federal Constitution, there had been no declaration regarding the Pennsylvania constitution. On March 21, 1962, the Pennsylvania Supreme Court ruled that the 1959 Sunday laws did not violate the Pennsylvania constitution. Justice Herbert Cohen writing the opinion said that the "reasonableness upon which the 1959 act must be upheld" was pointed out in the United States Supreme Court decision.

Once enforcement of the Sunday laws was resumed in the Allentown area, George Hubschman, manager of Two Guys, was the merchant most often cited—four times between October 22 and November 19, 1961. His alleged violations were the subject of hearings before one of Allentown's aldermen, and in each instance he was convicted and sentenced to pay a fine of $50, plus costs. Hubschman welcomed and, indeed, courted the convictions because they gave him an opportunity to charge discriminatory enforcement of the law and to appeal his case in the Lehigh County Court. In the end, however, he did not appeal.

The Pennsylvania legislature strengthened the Blue Laws by adding another Sunday sales statute, signed in September, 1961, by Governor Lawrence and going into effect October 26. This new law banned stores with ten or more employees from selling food on Sunday. This law, too, quickly ran into legal test. Twenty-one supermarkets in western Pennsylvania brought a complaint before three Federal judges. The judges held that no substantial Federal question was involved and that interpretation of the legislation would be up to the state courts.

By the end of April, 1962, the commissioners of Whitehall Township, where the Two Guys discount house was located, announced a new policy of arrest. Briefly, this policy called for the police to make arrests whenever they saw the law violated, "without going out of their way to look for violations." This was not a policy the commissioners favored but one they adopted because they claimed "Harrisburg" had brought pressure upon them. They voiced their objection saying, "A municipality should not be placed in a position of police-state tactics to enforce legislation which benefits private interests, and this is especially true when the legislation is highly controversial."

In May the state police also adopted a new policy, namely, to remain alert to violations of the Sunday laws and to arrest offenders. Previously the state police arrested violators only when complaints were filed or when local authorities requested them to act. The new policy could help to bring uniform enforcement throughout the state. Morris Efron, counsel for Two Guys discount house, took a different view of it. According to Efron, on May 27 the state police visited the discount house and "insisted" that certain departments be closed or they would make arrests on every sale. In Efron's opinion arrests other than at the Two Guys were "token" arrests. He continued to insist "that all the powers of the enforcement agencies, as far as I am concerned, are being directed against this one store."

### The Cases in Perspective

The Sunday closing cases by their very names will always carry a religious aureole. To ignore this would not be honest. The Supreme Court, however, by its opinion decided that they belong as much with the maximum-hour cases of some decades back as they do with flag salutes, school buses, and released time. It may be profitable for Sunday law opponents to play up the religious aspect in order to place the legislation in its most unpalatable light. The fact remains that the Court declared that the laws under its consideration, although admittedly religious in origin, had evolved into social and economic laws. To say this, the Court used nearly 200 pages—no small number when one considers that for ten years the Court had been ruling out consideration of the Sunday question because "no substantial Federal question was involved."

The Court did not, on the other hand, close the door to the possibility of a religious question arising from Sunday legislation. The last sentence of the Chief Justice in the first of the four opinions that he wrote for the four Sunday cases was

> We do not hold that Sunday legislation may not be a violation of the "Establishment" Clause if it can be demonstrated that its purpose— evidenced either on the face of the legislation, in conjunction with its legislative history, or in its operative effects—is to use the State's coercive power to aid religion.

That this was a final sentence, almost a punch line, appears to give added potency to the warning it carries. The sentence would also save the Court, if need be, from another *Gobitis*. The line, nevertheless, carried little consolation for the seventh-day Sabbatarian who weekly might be confronted with what Justice Stewart in dissent called the cruel choice between faith and his economic survival.

It is possible that the Sabbatarian cases might have fared better had they not been linked with the discount house cases. As it was, the former produced three dissenters, whereas the latter had only one. Certainly the presence of the discount house cases pointed up the economic character of the laws and of the struggle provoked. Perhaps they even drew sympathy away from the Sabbatarians. On the other hand, without them the Sabbatarian cases might never have reached the Court. The combined, persistent clamors of the two groups, Sabbatarians and discount merchants, would have been difficult for the Court to ignore much longer.

In speaking from its Jovian heights the Court offered no solution to anything but the legal problem. Where has this left public policy with respect to Sunday laws? Obviously, in the hands of the voters if they wish to avail themselves of the democratic process and speak through their representatives.

Voters and legislators, however, may have an even less easy time of it than judges. Several questions face them, both major and minor. Do they wish to shop on Sundays? Do they wish to sleep on Sundays? Do they wish to be able to work any day in the week? Do they wish a common day off? If they are not themselves seventh-day Sabbatarians, do they wish, nevertheless, to accord a respect to the sincere religious beliefs of some of their fellow Americans? Do the old-time retailers wish to keep their traditional ways? Do they feel the only way to compete is "not to fight 'em but to join 'em"?

Part of the problem of finding a suitable solution to the Sunday question lies in the difficulty of giving an unqualified yes or no to some of the above questions. That difficulty may result in voters and legislators both shelving the problem, and letting practice and custom (be it new or old) take over and solve the problem. So doing might produce the truest replica of people's preferences. Whichever way the problem will be handled, the losers in the Court may not necessarily be the losers out of Court.

### Table of Cases, in Order of Citation in the Text

*Hennington* v. *Georgia,* 163 U.S. 299 (1896).
*Petit* v. *Minnesota,* 177 U.S. 164 (1900).
*Soon Hing* v. *Crowley,* 113 U.S. 703 (1885).
*Gallagher* v. *Crown Kosher Super Market, Inc.,* 366 U.S. 617 (1961).
*Two Guys from Harrison-Allentown Inc.* v. *McGinley,* 366 U.S. 582 (1961).
*Braunfeld* v. *Brown,* 366 U.S. 599 (1961).
*McGowan* v. *Maryland,* 366 U.S. 420 (1961).

*Commonwealth* v. *Chernock,* 336 Mass. 384; 145 N.E. 2d 920 (1957).

*Crown Kosher Super Market, Inc.* v. *Gallagher,* 176 F. Supp. 466; 178 F. Supp. 336 (D.C.D. Mass. 1959).

*People* v. *Friedman,* 302 N.Y. 75; 96 N.E. 2d 184 (1950); app. dism'd for want of substantial Federal question. 341 U.S. 907 (1951).

*Commonwealth* v. *Bauder,* 14 Pa. District and County Reports 2d 571 (Court of Quarter Sessions, Lehigh County, 1958); 188 Pa. Super. Ct. 424, 145 A. 2d 915 (1958).

*Commonwealth* v. *Mills,* 14 Pa. District and County Reports 2d 571 (Court of Quarter Sessions, Lehigh County, 1958); 188 Pa. Super. Ct. 424, 145 A. 2d 915 (1958).

*Everson* v. *Board of Education,* 330 U.S. 1 (1947).

*Illinois* ex rel. *McCollum* v. *Board of Education,* 333 U.S. 203 (1948).

*Commonwealth* ex rel. *Woodruff* v. *American Baseball Club of Philadelphia,* 290 Pa. 136 (1927).

*Specht* v. *Commonwealth,* 8 Pa. 312 (1848).

*Two Guys from Harrison-Allentown, Inc.* v. *McGinley,* 179 F. Supp. 944 (D.C.E.D. Pa. 1959).

*Minersville School District* v. *Gobitis,* 310 U.S. 586 (1940).

## Sources

The primary sources for this treatment of the Sunday closing cases have been the records, petitions, and briefs filed in the Supreme Court. The copies I used are in the Supreme Court Library. I also attended the oral argument before the Supreme Court. Edward McCormack, Attorney General of Massachusetts, kindly put his files on the *Crown* case at my disposal. George Joseph, District Attorney of Lehigh County, Pennsylvania, and prior to that, counsel for the Two Guys, contributed generous and valuable help by going through his files on the *Two Guys* case with me. Many were helpful in their recollections and comments when I talked to them. Among these were Edward McCormack, Joseph Elcock, Professor Arthur Sutherland, Herbert Ehrmann, Raymond Gallagher, Milton Chernick, Judge William McCarthy, the Rev. John Grant of the Boston *Pilot,* the Rev. Vaughn Shedd, Leo Pfeffer, George Hubschman, and Paul McGinley. Rabbi Moses Sheinkopf gave helpful information to a research assistant of mine when I was unable to see him personally.

Relevant files of the Boston, Springfield, and Allentown newspapers were consulted. For a three-month period beginning in January, 1962, use was made of a national clipping service. That the Sunday laws were in the news could be seen in the blizzard of nearly 800 clippings supplied for January alone.

I have been aided financially in this study of the Sunday closing cases, which is part of a larger study that I am doing, by a fellowship from the American Association of University Women. (It should be pointed out that the data of this study do not extend beyond July, 1962.)